ADG-7788

LO

D0455377

0000118578958

**BIO
TUBMAN**

Lowry, Beverly.

Harriet Tubman.

C.2007

DATE			

3/08 LO

DISCARD

SANTA CRUZ PUBLIC LIBRARY
SANTA CRUZ, CALIFORNIA

BAKER & TAYLOR

HARRIET TUBMAN

Also by Beverly Lowry

*Her Dream of Dreams: The Rise and
Triumph of Madam C. J. Walker*

The Track of Real Desires

Crossed Over: A Murder, a Memoir

Breaking Gentle

The Perfect Sonya

Daddy's Girl

Emma Blue

Come Back, Lolly Ray

HARRIET TUBMAN

Imagining a Life

BEVERLY LOWRY

DOUBLEDAY

New York London Toronto Sydney Auckland

PUBLISHED BY DOUBLEDAY
a division of Random House, Inc.

Copyright © 2007 by Beverly Lowry

All Rights Reserved

Published in the United States by Doubleday, an imprint of The Doubleday
Broadway Publishing Group, a division of Random House, Inc., New York.
www.doubleday.com

DOUBLEDAY and the portrayal of an anchor with a dolphin are registered
trademarks of Random House, Inc.

Pages 417–18 constitute an extension of this copyright page.

Book design by Donna Sinisgalli
Maps by Virginia Norey

Library of Congress Cataloging-in-Publication Data
Lowry, Beverly.
Harriet Tubman : imagining a life / by Beverly Lowry. — 1st ed.
p. cm.
Includes bibliographical references and index.
1. Tubman, Harriet, 1820?–1913. 2. Slaves—United States—Biography.
3. African American women—Biography. 4. Underground railroad.
5. Antislavery movements—United States—History—19th century.
I. Title.
E444.T82L68 2007
973.7'115092—dc22
[B]
2006024778

ISBN: 978-0-385-50291-7

PRINTED IN THE UNITED STATES OF AMERICA

1   3   5   7   9   10   8   6   4   2

First Edition

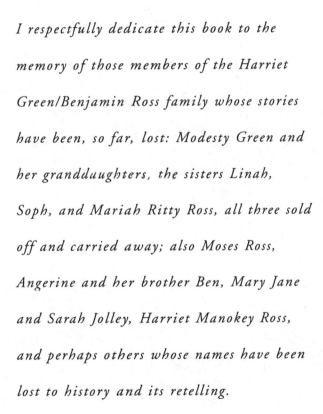

I respectfully dedicate this book to the memory of those members of the Harriet Green/Benjamin Ross family whose stories have been, so far, lost: Modesty Green and her grandduughters, the sisters Linah, Soph, and Mariah Ritty Ross, all three sold off and carried away; also Moses Ross, Angerine and her brother Ben, Mary Jane and Sarah Jolley, Harriet Manokey Ross, and perhaps others whose names have been lost to history and its retelling.

Contents

Author's Note   1

Prologue   3

I. Araminta

1. Owasco Lake   13
2. Dorchester: Birth   23
3. Childhood   47
4. At Polish Mills: A Shower of Fire   64
5. The Weight: At the Bucktown Crossroads   77
6. Sold and Carried Away: The Slaveholder's Choice   93

II. Harriet

7. Marriage   115
8. Over the Line   138
9. Family   153
10. Rescues, Promises   171

III. Moses

11. Becoming Moses   193
12. Escapes, Rescues: The Stampede   217
13. With John Brown: Dreams, Metaphor   228
14. Last Rescue   257

IV. The General

15. Beaufort, South Carolina   283
16. The Proclamation, the Raid   309
17. Raining Blood   328

V. Araminta Ross Davis,
Better Known as Harriet Tubman

18. Auburn, Last Days   360

19. March 13, 1913   375

Acknowledgments   379

Notes on Sources   383

Selected Bibliography   391

Index   405

HARRIET TUBMAN

Author's Note

*T*his book does not pretend to be a work of intense scholarship. It is the story of a life as I have studied and reimagined it, based on documentation and previous publications and told, as best as I could, scene by scene. I have tried to emphasize the visual elements of Harriet's story—what things looked like, places and clothes, faces, plants, the sky—and to thread information from the sources listed in the Selected Bibliography through the narrative as seamlessly as possible. All this in order to come up with one version of what life might have been like for the American hero Harriet Tubman.

In his introduction to his very compelling biography, *M: The Man Who Became Caravaggio,* Peter Robb uses a phrase I wish I had thought of myself. He wanted to tell Caravaggio's story as it was lived, he wrote, using a minimum of what he called "weasly qualifiers." This has been my goal, too: to tell the story plain. In some passages, I have incorporated the language of the speaker into the text without quotation marks (as in Sarah Bradford's *keep it green* and Gerrit Smith's *badly frosted her feet),* in order to depict a scene with some accuracy, as the participants may have lived through it and as they remembered it afterward.

By necessity, because Harriet never learned to read or write, what information we have comes second- or thirdhand, mediated by "as told to" texts. In many instances, I have included source material within the body of the narrative, to indicate not just when something happened but also in what year Harriet told the story, and to whom. One decision a writer using slave narratives has to face is whether or not to duplicate the heavy dialect of the interviewees of that time. Finding dialect distracting, difficult, and in the end, patronizing, I have decided to render Harriet's stories and comments in plain English.

This act of simplification, I think, honors her great wish to exactly communicate what life was like for herself and her people, so that no detail would be lost or forgotten.

Prologue

*O*ur heroes come to us in flashes that fade fast. We remember the famous moments—some of them pure myths—and the visual images, which after repeated viewings become such a part of our lives, it seems we actually were there. So it often goes with the American hero Harriet Tubman. Even if you cannot say exactly who she was or precisely what she did, where she lived or when she died, you have doubtless seen her in photographs and drawings. You may even have witnessed a version of her onstage, channeled by one of her many delineators—that is, a woman who dresses in clothes like hers and stands there proclaiming, "I am Harriet Tubman."

In 1978, a colorized 1905 photograph of her appeared on a postage stamp, the first black woman to be so honored. Her likeness is featured in history textbooks covering slavery, the Civil War, the Underground Railroad, women's history, black women's history. Visual images are endlessly engaging and we study them carefully, looking for the real *her,* the genuine *him*—beyond appearances. In Tubman's case, we are also attempting if not to capture then at least to find her, not in wet, cold Maryland December, but on the page, standing in one spot in her guerrilla-warfare garb, clutching a long-barreled rifle or seated, facing us, old now, her bony face framed by the white lace shawl said to be a gift from Queen Victoria—in either case, immobilized, caught, ours.

There, we want to say, taking particular notice of her hands in the photograph with the shawl: how big they are, what pure strength in the knuckles, a man's hands. Now we have her.

Yet she escapes us. Just as she made it out of slavery, she dodges us now, however relentlessly we dog her footsteps or meticulously study what clues she left behind. We keep trying to fix in place the *definitive,* as biographers like to claim, Harriet Tubman. She is part of our history, after all; her life and legend contribute to ours.

She could not read, never learned to write, and so of necessity, others have acted as her scribe, each making a case for who she was, how she looked (one reporter says not one drop of white blood, while another makes a case for a white ancestor; one calls her handsome, while another says plain and toothless) and sounded, how she managed to do what she did, what it was like, how many times she made the dangerous trek back into slavery and then to the North again, how many people she brought out—eighty, ninety, three hundred? In her time, some dismissed the claims altogether. How could one small, illiterate woman, an ignorant black person, do such a thing? Questions roll into one another; answers skitter away. And so we are constantly interpreting whatever we read or hear, seeing her as if through a warped glass.

The first book-length biography of her, called *Scenes in the Life of Harriet Tubman,* was written by Sarah Hopkins Bradford from personal interviews and published in 1869, its costs covered by local subscription. The book came illustrated with that frequently reprinted woodcut of

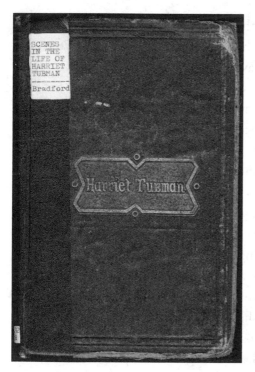

Tubman holding the rifle and dressed in her Civil War military garb. To substantiate her subject's version of events, Bradford inserted a number of letters from abolitionists and wartime colleagues, as well as the full text of a previously published biographical article from an 1863 Boston *Commonwealth,* written by its editor, the abolitionist schoolmaster and editor Franklin B. Sanborn.

Sarah Bradford was a white

Cover of *Scenes in the Life of Harriet Tubman* by Sarah H. Bradford, published in 1869.

woman, Franklin Sanborn a white man. Without question, freed slaves told white people stories they wanted to hear. But we take what we can get, and what has been given to us in Harriet's case, but for one occasion late in her life, are stories told to white interviewers. There is nothing to do about this except keep it in mind. Maintaining racial vigilance, relying on backup testimony from family and friends, we compare one version of an occasion with another. Noting especially that her stories remain the same, for the most part, throughout her life, we depend on and value that consistency, backed up by whatever documentation we can come up with. And in the end, choose pretty much, even if not entirely, to take her stories at face value.

At the request of Tubman—who spent much of her life trying to gather money enough to support herself and the many others she took care of—Bradford later issued two revised versions of her book, one in 1886, the other in 1901. The 1886 edition, entitled *Harriet Tubman, the Moses of Her People*, included significant, often unfortunate revisions, and today is the only version of Bradford's book in print. *Harriet, the Moses of Her People*, from 1901, replicates the 1886 edition, then offers an addendum of what the biographer calls "some additional incidents in the life of Harriet." While these supplemental stories— many of them never having been previously reported—are of crucial importance, they are included almost as an afterthought and are currently available only to those willing to ply the waters of the Internet.

Taken together, the three editions of the Bradford books are instructive, if problematic. A

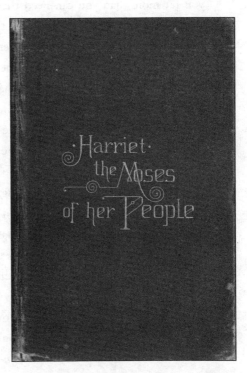

Cover of *Harriet: The Moses of Her People* by Sarah H. Bradford, published in 1901.

socially conscious middle-class woman, Sarah Bradford, prior to writing the biography, had published only moralizing, sentimental novels and stories under the name Cousin Cicely. In addition, her schedule allowed her a scant three months to research and write her book before leaving on a trip to Europe. Nonetheless, she was there: Sarah Bradford sat face-to-face with Harret Tubman for many hours, encouraging her to talk, listening to and recording her stories.

We can also be grateful to her for soliciting testimonials from some of Harriet's colleagues and friends, including Wendell Phillips, Thomas Garrett, Susan B. Anthony, Gerrit Smith, and the eloquent Frederick Douglass, who wrote the following:

ROCHESTER, AUGUST 29, 1868.

DEAR HARRIET: I am glad to know that the story of your eventful life has been written by a kind lady, and that the same is so soon to be published. You ask for what you do not need when you call upon me for a word of commendation. I need such words from you far more than you can need them from me, especially where your superior labors and devotion to the cause of the lately enslaved of our land are known as I know them. The difference between us is very marked. Most that I have done and suffered in the service of our cause has been in public, and I have received much encouragement at every step of the way. You on the other hand have labored in a private way. I have wrought in the day—you in the night. I have had the applause of the crowd and the satisfaction that comes of being approved by the multitude, while the most that you have done has been witnessed by a few trembling, scarred, and foot-sore bondmen and women, whom you have led out of the house of bondage, and whose heartfelt *"God bless you"* has been your only reward. The midnight sky and the silent stars have been the witnesses of your devotion to freedom and of your heroism. Excepting John Brown—of sacred memory—I know of no one who has willingly encountered more perils and hardships to serve our enslaved people than you have. Much that you have done would seem improbable to those who do not know you as I know you. It is to me a great pleasure and a great privilege to bear testimony to your character and your works, and to say to those to whom you may come, that I regard you in every way truthful and trustworthy.

Your friend,

Frederick Douglass.

There have been other biographies since that time, but until recently (except for *General Harriet Tubman,* written by former union organizer Earl Conrad and published in 1943), they were all aimed toward a young audience—children to young adults—a fact that doesn't yield all that easily to simple explanation. Tubman's illiteracy certainly presents a problem for scholars looking for primary material. Beyond government records, court documents, property assessments, and census figures, everything we have has been interpreted or—as historians say—*mediated,* even when the writer interviewed Tubman directly or took down a dictated letter.

My own sense of her is that she is one of those historical figures whom—if we really want to form an idea of what she was like—we have to catch on the fly. Of course, we must listen to those people who insist, "This is what she told me and this is how she said it," or "This is what I know from stories I heard as a child, and I know those stories are true," but we also must keep in mind that some of the stories are indeed true and some are not, and that many contradict one another, forcing us to make a choice. And also, that most of them are so set in stone, they cannot be dislodged or negotiated with in order to accommodate whatever new information is unearthed. Too much has been invested, one way or another, in a certain version of the facts. Nobody wants to budge, no matter what.

And in the end, none of the tellers know, whether kin, scholar, composer, or poet, and none of them knew even then—when she was doing her work. For the fact remains, Harriet Tubman worked alone. Having taught herself to develop and maintain an indifferent, almost casual attitude toward circumstance—a rare skill and perhaps the real test of a genuine hero—she ran too fast to catch up with, listening only

For Sarah Bradford's 1901 biography of Tubman, *Harriet, the Moses of Her People,* Susan B. Anthony wrote a tribute to "this most wonderful woman Harriet Tubman," which appeared on the first page of the book. (*Transcription of letter appears at bottom of page.*)

to the voices inside her head—God, she said, spoke directly to her—operating beyond sense, reason, and the boundaries of community, family, and marriage. When others pondered dangers, risks, options, alternative possibilities, she did what she felt she had to and simply *went*.

Araminta. Harriet. Moses. Old Chariot. The General. See her as she turns her back and, facing north, on a cold night, pitch-dark, Polaris ever in her vision, goes.

Freedom in her heart. Knowledge in her feet. Laughing. Running.

Let us track her ourselves, her next mediators, scene by scene, avoiding commentary when we can, submerging direct quotes into the narrative say-so, trying more than anything to *see* her, understanding as we go that memory is a trickster, that perspective ever alters, and that point of view is everything.

(*Transcription*)

This most wonderful woman—Harriet Tubman—is still alive. I saw her but the other day at the beautiful home of Eliza Wright Osborne—the daughter of Martha C. Wright—in company with Elizabeth Smith Miller—the only daughter of Gerrit Smith—

Miss Emily Howland—Rev. Ames H. Thaw—and Miss Ella Wright Garrison—the daughter of Martha C. Wright and the wife of Wm. Lloyd Garrison Jr—all of us were visiting at Mrs. Osbornes—a real love feast of the few that are left—and here came <u>Harriet Tubman!</u>
Susan B. Anthony, 17 Madison Street. Rochester, NY.

We begin in the summer of 1900, our view telescoped by more than a hundred years, as from beyond the next millennial turn, we try imaginatively to catch or create a glimpse of her sitting with friends, casting back in her mind, telling stories of events of some seventy years before. To complicate matters even further, the scene and the stories have come to us by way of her biographer, Sarah Bradford, who was there on that summer day. Bradford, of course, does not just listen and report; she has her own ideas about what matters and why. And because she is not always a trustworthy reporter, we have to keep in mind her particular point of view.

From here in the twenty-first century, then, we focus on 1900, and then twist the telescope lens farther out, to focus on the time and place of the story being told, back to the late 1820s, when our subject was a child. Then return to the day of the storytelling. We, of course, cannot lay claim to objectivity, either; we hold on to our own beliefs and perspectives. Tricky, imprecise. But we have what we have, and it is one way to begin, by finding a time, a place to see from. And to listen.

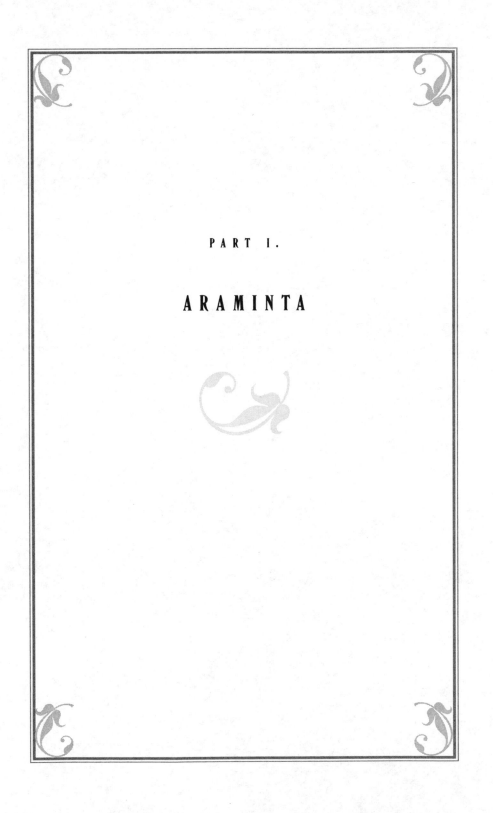

PART I.

ARAMINTA

Scene 1.

Owasco Lake

There is a quiet dignity about Harriet that makes her superior or indifferent to all surrounding circumstances . . . she was never elated, or humiliated; she took everything as it came, making no comments or complaints.

—SARAH BRADFORD, *HARRIET,*
THE MOSES OF HER PEOPLE, 1901

She is old now, near eighty, and feeble—illness and injury, brutality, oppression, and the constant cut of fear having taken their toll—her condition convincing many people that Harriet Tubman has lived out her time and will soon pass into history and legend.

They underestimate her stubbornness, the thick shell of the nut of self-preservation tucked into the curl of her heart. In Auburn, New York, where she lives with her brother William Henry Stewart, her presence is almost boringly well known, she having so memorably and so often performed the events of her life—dramatized, danced, sung in shouts, creating the shadows and cries and frosty streams between slavery and freedom—that she has become, even in 1900, only thirty-five years beyond Appomattox, outmoded, overexposed, a relic of another time and a victim of our country's old and continuing malady, a propensity for willed historical amnesia.

She has lived in central New York State, in the town of Auburn, for some forty years—more than half her life—even so, many people born since the war's end don't know who she is anymore but have to be told, and even then they shrug and wonder, Which war? What slavery?

Where? Maryland? And if they do know of her, some of them have wearied of hearing about the terrible days back then and down there. Oh, they think, her again.

The country is sick of hearing about slavery and the South, the war, the disenfranchisement of black men, the masked white terrorists who ride the night. People want to move on.

But not all have forgotten. Some are steady friends, and believe.

Aunt Harriet, as she is often called by those who would idealize her into safe, if nonexistent, kinship, lives a mile south of downtown Auburn, beyond the city tollgate on South Street, where she raises some crops and chickens and, despite her fragility, cares and provides for a number of indigent and infirm people, one of them blind. "Her beloved darkies," one woman calls them, though not all of them are black. Children, stragglers, panhandlers, the ill, the hapless and dis-abled, those with no homes or family, people unable to take care of themselves—they wander into her yard, gather beneath her fig tree, and settle in. No one is turned away.

She has spent a good part, if not most, of her life on the road, alone. Today she is on the move again, on her way out of town, going downstate to visit two old friends.

An old woman, small, compact, keen-footed. Layered in clothes: dress buttoned to the neck, boots, dark straw hat, flat-brimmed against the sun. Moving at a quick clip.

Her mother and father and other members of her family once lived with her in Auburn. Most are dead now, but her younger brother, William Henry, born into slavery as Henry Ross, still lives there. William contributes, but he is now seventy years old himself. Every-body in the household is old, infirm, or a child; nobody leaves. And so, ever the caretaker, despite her own age and infirmities, Harriet contin-ues to take to the road to solicit funds from her supporters and to sell eggs and chickens in town in order to keep the operation afloat.

In one photo, her chin is tucked and she looks up heavy-browed, as if wary. Others in the picture—lined up in a row, posing—look straight at the camera, taking it on. Harriet stands at the end, holding a washbasin tightly in her grip, their protector.

The month is June, maybe early July—early summer, at any rate,

A family photograph of Harriet and residents of her home in Auburn, in about 1887. Harriet stands guard on the end. Next to her is her adopted daughter, Gertie, and next to Gertie, her second husband, Nelson Davis, then Lee Cheney, "Pop" Alexander, Walter Green, Blind Aunty (Sara) Parker, and Harriet's great niece, Dora Stewart.

and halfway through the first year of the new century. One of the people she is going to see is Sarah Bradford, author of *Scenes in the Life of Harriet Tubman* and *Harriet Tubman, the Moses of Her People*. Bradford has traveled from nearby Geneva, New York, where she lives, to visit her brother, the Reverend Samuel Miles Hopkins, Jr., who introduced her to Harriet in the first place. Harriet's visit is not entirely social; she has been poking at her memory the way we bother a dying fire, searching for stories she forgot to tell Bradford, so that they might be included in yet another edition of the biography, which will be called *Harriet, the Moses of Her People* and which might sell well enough to pay off some debts and keep the operation of her household afloat a while longer.

Her pace is steady, determined. She cannot read and does not know the train or steamboat schedule; when she travels, she does not seek out such information ahead of time, but—trusting God and a sense of time grander than clocks—sits at depots or on docks, waiting

Sarah Hopkins Bradford

for transportation to arrive. In order to get to the summerhouse in time, she had to leave early, midmorning latest, to be sure of catching the train and steamboat.

By the end of the nineteenth century, the more prosperous citizens of central New York state are fleeing the muggish funk of town summers to settle themselves in mostly unspectacular homes on what are known as the Finger Lakes— eleven bone-slender lakes that yearn toward Ontario, Canada, like reedy children cast from home. Once north-flowing rivers, the lakes were created by the incursion of gouging, south-moving Ice Age glaciers, and in time were tagged with Indian names, among them, Seneca, Cayuga, Canandaigua. The Finger Lake closest to Auburn is Owasco.

A train runs from town to the lake, the Lehigh Valley Railroad, the Owasco Lake depot of which yet stands on the western shore, a two-story rectangular building—wooden and slightly leaning—painted a seaside shade, something between teal blue and aquamarine, vibrant against the ordinary greens and blues of the countryside.

Perhaps Harriet takes the Lehigh Valley train from Auburn to the Owasco Lake depot, then walks to the dock, where she will board one of the small underpowered steamboats that ply the Finger Lakes during the resort season. Or she may simply walk the five miles from town to the landing and then ride the boat, disembarking near the house on the point where the Reverend Samuel Hopkins summers.

This seems likely. And so we see her on foot. And then at the dock, staring at the lake and waiting. And on the boat, looking out, poking a little harder at her memory, squinting into the horizon until hazy pictures come clear.

Often, she seems to be frowning as if in disapproval, when actually she is only thinking.

An injury from slavery days, clearly visible along the middle of her forehead, has left her somewhat incapacitated. She is given to fits of sleeping, which come on her unawares, sometimes mid-sentence. Her head drops, she goes off farther away than sleep, then returns to finish her thought exactly where she left off.

A jokester, memory plays hide-and-seek. Incidents disappear, it seems, forever, then, even unbidden, return, fully colored and intact, down to conversations, colors, the buzz of a mosquito. The incident Harriet is so keen on remembering is one that occurred some seventy or so years ago, the details of which she comes up with on the boat: the kitchen, the voices raised in anger, the look of the baby on its mother's hip, the sugar bowl on the table seen from the eye level of a seven-year-old.

A recent (2001) photograph of the two-story depot at Owasco Lake, New York, located a few miles south of Auburn, where Harriet lived. When in 1900 she went to visit Sarah Bradford and provide her with additional stories, Harriet may have taken the Lehigh Valley Railroad train to this depot before boarding the steamboat across Owasco.

A Town of Auburn, New York. Harriet lived just south of the city limits in Fleming (see detailed map, pages 244–245), from 1859 until her death there, in 1913.

B Owasco Lake, one of the threadlike Finger Lakes, where in 1900 Harriet met with Sarah Bradford and her brother, Samuel Hopkins, to discuss a new edition of her biography.

C Rochester, New York, home of Frederick Douglass during Harriet's Underground Railroad years.

D Niagara Falls, Niagara River, Harriet's escape route into Canada.

WESTERN NEW YORK

D

Niagara Falls

Lake Erie

The boat docks.

Hopkins and his sister have finished their lunch, but they are waiting. In her remembrance of the day, Bradford has her brother ordering a table set for Harriet when she arrives, then—the two women sitting together—waiting on her himself.

"As if," she writes, "it were a pleasure and an honor to serve her."

Hopkins brings cups of tea and some food. And the three friends sit together on what Bradford calls a broad, shaded piazza, overlooking the lake. An enchanting scene.

We may well sniff at the presumptive snobbery of Bradford's "as if." turning the pleasure and the honor into a virtue on her brother's part. Without question, the woman who sometimes called herself Cousin Ciceley could be precious. And while steadfast in her devotion to Tubman, the biographer was not immune to the casually accepted racial stereotyping of her time, a practice common even among abolitionists. Beyond that, in any case, "ordered a table set" misrepresents the truth and "piazza" turns out to be wishful thinking.

In fact, Hopkins's summerhouse is purposefully rustic, a retreat from worldliness and privilege that the minister happily imposes not only on himself but his grandchildren, one of whom—Samuel Hopkins Adams—hated the summerhouse. Young Adams considered the month he spent there every year a kind of sentence, especially since he so enjoyed staying in his grandfather's grander digs in Auburn, where there were servants, soft beds, and good china. For the grandchildren, the Owasco house meant only tin dishes to wash, grimy kerosene torches to fill, potatoes to peel, garbage to bury. A Spartan regime, inflicted by a learned Presbyterian given to preaching in a swallowtail coat.

Piazza or porch—let us not be too harsh on Sarah Bradford. She has been to Europe and is by birth and upbringing of a class-conscious nature, and so when she describes this scene in 1900, she upgrades.

Maintaining her usual demeanor, Harriet eats her lunch and drinks her tea.

She likes chicken. Maybe Hopkins serves her some.

Eating, she remains quietly impervious to and apart from the attitudes and wishes of her hosts. Her dignity, the ability to maintain a steady indifference to circumstance, helped keep her safe on the road to the North, and after. Had she entertained visions of the tracking dogs, the men on horseback carrying guns, had she responded to the certainty of their presence or imagined what would happen if they caught her, she might never have made it safely out. Or gone back.

Because of their history, the Finger Lakes are spectacularly set but high in humidity. Summer afternoons tend to be close in the countryside between the lakes, so shade would be welcome. Sitting there while their guest takes her lunch, brother and sister watch the little summer steamboat move back and forth across the lake, zigzagging south and then putt-putting back up.

When Harriet pushes her plate away, the three of them sit a bit longer, enjoying the view, perhaps watching the setting sun darken the lake, watching for the boat that will take her back home.

And then she gets to what she has come for.

I often think . . . she says to Bradford, *of things I wish I had told you before you wrote the book. . . .* Things that happened all those years ago, like the incident she just remembered on the boat on the way over, after all these years, something that happened, she says, when she was very little.

Clearly, Harriet has come to Lake Owasco to pass this story on, hoping to get it into print in the new edition of the biography. Perhaps also—when it came to money, she had to be crafty, diligent, and mindful of keeping her wits about her—she is thinking that new information will create more sales. As she begins—*When I was only seven years old I was sent away to take care of a baby*—Bradford and Hopkins pay close attention, keeping in mind the importance of imprinting the scene in their minds in order to recall it someday, whether for the page (for *us,* with our computers, all these years later) or parlor conversations.

Since one of Bradford's stated goals for the new book is to put up what she calls a fitting monument to Harriet's memory and to keep it green, she is particularly anxious to hear of the incident.

The past is alive in the present, of course, and it sits at table with brother, sister, and their guest. As Harriet revisits the earlier time, a thousand thoughts and pictures must fly through the minds of the listeners—

memories, descriptions, previously known details—and they fill in blank spots as she goes, just as the words to a song dwell beneath the strains of a tune played instrumentally and emerge unbidden in the listener's ear.

And so, for the moment, we depart the scene on the Owasco porch and fly back to earlier times with Harriet, to revisit and fill in the blanks of the past that lives there with them all, in order to envision the moment and especially to see, reimagine, and try to know her.

Scene 2.

Dorchester: Birth

I do not remember to have ever met a slave who could tell of his birthday. They seldom come nearer to it than planting-time, harvest-time, cherry-time, spring-time or fall-time.
—FREDERICK DOUGLASS, *NARRATIVE OF THE LIFE OF FREDERICK DOUGLASS, AN AMERICAN SLAVE,* 1845

I was born in Cambridge, Dorchester County, Md.
—AFFIDAVIT, HARRIET TUBMAN, NOVEMBER, 1894

I was born and reared in Dorchester County, Md. My maiden name was Araminta Ross.
—AFFIDAVIT, HARRIET TUBMAN, 1898

In the Eastern Shore of Maryland Dorchester County is where I was born. —HARRIET TUBMAN TO EMMA TELFORD, 1905

Aunt Harriet was born in Bucktown Dorchester County . . . the property of Edward Brodas . . .
—HARKLESS BOWLEY, GREAT-NEPHEW OF HARRIET TUBMAN, TO EARL CONRAD, 1939

She was born Araminta Ross—called "Minty"—not Harriet. But when exactly? What year and in which season? And where? Dorchester County, Maryland, but which town and on whose property? At her birth and even before, while still in her mother's womb, Araminta

The first letter written by Harriet's nephew, Harkless Bowley, to biographer Earl Conrad, in 1939. (*Transcription of letter appears at bottom of page.*)

was considered property pure and simple, a taxable asset belonging to a young man named Edward Brodess—sometimes spelled Brodas, Brawdis, or Broadas—who also owned her mother, Harriet Green. But in the year of Araminta Ross's birth, Edward had not yet come of age, and so another master controlled the life of her family at that point: a man named Anthony Thompson, who owned Minty's father, Ben Ross.

(*Transcription*)

519 N Carrollion [sic] Ave
Baltimore Md.

Aug 8—1939

Mr. M. Earl Conrad
Dear Sir My Dear Sir

My son received your letter of the 3rd mst [???] and turned it over to me to answer. My son is sick and goes to the hospital today for 10 or 12 days I will try to give you all the information concerning my great aunt, Harriet Tubman, that I can. Aunt Harriet was born in Bucktown Dorchester County about the year of 1812 the property of Edward Brodas who owned so many slaves he hired those he did not need to other farmers. Aunt Harriet was hired out at the age of 9 years to a woman as a nurse in connection with this to do general house work after working all day was required to attend the baby at night this woman was a particular cruel woman. Whipped as often as 5 or 6 times a day when She was nearly starved to death an unable to perform the heavy task She was sent Home to Her master. When She had recovered She was hired to a man who was even more cruel to her requiring Her to do the work of an able bodied man Hauling wood splitting nails and other kinds of laborious work. . . .

[Note: Punctuation added by author.]

Establishing this essential data turns out to be an especially thorny endeavor, largely due to the stubbornly held notion mentioned above: that, from the moment a newborn slave baby sucked air into her lungs, she was property, liable to sale, trade, or bequeathing. Thus, as far as most white people were concerned—and they, after all, were the ones who read, wrote, governed, bought, sold, and decided—there was no reason to keep personal records distinguishing one enslaved child from another, since in every measurable way but for their marketplace value, all slaves old or young were the same.

We must, then, depend on meager statistics and the word of existing accounts, many of them court documents recording the testimony of old and middle-aged white men who, in the interest of their own pocketbooks, had come to court to recount memories of an earlier time and give information about who was born when and who was whose great-grandfather and what the estimated selling price of a certain human being was in the marketplace assessment of the day. The data comes scattered and for the most part will not stand on its own, but must be applied, interpreted, and merged across the years.

COUNTY OF DORCHESTER

CAROLINE

Poplar Neck
◆ I

MARYLAND

DELAWARE

Federalsburg
◆

Trappe
◆ G

H

Choptank River

East New Market

F
Cambridge

DORCHESTER

Harrisville Road

Bucktown A

B C

D E

WICOMICO

Chesapeake Bay

A   Home of Edward Brodess.

B   Home of Atthow Pattison.

C   Bucktown store, where young Harriet received the blow that changed her life.

D   Anthony Thompson place, where Rit Green met Ben Ross, and where Harriet was born.

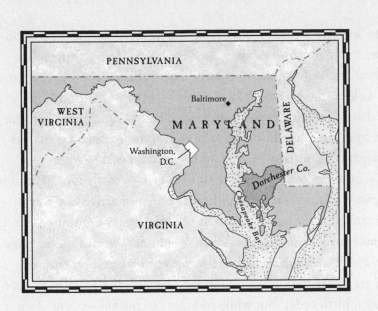

E   Harrisville Road, in the vicinity of which Ben Ross was given use of a cabin, and home of Harriet's first husband, John Tubman.

F   The town of Cambridge, on the Choptank River, down which John Bowley—the husband of Harriet's niece Kessiah—rowed his family to freedom, the town also where Harriet's brother Benjamin was held in jail as collateral for his owner's debts.

G   Trappe, where Mary Manokey Ross gave birth to her third child, Harriet, on Christmas Eve, 1854, the night the newborn's father, Robert Ross, escaped from bondage with his brothers.

H   East New Market, home of Reverend Samuel Green, who sheltered the Dover Eight during their run for freedom in 1857 and who was subsequently arrested for owning a copy of *Uncle Tom's Cabin*.

I   Poplar Neck, Caroline County, where Ben Ross lived with his wife and some of their children and grandchildren on acreage owned by Anthony C. Thompson. Harriet left for the North from here in 1849 and slept overnight in her parents' corn crib with her brothers on their way out of bondage in 1854. It was from here that she also set out for the North with her parents in 1857.

The surprise is that—considering the fact that, as the great abolitionist writer, orator, and escaped slave Frederick Douglass put it, he never knew a slave who knew his birth date, it being "the wish of most masters to keep their slaves thus ignorant"—any information exists at all. But thanks in part to several prolonged family squabbles, there are snippets from here, bits from there, last wills, those court testimonies and newspaper advertisements, an ad for a runaway slave.

The information has come to us over many years' time, most of it in a sideways manner—some of it having only just arrived by way of one woman's nervy search for artifacts in a neighbor's Dumpster—and despite numerous obstacles: conflicting opinions, a great fire, the passage of time. Names are spelled one way and then another; enslaved children are either forgotten or confused one with the other in terms of age, gender, birth order. But while resistant to chronology and often difficult to unravel, especially into a linear telling, the scraps, if carefully studied, eventually adhere well enough that we can piece together some pretty well-founded, if somewhat bold, assertions, a birthplace and date among them.

The season is winter, late February or early March; the year, 1822; the place, not Bucktown, Maryland, where Harriet grew up and where her great-nephew Harkless Bowley says she was born, but an area west of there, the Parsons Creek district of Dorchester County, south of Cambridge and the Little Choptank River, south of Tobacco Stick and Woolford, south down what we now call the Harrisville Road, which at this time is still known as Thompson's Road. Harrisville, the area is also called, or Peters Neck, in which is located the plantation of the landowner and slaveholder Anthony Thompson.

There. Her family—mother, father, sisters, one brother—live there. Harriet—Araminta, Minty—is not yet born.

In 1822, Anthony Thompson is sixty years old: not young as age goes at this time and under these circumstances, but he's an exceptionally robust and forceful man, who will live for another fourteen years. His family has been in Dorchester County since the mid-1600s, when, in the first days of the tobacco boom, single men in their twenties fled their lives in England and Scotland and came to settle on the eastern banks of the great Chesapeake Bay. There, they applied for acreage granted by what Maryland law called "headright count"—fifty acres for every relative or servant—often bringing indentured servants with them.

Of Maryland's Eastern Shore counties, Dorchester's a kind of lost and anomalous one, settled between the richer counties to the north—Talbot, Queen Anne, Kent—and the pretty much pure swamps of Worcester and Somerset. Bounded on the south and southeast by the Nanticoke River, on the north by the Choptank, and on the west by the bay, Dorchester is webbed with waterways, seventeen of them navigable, including the Transquaking River, the Chicamacomico River, the Big and Little Blackwater rivers, and Marshy Hope Creek. The rivers and creeks yield advantage to those who have emigrated there, hoping to repair their families' fortunes by transporting crops and timber to the Chesapeake and eventually the Atlantic. Water, however, makes for the county's curse as well as its blessing, and much of its southernmost sections remain uncultivated at this time, due to the rank impossibility of settling well or prosperously in swampland and marsh.

Cambridge, the Dorchester county seat and major port city, sits on the southern bank of the Choptank, in the high part of the county jutting into the Chesapeake. Anthony Thompson lives in the lower countryside, southwest of Cambridge, on the margins of, but well above, the marshes. So do the other white property owners and slaveholders of Harriet's early life.

Anthony Thompson owns Harriet Tubman's father, Ben Ross. At this time and for a little while longer, Harriet's mother lives on the Thompson place as well, but she does not belong to him, being the property of another man.

Language changes with perspective and in time. We pay attention, and make apologies when necessary. *Own* is a painful word to use, and it is good to repeat it—and other slaveholder's terms, such as *owner, master, mistress*—in order to understand exactly what kind of world this family and others like it inhabited. Such language makes an awful sound in our modern ears, as it should. But because it correctly characterizes the legal condition of slaves and the general oppression and categorizing that accompanied their every breath, we will use it, maintaining our own perspective as we go, understanding that these terms are not only shameful but, in the larger sense, inaccurate.

Thompson has done well. Having inherited a sizable chunk of land, he has shifted his feet to keep tune to the changing dances of the marketplace and by now has moved from the growing of tobacco and grains into the timber business, which—now that the more prosperous and fertile Talbot County has been timbered over—has become, along with shipping, Dorchester's most viable industry. The road Anthony Thompson built in 1816 (running from the Baptist Meeting House in Loomtown south to the Indian Landing, just beyond his home) gives him even easier access to several of those waterways—the Blackwater and Choptank rivers, Tobacco Stick Bay, and eventually the Chesapeake.

Prosperous, respected by the white community, Thompson is considered by his slaves to be relatively decent, a steady man to work for. Not that he hasn't had his difficulties. In 1817, he was imprisoned for debt, perhaps from overextending himself when he built that road. But times are hard all over the Eastern Shore. A war has recently come and gone, markets fluctuate, the land grows weary from overuse; in time, even a respected landowner makes a misstep and lands in jail for a few days.

But Thompson has kept his balance. By now, his landholdings are large, and his sons have been educated; the census of 1820 gives him thirty-nine slaves, many more than the average Dorchester plantation owner possesses and up by more than double from his holdings of ten years before, when the count was fifteen.

Ben Ross has been the property of Anthony Thompson for many years, perhaps his whole life. His wife, however—Harriet "Rit" or "Rittia" Green—belongs to Thompson's young stepson and ward, twenty-year-old Edward Brodess.

The word *wife* is not casually applied here. That slaves were not allowed legally to marry is of no concern to this story, or to the lives of the many enslaved people we will chronicle and follow. Even in the early 1800s, when Ben and Rit first met, marriages between couples held in bondage were recognized as such, not only within the slave community but among many slaveholders. In Anthony Thompson's 1839 inventory—called "Negroes of Anthony Thompson"—he will record the marital status of each slave, listing Ben Ross's name first, with the notation, "wife and children belonging to Edward Brodess."

In 1822, Ben and Rit have known each other for nineteen years, since 1803, when the widowed Anthony Thompson married the widowed Mary Pattison Brodess and the two merged their separate households. After her marriage, Mary moved into the Thompson place with her only child, Edward, who was almost two years old, and her five slaves, one of whom was her personal attendant, Rit Green.

Within a few years, Rit Green and Ben Ross had entered a marital union that will last the rest of their lives, and by 1808 they had begun having children. By this time, 1822, they have four—three daughters (Linah, fourteen; Mariah Ritty, eleven; Soph, nine) and one son (Robert, six)—with another on the way. Since under Maryland law, ownership of the mother determines the status of the children, all of their offspring, including the one in Rit's womb, are also considered the property of young Edward Brodess.

Early winter, 1822. Edward Brodess is still a minor. In a matter of months, however—June 14 of this year—he will reach the age of maturity, at which time he will claim his inheritance, including his slaves . . . and after which time, Rit and her children will live and work wherever young Edward tells them to and at his prerogative.

Straight chronology is comforting. It would be nice simply to jump into the year when Harriet Tubman's parents met and move forward to her birth. But once again, the terms of slavery remind us that an enslaved family had no legal rights, not being considered citizens, or even as people. And so to discover anything at all about them, we have to examine the archives and the wills, the accounts and testimonies of the white people who considered them property.

To find out how the mother of Araminta Ross—and Minty herself—came to be the property of Edward Brodess, we turn to a section of the will of Edward's great-grandfather Atthow Pattison, written in January 1791 and probated February 1, 1797:

> Item. I give and bequeath unto my granddaughter Mary Pattison one Negro girl called Rittia and her increase until she and they arrive to forty-five years of age.

And this:

> Item. I give and bequeath unto my daughter Elizabeth Pattison one Negro woman named Bess until she arrives to the age of forty-five years of age to be her housemaid and her children until they arrive to the same age, also one Negro woman named Suke until she and they arrive to forty-five years of age.

Also, to his grandson Samuel Keene and his heirs:

> . . . one Negro woman called Minty and her increase until she and they arrive to forty-five years of age, using them kindly, also my desk, also a gun . . .

We should note as we go the words "Negro woman" in two of the items and "Negro girl" in the other; the phrase "and her increase"; and, even more especially, the crucial "until she and they arrive to forty-five years of age."

In 1791, when Atthow Pattison wrote his will, his family had lived and owned property in Dorchester County for over a hundred years. The Pattison land—more than four hundred acres—is located near Anthony Thompson's place, about eight miles east of there and west of the Transquaking River at the confluence of the Little Blackwater with the Big. In the two generations following patriarch Thomas Pattison's time, the family has increased and held on to its inheritance, in some measure by adhering to the patriarch's policy of keeping property within what Atthow calls the "line and blood" of his family, by encouraging offspring to marry their cousins.

By 1791, Atthow Pattison's daughter Mary is dead. His surviving daughter, Elizabeth, has hewn close to family tradition by marrying her first cousin, William Pattison, thereby assuring that the Pattison name will live beyond Atthow's death. Her husband, William, however, has died, leaving Elizabeth to cope with the rearing of five children: two sons—Gourney Crow and William—and three daughters—Elizabeth, Acsah, and Mary.

We must remember these names, these people, these owners of slaves bequeathed to them by Atthow Pattison. They are the decision makers, who will determine how the lives of Rit Green and her children, including the one born Araminta Ross, later to become Harriet Tubman, will go, and where they will live and work, according to whose directives. And we should remember especially the name of Atthow's beloved granddaughter Mary, on whom ownership of the slave girl Rittia has been bestowed, along with her increase . . . until, that is, "she and they arrive to forty-five years of age." Important, that *until*. But vague when left without subsequent clarification: until forty five years of age and then what?

Atthow doesn't own many slaves: five in 1776, seven in 1790, and his will mentions only five, all of them female, all to be held in bondage until they are forty-five. To prevent owners from setting aged and ill people free to wander helplessly about the state, panhandling and seeking shel-

Atthow Pattison's will, in which he emphasizes the need for descendants to marry "within the lines and blood" of his family and bequeaths to his children and grand-children such "possessions" as land, heifers, a writing desk, a still . . . and several enslaved people, among them Harriet's mother, the "Negro girl called Rittia."

ter, the laws of Maryland have set fifty as the maximum age for the free-ing of slaves. Atthow, however, has instructed his descendants to manu-mit his slaves five years earlier than that.

Although her exact birth date has not been established, the "Negro girl called Rittia" is probably slightly younger than her mistress. In 1791, when the will is written, she may be six years old and Mary Pattison seven. Clearly, the slave child is meant to be a companion to her mistress.

Young Mary's mother, Elizabeth, enjoys the services of a personal servant of her own, a woman who will be called Modesty by all who re-member her, even though she is not mentioned by that name in Atthow's will. Some will even call up Modesty's last name, which, while the deri-vation of it is unknown, is Green. As for why Modesty Green is not men-tioned in Atthow's will, she may already belong to Elizabeth—given to her perhaps by her own mother—or perhaps Atthow knows her as either Bess or Suke. Much is unknown about Modesty Green; in fact, almost everything, including where she was born—presumably West Africa, but which part and what tribe?—and when she came to Maryland.

The one fact to hold on to is that Modesty Green is the mother of Harriet (called Rit or Rittia) Green and the grandmother of Harriet Tubman.

When in 1797, Atthow dies, Rittia becomes Mary's property. The girls—one enslaved and one free—are in their early teens, still living in the same household under the comforting presence and guidance of their mothers.

They grow up together, certainly not playmates, but girls together nonetheless, watching each other move past puberty into physical matu-rity. Rit learns domestic skills—to cook and clean, sew, mend, patch, iron, to tend to her mistress's hair and toilet. It is unlikely that Mary Pat-tison was sent to school, but she certainly would have learned to read and write, skills that separated her from her playmate inextricably.

And so, in the marshy district of southern Dorchester, the young Rit Green becomes a domestic servant, who by the time she is well into her teenage years, has become exquisitely trained in skills far more im-portant than stitching and stirring. Living intimately with a white fam-ily for that many years, she has picked up on their ways and has learned

how to know what they mean when they speak, the nuances that go beyond language: the tone and rhythms they use, the looks they cast, their
gestures and facial expressions, the secrets they think they are keeping,
which to their servants seem as obvious as breakfast mash.

These skills she will pass on to her children, especially her daughters.

In March of 1800, Mary Pattison marries a young man named Joseph
Brodess, whose family has not prospered. Joseph's legacy is one of scram-
bling for respect and money and of skirmishes with the law, including a
charge of child abuse against an uncle. While he and his siblings have inherited some four hundred acres of land several miles east and somewhat
north of the Pattisons', in an area named Bucktown, Joseph himself did
not receive the homestead, and his parcel of two hundred or so acres has
not been improved. In the year of his marriage, his older brother Edward
has begun selling off the family property (the dwelling house, two slaves,
five horses, seventeen sheep, twenty-three hogs, a mahogany table, as
well as all of the wheat seeded and growing on his land) and is planning
to move west to Mississippi, where opportunity seems brighter and new
starts both possible and perhaps—as rumor has it—easier.

Joseph Brodess, however, has decided to stick it out in Dorchester,
perhaps because of the greater prosperity of his bride's family, and maybe
because Mary refuses to go.

At sixteen, Mary Pattison enters her marriage accompanied by Rit
Green, who is not only her companion but also a connection to her previous life. In addition to his two hundred acres, Joseph Brodess adds four
male slaves to their combined holdings: Shadrach, Sam, Frederick, and
one other man, whose name has not been recorded. Because there is no
house on his property, and since Mary's widowed mother is struggling to
take care of a household of fifteen, perhaps the newlyweds live with her
so that Joseph can help out. In which case, the four women would remain in the same household: the mothers, Elizabeth and Modesty, as well
as their daughters, Mary and Rit.

We should take note of some names at this point—the slave named
Minty, whom Atthow bequeathed to Samuel Keene (asking specifically
that he treat her and her increase kindly); a teenage slave girl named

Modesty, sold to a trader by Gourney Crow Pattison—and the frequent repetition of the names Harriet and Minty. There is no proof, but surely these women are kin and connected—if not blood relatives, then family, one way or another. For enslaved people, family counted more than anything else except religion. Church and family ties provided hope, grounding, a life beyond dailiness.

Within six months or so, Mary Pattison Brodess is pregnant, and in June 1801, she prepares to give birth. A midwife would have been called. A seventeen-year-old girl might well have suffered a difficult, possibly lengthy labor. The three other women help out, especially her personal servant and companion, Rit, who attends to her mistress and gives her comfort.

On June 14, Mary gives birth to her only child, a son she and her husband name Edward, for his grandfather on his paternal side. Thus does Rit observe the birth of her future owner as he squalls his way into the plantation world of the Eastern Shore.

Edward Brodess. Only child. His father dies the next year, leaving his property—including land and slaves—in trust to his baby son, who will be christened in the Episcopal parish church the following June and, within a few years, will be the last Brodess remaining in Dorchester County.

On March 19, 1803, a little more than a year after Joseph's death, Mary Pattison Brodess—who owns property but no home—makes a practical move. She marries the forty-one-year-old landowner Anthony Thompson, who has sons not much younger than she. With young Edward and her five slaves, she moves to the Thompson place.

Thus does the approximately eighteen-year-old slave girl Rit move with her mistress to the farm where her future husband, Benjamin Ross, lives and works.

And there, in a way, the story of Harriet Tubman begins.

For a while, Rit is separated from her mother, and Mary from hers. But the four women are soon reunited when Elizabeth's health begins to fail and she and Modesty move to the Thompson place so that Elizabeth's daughter, and Modesty's, can help watch over her during her last days.

After Elizabeth Pattison's death, except for a brief appearance in a lawsuit, the name of Modesty Green disappears from all known records and family stories. The only mention we so far have of her appears in an 1852 lawsuit in which Gourney C. Pattison, the grandson of Atthow, files a claim against his cousin Mary over ownership of Rittia Green and her children. In sworn testimony during the course of this nasty, protracted business, one of Anthony Thompson's sons, Anthony C., will swear that he knew Rit's mother, Modesty. In court, he calls her by name. Anthony C. Thompson was only a boy at the time, but he remembers that his step-grandmother, Elizabeth Pattison, came to live for a short time in his father's home, bringing Modesty with her, and that she died soon after.

After that, there is nothing. Anthony C. Thompson doesn't say where Modesty went next, how long she lived, where she came from originally—nothing.

Presumably, almost certainly, Rit talked of her mother to her husband and her children. But no one remembered to keep the story alive through its retelling, and no one seems to have written it down.

In 1808, Ben and Rit's first child is born into the slave community at Thompson's place, a daughter they name Linah. Since Anthony Thompson is known to hire a midwife to service enslaved women, perhaps Rit's labor is attended by a black woman who lives close by. In years to come, Linah will be described as of a weakly constitution, and perhaps she begins her life that way.

And so for maybe five years or so the two young women who grew into puberty together on the Pattison plantation watch as one generation gives over to the next in both of their families. But by the time Linah is two years old and her owner, Edward, nine, Mary Pattison Brodess has died. There is no record of what killed her or even exactly when her death occurred. She is not mentioned again, except in relation to her property rights. Mary's seems a sad life somehow, even given that we know so little about it. Perhaps especially since we know so little, for we are left to wonder why her death—twenty-six years prior to her husband's, even though he was more than twenty years older—has not been recorded, or if it was, then where?

Testimony of Anthony C. Thompson, who at age sixty remembers when Harriet's mother, Rit, came to live in his father's home with Mary Pattison Brodess and her son, Edward. After recalling the names and ages of the children of Rit Green and Ben Ross, he also estimates their value in the slave marketplace. (*Transcription of testimony appears at bottom of page.*)

(*Transcription*)

. . . afterwards married Joseph Brodess the father of Edward Brodess, and the said Joseph having died leaving her a widow she afterwards married Anthony Thompson the father of the deponent. Upon the death of Joseph Brodess, in the division of Negroes belonging to the estate, Rit and Linah, her daughter, were allotted to Edward Brodess. The said Joseph Brodess having left his widow and the said Edward Brodess, his only child, his only heir and legal representatives, witness has always understood that said Rit was the

mother of Linah, Soph, Robert, Ben, Harry, Minty and Mose . . .
Linah I think if living must be 45, Linah and Soph are sold out of
the state and I understand by Edward Brodess. Mose and Minty
since the death of Edward Brodess have run away from the possession of his widow, Robert, Harry, and Ben are still living and always
claimed by Edward Brodess and in his possession or hired out by
him, and since his death hired out by his widow. Witness had in his
possession at one time three of them, two boys and a girl, for which
he paid $120 a year, he has now Robert in his possession for which
he payd [sic] $53 per year. All of the said children were born while
their mother, Rit, was under 45 years of age, except Moses, the
youngest, he may have been born after his mother was 45 years but
witness cannot say. Witness has always understood that the said
Mary Pattison claimed the said girl Rit as coming from the Pattison
estate, the other Negroes which she had, she got from Brodess, as far
as he knows, Rit was the only female servant that Mary Pattison had
when his father married her. The Negroes belonging to Brodess estate and . . .

She leaves her only child in the care of her husband, Anthony
Thompson, under whose legal guardianship the boy will remain until he
reaches the age of maturity at twenty-one. At which point, he will also
come into full possession of the land and slaves left to him in trust by his
father.

Edward grows up alone, the only white child in the house. Perhaps
spoiled, perhaps miserable, missing his mother, living with an old man
for a father, his stepbrothers—who are smarter and more ambitious—off
at school a great deal of the time. Loneliness can make a child cranky, ar-
rogant, perhaps even a brat.

Rit keeps her eye on the boy owner.

In 1822, Ben and Rit have been a steady presence in the large Thompson slave community for nineteen years. During that time, they have certainly formed close bonds with other members of that community,

creating a kind of extended family there. And they have earned some status. Though illiterate, Ben Ross has become Anthony Thompson's chief timber inspector, respected for his skills. As a domestic servant, Rit garners privileges not given to field-workers. Under these circumstances, and given Thompson's disinclination to sell his slaves, as long as Rit and Ben remain on his place, they can hope for some measure of stability.

But in June of this year, when Edward Brodess turns twenty-one, there is no knowing what he or the times will be like or what changes he will make.

We were always uneasy, Harriet will tell a man who, in 1855, has come to Canada to talk to her and other refugees from slavery. *Every time I saw a white man I was afraid of being carried away.*

Unease dogs the footsteps of Rit and Benjamin Ross, jags into their sleep. More than anything else, they, and all others living as they do, are haunted by a vision of the auction block. This often was not a formal wooden platform as we might imagine, but, more specifically, an event, one that took place in a central location, close to hotels where slave traders stayed—in this case, the steps of the Dorchester County courthouse in downtown Cambridge. The seat, as white citizens would have it, of justice.

By limiting their time of bondage, Atthow Pattison had decreed that Rit and her children be considered term slaves, not slaves for life—a crucial distinction. By Maryland law, term slaves could not be sold beyond state lines. When their time of bondage expired, they were to be set free. But there is no real assurance that anyone will abide by that law, and no way for Rit to prove her status, since she can't read or write and the white women who valued her most, Elizabeth and Mary, are dead.

There is the added complication that Atthow Pattison did not specifically say what should happen to Rit and her increase once they reached the age of forty-five—his use of the conjunction *until* leaving unfortunate room for interpretation and, in the future, disgraceful courtroom maneuvers.

By June of 1820, when Edward was about to turn nineteen, the fifty-eight-year-old Thompson began to make plans for his ward's adult years, in all likelihood looking forward to the time when the young man would move out. As Edward's legal guardian, Anthony Thompson's mandate was to use his stepson's estate solely for the maintenance and education of his ward, and to secure and preserve his assets for his use when he reached the age of maturity. In no way was he to reduce the net value of his ward's inheritance.

Regarding Edward Brodess's finances, the Orphans Court would remind Thompson of the law: "The interest or income of a minor's estate is the fund out of which he is to be maintained and educated, and under no circumstances [can] be exceeded. . . ." Further, the guardian, whose province it was to "take care of the person of his ward," should keep together and preserve his property of every kind and description. "Repairs necessary for those ends, within the compass of the ward's income, ought to be attended to, but *schemes of improvement* under no circumstances ought to be engaged in. . . ."

In 1820, Anthony applied for and received permission from the Dorchester Orphans Court to use his ward's money to build a house for him on his land, a modest one-story structure—thirty-two by twenty feet, with plank floors and a brick chimney—as well as a barn. To ensure that the house was properly constructed, the process was to be overseen and supervised by Edward's uncle, Gourney Crow Pattison, the work and materials to be examined by inspectors who would then report back to the court. In the end, the cost of building the house and barn came to some thirteen hundred dollars, a greater amount than the value of Edward's estate, which the supervisors and the court presumably believed would be regained by rentals and future sales. In the meantime, Anthony Thompson rented out his ward's new house and credited the rent to Brodess's account.

As the date of Edward's twenty-first birthday draws near, the Ross family grows uneasier still. Rit and Ben certainly know of the new house. Ben may even have participated in its construction. Although the written plans make no mention of slave quarters, the building of the house increases the possibility that Edward will soon move Rit and her children there, some ten miles from Ben, east across Church Creek and over the Little Blackwater River, to Bucktown, a harsh move, away from the community she knows and deeper into the marsh, where the land is unimproved, the work harder, the master young, undisciplined, and unpredictable.

By the winter of 1822, to which date we now return, Rit and Ben have been married for at least fifteen years. Their four children range in age from fourteen (Linah) to six (Robert).

Rit is about thirty-seven years old, and by January, she is heavy with the new baby, due to deliver in late February or early March, still deep winter, the ground yet unyielding, the air icy even when temperatures come up a bit. There are no pictures of Rit, but it is hard not to imagine her small and sturdy, like her daughter, pregnancy causing her to ache and cramp as the baby fills up her midsection, pushing against her ribs and pelvis.

In April, Anthony Thompson will turn sixty. One of his sons, Anthony C., a medical doctor, lives in Talbot County on rich and valuable property inherited by his wife. Another son, Absalom, is attending college, and he will also be awarded a medical degree. Anthony C. is, in addition, a sometime Methodist minister. And so the father must feel that he has done well by his own sons, and while his life and theirs has certainly rolled into debt and trouble with the times, and will continue to do so, he has fared better than many, perhaps even than most.

But what a bother his second marriage has turned out to be, and who'd have thought his bride, so much younger, would die first, leaving him to track down and see to her scampish and ungrateful son!

For Thompson, his stepson is a constant worry, traveling nobody knows exactly where, perhaps visiting Brodess relatives in Mississippi, or—based on 1820 U.S. census figures—living for a time with his stepbrother Anthony C. Although there is no record or indication of an inclination toward higher education, he might be off at school or—a more likely possibility, considering the fancy silk duds and yards of red ribbon charged by his stepfather to his account—off in some city, having a good time.

To abide by the laws of his guardianship, Anthony Thompson is keeping an account book in which tallies up debits and credits as they are charged to his stepson. Every time Edward buys a length of ribbon or a pair of boots on credit at a local store, that amount is recorded on the red side of the ledger. And when Thompson employs slaves who belong to his stepson, he gives Edward credit for the hire and the work those slaves do for him.

In 1821, and again in 1822, Thompson hires Rit. In his ledger, he credits Edward's account for her services, which he has set at sixteen dollars a year.

He also hires her firstborn, Linah at twelve dollars a year, and four unnamed male slaves, presumably the men Joseph Brodess brought into his marriage to Mary Pattison. On the debit side, Thompson charges Edward two dollars a month "board and clothing for two Negro children" for eleven months. These children are certainly Soph, nine years old, and Robert, six. Ben and Rit's second daughter, Mariah Ritty, who is now eleven, is not mentioned, and since she is old enough to handle heavier work, she may be otherwise hired out in the area, even though she, too, is said to be somewhat fragile.

Financially strapped, the planters of the Eastern Shore consider hiring out slaves an economic necessity if they are to hold on to their land and keep their own families properly housed, fed, clothed, and educated. Since slaves are their biggest asset, farmers rent out their services to neighbors and friends, using them, as one slaveholder will attest, to "make a little money until [they can] turn them into real estate."

The list of Thompson's charges against Edward Brodess includes the following:

1821

March 1	pair of shoes $2. Repairing boots $2	$4.00
April 24	1 3/4 blue cloth at $4yd, 1 h yd brown ??? 37c	7.37
	1/4 yd ???ing 12c?, ???? buttons 75c	.87
	Silk ??? 75c, pair pantaloons 4.50	4.75
May 19	Hat 2.50, pair shoes	3.75
	Pair stockings25c, Cash? 50c	.75
	1 comb 25c, ???? $1, pair shoes $2	3.25
Sept 6	5.2 yds linen @ 2c, lb ?? ?? tobacco? 8 buttons 18.	3.58
	Thread 18c, rd ribbon 18 3/4, 1/4 ? powder 12	.39
	Cash $1, pair shoes, 1.34, 1 lb. ??12c	2.50

Dec. 10   Pair of yarn stockings $1, making pair

pantaloons 50 cls   1.50

To James Landers bill for the following sundry,

I yd cotton ca???? 25c. Silk cape? 1.25   1.50

1 Swiss? and 1 silk@ 10¢. Thread, 4 1/4c   .22 1/4

3/8 linen 18, cash borrowed 12c,

making pantaloons 125c   1.68 1/4

But Edward Brodess cannot be found and does not respond to the charges.

Reading the list, it is not hard to envision an outraged Anthony Thompson, who clearly believes that his stepson, by whom he feels he has done well, has, in return, bolted from financial responsibility and filial obligation. He has also charged Edward for the cost of building his house, which amount Edward has refused to pay, claiming that the cost of the house exceeds his inheritance. A man of action, the stepfather takes the matter to court, where his account book is presented as evidence.

While the two white men scrap, Ben, Rit, and their children face an unwanted separation.

After crediting Edward's account for sixteen dollars for the hire of Rit in 1821, Thompson has subtracted $5.73 for forty-three lost days in 1822. And on March 15, 1822, he inserts a charge of two dollars in cash paid to a midwife to attend to "negro Rit." And so it is that we come up with

Anthony Thompson's ledger entry for March 15, 1822, in which he charges his stepson and ward, Edward Brodess, for work on a road, a pair of stockings, and $2 paid to a midwife for Harriet Tubman's mother, here called "Negro Rit." This ledger sheet goes a long way in establishing the place and date of Harriet's birth.

information from which we can make a determination of the approximate birth date of Araminta Ross.

We can merge these two entries easily enough. Rit, it clearly seems, missed forty-three days of work in the winter of 1822 because of her advanced state of pregnancy, which culminated in her giving birth to her fifth child.

This date jibes with other, later testimonies giving the birth order of Ben and Rit's children, putting Araminta "Minty" Ross square in the middle of nine siblings, her birth occurring not in Bucktown as has often been claimed, not only by local residents but by Harriet's great-

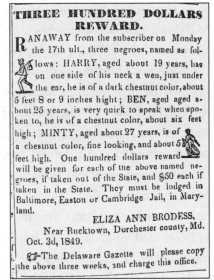

THREE HUNDRED DOLLARS REWARD.

RANAWAY from the subscriber on Monday the 17th ult., three negroes, named as follows: HARRY, aged about 19 years, has on one side of his neck a wen, just under the ear, he is of a dark chestnut color, about 5 feet 8 or 9 inches hight; BEN, aged aged about 25 years, is very quick to speak when spoken to, he is of a chestnut color, about six feet high; MINTY, aged about 27 years, is of a chestnut color, fine looking, and about 5 feet high. One hundred dollars reward will be given for each of the above named negroes, if taken out of the State, and $50 each if taken in the State. They must be lodged in Baltimore, Easton or Cambridge Jail, in Maryland.

ELIZA ANN BRODESS,
Near Bucktown, Dorchester county, Md.
Oct. 3d, 1849.

☞The Delaware Gazette will please copy the above three weeks, and charge this office.

Eliza Brodess's runaway advertisement for Minty (Harriet Tubman) and her brothers Ben and Harry (Henry).

nephew Harkless Bowley, but in Peters Neck, on the property of the outraged, litigious, aging stepfather, Anthony Thompson.

The date also corresponds exactly with an ad that will run in the October 3, 1849, *Cambridge Democrat* offering a reward for the capture of "MINTY, aged about 27 years," and her brothers. Until January 2003, no ad mentioning Harriet Tubman as a runaway had been found. But in that year, a determined Tubman researcher and Bucktown resident, Susan Meredith, began keeping tabs on a house in Cambridge whose owner was stripping his attic of items he considered too old to be of any use or interest. To hold his discards, the man had rented a Dumpster and installed it on the curb in front of his house. Susan Meredith made it her business to conduct regular raids on the Dumpster, among which recovered treasure was the newspaper containing the ad, which was placed less than seven months after Edward Brodess's death, by his widow, Eliza. The ad also states that two other slaves have run away as well: "Harry, aged about 19 years" and "Ben, aged about 25 years." These two men can be reliably identified as Harriet's brothers Henry (called Harry in the ad) and Benjamin.

Harriet Tubman: born February or March, 1822, Dorchester County, Maryland, below Tobacco Stick, in Peters Neck. Escaped from slavery at age twenty-seven, 1849, having left for the North, in all likelihood, from Dr. Anthony Thompson's plantation in Caroline County, Maryland.

By piecing together these various scraps of information, we establish the birth date of "the Moses of her People." And then we can circle back to the beginning of our exploration and—while somewhat surprised to find that Anthony Thompson bothered to hire a midwife for the thirty-seven-year-old slave woman, Rit—state with a fair amount of certainty and confidence that in the late winter of 1822 (giving the plantation owner leeway and time to record the charge as a debit to his stepson, Edward Brodess, who, by the way, will never prosper enough to move out of or even enlarge the cracker-box frame house built for him by his stepfather), a pure and wonderful event occurs: Araminta Ross, aka Harriet Tubman, is born.

Scene 3.

Childhood

I grew up like a neglected weed . . .
—INTERVIEW WITH HARRIET TUBMAN, IN BENJAMIN DREW,
*A NORTH-SIDE VIEW OF SLAVERY. THE REFUGEE: OR THE
NARRATIVE OF FUGITIVE SLAVES IN CANADA,* 1856

In 1905, Harriet will say that her first memory is of lying in a cradle.

"You've seen these trees that are hollow," she tells her Auburn neighbor Emma Telford. There is no knowing what Telford's response is, but in any case, Harriet proceeds to describe what next to do: You take a big tree, cut it down, put a "bode" in each end, and make a cradle. She remembers, she says—perhaps having been asked for her earliest memory by her interviewer—lying in that there.

Harriet is eighty-three years old when she relates that memory, one that in all of her many other interviews and performances she has never before reported—at least not to anyone who took notes or remembered. Why, then, would it come to her now? Why this late in her life, as she tells her story yet one more time, would her oldest, earliest memory suddenly come to mind?

There is no way to figure it with anything approaching certainty. But even as we ask the question, shading our eyes against the glare of so many versions of the truth, we must respect Harriet's *The first thing I remember,* before breezing by it to land on documented dates and times and the sworn testimony of related likelihoods. We have to linger awhile, if for no other reason than how can we not?

Harriet Tubman saw things. She was, to squeeze her talents into a known category, a visionary, if not, as some believe, a true psychic. The visions she described were sometimes nightmarish, dreamlike or prophetic. But the voices she heard and the messages she received were pragmatic and specific. They told her what to do next, something like the ones heard by the young Jeanne d'Arc. Through letters and published accounts, her contemporaries—hard-nosed realists among them—verify the indisputable presence of these extrasensory powers and offer sound footing for the choice to believe that, in Harriet Tubman's eighties, a vision appeared to her, in which she actually *saw* herself—and why not?—sleeping in a hollow tree cut and shaped for a bed, which, when she grew too big and active, would be handed down to the next child.

A devoted parent, Ben Ross was also, as we have noted, a skilled timber inspector who, of necessity, had secured for himself a practical knowledge of trees, a quick eye for making snap judgments about which kind to cut for what purpose. And so surely he was the one who selected the proper tree, or hollow log, he who measured and cut it the right size, smoothed away the splinters, cut the necessary "bodes" the right size, one for each end to hold the baby safely in.

In the memory, Minty is perhaps a year old, maybe less. Say the winter or spring of 1823. Edward Brodess having yet to show up to claim them, Rit and her five children are still on the Thompson place, living with Ben. Harriet remembers lying in the tree cradle when "the young ladies in the big house where my mother worked came down, caught me up in the air before I could walk."

Harriet doesn't say why the young white women—probably Anthony Thompson's daughter-in-law and niece, Anne Gurney and Barsheba Thompson, who lived there for a time—bothered to come to the slave quarters, only that they did. They surely did not enter a house in the quarters, since few white women did, but found her outside, where someone, maybe one of her big sisters, rocked her. Finding the child in her cradle out under the trees, they "caught me in the air before I could walk."

See her: a special child with a large spirit, irresistible to the young white women. Her small, compact body in flight, airborne, like a ball pitched to the sky, the baby who would one day find her own way to fly.

Arms out, she catches at the air, aloft.

In October 1823, when Minty is about nineteen or twenty months old, Edward Brodess is subpoenaed to appear in court to answer his stepfather's charges. But the upstart absconder remains in hiding. Another subpoena is issued. Finally, Edward comes home and, at twenty-two, gains control of his assets and moves into the Bucktown house his stepfather built for him.

In March of the next year, he marries Eliza Keene, a Catholic girl who has wed rather below her family's expectations. After the nuptials, he and his new bride go to Bucktown to begin married life.

In April, Edward shows up in court with Robert P. Martin, his attorney, but he refuses to pay up.

As the hostilities between stepfather and stepson intensify, Rit and Ben face the certainty that the stability and continuance of their life as a family as it has existed for fifteen years will soon end, and that things will never again be the same.

The ten miles between the Thompson place and Bucktown are watery and uncertain, as much of the land is given to tidewater marshes, which swell and sink with the Chesapeake as it obeys the rhythms of the Atlantic. From now on, visits between Ben and Rit will be difficult at best, often impossible.

When Rit is ordered to leave, Ben may walk the ten miles with his wife and his five children to help them on their way. The four male slaves who belonged to Edward's father travel to Bucktown, as well. Linah is sixteen, Mariah Ritty thirteen, Soph eleven, Robert eight, and Araminta two. There is a new baby, Benjamin—named for his father—and Rit is pregnant again. They go part of the way either on a wagon or on foot and then—there is so much water!—undoubtedly into a boat, if saltwater tides demand or allow it. A long trip, exceedingly difficult, mother and children traipsing into no telling what kind of future, with who knows what kind of hiring out and sales ahead, given Edward's youth and brashness.

There is no record of the construction of a slave quarter on the Brodess place, only the disputed house and barn built by Anthony Thompson. No community, no children for Minty and her siblings to play with, no women to share child-tending duties. Ben Ross may fashion a home for his family in the barn, but there is nothing that says so. His heart must break to leave his wife and children there, in surroundings so brutally meager. But once he has settled them in as comfortably as he can, he has no choice but to make the long and tediously slow journey back to the Thompson place, alone.

Unsurprisingly, Edward turns out to be ill-suited for the business of farming. In addition, the whole of Dorchester County continues to suffer from hard times and bad markets. And so from the beginning, the newlyweds, Edward and Eliza, live a hopeful would-be life, ever waiting for luck, the big score, a good crop, meantime continuously borrowing, in debt to their eyes, always up against lawsuits and bankruptcy. This will never change. And when the children keep coming—eight in all—their life will become more and more difficult. Edward will eventually die after a brief illness, at age forty-seven, in the same small house built for him by his stepfather, before a number of his offspring have reached puberty. Eliza will inherit only debt and trouble. By then, whatever goodness had found a place in her heart will have long ago been wrung out, leaving only rage, greed, and disappointment to sustain its pulse.

In a constant struggle to pay off debts and hold on to his land, Edward, like other Eastern Shore slaveholders, regularly makes use of his greatest assets, his slaves. Officially, Rit and her children live on his land and are counted in federal and state assessments and censuses as belonging to him, but during this time and into the future, they are all more often gone than present, as Edward hires them out for ready cash, even the children, and occasionally—unlike Anthony Thompson—sells one or two.

This strategy begins immediately as, within eighteen months of his marriage and during the still-unsettled court battle with Anthony Thompson, Edward makes his first attempt to dig himself out of trouble. He sells two slaves: a boy named James, who is about fifteen, and a girl, Rhody, whose age is listed in the Dorchester County Land Record of 1825 as sixteen. The young people are bought and paid for by Dempsey Kane, a slave trader from Mississippi, for $610.

There is no record of these teenagers having been advertised for public sale. Since many of Brodess's kin have moved to Alabama and Mississippi, he and Kane—who comes often to the Eastern Shore— probably have struck a private deal. Kane may have come to Maryland as an agent for a particular buyer, perhaps a Brodess relative, or he may be speculating, hoping to turn his purchase into the going rate of profit, 20 percent or more.

The money having changed hands, Kane goes to Bucktown, where he secures the boy and girl—ties them, chains them, either to himself or together, perhaps with others—and takes them away. The transatlantic slave trade has been outlawed for almost twenty years now, but within the states of the South, it not only continues but is on the steady increase.

Edward and Eliza don't have many slaves. Almost certainly, the name and age of the girl being sold have been dashed off in haste, and she is, in fact, not Rhody but Rit and Ben's second child, fourteen-year-old Mariah Ritty. Probably because she lived for so short a time in Bucktown, Mariah Ritty's name is missing from many of the court documents and testimonies in which Brodess's neighbors establish the existence of her brothers and sisters. But the Pattisons remember her, and they will supply her approximate birth date.

She was, as they remember her, a somewhat fragile girl. Once she's sold she may not live long enough to complete the long journey south and then west from Bucktown.

As for James, what is there to say except that we don't know? His name is given only as James, and he may be an enslaved boy whom Eliza brought into the marriage.

There is nothing Ben and Rit can do. They may not even have known their daughter was up for sale until after she was taken away. Ben has won the respect of local slaveholders and so, in her way, has Rit. But Ben is ten miles away at the Thompson place, and since all mothers loudly protest the sale of their children, Rit's grief is dismissed. In the end, respect counts for nothing. Nor, it seems, does the law.

Like a death, those slaves who found freedom testified when describing the selling of family members. Worse than death, some said, especially when your loved one was taken to the barbarous Deep South— *to Georgia!*—even more so when the one sold was your child, her life debased, her very soul reduced to flesh and service.

Like her grandmother Modesty, Mariah Ritty Ross will never be heard from again. Her recorded history ends here, and now.

Minty is three and a half years old. At forty, assuming Edward will honor his great-grandfather's will, Rit is five years from manumission.

A mother does not heal from the loss of a child. The surviving sibling suffers in her own way, helpless to fill in the loss however she tries. Imagining how Rit must have mourned, it is easy to understand why Harriet later speaks of her family's unease any time they saw a white man.

Once she has escaped slavery, Harriet will go back time and again to Maryland to rescue members of her family. To understand the ferocity of her determination, we must remember this event—the sale of her big sister at a time when she was too young to understand why or how a person could simply *vanish*—and how it must have affected the little girl to lie awake wondering what happened and to watch helplessly as her mother and her older brothers and sisters give themselves over to inconsolable despair, calling the name of the vanished sister.

She is a fix-it child, on the lookout for ways to make things right from her earliest days. This time, nothing helps.

As a domestic servant, Rit leaves for work in early-morning darkness and doesn't come home until after nightfall, once the dishes are washed and the Brodess's first child has been put safely to bed. More than likely, she takes the new baby, Rachel, with her, to watch over and breast-feed. In slave narratives, many people testify to the fact that while domestic work was less physically taxing than field labor, its terms were more onerous, in that they felt always on call, always at work, considered a part of the white family instead of their own.

Benjamin is a baby, at least two years younger than Minty, who is four, both of them too young to be hired out or to work in Eliza Brodess's kitchen.

Linah, Soph, and Robert work the fields or are hired out. Mariah

Ritty is gone forever. And so Rit has no choice but to make Minty the baby-sitter of Benjamin.

A fierce and careful mother, before going off to work, Rit undoubtedly leaves instructions for her young daughter, repeating them and making sure the little girl understands.

Impatient Minty waits out the repetitions. In her storytelling years, Tubman often commented on her mischievous nature, and about her baby-sitting with Ben; she said was always in a hurry for her mother to get out of the house so that she could start to have fun with him.

Once her mother is out of sight, she gets to her games. One frolic she particularly likes is to hold her baby brother upside down by the bottom of his dress and, closing the hem into a bunch in her fist, swing him round and around, pretending he is a pig in a bag. If Ben objected—cried, vomited, screamed—Harriet doesn't say so and maybe didn't care. She just remembers having a swell frolic with her baby brother, his feet in the dress and his little head and arms touching the floor when she whirled him around and around because she was too small to hold him higher.

By late afternoon, the day drags and the frolic gets old. By dusk, Minty is bored with games. And when night falls and still their mother hasn't arrived, the baby begins to fret. To settle him down, Minty sometimes toasts a fat chunk of pork on the coals and, once it has cooled, sticks it in the baby's mouth to suck on. This calms him for a while. Sometimes he even drifts off to sleep.

One night, Rit comes home and finds the baby deeply sleeping, the chunk of meat hanging from his mouth. Believing the pork to be Ben's tongue, Rit panics. Assuming Minty has killed her baby brother, she begins screaming and yelling and raising all kind of ruckus, until Minty can calm her down.

The pig-in-a-bag game remains Harriet's secret, one she will not recount until 1905, nearly eighty years after the fact and long after Rit, Ben, and Benjamin have died. Even then, she remains unrepentant. Remembering the incident with obvious glee, she says she "nursed that there baby till he was so big I couldn't tote him any more."

These are better years than Minty can possibly know, when she lives with Rit and can nestle with her on the straw mat she uses for a bed and try to comfort her over the loss of her daughter. Rit is home, safety, love. As long as Minty lives with her, she does not feel owned, except by Rit's love.

Small Minty, a rapscallion little girl. In very old age, when she seems utterly wheelchair-bound, she will step secretly from her chair and slither through the grass like a snake, coming upon a child unawares to stir up monkey business and scare her; she is still that lithe and can move that swiftly and without sound. Physical agility is pretty much a quality that comes, or doesn't, at birth, and in her case, it surely showed itself early in her life and may well have saved her baby brother from injury as she swung him around by the hem of his dress, whirligig-style.

But Minty remains small for her age and soon the baby has grown too big for her to lift, so the pig-in-a-bag game ends, and not long after that, so do her baby-sitting duties, as her mother realizes that she is simply too much of an outlaw child to be trusted.

Anyway, her life is about to change.

At six, Minty, hired out, leaves home.

Her first boss, James Cook, comes on horseback to fetch her from her mother's household and take her back to his house, where his wife will teach her to become a weaver. Rit may even have encouraged this particular training for Minty, given the limited range of choices for a slave child, believing that for a woman, any domestic job was preferable to one in the fields. In discussions with Cook, Edward Brodess has set the terms of her hire, probably at about one dollar a month.

A restless child, now that she is old enough not only to work on her own but to learn a new skill, Minty's keen on the idea of going to a new place. *Anxious* is how Harriet will describe her feelings to Bradford; she was anxious to go. And when Eliza Brodess realizes that Minty has no clothes to wear, she makes her a petticoat—a little dress, her first.

Ahead of the event, she is atremble, lost in imagining what will happen next.

When James Cook arrives, he lifts her up to ride horseback in front of him, then nudges the pony, and like that, they ride off together. Does Minty look back and wave? Probably not. A born road warrior, she moves on. Rit might watch, hoping for a lucky hire. Her fourth daughter's first trip from home.

James Cook lives two or three miles west of Bucktown, deeper in toward the Blackwater swamplands, near the property belonging to Edward Brodess's uncle Gourney Pattison. The land there is rich but marshy, mosquito- and snake-ridden; the air thick as clabber, steamy hot in summer, bone-deep cold during winters—a chill beyond numbers and gauging—from the cloying dampness.

Two, three miles is not a huge distance on horseback, but longer than in our modern speed-trap minds we might first imagine, considering that they make the trip on dirt or mud roads, and sometimes through the woods that grow thick and almost impenetrable in that part of Maryland. As for possible impediments of the season, since there are no records of Cook's transaction with Brodess, there is no way to know what month he came to fetch the new girl, or if the new cotton dress was clothing enough for the day.

Called a "poor white" by the writer Franklin Sanborn, James Cook owns no property. He is a renter, a fact that, in a time when property ownership was valued even more highly than it is today, likely grates like sandpaper on his skin. Defined by class, he, then, would not be an especially kind man nor an educated one. He might well be an overseer, a necessary profession in the plantation setup, but one neither respected by nor socially acceptable to slaveholders or, especially, their wives. The horse, then, would be a workhorse, a field horse, slow and plodding, and so the trip might take a couple of hours, maybe longer.

During the ride, if Minty asks to relieve herself, James Cook will not pay attention. Knowing her, she probably says nothing. And while it's hard to imagine that a six-year-old wouldn't have fallen asleep during such a trip, leaning her head back against the man's middle or forward toward the horse's neck, Minty probably focuses her considerable energies and determination on staying awake. One former slave testified that once he saw family members sold away, his mind turned to iron; so might the child Minty have gathered her instinct for resistance and self-control once her sister had been sold.

It is unlikely also that her natural curiosity allows itself to emerge in the guise of the questions that surely nag at her: What is this? What is that? How much farther? What is weaving like?

It is evening when Minty and James Cook arrive. Once the man has put the horse away, he and the little girl walk directly into the kitchen, where his family are taking their evening meal.

And there they sit—white people, a wife and two sons younger than Minty—at table.

As a mother, Rit is fierce. Having worked as a domestic, she knows how white people operate and talk, and she has schooled her children well, giving instructions in how to deflect humiliation and fear, how to mine the subtext of a white man's conversations, to speak to one another in code, in language slaveholders cannot decipher.

Minty stands waiting, a child trying to make an adult adjustment, to scope out a situation that no longer seems exciting to her. Imagine how desperately she wishes for only one thing: to go back home again. Four other slaves are counted as Cook's in the 1830 census, but they are field-workers and therefore eat in the quarters in their own world. She is utterly alone.

Waiting, fighting instinct, which tells her *Run. Now.*

The Cook woman offers her a glass of milk.

Having never before eaten in the presence of white people—not without her own family nearby—Minty draws back, hesitant to do so now, fearing perhaps that she won't do it properly, or that they are in some way trying to trick her.

Or, more than likely, she doesn't know what she fears or why exactly she backs off from their offer, but is only reacting to a kind of preternatural quickness.

She says no to the milk for a simple reason: She does not want to—will not—make herself vulnerable to or part of the new family, even to admit to hunger, thirst, or a liking for a particular kind of food or drink. They will not come to know her easily if she can help it.

She has never, she tells the Cook woman, liked sweet milk. *I don't,* she says, *drink it.*

She is, of course, as she will later attest, as fond of milk as "any young shoat." But by refusing their offer, she remains somewhat in control and impervious to their desires and gestures, no matter how tempting.

Once again, the Cook woman makes her offer, but Minty holds out.

The weaver may, at that moment, envision trouble ahead, having to deal with a slave child so recalcitrant, she even refuses to accept their generosity.

Milk, after all. How many slaves are offered sweet milk?

The Cooks finish their supper and go to bed, leaving the new girl alone in the kitchen with only a low-burning night fire for company. That night and every night to come, Araminta sleeps on the hearth in the Cooks' kitchen. Keeping warm there, she cries all night, lonely, miserable, missing her family and home.

Here is what she will tell Emma Telford about that time: "Whenever you saw a child worse homesick than I was, you seen a bad one. . . . I used to think all the time if I could only get home and get in my mother's bed, and the funny part of that was, she never had a bed in her life. Nothing but a board box nailed up against the wall and straw laid on it."

The longing for home transforms her mother's straw mat, which in her mind becomes a bed, as Rit becomes home itself. And she compares herself to "the boy on the Swanee River, 'no place like my ole cabin home.' "

It is good to remind ourselves, she is six years old.

Weaving lessons begin, but Minty either can't or won't get the hang of it. She may be ham-handed, her fingers too thick for weaving, or she may be refusing to learn as a form of resistance, the same as not drinking the milk. At any rate, after many days of useless teaching, the Cook woman becomes fed up and tells her husband he can have her.

James Cook gives Minty a new job. He sends her out to check his muskrat traps, an unpleasant assignment for an adult, much less a child. Muskrats burrow in the soft banks of river- and marsh beds, then swim out. They are evil-toothed creatures, valuable for their pelts, especially during winters, when their coats are thick. Muskrats are practically extinct today, unmissed by most of us. But in the nineteenth century, trapping them brought money to those willing to deal with the nasty rodents—a practice generally looked down on by plantation owners and the social elite, a fact that might have given Sanborn the idea that Cook was a poor white.

Minty likes being outside and hates weaving, and so she doesn't mind her new job. But in no time, she comes down with the measles—a disease about which there is no room for doubt, given the red pocks marking the skin. But Cook has no time for a slave girl's illness. Whatever her physical condition, with however many red spots, he needs the traps checked.

Ill already, her immune system weakened, she does as she is told. Wading barefoot in the chilly water, trying to steer clear as some of the trapped muskrats fling themselves about, trying to dive into the water and swim free, Minty catches a terrible cold.

She lies by the fire, shivering, hoping to heal. But the cold, combined with measles, stirs up other infections, and soon she is seriously ill. In their courtroom testimonies, white men from Dorchester County will describe several female slaves as being of a weakly constitution or somewhat fragile, as if nature declared them so, instead of the unrelieved harshness of their everyday lives. Minty's health, untended, declines further.

Although slaves were forbidden to learn to read, news spread reliably fast, up and down secret paths as if on birds' wings, through the trees in whispers. One of the other slaves living on Cook's property might have sent word, or perhaps Minty's sister or brother was working nearby. However it happens, Rit finds out about Minty's ill health. Powerful in her way—perhaps reminding Edward Brodess that she was a companion to his mother—Rit uses her position to get Minty back to Bucktown, probably emphasizing the obvious—that the child is of no financial value to him if she dies. Thus convinced, Edward Brodess allows Minty to come home to her mother.

She returns, a shadow of the saucy girl who left riding horseback in her new frock such a short time ago. There, in familiar surroundings—*home*—she is nursed and comforted by her mother.

But her happiness at being granted her fervent wish is quickly curtailed, as once she rallies, she is sent back to the Cooks in another attempt to turn her into a weaver.

By now, Minty has come to despise the Cook woman. Once again, she balks, refusing to learn. Furious, unwilling to shell out another farthing on her, James Cook sends her away from his home for the last time.

Harriet Tubman had a quick mind, a sharp wit attuned to subtext and its messages. You have to wonder what she, as the child Minty, thought when she was sent home the second time. That she had beaten the system? That flunking out of her first job would discourage Brodess from sending her away again? Or did her child's mind create a fantasy in which she burrowed down so deeply with Rit that no one noticed or even saw her, not even Edward Brodess?

Maybe she thought she could wish invisibility on herself, like a cloak.

Whatever her thoughts, she will not long be allowed to play out her fantasies or comfort her mother further for the loss of Mariah Ritty. She has hardly settled back into life with Rit and her brothers when a woman whom Bradford calls "Miss Susan" comes by in a carriage.

Perhaps calling out from her carriage, not deigning to step inside the Brodess house, Susan says she needs someone to take care of her baby and do domestic chores—sweeping, dusting, setting the table—a young slave she might eventually want to buy, so that her baby will grow up with a familiar nursemaid. The appearance of this Susan is fortuitous for Brodess, who names his price and sends Araminta once again from her family and her home.

Minty is used to being a nursemaid and won't have to be taught what to do. But Susan's child is large—perhaps a toddler—and at seven, Minty can't lift it, so she has to sit on the floor and wait for the baby to be put in her lap.

She can handle this well enough, but other duties confound her. She has no idea how to sweep and dust properly, having never done it in her life, and so on her first day, she improvises, working fast to finish one chore in order to move on to the next.

Miss Susan comes in to inspect her work. After looking around and seeing what a mess she has made of the job—believing, like most slave-holders, that since black people learn only through application of the lash, there is no reason to make explanations or try to teach them—she takes her rawhide whip from the mantel and beats young Minty about the face and neck. These are hard blows, leaving welts that turn to permanent scars.

Minty cowers but does not cry out. Many years from now, she will tell the grandchildren of Bradford's brother, Samuel Hopkins, that the slaveholders who beat her never made her holler, not once.

Without explaining anything, Susan tells Minty to do the same job all over again. Minty obeys, repeating her tasks. But when Susan returns and finds that the hired girl has failed once more, she beats her again. No further lessons are given, no questions asked about how Minty did the job, no calculation or figuring. Reasoning is not applied, nor is thought. Only the lash.

Minty tries again. Fails again. The white woman again strikes her.

This scene is repeated four times and might well have recurred until Minty fell unconscious without knowing what she'd done wrong.

Ladies Whipping Girls.   Page 109.

This engraving, called "Ladies Whipping Girls," gives us an idea of what happened during slavery, when all of the men had gone to the fields, and women were left to dole out punishment at home.

Fortunately, however, at this point, Susan's sister Emily arrives. Emily seems not only to be in possession of a more compassionate heart than her sister but also to have a better mind. Appalled at the sight of the little girl's knotted and bruised face and neck, she asks her for a demonstration.

Once again, Minty takes up the broom and dusting cloth and patiently—despite her injuries—obliges.

Emily stops her. It turns out that Minty is doing her work exactly in the order that her mistress told her: She moves the furniture to the middle of the room, sweeps vigorously, then quickly dusts, but she does not leave time for the dust to settle. Emily gives Minty a lesson, teaching her to wait before dusting, thus saving Minty from yet another beating.

Thus does Araminta Ross experience her first morning in the employ of Miss Susan.

Like her mother, she works from before breakfast until late at night, when she is obliged to watch over the child as he sleeps. One night, when the child has become ill, she is to sit close to her mistress's bed on the floor beside the child's cradle and rock it all night.

The house grows quiet, the even breath of the adults making a kind of lullabye in the night. Minty's head drops. She wakens. It drops again, and stays there. The cradle goes still.

Used to the rocking motion, the baby wakens, cries out.

Before Minty can get the cradle going again, Susan has taken the rawhide from under her pillow and reached over to slam it on Minty's face, head, and neck. There are scars, of course, from these beatings, knots and raised welts, which have often been described by people who knew Harriet in her adult years.

When I was only seven years old . . .

And so we return to the terrace overlooking Lake Owasco, where Harriet sits with Sarah Bradford and her brother, passing on the story she forgot to tell her biographer in 1868, which she has come in 1900 to pass on.

She has been sent to Susan's to take care of the baby, who was "always in my lap except when it was asleep, or its mother was feeding it."

Morning. The family has finished breakfast, and Susan is holding the baby. Minty is standing close by, waiting to be handed the child, when Susan and her husband get into a noisy row. The clearly hotheaded wife begins to storm about, scolding her husband for who knows what real or imagined transgression, wildly accusing him, calling him names.

Minty stands beside the table, waiting for the fury to subside, keeping her eye meanwhile on a bowl on the breakfast table. About at her eye level, the bowl is filled with lumps of white sugar.

"Now you know . . ." says Harriet to Hopkins and Bradford on the shaded porch in 1900, "I never had nothing good; no sweet, no sugar, and that sugar, right by me, did look so nice. . . ."

Sugar! Sparkling, exotic substance, as desirable an importation as slaves themselves, in the late seventeenth century when both came highly valued to Maryland and other states of the eastern seaboard. The first crop for which Africans were gathered, chained, and shipped abroad.

But for a child, the lure is mystery and sweetness, within irresistible reach of her fingertips.

Her mistress's back is turned and she is still occupied with railing away at her husband, and so Minty's bold desire overrides common sense and she puts her fingers into the sugar bowl, hoping to filch just one lump, when Susan either hears a clink or, detecting movement, turns and catches the little girl in the act. At that point, the husband is off the hook, for his wife's attention instantly moves toward the rawhide lash, hanging—as always—conveniently close by.

But this time, Minty, who is nearest to the door, darts out into the morning. "I just flew" is how she puts it, and neither Susan nor her husband can catch her. Her little legs pumping, she never bothers to stop or take stock of where she is, but keeps going, past one house and then another, not knowing where or what is out there, not heading home to Rit or Ben, having no idea where they are or where home is located, just speeding ahead from a situation she knows will never change, away from the next beating and the woman who controls her life.

Eventually exhausted, she slows down. The master and mistress are out of sight, but they will not, she knows, give up until she is found. And so, because she is, in her words, "clear tuckered out," she finds a way to scramble up to the top board of a pigpen fence and—too small to climb down—lets go. She simply tumbles in.

Pig excrement and mud pillow her fall, coating her skin, entering her nose and eyes. Rotten scraps of food litter the ground. But Minty feels safe with the pigs and there she remains with the sow and her eight or nine piglets for four days, fighting the sow for scraps, steering clear of her angry, omnivorous snout. But there isn't much to keep her going, and eventually hunger forces her to pull herself together and, having nowhere else to go, find her way back to Susan's house.

Harriet may pause in her storytelling, while Bradford and her brother sit quietly listening, waiting to hear what happened next. But when Bradford suggests the inevitable, that surely Susan gave her an awful flogging when she returned, Harriet says no, she didn't, but the master did, suggesting that the lashing was more severe.

But, she reminds her listeners—or so Sarah Bradford tells us—it was of no use to chastise the slaveholders for being cruel, because, she says, they didn't know any better. "It's the way they were brought up. 'Make the little nigs mind you or flog them,' was what was said to the children and they were brought up with the whip in their hand."

And then she catches herself.

Perhaps, she says, this wasn't the case on all plantations; she has heard there were good masters and mistresses but, she says—and here the flippant, ironic Harriet emerges—"I didn't happen to come across them."

The steamboat chugs toward them and Harriet says her farewells and makes her way from the Hopkins summerhouse to the dock, back to South Street, where the residents await her. Bradford does not indicate that she and her brother send funds or food with her, but in all likelihood they did. Bradford will pay a surprise visit to Harriet's home in May of the next year, 1901, when she is between trains in Auburn. The house on South Street, she will report, was, as always, neat and comfortable, the parlor nicely ("rather prettily") furnished. When Bradford tells Harriet to go out to the carriage to receive some provisions she has brought, Harriet turns to one of her tenants and reminds them how worried they had all been that morning that there was no food in the house, and what had she said to them? " 'I've got a rich Father!' "

Bradford professes not to feel slighted, knowing that Tubman rarely gave thanks to anyone except "the Giver of all good," with whom she seemed to be in daily correspondence and whose intervention she seemed able to predict.

By nightfall, having passed on the story of the sugar and the pigpen in time for it to be included in the new version of her book, Aunt Harriet is home, surrounded by the circle of unfortunates she has taken in, who press her for food, hope, and help, not stories.

Scene 4.

At Polish Mills: A Shower of Fire

. . . and the Holy Ghost was with me, and said, "Behold me as I stand in the Heavens"—and I looked . . . and there were lights in the sky . . . and shortly afterwards, while laboring in the field, I discovered drops of blood on the corn . . .
—*THE CONFESSIONS OF NAT TURNER,* 1831

In the wooded marshlands that hog the southern half of Dorchester, autumn nights settle in early, beginning at an hour when, only weeks before, daylight yet held out against the opening-act fandango of sunset. The long days of summer and early fall have been narrowing since the equinox and now, by six o'clock or so, beyond the trees the sky darkens fast, bringing a chill.

But the laborers out in it ignore the cold and can't see the sky, treetops of white oak, hickory, and yellow and white pine having thatched together high above their heads, obscuring the moonrise. The trees have become Dorchester's main industry, waiting to be cut, loaded, hauled onto oxcarts, hauled from the carts, transferred to boats, shipped via canals and rivers to the Chesapeake and on to Baltimore, Annapolis, or into the Atlantic to be transported to the industrial Northeast. Sometimes in this wet world, the laborers stand in water up to their knees and sawing has to wait.

The date is November 12, 1833, one day after the second anniversary of the hanging of Nat Turner in Southhampton, Virginia.

In the growing darkness, field-workers straighten from their labors, call to one another, pull their bare feet from the muck, lay tools

The capture of Nat Turner, two years almost to the day prior to the stellar event named by many "the night the stars fell."

across their shoulders and, knowing nothing of clock time, peel off down paths so familiar, they need no marking.

From among the laborers, most of whom are men and boys, a young girl—compact, tightly wound, her low center of gravity a certain sign of surefooted speed—sets off at a quick clip.

The chill deepens. In their homes, people hug their own arms, cover their shoulders, grab for shawls, kick up a flame in the fireplace. The workers, however, take no notice. Cold is irrelevant. Darkness is all that matters. With no more light to work by, they can go home.

Emerging from the trees, the young Minty Ross makes her way barefoot through the wet, sucking earth, perhaps looking up as she goes, searching the night sky for constellations—the Big Dipper, the North Star—under the guidance of her father, who may be close by, on his way to his own residence. But the hour is early yet, the moon on the rise, constellations saving their light for later.

Life has changed for the enslaved people of Maryland and other states throughout the South. As trouble and imagination come into play, fueling the fears of the people who call themselves master, causing them to tighten up, bear down, and become more closely scrutinizing, more care must be taken. Statistics partially explain the general unease. By now, the census shows some 291,000 white people living in Maryland, compared with almost 103,000 enslaved and 53,000 free blacks. It's that last number the slaveholders worry about, the highest of any state in the union and almost double what it was ten years ago.

Communities of free blacks dwell in tightly protective clumps throughout the Eastern Shore, including the Bucktown area. But when they can and if they are not married to an enslaved spouse, most free black people make their way out of the remote counties like Dorchester and go up to the city of Baltimore. Thirty percent of the free blacks in Maryland live in Baltimore. There, where some white people are entertaining slightly more enlightened views about race, a free black man or woman can find work and a welcome sense of anonymity, on the docks or in private homes.

But manumissions have increased in Dorchester, as well, and the Methodists are getting into the fray alongside the Quakers, calling meetings to tell their members to stop turning people into slaves. The abolitionists are gathering, mounting their campaign: William Lloyd Garrison, publishing the newspaper *The Liberator;* northerners coming South to meddle and stir; ministers at campground meetings giving black people reason to believe they are precious in God's eyes, same as white people. No wonder slaveholders grind their teeth in their sleep, while slave-owning women reach for the kitchen whip more often even than before. They consider free blacks troublemakers pure and simple; in Maryland, there has been a movement to oust them legally from the state.

But they also fret over the burgeoning enslaved populace. The larger their numbers, slaveholders reason, the greater an opportunity to congregate, pool resources, and stage an uprising like the one in Virginia.

The recent past makes them wonder what will happen next. In February 1831, in nearby Vienna, an enslaved woman named Henny— after being whipped by her master for allegedly complaining about the

From the Cambridge (E. S.) Chronicle.
MOST HORRIBLE.—On Tuesday morning last, between nine and eleven o'clock, a Mrs. Insley in the absence of her husband, was murdered at her residence, near Vienna, Dorchester county, Md.— At the time of this foul and horrible transaction, there appears to have been on the farm, beside the unfortunate lady and her infant child, a white man and black lad, a negro man, woman and nurse.— The first two were at work in the woods, some distance off—the latter were near or about the house. Upon passing or perhaps entering the door of which, one of these heard an unusual noise, and turning to ascertain whence it proceeded, saw Mrs. I. prostrate, under the bed, bleeding profusely—This was speedily communicated to the rest, and she, shockingly lacerated, speechless, exhausted, dying and insensible to all but agony, was removed to a chair and placed in it, where, her deadly contusions and gaping wounds still issuing copious streams of blood, she survived but a short time. The instrument used to consummate the diabolical sacrifice of this unhappy victim of an incorrigible passion, was an axe—With which, horrible to relate, her scull was fractured, her throat cut and one of her arms broken. Thus, in cold blood, was she butchered, for the love of filthy lucre; for, a desire of money, supposed to have been in her possession, it seems, was the cause which led to the deed; and it must be added, that she upon whom it was perpetrated, was in quite an advanced state of pregnancy.

The negro man and woman alluded to above were immediately apprehended and are now in prison, to await their trial, which will doubtless take place at the next session of our County Court, which is to commence on the first Monday in April. This being the case, we have endeavored to avoid using such expressions and, to us, irrelevant facts, as might possibly give direction to public opinion, in reference to the guilt or innocence of any one.

Newspaper account describing the actions and execution of the slave woman Henny.

absence of sausage on her breakfast plate—threw lye in her mistress's face, then hacked her up and stuffed the pieces in a closet. It was Henny's plan, then, to behead the dead woman's child, but a surge of empathy prevented her from lowering the ax across the child's neck, which lay white and smooth on the chopping block. In June, Henny— forever after to be known in the white world as "Bloody Henny"— was hanged in Cambridge, the Dorchester county seat.

Two months afterward, the slave Nat Turner led his rebellion through Southampton County, Virginia, attacking white people in their beds, leaving nearly sixty men, women, and children dead. Within months, Turner was captured and hanged; hundreds of black people were killed in response to the uprising. But the bloody aftermath of the revolt did nothing to comfort the agitated hearts of the slaveholders. As one writer put it, the insurrection "shook slavery to its foundations."

Imagining similar plots being hatched in every corner of their world, slaveholders have become suspicious and broody. There is no reason to expect kindness to make for contentment, they grumble among themselves, since Turner, by their lights, had been well treated, even taught to read. And so they are sending out more patrols, setting up tighter restrictions, looking for new ways to prevent slaves from assembling for any purpose, spending more time issuing warnings of harsh retribution and making dire, if often unspecified, threats.

It is a Tuesday, November 12, 1833, the day after the new moon. Many years from now, Harriet will tell an Auburn neighbor that she always knew how to find the North Star. "That was one thing she insisted," the neighbor will report, "that she was always sure of." We might assume there was emphasis on the word *always* to indicate the doggedness of Harriet's insistence that her knowledge went as far back as she could remember. But from where did she receive it? Early on, more than likely, somebody taught her how to read the night sky, and especially to recognize the star that lay in the direction of liberty, which Harriet will say she was ignorant of, having no experience of it. Perhaps her teacher was Ben Ross, who would have had more occasion to be outdoors at night than Rit, and who had a wider range of knowledge, having traveled farther from home.

Other slaves who, in slaveholders' terms, managed to "steal" themselves to freedom reported the same thing: Every slave knew where the North Star was, without the help of telescope, lessons, or the written word, and before there was an organized path to freedom, like the Underground Railroad.

Once again, the Ross family has been splintered, Minty's mother hired out to a neighbor, along with a sister of Minty's and her two youngest brothers, Minty working either for Edward Brodess or someone else. Having come to understand that, unlike her mother, Minty either cannot or will not perform domestic chores, Brodess is instead sending her to do the roughest, bottom-rung fieldwork, as he would a boy of her age, to lift, dig, haul, and chop.

At only eleven years and eight or nine months of age, Minty has learned how to use field tools, the hoe and shovel, pitchfork and baling pick. Her body has already begun to show the results of this work, her muscles hardening, her legs growing more powerful, her strength increasing so impressively that at the insistence of her boss, she often performs tricks for grown men to prove how many pounds she can lift, small as she is.

Lithe as a budding athlete, proud of her skills and strength, accompanied by people she knows and respects, the alert young girl heads home, paying attention as she goes, marking her way, teaching herself to see what the eyes of others only drift past, to hear and feel the peculiarities and gifts of the night, her school and teacher.

Since Rachel's birth in 1825, Rit has borne two more children—boys, Henry and Moses—making a total of nine. In May of this year, Edward hired her out with three of her children to a young man named Polish Mills, receiving no cash in the transaction, only releasing himself from the obligation of providing these particular slaves with food and clothing. In the meantime, he and Eliza are producing babies as well, three sons under five thus far, five more children to come. Overextended in every way, they strive and thrash for equilibrium. As troubles deepen, Eliza becomes more and more devilish and snappy, while Edward is said by one of Minty's brothers to be a man not fit to own a dog.

Rit's four youngest children range in age from nine down to about a year. She is forty-eight years old now, and under the provisions set down in Atthow Pattison's will, should have been freed three years ago, a fact of obviously crucial importance to Minty and her brothers and sisters.

By all accounts, Rit was a talker. As it turns out, she also listened well. Somewhere along the way, word came down. Somebody told her that Atthow Pattison had bequeathed her to young Mary Pattison for a limited period of time, only until she, and any children she had, reached the age of forty-five. And while Atthow complicated matters considerably by not spelling out what should happen next, it was generally assumed that at that point, she and her "increase" would be free.

Who told Rit about the will? Modesty may have known, or heard. She might have then passed the information on to her daughter, perhaps repeating Atthow's instructions many times, so that the girl would remember.

And who told Modesty? My guess is, the writer of the will himself, the only person we know of, in this large, intermarrying, squabbling family, who desired and ordered manumission for his slaves. And so perhaps Atthow Pattison told Modesty and Modesty passed on the information, and then disappeared, leaving no footsteps to follow. Maybe Elizabeth Pattison manumitted her. Maybe she changed her name and went off. Maybe at age forty-five, she vanished, by example reminding her daughter that she could leave at the same age.

Minty will stir up a lot of trouble in the years to come when she pays a lawyer to dig up Atthow Pattison's will and find out the truth.

Clearly, she knows about the provision, has probably known for years. Rit would have clarified the point again and again and would have told all of her children that they were special. *You are term slaves, not slaves for life. When you are forty-five years old, you will be free.*

Some of Rit's children may be skeptical, thinking either that their mother may only be going on in her garrulous way. Or they may just shrug her off and stop listening, since no matter what the will says, what difference does it make if they have no proof beyond spoken promises that Brodess doesn't honor? But Minty listens. Makes a vow to find out, someday, what the will says.

Instead of being freed, Rit is hired out to a neighbor who is only twenty-two years old, younger than at least one of her children. Her last baby, Moses, still at the breast, goes with her. Henry, about two years old, goes as well, as does Linah, whom Mills has hired.

Rit, Linah, Henry, and Moses sleep at the Polish Mills place, apart from their family.

And so, with no parents nearby for instruction and comfort, Minty scrambles to move into adolescence on her own. Her mother and father otherwise and helplessly occupied, she is being raised, as she will one day say, like a neglected weed, ignorant of liberty, having no experience of it, living within the terms that have been set down for her, her family and her people, pushing against the rules when and as she can.

I was not happy or contented, she will also say, as if that possibility had somewhere been raised.

In the past four years, as more laborers are needed for Mississippi and Louisiana cotton plantations, slave traders have begun setting up shop in downtown Cambridge in a hotel conveniently kitty-corner from the courthouse steps. The prosperous Woolfolk Brothers from Baltimore have established a branch office there and regularly run an ad proclaiming that Austin Woolfolk "lives to give [slaveholders] cash and the highest price for their NEGROES." They and others—Dempsey Kane, among them—hope to go back home with bondmen and -women to sell, hoping especially to bring back young men and women of an age to withstand the rigors of cotton-field life and to produce children.

November 12, 1833. Daylight yields. Darkness deepens. Ben Ross heads to Peters Neck, Minty to Bucktown.

In her own way, Minty has challenged the limitations and margins of the system that enslaves her. By failing to learn to weave, to dust and iron properly, and to keep her fingers out of the sugar bowl, she has successfully defied her master's wishes, and has in this way taken for herself one of the only kinds of agency open to her, that of refusal. When they whip her, she refuses to give them the satisfaction of crying out. When they attempt to put her to work indoors, doing what is thought of as girl's work, she botches the job magnificently, so that they have no choice but to send her outdoors, where—working beneath God's roof—she is content.

Twenty years from now, in 1853, the forty-two-year-old Polish Mills will testify in a Dorchester County courtroom as to Rit's whereabouts at this time. His memory may well play tricks on him, however, when it comes to naming Rit's children, since he mistakenly calls little Henry by a girl's name, Hannah.

In his testimony, he will say that he

> knows [the] Negro woman Rit and her son, Moses, [that] he hired the said Rit with her two children Hannah and Moses from Edward Brodess in the year 1833 for their victuals and clothes, [that] the said Rit with her children came to his home in the month of May in same year . . .
>
> Moses her youngest child was then suckling at the breast, he might have been one year-old or older, or somewhat younger. Hannah her next child was quite small and could run about, there was probably a year and a half or two years between them. Moses could not walk but crawl about. Witness also knew Linah the daughter of Rit, she lived with witness same year, 1833.

In May, when her mother, her little brothers Henry and Moses, and her big sister Linah were taken off to Polish Mills's farm to live and work, Minty likely was not around to say good-bye or witness their departure. She may have been in Edward Brodess's fields or timberland when they left or perhaps had been hired out to Joseph Stewart, for whom she would work for five or six years.

A prosperous, ambitious man, Stewart is having a canal dug on his property, the work on which has been in progress for twenty years. Running from Parsons Creek to Tobacco Stick and over to the Big Blackwater, the canal is a huge and important project, one that will provide a way for Stewart and other farmers and timber merchants to transport products from the interior of the county into the rivers and eventually the Chesapeake.

Anthony Thompson has been appointed by the county as an overseer of the canal work, along with Joseph Stewart, and in all likelihood many of his slaves have been hired out to work on it, including perhaps Ben Ross, in the cutting of trees to make a channel for the canal.

Too young to work on the canal, more than likely Minty labors in the fields.

Polish Mills describes Linah Ross as a woman of "rather weakly constitution." By this time, she has married a man named Harkless Jolley and has a child of her own, a seven-year-old daughter named Kessiah. But the child does not go with her mother, perhaps because Mills thinks Linah isn't up to doing her work on his place while caring for her daughter. Or perhaps—remembering how young Minty was when she was hired out as a nursemaid—Kessiah has been ordered to stay behind in Bucktown to help Eliza Brodess take care of her young sons.

By November, Rit, Linah, Moses, and Henry have been living on Polish Mills's place for more than six months.

Minty arrives home. There is no reason to imagine she would enter any dwelling place in any fashion except by blasting in, wherever she lives, whatever her destination. One or more of her brothers may be working for Brodess; if so, they would be there, as well.

There may be food for the returning workers, a piece of fatback, cereal of some kind. Time to settle for the night.

Outside, the celestial snowstorm has begun—one falling star, then another.

Minty is the kind of child who translates every sensation, whether boredom or fear, into movement. Happiness, as well as trouble, cooks up her energy, giving her no option but to move, to go, never to look back or second-guess.

In the in-between stage of preadolescence, she handles adult work during the day, but at night, like the child she was when hired by James Cook, she misses her mother. Loneliness sets her off, makes her edgy. She is particularly attuned to nighttime phenomena; perhaps she senses something about to happen. The quietness of the rural night pounds in her ears and prods her up. When the Brodess family is well asleep and unaware, she tears out into the night, running as always, hard and fast and without looking back.

By law, she has no right to go anywhere except the place to which the man who calls himself master has sent or assigned her. If she is caught, she will face punishment, perhaps a severe lashing. Because of the Nat Turner uprising, there are more patrollers, more horses, more whips, less patience.

But she is of a willful temperament and she goes, taking only one precaution: She sends one of her brothers ahead to stand guard by the door of the cabin in case the patrollers come by. Probably the brother is Benjamin who, being younger, minds his baby-sitting older sister without back talk or questions.

The starbursts begin at nine o'clock, perhaps just after Minty enters whatever kind of quarters Polish Mills has fashioned for the slaves he has hired. She visits with her mother and Linah, catching up on family news, playing with the baby. Perhaps she even falls asleep for a time, until her brother Ben calls to her.

The world may be coming to an end. Quick, Ben tells her, she needs to come outside and see.

Startled by her brother's tone, she may assume that Brodess is out there, or a patroller, and maybe as she runs to the door, she is creating a fast cover story to protect herself and her little brother. But when she gets there, she finds Ben pointing toward the sky, which has become a dome of white fireballs and quick explosions, the stars shooting, she will say, in decided understatement, "all which way."

Imagine a moment in history when Abraham Lincoln, Frederick Douglass, Joseph Smith, and thousands of people all over the country are leaning their heads back to look at the same sky. Imagine stars careening westward, shooting like rockets, spewing tails of smoke, then falling, or so it seems, straight into the plains, the mountains, the rush of Niagara Falls. The long, dark night becomes as bright as noon.

On this very night, particularly during the four hours preceding the dawn of November 13, 1833, the Leonid meteor showers were viewed, discovered, described, and studied, their radiance determined to have come from a point in the constellation Leo, thus the name of the event, their reappearance predicted to occur approximately every thirty-three years. But this was the biggest night of all. And to this day, the night of November 12 into the early hours of the following morning is marked as the birth of meteor astronomy.

People wakened in the predawn hours, aroused by the suddenness of the light, thinking morning had come. In the West, when the light fell on the camps of the Oglala Tetons, they ran from their tepees and sat

A woodcut, made fifty years after the occasion, showing the spectacular effects of the Leonid meteor showers of November 12, 1833.

watching the meteor blizzard in dread, believing that the end of the world was at hand. The Mormon prophet Joseph Smith wrote of beholding "the stars fall from heaven like a shower of hailstones," a sign that the coming of Christ was imminent.

In Maury County, Tennessee, an enslaved woman yelled for people to come out and look, the stars were falling almost to the ground, burning up only seconds before they hit. Some people prayed; others screamed. Soon the white people came outside as well and they became so afraid that they called their slaves together and, as if to clear their record in time for Judgment Day, began giving them previously withheld information— who their parents were and where they'd come from, who'd been sold and to whom and where.

That same night, a man named Samuel Rogers, who had just sold his farm and stock in Antioch, Virginia, and was headed west, had been given a farewell party by friends, some of whom stayed behind to see Rogers and his family off the next morning. They had not been asleep for long when one of the guests woke up, declaring that daylight had arrived, even though the clock read 3:00 A.M. Rogers's children set off the real alarm, calling to their father to come and see, the world was surely coming to an end, the heavens on fire, the stars falling. Rogers, describing the event, said it appeared as if every star had left its moorings, some of them as large as a full moon, all of them heading in a westerly direction, gathering together in a cloud of snowflakes thick enough to obscure the sky.

Astronomers estimate between 100,000 and 240,000 meteors streaked across the sky every hour, making for a "fiery commotion," its "sublimity and awful beauty" viewed by some people with intense admiration and by others with dread and alarm. A fire-breathing Christian movement was moving across the country at this time. Camp meetings were held in every community, at which preachers issued dire warnings to the congregation, predicting the coming of the end. And they quoted the book of Matthew, which foretold that "the stars shall fall from heaven, and the powers of the heavens shall be shaken." And Revelation 6:13: "And the stars of heaven fell unto the earth, even as a fig tree casteth her untimely figs, when she is shaken of a mighty wind."

And so people knew the verses and, at this moment, recalled them. Roused from his sleep by a voice exclaiming, "Arise . . . the day of judgment has come," Abraham Lincoln rushed to his window and saw the stars falling "in great showers." And in Maryland, the still-enslaved Frederick Douglass witnessed "this gorgeous spectacle and was awestruck" at how the air seemed to be "filled with bright messengers from the sky," who had come to announce the coming of Christ.

Nat Turner was hanged on November 11, 1831, two years and two days before the shower of stars made people think the sky was falling to the earth and that the Day of Judgment was at hand. Turner went to his death believing that Christ spoke directly to him and that it was his duty to fulfill the prophecies and revelations he had been given.

The published confessions and prophecies of Nat Turner linger in the common memory, especially in the slaveholding states.

A young girl stands looking up, holding her balance to keep from falling backward as above her the stars zigzag and fall. Since she is of a deeply spiritual nature herself, it is unimaginable to think that the celestial uproar doesn't speak to her the way the voice of heaven spoke to the visionary Nat Turner.

It is a night like no other, before or since.

Minty and Ben stand watching.

They make it back to their own straw beds without being discovered.

Scene 5.

The Weight: At the Bucktown Crossroads

... she used to dream of flying over fields and towns, and rivers and mountains, looking down upon them "like a bird..."

—FRANKLIN SANBORN, "HARRIET TUBMAN,"
THE *COMMONWEALTH* (BOSTON), JULY 1863

Flax comes up pretty and it comes up fast. Planted in early spring, by June its grassy yellow stalks have grown to about a farm dog's eye level and are whispering in the wind. Soon after that, tiny flowers emerge: tight white buds that quickly unfold into pale blue blossoms lifting faceup to the sun, giving the field a look of clear water gently stirred.

An observant girl like Minty would take notice and be grateful. She whose life is attuned unalterably to the seasons, whose eye is sharp and whose heart is ever open to signs of hope and proof of God's grace, would stand for a moment simply to take in the beauty of the cool— almost icy—blue. Like a gift from above, beauty gives notice of other priorities, larger notions of what matters, in contrast to the immediate exigencies of constant work, and as visual relief against the blazing yellow sun, the smoky, edgeless summers of hot, humid Dorchester County.

The year is most likely 1835. At thirteen, Minty has been hired out again; her current job, to work a flax patch. She is a small girl who at her tallest will measure only about five feet, so now she would be maybe fifty inches tall—at any rate, only half again taller than the plants. To fulfill her duties, she has to wade through the stiffening stalks, which hit high on her bare legs and scratch her thighs.

Flax is a labor-intensive crop and poorly valued, one that Maryland and Virginia farmers don't grow to sell. But some of them dedicate an acre or two for personal use, the finer fibers to be extracted from within the stalk, then woven into a rough-grade linen used primarily to clothe the people who are enslaved to them and have no say about their attire; the shorter, external fibers to become bags—"tow sacks," they are called—and rope. Usually, the flax patch is planted near the back door to the main house, where women's work is done: cooking, spinning, weaving.

The blue flowers don't last. Not long after opening, they curl and fall, yielding to pods filled with next year's seeds. Once the delicate job of collecting the tiny grains is done, harvesting of the plants begins— slave work—each stalk to be pulled up separately by the roots in order to preserve the length of the fibers within. If the patch is only an acre or two, a strong girl like Minty can handle the pulling on her own, perhaps with only an overseer coming by from time to time to make sure she makes no mistakes and doesn't slack off.

When people fly in the face of her reputation and make her do indoor work, Minty sometimes indulges her outlaw proclivities to relieve her boredom—for instance, the time when, after making a bed and covering it with a down comforter, she jumped up and plopped herself in the dead middle of it to feel the softness as it puffed up around her. Nobody caught her at that, but in her later years she told the story.

Outdoors, however, she can work unobserved, using her increasing strength and know-how. There, she performs her tasks diligently. The overseer may well leave her alone to think her own thoughts and perform the assigned flax jobs on her own.

After gathering the plants, she lays them in water, either in a slow-moving stream or spread out in the grass, where they will be exposed to the morning dew. There, dampness and bacteria do their work, retting the flax until the gluey substance holding the stalks together falls away, revealing the fibers within. In the coming weeks, she will keep a close watch, making sure the plants do not entirely rot. In a damp climate, this doesn't take long. In less than a month, Minty will gather the carefully rotted plants and hang them to dry, either in the barn or over a stove.

Between flax-processing jobs, she moves to other assigned work—shucking corn, weeding the wheat crop, shoveling manure.

Flax: slave-tended, requiring little expertise or strength, only constancy—whether voluntary or enforced—and the patience for the endless and unchanging routine, a trait that, to get by, all slaves had either to learn or to fake. A perfect task for a slave child or adolescent, who will eventually don the rough garments woven from the fibers she is extracting, making an unending circle of involvement in a product that never leaves the place of its cultivation.

In the fall of 1835, then, young Minty has again been put out for victuals and clothes, this time to a Bucktown farmer whom, in 1863, she will describe as the "worst man in the neighborhood," whoever he may be. In any case, he is a neighbor, somebody whose plantation is located near the Bucktown Crossroads.

A father and son named Barnett live on separate farms in District 8, the same as Edward and Eliza Brodess, Polish Mills, and the descendants of Clement Waters, to whom much of the original Brodess land and homestead were sold when Joseph Brodess's brother pulled up stakes and went west to the Deep South. Thomas Barnett, Sr., owns a big piece of property south and east of Brodess, while his son, Thomas Barnett, Jr., is leasing a large piece of land close by. Polish Mills will eventually buy some of the Barnett property. His brother, John Mills, will operate a general store at the central meeting place of the neighborhood, an intersection of three roads, known as the Bucktown Crossroads. When Edward Brodess dies in 1849, John Mills will act as Eliza Brodess's business partner and adviser, until the two fall out over the usual issues—money and property—and lawsuits begin.

A prosperous farmer named Pritchett Meredith lives hard by the Bucktown Crossroads, as well. Pritchett Meredith's family will remain in the Bucktown area for two generations. It is Pritchett Meredith's great-great-

A nineteenth-century general store, renovated and currently standing at the Bucktown crossroads. More than likely, this is not the actual site of Minty's injury, but it has come to represent that historical event and, in many people's minds and imaginations, the store she *might* have gone to.

grandson's wife, Susan, who in the year 2003 will recover from a Dumpster the newspaper containing the "Minty" runaway ad.

An interlocked neighborhood, then, circles within circles. Brothers, sisters, fathers, and sons. Generation to generation. Slave families separated, put out to different white farmers to work the land and care for the babies. Then coming back, never breaking the deeper connection. The black world, the white one, linked.

All of these Bucktown white people and those enslaved to them know one another by name and live near one another, either close to or at the crossroads. There—after running crookedly through swamps and marches, following the riverbeds and creeks—three roads come together at a point just beyond the Brodess place. At this time, the mid-1830s, a general store sits there, and a blacksmith shop. Other businesses come and go. Sometimes records show a shop on each corner. The crossroads constitute the heart of the neighborhood and district, the place where farmers go for home and farming supplies, to have their horses shod and tools repaired, and, more informally, to congregate. To gab, complain, boast, make predictions and deals. The usual.

One store still stands there today, the date of its erection unknown. Although an architectural preservationist has found in the store's structure some wood that probably dates back to the mid-1830s or even earlier, the interior seems to have been built much later, perhaps during or after the Civil War. But the store has become a landmark, and even in the twenty-first century, people come to it to breathe in its air and envision the scene they think took place there. They like to imagine that the store now standing at the Bucktown Crossroads is the exact one—including counters and walls—that the young Harriet Tubman will visit on this important, flax-breaking autumn day in the year 1835. They stand on the wooden floor until they think they can actually feel her presence there, so great is our constant desire not just to *know* or study the past but to reimagine it and therefore, we hope, as if by historical proxy, to have some experience of it.

To feel the ghost of her there, when the thing happens that will forever change her life.

The three roads that meet and form the Y-shaped intersection are the Bucktown Road, the Bestpitch Ferry Road, and the Greenbrier Road. Trace them through Dorchester from source to finish and, in a sense, you trace the in-county migration of the Ben Ross–Rit Green family.

Forming the right wing of the Y, the busiest of the three, the Bucktown Road, follows the Transquaking River east and north past Indian Bone, to the main highway leading to Cambridge—and to the courthouse/auction block where Ben and Rit's granddaughter Kessiah will be assessed and price-tagged—and the great Choptank River, which will provide Kessiah and her husband with a path to the Chesapeake and from there on north. Today, the Bucktown Road is still the road you would take from the crossroads to Highway 50 west into Cambridge. A sign now stands on that highway, directing people down the Bucktown Road to what some people still maintain is the birthplace of Harriet Tubman.

The Bestpitch Ferry Road originates deep in the marshes south of

Bucktown, beyond Griffiths Neck and Hog Island. After passing Squirrel Point Marsh, the Bestpitch ends at the point where it bisects the Bucktown Road. The third road, the Greenbrier, runs mostly west toward the Little Blackwater and Anthony Thompson's place, where Ben Ross lives and works. Today, it is one of the roads that runs along the northern edge of the Blackwater Wildlife Refuge. In Minty's day, the Brodess farm was situated on Greenbrier Road and on a clear day was discernible from the crossroads.

Thus, all roads in Minty's life so far seem to cluster and meet at this particular crossing.

Early fall of 1835, maybe October, a little less than two years after the stars fell, Minty would have showed up in the flax patch early. Despite having begun work right away, by late afternoon she is still at her job.

The jitters that crept into slaveholders' hearts when Nat Turner went on his raid have not subsided. In fact, if anything, now that outsider meddling is on the rise, with people coming south from all over the country to preach abolition and the sanctity of every living soul, slaveholders and proslavery advocates have become testier even than before.

From our vantage point, it is hard to imagine how wounded they must have felt, how misunderstood and maligned, how unfairly intruded upon by dangerous, know-nothing meddlers, how justifiable they considered their anger and dismay.

The arguments for and against slavery have grown more and more complex. Gradualists believe in abolishing slavery, but not all at once, fearing the release of ignorance and barbarism upon the land. Immediatists and come-outers, however, decry foot-dragging and consider postponement only a veiled justification for continuing the sin being committed against God's children.

In the coming weeks, on October 21 of this same year, fervent abolitionist William Lloyd Garrison—publisher and editor of *The Liberator*—will be dragged through the streets of Boston by a mob protesting his antislavery views, his use of Christian evangelicalism to vilify gradualism in favor of the immediate freeing of slaves. At this same time, Baptist and Methodist ministers are riding into the backroads of the upper South, preaching free will and choice, personal morality and equality in the eyes of God. The proslavers in Congress are reacting—no surprise—furiously to all of this, passing a "gag rule" prohibiting further discussion of slavery. One southern state has called for a law prohibiting the printing of any publication that might "have a tendency to make our slaves discontented." Mob violence has escalated and spread, its intent to "terrorize and therefore silence" abolitionists.

Enslaved people listen, talk among themselves, and wait. Evangelists are bringing promises of God's unconditional love to camp meetings, whatever the color of a person's skin. Quakers take their stand, as do Methodists.

The waves roll, the tide turns. Panicky slaveholders bear down.

Late afternoon: Minty in the flax patch, or in the backyard, near where the flax once grew, the plants having been already harvested, retted, and dried. Evening coming on and she is still at work.

Were you to pass by on the Bucktown Road, you could pinpoint the young girl's exact whereabouts by the small cloud of yellow dust that suddenly flies up into the air, then gradually descends, after which there is a brief silence, then a banging sound and another cloud. Follow the sifting dust and there you will find thirteen-year-old Minty, bits of flax gathered upon her nose and face, collected in her eyelashes, garnishing her hair. Alone or overseen, she's doing the job she has been assigned by the "worst man in the neighborhood," who has, in her words, spoken in 1905, "set me to breaking flax."

Not all people who raise flax weave their own cloth—most, in fact, send the spun thread out to weavers—but, as we will see, Minty's employers own a loom, and so, like the James Cook family, they apparently do the job at home. Certainly, then, they own the much more commonly used mechanism, a flax break, a low wooden benchlike instrument, no more than eighteen inches high, designed to break up the skin along the length of the flax plant, softening it so that the long spinning fibers within can be separated from the shorter, tougher exterior tow.

Breaking flax is grueling work, tedious, time-consuming, rough on the shoulders and lower back. In the West, farmers help one another out by gathering together for a flax-breaking bee, and in many places, the task is considered strictly man's work. But in the slave states, there is

When Harriet was sent to the fields to break flax, this is probably the device she used. On her knees or squatting, she would lay a bundle of flax across the instrument—called a flax break—then slam the lever down upon the stalks.

no need for neighborhood bees, and young female slaves often do the work of grown men.

Built from hardwood, the base of the break sits on four stumpy legs and holds seven blades about four feet long and five inches wide, the top one designed to be lifted by means of a hinged handle. Minty's job is to lay a small bundle of cured stalks across the lower blades with one hand and with her other one slam the hinged blade down upon the plant, breaking its skin. Then she slides the stalks a little farther across and slams the top blade down again, repeating the process until the skin is broken along the full length of the bundle.

She is small, but the break is low, and in all likelihood she works it on her knees and, because of her size, has to raise the top blade awkwardly high in a shoulder-straining pose in order to establish the leverage required to slam it down hard enough to do the job. The work requires certainty, perhaps even more than skill, an ability to concentrate and not flinch from imagined possibilities.

As Minty works, her hair stands out around her small round face, frizzed and wild. After breaking the plants, she scrapes and beats them against a wooden board, using a scutching—or swingling—knife to flay away more of the tow. Finally, to complete her work, she pulls the swingled flax through a metal-spiked brush known as a hatchel. The hatchel is simply a board, about eighteen inches long, wide at one end, narrow at the other; the wide end is filled with three-inch square nails that have been hammered into it. The spikes are tapered from head to point, and it is through them that the swingled flax is drawn. Avoiding jobs and cuts takes skill; most injuries occur across the back of the hand or in the fingertips. And even those who have learned well cannot always keep from being punctured or scraped.

When hatcheling, Minty takes care, but at thirteen, a slave girl who has been lashed repeatedly since she was five years old has, of necessity, developed an intimate relationship with pain. Such a girl would pay scant attention to small cuts and minor slices.

She takes the processed flax to the overseer to be twisted into ropes and eventually fed into a spinning wheel, after which it is loomed into cloth—jobs usually tackled in winter, when fieldwork is over.

Like a factory whistle, the sun falling in a red ball into the stand of trees between the Barnett and Brodess farms announces the end of her work day. In rural areas, fall evenings take a while to digest the

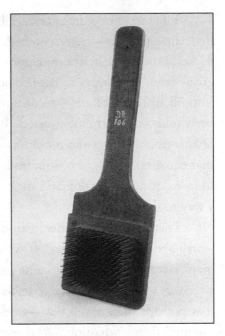

The hatchel was simply a comb used to detangle and align flax fibers before spinning them into linen thread. Harriet may well have employed such a tool after she had finished her duties working the flax break.

day's dust. Still smoky with grain residue, the light goes gray before it dims, the sun seemingly stuck in place, as if held there by field detritus.

The story that is about to unfold before us is a famous one, which Minty was asked about and retold a number of times. In some ways, the various versions of the tale contradict one another in the matter of details. But the main points remain and are consistent enough to take for the truth.

On her knees, then, beside the flax break, she looks up to see the cook coming toward her from the great-house kitchen. She's on her way to the crossroads, she says, to get some things for the house. Does Minty want to go?

Thirteen. Her breasts have plumped out; she is moving toward but has not by any means entered womanhood. Of course she wants to go. But look at her, all flecked out with tow, her hair uncombed, untended.

Some seventy years later, recalling this particular day, she mentions her hair especially—never combed, she says, it stood out like a bushel basket. And further, she remembers how, after meals, she wiped the grease from her fingers across her head, trying to tame the wildness and smooth it down. She is—according to the tales we have, as they have been told—not just embarrassed about but *ashamed* of her appearance. Shame can sabotage—even obliterate—dignity, but Minty won't yield to that equation. Being an obstinate girl, one who always seems to find ways to face down degradation and turn it in the other direction, she will find a way to do that now.

There may be another reason both to go with the cook and to worry about her appearance. If we set aside her enslavement for a moment (actually forgetting it being impossible), long enough to see her as a teenage girl with predictable teenage fears and desires, we can imagine that perhaps there was a boy—whether he knew or not—one who had caught Minty's attention. Who might be at the store or on the road. Whom Minty would rather die than accidentally run into with her hair all out like a bushel basket.

This makes sense, but sense contributes only one more speculative possibility. A nice thought, little more.

Minty covers her head. "I had a shoulder shawl of the mistress's over my head," she will later tell Sanborn.

Since the flax patch is small and the product itself a domestic one, perhaps the owner's wife is in charge of its cultivation and processing, from seed broadcast to weaving. Minty may, then, work at least part of the time for her, a possibility that would go some distance toward explaining how a young slave girl has managed to be in possession of her mistress's shawl. Or maybe the cook, sympathetic to Minty's worries about her appearance, brought the shawl from the main house, with or without the mistress's permission.

In any case, when the cook and Minty head toward the crossroads, Minty has draped her mistress's shawl over her head.

And off she goes, barefoot down the Greenbrier Road. And as she makes her way, we see a strange sight: a slave girl wearing her usual shapeless work dress, accessorized, however, with a white woman's shawl, which the girl has pulled down over her forehead and is keeping in place there, clutching its tail ends at her chin.

Thirty years from now, when she is asked how she managed to survive so many trips into and out of slavery without being caught, she will tell Franklin Sanborn that she always knew when danger was near, and she describes the warning she received as a kind of *flutter, flutter* in her heart. Along with these warnings came an ability to see into the future, a skill she says she inherited from her father, who could predict the weather and who foretold the Mexican War. Men and women who had been brought out of slavery by Tubman would refer to her gift as "the charm." "The Lord," said one of them, "has given Moses the power." Whites couldn't catch her, he assured his interviewer, because she was "born with the charm."

Born knowing how would seem to be a way of describing her extrasensory abilities, a kind of genetically gifted sixth sense.

Her psychic abilities will not come through for her today. Although trouble lies ahead at the Bucktown store, Minty's heart provides no warning. Or perhaps she is too young to decipher the signals. Maybe her heart is, in fact, going *flutter, flutter,* but, at thirteen, she is not yet attuned to the full meaning of its signals and reads them instead as nervousness and shame, because of her hair. Or anticipation of whoever might be present in the store when she gets there.

In any case, whether her heart beats normally or is wildly seeking to alert her, she goes on, keeping the shawl not only *over* her head but down across her forehead.

Her destiny, it seems, is to go to the Bucktown store with no notion of impending danger beyond the ongoing sense of unease she knows that all slaves feel in the presence of white people. Perhaps the path has been laid out for her—she would say that God commanded that she walk it—and it is her fate and the necessity of history that she suffer the injury about to be inflicted upon her. One other important thing to remember is that she is entering puberty, an age when historically girls have experienced a powerful susceptibility to psychic eruptions and dreamy thoughts—stigmata, visions, prognostications, direct conversations with God.

At the intersection where Greenbrier meets the Bestpitch and the Bucktown, Minty and the cook come onto the porch of the store, but Minty refuses to enter. Despite her head covering, she is still "shamed to go in."

And so when the cook enters, Minty stays where she is, lingering in the doorway, peering in, scoping out the situation within, behind her the open and harvested fields of Bucktown and, beyond them, marshy woodlands. If the setting sun moves into an open space between the trees about now, it might well blind a man looking out the front door and cause him to make a great mistake.

Nastiness and trouble do not arrive on a scene discreetly, but come making screeches and howls, mouthing off awkwardly in guttural tones. Raised voices turn harsh, pants are hitched, arms fly out, and bystanders scurry mouselike out of range of whatever has been primed to occur. Inside the store, something is about to happen; Minty needs no supernatural powers to foresee it. Still, she stands there, perhaps merely out of curiosity and the desire to be in on whatever's afoot. Perhaps thinking she might be of some service to the black man inside, who seems to be the target of the menacing language now being hurled about the small room.

Besides which, there is no time for second thoughts. Starting now, things happen fast.

A slave from the Barnett place, it seems, has either quit work before he was supposed to or is simply in a place that is off-limits to him. Maryland slaves often convinced their masters to let them hire themselves out for extra money, beyond what was paid to their owner. Perhaps the slave has coins to spend at the store. One story says he was trying to escape.

At any rate, whatever the reasons, it seems that Barnett's overseer has traced the man's path and, having followed him into the store, wants him hauled back to the farm for a whipping. But the black man is not yielding easily to capture, and he turns away, giving all the appearance of a man about to flee. Irate, indignant, the overseer reaches to the counter beside him and picks up whatever his hand lands on, which turns out to be a two-pound weight—an irregularly shaped chunk of lead used in a balance scale to figure the cost of small items, say tobacco or salt—and hauls back to throw it.

Years later, Harriet will describe the moment as one of those in which, upon reflection, time seems to come to a standstill. She saw, she will tell her interviewer, "the overseer raising up his arm to throw an iron weight."

And then nothing. "That was the last thing I knew."

The overseer's follow-through sends the weight hard through the air and out the open door, but he has aimed low, missing the fleeing slave altogether. The weight instead strikes Minty hard, splitting her skull, cutting off a piece of the Barnett woman's shawl and driving it into the jagged wound.

"A stunning blow," Sanborn describes it.

The girl falls to the porch floor, blood pouring through her hair, soaking the floorboards. People gather around, the cook presumably taking particular care to see to Minty's condition and provide what help she can, brushing flecks of yellow from the wound, removing the bit of cloth embedded in her skull, dripping water on the broken place in her forehead to wash it.

Minty remains out cold. She is small and, as we have seen, she has had a number of spells of illness. Perhaps this injury will do her in for good. But she's also strong, so no one can say how things will go.

When she revives enough to be moved, the cook and others take her back to Barnett's, "all bleeding and fainting."

There is no bed for her at the place where she's working, but because she is badly hurt and still bleeding and there is nowhere else to put her, they (it is Harriet who says "they put me," but who—the mistress, the cook, the overseer?) lay her on the seat of a loom, a wooden bench for the weaver to sit on while working the foot pedals that drive the shuttle. The bench is wide enough for a small girl to fit on, even to curl up on if the wound will allow it. Because of their bulky size, looms are often placed in the barn. If this one has been so located, Minty sleeps outside the walls of the main house and the white family within, her preference.

Although some testified to having seen or felt the dent in Harriet's skull, even when she was very old, no one—neither Harriet nor anyone else—would ever say exactly where the lead weight hit Minty. Was it on the side of the head? The front? In his 1913 eulogy, Sanborn reported

A late photograph of Harriet, taken in about 1905. The scar on her forehead—a little like a gull in flight—seems etched particularly deep in this photo.

that the wound was "ever after visible," indicating that the hurled object had hit her in the face. Further to that point, in photographs taken years and years later, you can see a crease in the exact middle of her forehead, about an inch above the bridge of her nose, a kind of wide V, like a bird in flight, its wings spread. Thus might the balance weight have been shaped and thus split her skull, not wide, but deep enough to cut a jag in the bone and to rob her of consciousness and send her into another world, beyond sleep and thoughts.

She remains on the loom bench in a twilight state that comes and goes for, she says, two days. On the third day, she rouses enough to ease herself up off the bench and back to work in the fields, with "blood and sweat rolling down my face till I couldn't see."

Head wounds bleed copiously. In two days' time, an injury this serious would not have had time to scab over. Whatever she is doing in the fields, the work will require her to bow her head, causing the blood to pour even more profusely.

Her hiring-out boss wants nothing to do with a girl thus damaged and sickly. And so he returns her. And when Edward Brodess sees how thin this small young girl of his has become and when he notes the strange cast in her eyes, also taking into account how obstreperous she can be, he longs only to rid himself of such a useless, balky slave girl. And what was she doing at the Bucktown store to begin with?

He offers her for sale to his neighbors.

There are no takers. Harriet wryly sums up her situation: "They said they wouldn't give sixpence for me."

Rit, Soph, and Linah presumably still work for Brodess and live on his land, and will be there to care for Minty.

But their little sister comes home a changed girl. She has become a kind of stranger even to her family, a girl who wanders in her mind, falls asleep in the middle of a sentence, then comes back from her quick doze speaking of music she has heard and visions she's had, of flying and of white ladies who help her over a fence, to flee from slavery. When questioned, she explains that when she seems to drop off into sleep, she has actually left and gone traveling, her spirit having left her body to make its way beyond boundaries of space and time to wonderful places, making visitations in both the real and spirit world.

To the abolitionist poet Ednah Dow Cheney, Harriet will talk about the psychic fallout from her wound, describing a day when after carting manure with another girl all day long, she was riding on the side of the cart when she "heard music as filled the air" and saw a vision she described in "language which sounded like the old prophets in its grand flow." And when the other girl tried to rouse her and even when the master came over to command the young slave girl to wake up, she told him she wasn't sleeping. Not sleeping at all.

They stand back away from her.

Who would believe such stories?

At thirteen, Minty has become a child apart, either a visionary or a slightly crazed girl, alone with her own certainty and the sights and sounds only she can see and hear.

Those who met Harriet Tubman during the years after her escape spoke of the periods of narcolepsy she experienced, when in their presence, in the middle of a sentence or thought, she would drop off into what seemed like the deepest kind of sleep. Her head would fall forward and for minutes at a time, sometimes twice in an hour's time, she would be as if gone. And then she would come to again, taking up exactly where she had left off, as if nothing had happened. People said that even in her last days the indentation was still there and that they could lay a hand into the crease in her head and feel where the weight had hit her.

Whether by hearsay or interview, all testified that it was at this time, in the fall of the year—probably 1835—when she was about thirteen years old and after she was smacked in the head by a flying weight, that Minty Ross began having visions and speaking with God on a daily basis, as directly and as pragmatically as if he were a guardian uncle whispering instructions exclusively to her and in the most concrete terms about what to do and not do, where to go and not go.

Visions can be destabilizing, sometimes terrifying. Or they can lift us out of unacceptable circumstances into a new and sometimes better world, one in which we can imagine—*see*—ourselves living entirely different lives. Those among us who are clairvoyant or to whom visions come may, in the beginning, dread such a visitation and try to find ways to stave it off.

But the insight comes. There is nothing to do. Like a busybody neighbor the caller arrives when it will, on its own schedule. Soon the hostess relinquishes her resistance and accepts the suspension of her regular life as a given.

Minty nods off, yields. The vision arrives.

When it departs, she rejoins daily life. Slavery. Until the next time.

Scene 6.

Sold and Carried Away:
The Slaveholder's Choice

The estate being in debt, I was imprisoned. Before I went to jail, my niece was hired out; then her owner concluded to sell her. She was taken away from her children, handcuffed, and put into the jail where I was. She was sold and carried away, leaving her children behind.

—INTERVIEW WITH JAMES SEWARD, AKA JAMES STEWART,
BORN BENJAMIN ROSS, IN BENJAMIN DREW, *A NORTH-SIDE
VIEW OF SLAVERY. THE REFUGEE, OR THE NARRATIVE OF
FUGITIVE SLAVES IN CANADA,* 1856

This is a story almost too sad to tell.

It begins in 1842. Christmas Eve. A Saturday, ending a week of public humiliation for the slaveholders Edward and Eliza Brodess, irretrievably spoiling whatever holiday festivities they might have planned for Sunday.

Not that we need harbor any particular sympathy for the Brodesses and their embarrassments. The sad story is not theirs, but it begins with them.

In the slave states, Christmas served as the one dependably sacred day of the year, a day when nobody worked; everybody, black or white, slave or free, got time off to spend with their families. By then, the crops had been gathered and sent to market, the land cleared for the year. People gathered with family to celebrate and eat together, to take time off for reflection, prayer, some rest.

There will be no rest on this particular holiday for Edward Brodess, who is down to last-ditch options: what to sell, what to keep, how to regain lost face and, one way or another, hold on to what he has. Owning too little land to turn a profit and no money to buy more, once again he's had to play long-odd possibilities, mortgaging one year to finance the next. And with no nearby Brodesses to back him up, he's down to the tapped-out farmer's prayer: lobbying the gods for a miracle. Now the father of seven children—six boys from age fifteen down to four and a two-year-old baby girl—all nine members of the family still living in the thirty-two-by-twenty-foot dollhouse his now-deceased stepfather built for him twenty-two years ago, Brodess has to be desperate.

His home life doesn't take much imaginative stretch to picture. Eliza certainly grew up expecting more from life. She's testy to begin with, uncertainty having made her even edgier. She must have been agitating for better circumstances for some time. After all, Anthony Thompson built their house before she and Edward were married, when they were barely into adulthood. And here they are still, forty-one and forty years old, living with seven kids in a house built for one person or maybe two. Raised Catholic, Eliza, furthermore, cannot rule out the possibility of more children in the future—who knows how many—leaving them with even less room, more tension, no change.

If Christmas expectations often prove daunting, imagine the sleepless Christmas Eve of the debtor—speculator, hustler, husband, father—who has no financial safety net to catch his fall and who therefore cannot afford, ever, to be wrong.

In the current issue of the *Cambridge Chronicle,* Dorchester County sheriff William Dail has placed a Christmas Eve notice announcing that "Edward Brodess and cousin Richard Pattison are being sued for debt and must sell a good bit of land." The announcement further notes that to satisfy the suit brought namelessly against them, Edward and his cousin—a frequent business partner who is also married to a Keene, Mary—must sell some 216 acres. This land includes twenty-one acres of marsh pasture and thirteen on the west side of the Transquaking River adjacent to the property called Taylors Delight, land that has been in the Brodess family since 1792.

By the time the newspaper notice appears, William Dail and two deputies have already gone out to Bucktown to declare official seizure of the land as well as of certain other kinds of property: one yoke ox and one "negro man, Ben, 19 years old."

Benjamin, the sixth child of Rit Green and Ben Ross, who as a baby was spun around in a sack whirligig-style by his five-year-old baby-sitting sister, playing pig in a poke.

This same sister will help Benjamin and two of his brothers escape slavery exactly twelve years from now, in 1854, on another Christmas Eve, one that also falls on a Sunday.

At eighteen, Benjamin may well be the only male member of the Ross family currently living and working on the Brodess place. The 1840 census shows Edward owning one male slave, age ten to twenty-four. And since most of the Ross family is hired out and living elsewhere, and because Benjamin's the right age and the only slave mentioned in the lawsuit, there's a good possibility he's the one working for his desperate owner in Bucktown.

How the sheriff goes about taking Ben up the Bucktown Road to Cambridge to be locked up for safekeeping is not noted, nor is the disposition of the ox. Presumably, Brodess simply calls Ben from the fields and tells him to go. As for the ox, Sheriff Dail might have left him where he was. Or perhaps he had Ben take the animal to the Bucktown Crossroads so that the two of them can be led away together. In any case, however the seizure is carried out, it's safe to say that three white male officers of the law will have little trouble taking an enslaved black man into custody, no matter where they are headed or for what reason.

This notice of seizure appeared in the Christmas Eve edition of the *Cambridge Chronicle*. Note the inclusion of "Negro man Ben, 19 years old."

SHERIFF'S SALE.

BY virtue of a writ of Fieri Facias issued out of Dorchester County Court and to me directed, at the suit of Stephen Hurley use of William T. Staplefort use of Jeremiah C. Wright, against the goods and chattels lands and tenements of Edward Brodess and Richard Pattison, I have seized and taken in execution all the right title, claim, interest and estate, at law and in equity, of the said Brodess, of in and to the following property, to wit—one yoke of oxen and cart, 1 horse, carriage and harness, 1 cow, 1 negro man Ben, 19 years old, one tract or parcel of land called "Eccleston's Regulation Rectified" 216 1-4 acres, "Marsh Pasture" 18 1-4 acres, Brodess's Goodwill 21 1-2 acres, "Taylors Delight" 13 1-4 acres, house and lot at Bucktown, from Thomas Basset, and I hereby give notice that on Saturday the 7th day of January 1843, between the hours of 10 and 4 o'clock, on the premises of the said Edward Brodess, I will offer for sale at public auction to the highest bidder for cash the said property so seized and taken in execution to satisfy the said writs of Fieri Facias and costs due and to become due.

WILLIAM B. DAIL, Sh'ff.

Dec. 17th 1842.

And so Christmas of 1842 finds Benjamin Ross, Jr., in downtown Cambridge, locked up in the Dorchester County jail, looking out a barred north-facing window, from which he may cruelly catch a glimpse of the courthouse steps, which serve as Dorchester's auction block. There, he waits to find out what will happen to him, fearing that in partial payment of Brodess's debts he will be among the items put up for the property auction to be held on an unnamed date in Bucktown—perhaps in the Brodess's front yard—there to be sold away from his home and family for the rest of his life.

Much has changed for the Ross family in the six years since Minty's injury. Of special note is the death of Anthony Thompson in 1836 and the early manumission of Ben Ross.

Anthony Thompson wrote his will on April 21, 1836, three weeks after his seventy-fourth birthday. He must have had an inkling: Five months later, he was dead. In his will, Thompson divided most of his property between his sons, Anthony C. and Absalom, both doctors, and ordered that, excepting slaves, his personal property be sold to pay his debts and funeral expenses, the remaining balance to be divided between his sons. Decisions concerning the slaves were to be made by his eldest son and executor, Anthony C.

At his death, Thompson owned more than forty slaves, almost all of whom he manumitted in his will, slave by slave and according to a carefully detailed schedule. Some people he freed immediately, while others were to remain in bondage for anywhere from one to forty-four years, thus making certain that infants and babies remained enslaved until they turned forty-five, the maximum legal age limit for manumission. To favored slaves, he bestowed immediate or quick freedom, while postponing it for others, possibly as punishment for intractability or bad behavior.

As for "my man Ben" Ross, Thompson decrees that he is "to serve five years and then free"—in 1841, that is, at which time Ben would be at least fifty years old, even though Maryland law prohibited manumission for slaves older than forty-five years.

Ben probably knows the law and can come close to guessing his age, but there is no reason for him to challenge or question Thompson's request. In any case, birth dates can always be fudged, making them earlier or later, according to the needs and wishes of the people in charge.

Thompson also devises to Ben Ross the use of ten acres of land "for and during his lifetime," there to be allowed peaceably to remain, on the west side of the Harrisville Road, with the "privilege of cutting timber on any part of my land" for the support of himself and his family.

An extraordinary bestowal. Ten acres, on which Ben Ross will be allowed peaceably to remain, from which land he will excise whatever timber he may need in support of his family and himself. *Home.*

Jerry Manokey, another of Thompson's slaves, comes in for even more favorable consideration. Thompson frees Manokey and his wife Polly immediately and bequeaths lifetime use of ten acres to him as well, with the added privilege of cutting timber for his own financial support. In addition, if in the year after Thompson's death, Jerry Manokey needs assistance, Thompson's son, Anthony C., is to supply bread sufficient enough to feed Polly and the Manokey's two young daughters, Mary, eight (one day to be the wife of Robert Ross), and Susan, seven. Later in the will, while keeping them in bondage for their full terms, Thompson declares his wish that Mary Manokey be allowed to stay with her parents until she is fifteen years old and Susan until she is eleven.

Anthony Thompson, it turns out, was a more humane (if we can allow ourselves to make use of the term) slaveholder than some others. On the other hand, it is important to note the limitations of his dispensations, and the personal gains inherent in them. By requiring babies to serve for forty-four more years, Thompson awards his sons the unpaid use of their labor for that many more years, as well as any money to be gained from their sale or hiring out. And when those children grow into adults, Anthony C. and Absalom will benefit from the labor and accrued value of *their* offspring, and after that, the children of those children, on and on irrevocably, or so goes the thinking, through the coming generations.

But Drs. A. C. and Absalom Thompson have looked ahead, and neither their wives nor they envision Dorchester County in their future. Both have traveled beyond the limits and the swamps of Harrisville. They are educated, have medical degrees, and are married to sisters, Martha and Mary Kersey, who have inherited land to the north of Dorchester, in more civilized, wealthier Talbot County. Both men have lived and breathed more rarefied air and are thus anxious to move their families from the lower Eastern Shore, if not all the way to Talbot, then close, into the richly timbered Poplar Neck district of Caroline County.

When his father dies, Dr. Anthony C. Thompson is running a drugstore on Race Street in downtown Cambridge. He will also hold on to a fourteen-acre piece of property, Bellefield, not far from there. But no sooner is his father buried—the whereabouts of his grave, strangely enough, as yet undiscovered—than A.C. begins putting the Dorchester farm and timberland he has inherited up for sale. When, in 1837, he sells to his neighbor Joseph Stewart the acreage upon which Jerry Manokey and Ben Ross were peaceably to have been allowed to remain for the rest of their lives, he makes no reference to the demands of his father's will. There is, on the other hand, no indication that Stewart forces Ben Ross, Jerry Manokey, and their families to move. The Thompsons and the Stewarts are friends, and often act in concert to help each other out. Minty is working regularly for Stewart at this time, and perhaps so are some of her siblings. Stewart probably leaves things as they are, for the time being.

Less than a year later, in 1840, Ben is no longer a slave, perhaps having made a deal with Dr. Thompson to yield any future claim on Stewart's ten acres and to move to Thompson's new plantation, after he sells the one in Dorchester.

In September 1842, after selling a large chunk of his Dorchester land, the fifty-three-year-old Absalom Thompson writes his own will. Like his father, Absalom also manumits his slaves on a staggered schedule, bequeathing as well property and money to an enslaved black woman named Elizabeth More. In all likelihood his mistress, Elizabeth, is also to receive support to provide for her two children, and perhaps Absalom's, with a suitable English education.

Obviously ill, Absalom dies in Talbot County one month after writing his will.

And only two months after that, a creditor lowers the boom on Edward Brodess, who, instead of celebrating Christmas, is spending his holidays looking for quick cash and snappy solutions.

Public humiliation, however, is a quick sting, and the Brodesses are not worthy of our deepest concerns. Those we save for Ben Ross and the illegally enslaved Rit, who are living together, presumably on the land Ben has been given use of, along with five of their children, all hired out, including a female between twenty-four and thirty-five, almost certainly their eldest, Linah.

Rit always made big plans for Christmas, but with her son in jail, this year will be different. Nobody in the family reads, but with relatives and friends working up and down the length of Dorchester County, they do not need the *Cambridge Chronicle* to alert them to what is happening on the Brodess place.

Having already lost Mariah Ritty in an illicit out-of-county sale, if Benjamin is not freed before then, they will spend this Christmas gathering together to fret and pray harder than ever for the safety of their son and his continued presence in their lives.

As for twenty-year-old Minty, since her recovery from her injury, Brodess has hired her out to Anthony C. Thompson, who, in turn, subleases her to the shipbuilder and timber man John T. Stewart, in whose employ she will remain for five years, maybe six. Sometime during the years of her hire to Thompson, she comes up with a new idea, which she takes not to her unimaginative owner but to Dr. Thompson.

Performers are born, not made, and certainly by all reports, Harriet Tubman was a sublime actress who could make use of language and its tricks—irony, metaphor, repetition, jokes—at will to dramatize, embroider, distract and, when necessary, deceive. The dreams she has of flying over fields and looking down upon them like a bird, as related by Frank Sanborn, may more nearly refer to her ability, while serving under the strictures and terms of slavery, to rise above those strictures, rather than serve as a prediction of her future flight to freedom.

To A. C. Thompson, she proposes that she act as agent for herself, hiring out her own time on a freelance basis, gambling on her well-known skills and self-confidence to bring in enough money to guarantee her hire, and put back a little for herself. To do this, she needs someone to stand for her, someone who will act as her guarantor and secure the annual fifty to sixty dollars owed to Brodess, so that the two of them—she and Thompson—can then pursue their own contractual arrangement.

While unheard of in the lower South, this kind of negotiating between slave and owner or boss—which, by blurring the borders between them, challenges both the efficacy of the old labor system and its philosophy of white supremacy—was not uncommon in Maryland and the other border states. The population of free blacks in Maryland had continued to increase, until by now it was the largest in the country. Slaveholders feared the influence free blacks might have on their slaves, and so, to hold on to their property and because of the continuing downturn in the agricultural economy, some of them were willing to make deals with their laborers, especially those who had proven themselves skilled in a particular area.

In the end, A. C. Thompson's a little hard to figure. Ben Ross says he was rough on his slaves, sold them, stinted them on food and clothing, and was, essentially, a wolf in sheep's clothing. All this as if to set the record straight about a man who otherwise might have been seen as more temperate than, say, Edward Brodess and other owners. As for Thompson's physical appearance, Ben Ross describes him as a spare-built man, bald and bewigged.

If Ben's description is accurate (and now we must picture him anew), he's fairly ridiculous-looking, a small man who rides a big horse while overseeing the work and operation of his plantation, making his slaves jumpy and on edge simply by riding by. (Does he clamp a hat down on the rug covering his pate?) He preaches the Methodist Gospel, doctors, sells ointments and magical elixirs, and sits on the local colonization board.

The son of a successful man must work hard to prove himself a worthy successor. And A. C. Thompson is busy thinking up ways to avoid trying to match his father's legacy by turning his back on it.

Thompson doesn't have to say yes to Minty's proposal, but he does, surely thinking that in addition to profiting from her labors, he can manage to needle his younger stepbrother, Edward, a little by making money off of *his* slave.

At any rate, for whatever reasons, he goes along with the plan. And so begins the next stage of Minty's life.

Hiring herself out, Minty manages not only to keep herself in jobs but even to save some money, enough to buy a pair of steers, which then she leads around the countryside as part of the package she offers to farmers. The steers, she says later, were worth forty dollars. How could she afford them? Say she was able to put aside ten dollars annually. Assuming that by "worth," she means cost, this would enable her, in four years' time, to purchase the steers for her own and her family's use—less if she convinces a farmer to sell her the animals on time, a not unthinkable possibility in her case—an incredible feat all the way around, if it happened. No way to know; the steers are never again mentioned. But we will remember them.

For a slave girl in her early twenties to negotiate such an arrangement speaks to Minty's intelligence and nerve, and her ability to work the white man's system to her own advantage. As a result of her taking a measure of control over her life, in her new line of work she sometimes works with her father, operating under his immediate authority as respected inspector and superintendent. Out in the thickets, she is learning about the woods and how to manage her way through them, where the trails are and how to find them, how to mark where she last was and look ahead toward where she will go next.

From time to time during her labors, a spell of blankness certainly must come on her, as it did when she was on that cart hauling manure. When that happens, her head drops and she is silent. When she comes to, she finds her thoughts shuffled into a kind of orderliness and clarity she interprets as messages sent from God. It is, perhaps, like looking up quickly into a sudden, sharp light.

The essence of slavery is to take over a life, to own its every breath. But dreams come on their own and cannot be bought. Hallucinations erase dailiness. We either learn from such psychic eruptions or, citing irrationality, brush the memory aside and move on.

Minty's usual woodcutting output is half a cord a day. Hauling, lifting, sawing, she grows even stronger, more muscular and athletic. Sometimes, John Stewart calls on her to demonstrate her abilities to his friends, which means lifting logs too heavy for grown men to handle. Enjoying the attention, Minty obliges, making use of Stewart's pride in her whenever and however she can.

Christmas, then. 1842. The perpetually overextended Brodesses consider their options.

The Ross family gathers, celebrates, prays, and worries while their jailed son and brother Benjamin awaits his fate. In 1856, when he has been out of bondage for two years, Benjamin—calling himself James Seward—will speak of his imprisonment and of a young woman being brought into a cell near his own:

"Her irons were taken off," he will say. "She was in great grief, crying all the time, 'Oh, my children! my poor children!' "

He refers to the grieving mother as his niece, but in all probability she is his big sister, Linah.

Polish Mills will confirm the sale of Linah Ross in his 1853 Dorchester County Circuit Court testimony. "Witness . . . knew Linah," Mills will state, "the daughter of Rit [and] . . . understood from Brodess himself that she had been sold out of the country for . . . $400 . . . and . . . that he thought it was best to turn her proceeds into land."

Linah. Fetchingly named firstborn, big sister to four boys and four girls, including the middle child Araminta. Wife of Harkless Jolley and mother

Polish Mills estimates the market value of various members of Harriet's family and tells of Brodess's sales of several of her sisters, including Linah.

of two daughters, Kessiah and Harriet. Grandmother of Harkless Bowley, who in 1939, when he is eighty-three years old, will write a letter to Tubman biographer Earl Conrad, telling him some of the stories he has heard about the life and times of his great-aunt, Harriet Tubman, the escape of his mother and father from slavery, and many other family incidents. He will not mention Linah Ross Jolley, the grandmother he never met.

The story of Linah Ross's life began, of course, on the Church Creek property of Anthony Thompson, where—working backward, from court testimony given by squabbling white men some forty-five years after the fact—she was born, probably around 1808.

A firstborn child claims special attention, perhaps in no other situation more powerfully than in this, in which mother and father, while married in their own hearts and within the rules and rituals of their tightly bound community, have no way to join together in a legal bond. Marriage, then, between the enslaved takes particular courage and an undaunted willingness to declare fidelity and love, despite knowing that at any moment and according to the needs and whims of a man who calls himself their owner, they may be sold and carried away from one another forever.

And so they defy the system, and the odds.

A child seals the bond between such couples. In the testimony of freed slaves, time and again we hear people tell of the need to hold family together and, when separated, to seek those taken away. Many years after her birth, in 1853, a white man will describe Linah Ross as being of "rather weakly constitution." Maybe she was, or maybe not. Once again, we must consider the source of this assessment, the Bucktown farmer Polish Mills, testifying on behalf of the Pattison family, perhaps with reason to temper his judgments according to their needs and wishes.

"Rather weakly" in these circumstances would indicate a lesser value in terms of monetary worth.

But perhaps he spoke the truth; maybe Linah's constitution was fragile from her first breath. Maybe she was tiny. A delicate baby, the firstborn of a young mother. To our ears, Rit and Ben named their first four daughters more fancifully than they did their sons. Linah, Soph, Mariah Ritty, Araminta. The last two appear to be family names, passed within the extended Pattison slave community from one generation to the next. Of daughters, only Rachel, born in 1825, is traditionally christened.

Some documents spell her name Linah, while others subtract the *h*, perhaps indicating a connection to one of the Carolinas. One branch of the Anthony Thompson family settled in Rockingham County, North Carolina, up near the Virginia line, in the mid-eighteenth century. Perhaps Ben Ross's father belonged to those Thompsons, or maybe Ben himself did as a baby.

If this is true and if Ben ever spoke of his past to his children, no one said so, or not for the record.

Certainly some people knew: Anthony Thompson, Rit. In private moments when they were forging the relationship that would result in their marriage, Ben surely spoke of his family and where they came from, where he had lived before Maryland, when and how he got there. And if he arrived in Dorchester by way of a North Carolina past, perhaps when the baby was born, they honored his family history by naming her Lina.

Speculation, pure and simple, based on a need to unravel the mystery and a love of the sound of the child's name, especially spoken with a vowely Maryland accent.

Between 1808 and 1813, Rit will bear three babies, all girls, all destined to be sold and carried away, presumably to the Deep South, never to be heard from again: Linah, Mariah Ritty, Soph.

And so we return to the Christmas of 1842. Benjamin Ross is still in jail, the ox has been seized, and the lawsuit remains unsettled. Edward Brodess considers his options.

Linah is about thirty-four years old. While she has been fairly profitable so far, being hired out regularly for about fifty dollars a year, a handy amount, she's said to be weakly, and while she has two children—daughters—she may not be healthy enough to bear more. In addition to which, there is the possibility that she could die. If he sells her legally—within the county, as a term slave—because of her fragility, she will bring no more than an estimated two hundred dollars. But if he ignores the law and her legal status as set down in the will of Atthow Pattison, he could double that amount by selling her to a trader who would take her to the

Deep South, where nobody would question her status or their own right to own her for the rest of her life, no matter Maryland law or ancient bequeathals.

With four hundred dollars in his pocket to pay off some debts, the remaining proceeds of which would be turned into land, Brodess could more happily write off the yearly income from hiring her out.

If he obeys Maryland law, he's hamstrung and may not select the more profitable option. In his will, his great-grandfather Atthow Pattison specifically ordered that Rit and her increase be held in slavery only *until* they were forty-five years old, not for life. Unfortunately and crucially, as we have noted, Atthow did not specify precisely what should happen to Rit and her children *after* they reached the age of forty-five, but in any case, they were certainly classified by him as term slaves and therefore never to be brought to the auction block as slaves for life.

And so the slaveholder considers his options. Does he defy the law and, before her health declines further, secretly sell the slave woman to a trader as a slave for life? Or does he hold on to her, assuming she will continue to bring hiring-out money for long enough to justify the choice? Or should he respectfully follow the terms of his ancestor's will and sell her legally within Dorchester County limits, thereby receiving the smaller amount?

Maryland property holders liked to think of themselves as more inclined to behave with decency toward their slaves than slaveholders in other states—particularly their rival neighbor, Virginia. In general, as a community, they do not look kindly upon the selling of term slaves to traders, or out of the county. But if Edward manages to conduct the transaction quietly and without public notice, no one will be the wiser. And once the woman is gone, she's gone for good—"sound of mind and body and a slave for life" being boilerplate terminology in many Deep South contracts—and, his thinking continues, who would notice then?

Perhaps they all meet: Richard Pattison and Mary; Eliza and Edward Brodess.

The sale of Linah does not appear to be registered on either side of the transaction, the seller's or the buyer's. More than likely, it happened fast and in secret, perhaps in the night. When in 1863, Linah's brother, William Henry Stewart, born Henry Ross, is interviewed in Canada, he says simply that he "had a sister, who had a young child, about two or three months' old, and the master came after her to sell her to Georgia . . . he comes and gets her and sells her down to Georgia, and leaves that young child."

The ages don't quite match up with the stories, Linah's and her children's, Soph's and hers. The interviews with the Ross brothers don't quite jell with the genealogy that years of research have pretty reliably established. Snags are everywhere. Contradictions jam the flow between stories and documentation. The family tree might contain errors. There might have been yet another sister who was chained up and sold south; another mother with other children to cry for. When people disappear without notice, there often is no way to be sure which one left when and in what sequence, how old she or the other one was, in this case whether Linah was sold now or earlier, whether Soph was sold this year or the one before or even back in the 1830s.

The estimated dates of birth of the women and their children also make for conflicting information, leaving us helpless to state outright that it was Linah whom Ben heard screaming and crying when he was in jail for debts of the estate by which he was owned.

What we do know is that in the early years of their life together, three daughters were born to Rit and Ben Ross and that all three were sold. White men under oath have told us so. We know that Linah was almost certainly the mother of two daughters, and she was married to a man named Harkless Jolley. One daughter, Kessiah, will figure largely in the story of Harriet Tubman in the coming years. Kessiah will have eight children, one named Harkless for her father, as well as a daughter, whose name has come down to us only as L, possibly—probably?—Linah.

It is also clear that this family passed down names from one generation to the next, to honor ancestors and establish much-yearned-for continuance. And that after the Civil War ended, Linah's daughter Kessiah and her family will return to Dorchester County, where they will live with Kessiah's father, Harkless Jolley, who owned property there.

Still, much can only be surmised.

Before Linah is taken away, her husband makes one final attempt to save her.

Having confidence in A. C. Thompson, whom he considers a "class-leader," Harkless Jolley gathers up his courage and boldly asks Dr. Thompson—who is the son of a man who did not believe in selling his slaves and who is a licensed minister in the Methodist Church, which has come out against slavery—to keep her from Edward Brodess.

We are listening again to William Henry Stewart, who was born Henry Ross some twenty-two years after Linah, as he describes his days as a slave in Maryland to the abolitionist interviewer Samuel Gridley Howe.

Thompson agrees to help. "Get your wife and bring her to me," he tells Jolley, "and I will take care of her."

But A. C. Thompson has his own financial difficulties to deal with. And the desperate Harkless Jolley has put too much faith in the white man's word.

After assuring Jolley of his help and taking Linah into his home to, as promised, "take care of her," A. C. Thompson "turns round and lets the master [Brodess] understand it and he comes and gets her and sells her down to Georgia and leaves that young child."

Having concluded, as Benjamin Ross puts it, to sell her and to make certain no further attempts are made to steal her from him, Edward places Linah Ross Jolley in the Dorchester county jail, where, as Benjamin Junior will remember, "She was taken away from her children, handcuffed, and put into the jail where I was. Her irons were taken off; she was in great grief, crying all the time, 'Oh, my children! my poor children!' till it appeared to me, she would kill herself for grief. She was sold and carried away, leaving her children behind."

Somehow, Edward Brodess slides out of the law's grasp and does not have to sell his land, his yoke ox, or Benjamin. The claimant, whoever he was, may have withdrawn the suit. Or perhaps Edward's and Richard Pattison's in-laws bailed them out. Whatever happened, there are no records to substantiate any particular version of the truth, the information having gone up in smoke three years after Edward's death, in the 1852 arson that will destroy the Dorchester courthouse.

And so Benjamin Ross, Jr., is set free and returns to Bucktown.

During that same season, probably before the first of the year, the Ross family faces the unthinkable. As Harriet will say with stark simplicity to Benjamin Drew in 1856, "I had two sisters carried away in a chain-gang,—one of them left two children."

Unacceptable loss. Firstborn, delicate daughter: Linah. Who leaves behind her mother and father and sisters and brothers, and her vendor, Edward Brodess, who—having chosen the more profitable slaveholder's option in order to preserve his standing and save his own financial skin— like Scrooge in Dickens's *A Christmas Carol,* will not escape remembering this particular Christmas, but in the not-too-distant future will experience a psychic disruption of his own as he lies dying in bed, a nightmare of damnation to haunt his last days.

Between now and then, however, the mother of the stolen girls, having had enough of it, will indulge what her daughter Minty refers to as her impulsive nature, in defiance of her so-called master's wishes and of his power over her and her family.

The story is told by William Henry Stewart, in 1863, to the Freedman's Inquiry Commission. After Brodess sold his sister, he says, another Georgia man came to Bucktown and bought his little brother, the baby

This woodcut shows a heartbreaking scene in which a mother in bondage is wrenched from her baby, to be taken to the auction block and sold away. Harriet's older sister Linah was taken away in this fashion, never to be heard from again.

of the family, Moses. Stewart doesn't say when this happened, but since Brodess was still alive, we can place the events sometime between 1842 and early 1849.

Moses Ross was born in 1832, when Rit was in her forties. A. C. Thompson says she might even have turned forty-five by then. This being the case, both she and her newborn child should have been declared free. But, as usual, the law and Atthow Pattison's will have been conveniently ignored. When Brodess tries to sell Moses, he is about twelve or fifteen years old, a prime age for boys to be put on the auction block.

The trader had come to Bucktown to scout out Brodess's stock. He did not identify himself as such to the slaves, of course, but any unknown white man was suspect, especially one nosing around the fields and slave cabins. Her senses sharpened by her overarching grief at losing her daughters, Rit had her eyes on this one. Determined not to lose another child, she did her own snooping.

Nothing escaped her notice. When the trader and Brodess were in the house negotiating a deal, Rit had stationed herself behind the house, where she could eavesdrop. She heard money being counted, then Brodess say he ought to have fifty dollars more. He and the trader dickered a bit, then eventually settled on a price.

At which point, Brodess shouted across the field for Moses to come up to the house; he was needed to catch up the gentleman's horse. "Hollered" is how Stewart put it.

But Moses doesn't come. His mother comes instead, the suspicious Rit having previously sent Moses deep into the woods—perhaps into the marshy Greenbrier swamp—to hide. She is the one who brings the trader's horse.

"What do you want of the boy?" she demands.

The somewhat intimidated and presumably embarrassed Brodess refuses to say, but asks Rit to bring him a pitcher of water, as if that was all he wanted to begin with.

Rit fetches the water, then goes back out in the field, where she is working.

After a while, Brodess shouts again for Moses to come to the house, this time to hitch the visitor's horse to his carriage. Once again, Rit shows up in his place.

"What did you come for?" Brodess asks. "I hollered for the boy."

Rit explodes, "ripping out an oath," in Henry Stewart's words, at Brodess and accusing him of only wanting to sell Moses to the lurking Georgia man.

After the third time he calls for Moses, Brodess goes out to look for the boy himself. But as Stewart says, "the mother had him hid" well enough that she will be able to keep him safe for about a month.

Holding on to the money, Brodess tells the trader to go on back to town and round up whatever flock of slaves he needs and that by the time he's ready to take them south, he, Brodess, will have rounded up the boy himself. Once the trader has left, Brodess finds a servant who is willing to betray Moses, certainly not one of his siblings, leaving us with the likelihood that the spy was a Keene slave, one of the men whom Eliza brought into the marriage.

But when the duplicitous servant (this is the word Henry Stewart uses) brings a dinner to take to Moses, Rit becomes suspicious again and sends word to her son to hide deeper in the swamps, so that by the time the servant goes where Rit has told him to, Moses is gone.

That night, Brodess himself comes to Rit's cabin with a neighbor, John Scott, saying that Scott wants to come in and light his cigar. Presumably, Rit has a fire in her cabin, or wherever it is the slaves live on the Brodess place, and thus the request for a light is an ordinary one, something that would gain them easy entrance.

But Rit stands firm. Guarding the door, she rips out another oath and issues a warning: The first man who comes into her house will have his head split open. She doesn't say what with, but clearly her tone of voice as well as Brodess's previous experience with her incline the two white men to take her seriously.

They leave.

Soon afterward, when the trader has gathered enough slaves to justify his trip to Maryland, he heads off with them to the Deep South—without Moses. At which point, Rit calls her youngest son in from the woods.

To smooth things over, sly Brodess comes to tell Rit he is exceedingly glad that she hid Moses, so that he couldn't be sold, and that when she sent him into the woods, he and his men actually knew where the boy was and that they were there to catch him but didn't. Strapped as Brodess is for cash, this is clearly a lie, intended to invoke gratitude and better behavior from a fierce and impudent woman.

As William Henry Stewart tells it, at some point during these years, Brodess also promises him and his brothers and sisters that if they will only be faithful to him during his lifetime, when he dies he'll "leave us to be free."

But in the end, Stewart tells the Freedman's Inquiry Commission, this does not happen. At his death, Edward Brodess manumitted no one, and thus "left us all to be slaves."

PART II.

HARRIET

Scene 7.

Marriage

About 1844, she married John Tubman, and lived with him.
—FRANKLIN B. SANBORN, "THE LATE ARAMINTA DAVIS,"
UNPUBLISHED MANUSCRIPT, 1913

Twenty-two years old, Minty's an adult. Compact, sturdy. Five feet, if that. The selling of her three sisters has tragically changed the makeup of her family, moving her from fifth-born child to second-oldest, from fourth-born daughter to eldest, therefore presumably—since so far Brodess seems inclined primarily to sell girls and women—next in line.

First daughter is the caretaker child. By nature, Minty fits the pattern—big sister, responsible, in charge. Whatever she feels she *can* do to care for her family, she must. She has inherited her mother's ferocity and daring, her father's strength and intuition.

Since the head injury, people look at her differently, not knowing what to make of the way she nods off in the middle of a conversation, then comes to saying she's been flying into the free-sky blue, while others see her sitting in the same place the whole time, stone-asleep and as unresponsive as if deaf, dumb, and blind. For her, those psychic trips constitute a special privilege, but since up to now she hasn't actually made use of her gifts, to others she must seem just . . . well, *odd*.

In the meantime, she watches, listens. Like the egg in the child's game Farmer in the Dell, within the family circle she stands not isolated, but alone. And the voices and visions that come are not strange to her. Not dreams. As real as a farm cat howling on a fence post.

After she finishes her hire to Stewart, she's off to others, much of the time in the same area, Peters Neck and around the canal. Few, if any, women work alongside her in the woods, where she does men's work, cutting and hauling timber, lifting barrels, carting. But unlike the dead-end day-in-day-out tedium of domestic work, outdoor labors provide a steady schooling. In the watery districts of Dorchester where she's hiring out, there are streams and creeks running through the trees and fields, things to study and come to know—currents, natural inhabitants, dangers, where the deep places are and where crossing on foot is possible—natural paths and trails, tricks to use to mark a trail. Her jobs often send her away from farms and timberland, to the great Choptank River where—loading wood, unloading—she can see how operations are carried out. Sometimes she rides to the Chesapeake docks, where she can watch transactions between people, finding out who's in charge of what and how papers are passed, giving permission, *by authority of*— saying this person has the right; let him or her board and go. Then she can stand there and observe a fully stocked schooner sliding out into the bay, finding the current and heading north, eventually disappearing into the horizon.

Ben Ross's house and ten acres lie on the west side of Anthony Thompson's Road—later (and now) to be known as Harrisville Road. The thirty-year building of the canal has attracted a large number of workers, black and white, slave and free, many of whom have settled in the area. Among them is a free black man, John Tubman, a darkish mulatto about ten years older than Minty; his father may have been a member of the large and prosperous white Tubman family of Dorchester.

A laborer, John Tubman might work side by side with Minty Ross, occasionally, if not more often. And because Minty sometimes lives with her father on the Harrisville Road, the two would have many occasions to come across each other.

Work in the back swamps is hard, hot, sweaty. Swarmy with mosquitoes that cluster in gangs. Beneath the umbrella-like leaf cover of the high trees, no breeze stirs. Working together in teams, the laborers saw and lift, haul, pull, load. Cooperation is a necessity, each worker applying his or her strength equally until all become a team, performing as one.

And so John Tubman meets Minty Ross, a small dark young woman, daughter of the man who oversees their work. He notices. She is not pretty; in no description of her does anyone make her out to be pretty. But she has spirit, wit. Strength beyond a woman's call. A sense of life as a drama—not an ordeal to succumb to, but an absurd set of circumstances to figure and then play out. An unusual imperturbability.

And then?

Some local oral historians and descendants of original Harrisville Road residents claim that Minty moved in with John Tubman before they were married. This bit of information—in the end, trivial and of no clear import beyond the who-knows-what arguments—has, however, never been verified and, given the Ross family's strict religiosity, seems unlikely.

From Minty's point of view, reasons to marry come fairly easy. A first daughter might feel the obligation to follow in her sisters' footsteps, to marry and have children as they did and as is considered normal and right for women, the natural order of things. At twenty-two, she is actually older than most nineteenth-century farm girls when they marry and bear children, whatever their skin color; older than Linah when her first baby was born; older than Mary Pattison Brodess was when she gave birth to Edward—who may also be issuing warnings that if Minty doesn't marry and propagate soon, he'll sell her like her sisters. This may seem a somewhat idle threat, since she is sickly and, at the same time, a little too assertive, not the kind of woman who might be assessed as a breeder type, therefore unmarketable as a slave for life. But remember how she describes her feelings to Benjamin Drew in 1856: "every time I saw a white man I was afraid of being carried away."

Now that she is the next sister in line, no threat is idle.

Perhaps Minty falls in love with the free black man, John Tubman, who seems to have had the kind of brashness and caustic wit that often attracts young women, at least for a time. Slightly haughty, aloof; quick to scoff; self-protective—that kind of man.

They could not be more different, John Tubman and Minty Ross. And so (can difference explain it?) her heart fills and then . . . she falls? And does he?

Possible.

Married. A wife. *Wife of*—with a new last name. Unusual for a woman warrior. But she likes men, and her heart has its own reasons. During the course of her life, she will marry twice—first in about 1844, to John Tubman, and in 1869, to a retired and fatally ill Union soldier, Nelson Davis.

She gives herself into marriage with John Tubman for life, as committed to the union as her parents were when they married. He will be shot dead by a white man in 1867.

Nelson Davis will succumb to tuberculosis in 1888.

John Tubman's motivations prove harder to figure. Minty's damaged—not so much because of the scars and the dent in her head, since most slaves have been similarly marked, but her behavior. She goes peculiar every now and then, first nodding off into the deepest snooze, then coming to in a bigger daze. John Tubman doesn't put up with nonsense. But who knows what he sees? Minty's small, alert, feisty. Maybe John Tubman simply admires her, gets a kick out of her ebullient spirit. There's no record of his having been married before; if he's held out until he's in his early thirties, he's either picky or a loner—like Minty.

But for him, there is an additional downside to marrying Araminta Ross: He is free, and she is not. Any children they have will be born en-

John Tubman is officially identified and declared to have been a free man since birth.

slaved to Edward Brodess, liable to be sold at any moment. Not a happy prospect.

Perhaps Minty energizes John Tubman. Perhaps he feels happier when she's around, singing her songs and telling her stories, doing her little jigs and jogs and tricks. He may appreciate that calmness she takes on when others panic in the face of the deepest kind of trouble.

Or maybe he wants to benefit from Ben Ross's favored status, including those ten acres loaned to him by Anthony Thompson. Perhaps John Tubman figures there is some way for him to gain personally from marriage into Minty's family.

She takes her husband's name but probably keeps her given name for now, or this is my guess. In an 1890s affidavit, she says when she married John Tubman, she became Harriet Tubman, but the affidavit was filled out by someone else, in her name, giving facts and figures in a governmental tone. The "I," then, is somebody else's idea of how she should sound.

The more likely possibility is that during the time of their enslavement, Rit retains her position as sole family holder of the name Harriet and that her daughter remains Araminta, or Minty, until she escapes from Maryland, at which time, from necessity, she renames herself.

Here, however, we take a small liberty and fly in the face of what seems most likely to be the case at the time. From now on, let us call her by her future name, the one with which we are familiar, the one that will become famous. Moving forward, we make a brash leap. From now on, let us call her Harriet.

A married timber worker in her early twenties, she has moved slightly away from her family, while still remaining utterly connected to it—through the bonds of slavery, if in no other way—to live with her husband, to become a Tubman, while working her own hires as she finds them and in her own time. She may be working even longer hours than before, since, to end up with a net gain, she must work even more fervently as a freelancer, not only to finish jobs but to acquire the next ones, as well.

Sometime around now, she gets it into her head to settle up one score. She wants to find a lawyer who will help her dig in the past and find out the truth of her mother's legal status. Born sometime between 1785 and 1790, Rit is now almost fifteen years beyond what's called the extreme age at which a Maryland slave may be legally manumitted. But in 1797, when she was bequeathed to the granddaughter of Atthow Pattison, what did the will decree, that she be given away as a slave for life? Or are Rit's claims based on fact? Did Edward Brodess's great-grandfather set up a particular period of years for her to serve in bondage, after which she should be manumitted, making her legally a term slave?

A later Maryland law (1835) ruled that because manumission during a slaveholder's last days might be "attended with many evils" (perhaps remorse, regret, affection), those manumissions be declared null and void. But Atthow Pattison wrote his will six years before he died, accompanied by two witnesses to help guard against "hasty and inconsiderate action." And so whatever he wrote was witnessed and sealed by the court, and should have stood.

Harriet will never say why she went on this mission at this particular time, only that she did it. Some possibilities come to mind: She's getting married or may already be. She wants not only to do what she can to help manumit her mother, if possible, but also needs to find out what her own status is, both now and in the future, so that she and John can make plans for themselves and for any children she may bear. After all, in twenty-three years, she may be legally free herself.

How she can find a Cambridge lawyer willing to do such a thing for a slave, even for money, is a thorny but interesting (if ultimately unanswerable) question. Also, even if she does, how does a slave girl come up with a lawyer's fee?

During this time, the years fold into one another, making exact delineation—precisely who did what in which exact year—impossible. In 1863, the year of her earliest interview, Harriet says she was hired out to John T. Stewart for five or six years, which would mean until, say, about 1842–1843. In that same interview, she says she worked for Anthony C. Thompson her last two years in slavery—that is, from 1847, when Thompson moved most of his operations to Caroline County, until 1849, when she bolted from enslavement and left Maryland altogether.

As for the lawyer's fee: If she is doing well enough on her own to buy two steers, she might not find the five dollars she will pay the lawyer so difficult to come by.

For the lawyer himself, we look back to the long-standing unpleasantness between Edward Brodess and the Thompsons. A. C. Thompson has a long memory. He remembers quite well—as he will soon testify in court—the time when Mary Brodess married his father and brought along her baby son, Edward, and her slave companion, Rittia, or Rit, to live in their home. He was eleven years old and was told or simply heard that Rit came to his stepmother through the Atthow Pattison will. Presumably, he would also have heard that Rit was to be manumitted at age forty-five.

Isn't it, then, very possible that, because of old grievances, Brodess's much more successful stepbrother might be willing to help Harriet stir things up by, if not validating her suspicions, then at least sending her to a lawyer who will help?

Ben says Anthony C. was rough on his slaves. That attitude may carry over to other aspects of his life, becoming an unalterable part of his personality. He may also be a man to hold on to a grudge, especially against an ungrateful upstart who had taken his father for a ride.

Harriet takes herself to Cambridge, to the lawyer's office.

The lawyer looks back a certain number of years (probably fifty) and, finding nothing, says it's time to give up. But his client wants her five dollars' worth. Look back further, she says. He goes back five more years, and there it is, witnessed, signed, and sealed. Atthow Pattison gives "unto my granddaughter Mary Pattison one Negro girl called Rittia and her increase until she and they arrive to forty-five years of age."

A triumph. Oral history has proven true. Rit should have been freed fifteen years ago. The sale of Linah, Soph, and Mariah Ritty beyond state lines was illegal.

And so? Nothing happens, but word gets out. Edward's relatives—especially his uncle Gourney Crow Pattison—study the situation. Mightn't there be a way for him and the other Pattisons to cash in on the new information and use it for their own benefit? Ignoring traditional Pattison fealty, considering that Edward is a blood relative, Uncle Gourney consults a lawyer.

By the end of 1846, Anthony C. Thompson has signed a $24,000 bond, enabling him to purchase 2,167 thickly forested acres in the Poplar Neck region of Caroline County from the daughters of former Maryland governor Charles Goldsborough. The land is spectacularly located, between Marsh and Skeleton creeks, on a wide, windy bend of the Choptank as it rolls down from Greensboro in a fat backward J, emptying past Cambridge into the Chesapeake.

In December, the doctor begins moving his slaves and free laborers—including Ben Ross—the thirty miles northeast from Peters Neck. There they will clear timber and construct outbuildings and a wharf and perhaps one day will have established a kind of self-contained village like the one John T. Stewart constructed, with a sawmill, a general store, and a blacksmith shop. A. C. Thompson will then be the John T. Stewart of southern Caroline County, serving as lord, master, and Methodist moral instructor over his slaves and employees, assisted by his son, Edward, who will live on the Poplar Neck property in a two-story house that still stands today.

Having been carved out of Dorchester and Queen Anne's counties in 1774, Caroline County came later than its neighbors. It has fewer plantations, fewer slaves, more free blacks (up to 75 percent of the total black population in 1850, many of whom own property), a large Quaker settlement. Less money. A seventy-five-year agricultural depression, having settled in in 1819, still has almost fifty years to go. But Thompson has done his research. In southern Caroline, there are waterways aplenty; land, trees; rolling landscape; a perfect creek on which to build a sawmill; the Choptank at his front door; propitious possibilities—for escape as well as profit, as he will learn.

Hope and ambition propel Dr. Thompson to, in the words of Ben Ross, "reach out too far." He loses a couple of other farms he meant to keep, gets called in on some debts. As the depression rolls on, he inches down bit by bit with it. In April 1847, barely four months after the move, he adjusts his situation somewhat by selling a slave away from a family his father greatly respected: eighteen-year-old Susan Manokey, younger daughter of Jerry and Polly Manokey, whom Anthony Thompson had set immediately free in his will.

In that same document, Susan and her sister Mary were given special treatment as well as a schedule of manumission; nonetheless, Anthony C. casually sells her to a man in nearby East New Market for two hundred dollars, and that man, in turn, sells her to the wife of a slave trader, who then transports her out of the state and sells her again. The trader is taken to court for illegally selling a term slave beyond the limits of the state, but by then, Susan is gone.

And Dr. Thompson pockets his two hundred dollars.

The Manokeys and the Rosses are closely entwined, Ben and Jerry Manokey having worked together both in Harrisville and now in Poplar

"1839, Jan. 1, Negroes of Anthony Thompson." Ben Ross, Harriet Tubman's father, tops this list of Thompson slaves.

Neck. Only four years prior to the sale of Susan, in 1843, Ben purchased two of Thompson's slaves, Maria Bailey and Aaron Manokey, for ten dollars, then went that same day to the courthouse to free them both. In an 1839 list of assets, Thompson describes Maria Bailey as "delicate" and Aaron Manokey, "a cripple," each with about twenty years left to serve in bondage. Ben may have freed these two young people out of compassion for their state of health. Or Thompson may have granted him the right to do so and at such a low price in return for certain favors. Whatever the reasons, Ben immediately sets Aaron Manokey free.

The closeness of the two families will only deepen in the coming years, when Susan's big sister, Mary Manokey, marries Ben and Rit's son Robert.

Some circumstance nonetheless convinces Dr. Thompson not only to sell Susan but cheaply, as well. Something else went into this deal, an old debt, a fancy for the girl—something in addition to the money. And if any member of either family had come and asked him to do something about Susan being subsequently sold illegally out of state, he would simply have shrugged. Once the girl was paid for, she was no longer his property. What happened to her next was out of his hands. Anyway, he wasn't the one who had sold her to a trader. And with that, the spare-built, bewigged man would have closed out the conversation.

Rough on his slaves, Ben will remember.

In late 1848, while working for Dr. Thompson, Harriet's health breaks down. It's winter—December—and since she is pushing herself hard, knowing that the only way she can turn a profit while hiring herself out is to work beyond the point of exhaustion, illness seems almost a given. Perhaps working barefoot in wet, cold ground has given her a chill, which becomes a cough and then worsens until her lungs fill and her recurring illnesses cause her to be all but bedridden. She may sell the steers at this time to pay for her hire. Thompson apparently keeps her on, allowing her to work as she can.

As for John Tubman, he is hardly mentioned during these years and there's no indication he is helping take care of his ailing wife even though he, too, might be working for Thompson at this time. Either way, Harriet says she lived in Poplar Neck on the Thompson place from 1847 until 1849, so presumably she's there now, living with her husband on property close to Ben and Rit.

December: the slack time, the selling season, traders checking into downtown hotels. Six years ago, on Christmas Eve of 1842, Benjamin Ross was put in jail. Soon afterward, his sister Linah was sold, and then Soph. For a slave, the season from Christmas to New Year's is a time for prayer, for groaning to God.

Not surprisingly, when Edward Brodess hears that Harriet is ill, he again gets the itch to get rid of her. He puts out the word, but finds no takers. She's twenty-six, with a birthday coming up, and if she hasn't had children by now, she probably won't. She may be strong, but she breaks down regularly and gets sick, a debilitating weakness in her system brought on by early inattention to symptoms, despite her muscularity. She's childless, rambunctious, stubborn—hiring her own time instead of by a master's order like the others—a troublemaker, meddling in the past, digging up wills and such.

Who would want to buy her? Brodess may hit Thompson up to make the purchase, but the doctor's in no position to do that, even as a favor to Ben.

Harriet hears everything. She may start thinking about running away, but now's not the time. She's sick, weak, not ready. But illness gives her time to study the situation. Edward Brodess, she figures, is determined to sell her. She is, after all, the next daughter in the family. Eventually, he'll find a buyer.

At first, she tries to alter her circumstances through spiritual intercession.

In December, during the day, she does what she can, working as she's able. At night, she solicits help from above, but not for herself.

"Oh, Lord," she prays, "convert master! Oh, Lord, change that man's heart!"

Wherever she goes, whatever she is doing, whether at work, at meals, or startled up from sleep, she prays. And she groans. When she goes to the horse trough to wash her face, she cups the water in her hands and, studying her reflection, asks God to wash her of her sins and make her clean. And when she takes up a cloth to wipe her face dry, she asks that all her sins be wiped away.

Once she has been cleansed she hopes God will intercede.

Prays, listens, acknowledges her own sinfulness, does not sleep. Startled awake by dreams, she hears sounds: footsteps, horses, chains. When she takes up a broom, she asks the Lord to sweep out whatsoever sin there be in her heart, clear and clean. And when her family is required to join in prayer with Dr. Thompson, she goes off alone and, kneeling on the Choptank landing, under the night sky, resumes her conversation with, her private petitions to, God.

Sometimes she takes a different tack. Like a soldier preparing for certain battle, she prays for courage, asking God to "make me strong and able to fight."

All during this time, Edward Brodess is sending people to size her up. Whenever a white man comes nosing around Poplar Neck for any reason, Harriet's unease grows and her heart kicks up its flutter, there being no way of knowing whether the man is only passing by or is there to chain her up on the spot and take her way.

The Second Great Awakening is rolling through the countryside, evangelicals promising certainty, redemption, God's unqualified love for all. To obtain it, grace is required, and forgiveness. Doubtless, the Methodist minister A. C. Thompson himself is preaching obedience, selflessness, and piety, especially to those whom he owns or employs. His slaves may be required to gather and hear his sermons.

A believer and a Christian, Harriet prays for her oppressor, for the heart of her master.

Christmas passes. Winter moves into its coldest months, January, February. Her twenty-seventh birthday approaches.

February closes out on a Wednesday.

The next day, March 1, 1849—she is very specific about the date— a rumor buzzes up the backroads and through the grapevine wires, reaching Caroline County from Bucktown that day. Brodess has made a deal with a trader and is about to sell Harriet and some of her brothers and perhaps her last remaining sister, Rachel, to go south on a chain gang, to the cotton and rice fields in Georgia, Mississippi, and Louisiana. There, they will be sold away from one another and lose their identity entirely. Who can know who they might then become? In the Deep South, slaves are not even given a last name. Without family, how will they ever know who they are anymore, and when they die, who will bury them, and beside what stranger will she lie for eternity?

Make me strong and able to fight.

Hearing the rumor, Harriet's heart turns to stone, and she changes her prayer. Turning her back on the precepts of forgiveness and mercy, she asks God instead for payback.

"Oh, Lord," she prays. "If you ain't never going to change that man's heart, kill him, Lord, and take him out of the way."

Kill him. Profane request. Blasphemy.

And yet she prays it, and in years to come is willing to repeat that petition to a fellow Christian, word for word. Not only because in truth she spoke them, but also because she knows their shock value and understands the need to shock in order to re-create the time and the situation and the extremes to which it drove people, even good ones, even Christians.

She does it for those reasons and because of what happens next.

Edward Brodess might already be sick. Or maybe he is suddenly struck down. Galloping pneumonia, heart attack, apoplexy. However it happens and whatever turn his health takes and for whatever reasons, less than a week after Harriet's appeal, Edward Brodess summons his lawyer to his home.

There, they write his will.

"Next thing I heard," Harriet tells Emma Telford, "he was dead and he died just as he had lived, a bad, wicked man."

One day after writing his will, on March 7, Edward Brodess dies.

It is now that Harriet Tubman begins to understand the power of her gifts, and the responsibility they have settled upon her. The message is clear: If she asks God to kill a man and that man is immediately struck down, then God has anointed her as a disciple. He wants her to ask for what she needs and to be prepared to receive it. But she must ask judiciously. And afterward take up the cause herself, for she is on her own then, and the rest is up to her.

But first, remorse. *Thou shalt not kill.*

"Oh, then," she tells Bradford, "it appeared like I'd give all the world full of gold if I had it, to bring that poor soul back."

But neither prayer nor the world's gold will do the trick. The master is dead. And, as in the case of so many others, from unknown causes.

In 1863, William Henry Stewart, born Henry Ross, will testify to the American Freedman's Inquiry Commission that on his deathbed, Brodess's "greatest cry was, 'Take this young child away from me!' " This may indicate that during his last days, a child whose mother he had sold into slavery—Linah's daughter Kessiah, perhaps—was brought to his bedside to beg him to pay heed to his great-grandfather's will and to ask that her family be kept together. The girl's uncle, Henry Ross, might well have brought the child as a last-ditch effort to appeal to Brodess's better instincts. After all, Henry also tells us, Brodess had made them all that promise: If they would be faithful to him, when he died he would leave them all to be free.

When Edward Brodess dies at forty-seven, he leaves behind an unfortunate legacy: massive indebtedness and eight children, five of them under eighteen. His will has not survived, having burned in the 1852 courthouse fire, but when subpoenaed to testify, Robert P. Martin will recall his client's last wishes. He leaves his estate to Eliza, excepting Negroes, the use and hire of whom she is to manage for the purpose of raising his children, until her death, when everything goes to the children. He is buried in an unknown grave, perhaps on his property somewhere, or—some say—in a churchyard. People go on searches from time to time, but the Brodess family is long gone from Bucktown, and even more than 150 years later, no one knows where he lies.

Perhaps he is buried beside his mother, Mary Pattison Brodess Thompson, both gone to mucky, wet Bucktown ground. Among the few people who will speak of him for the record are the black ones he owned, who—when their voices are finally sought out and heard—will refer to him simply as "master"—and white ones who call his name in court testimonies.

If Henry Ross was in Bucktown during Brodess's last days, he might well have heard the dying man call out in spiritual agony, in involuntary acknowledgment of his crimes. Perhaps a child was brought to his bedside to make her plea, but it is hard to imagine Eliza allowing such a meeting, knowing what kind of financial distress she would face alone, once her husband was dead. What is more likely is that the child appeared in a hallucinatory visitation, a reminder of that Christmas past, seven years before, when he tossed her mother in jail to be sold away, ignoring her cries of "Oh, my children! my poor children!" But the visitation is so real that Edward hears the mother's screams and the child's, as though it were happening all over again. And he calls out loudly enough for a slave outside his window to hear; in any case, fearing not for the girl or her family but for himself, his own damnation.

There is no further indication from any source other than William Henry Stewart that Edward Brodess made a promise to free his slaves, and no reason, based on his actions, to believe anything other than that if Brodess *did* make such a statement, it was only to keep his laborers in line. Other testimonies indicate that word passed through the slave cabins that while some of them might be sold, none would be taken out of state.

The death of a master made all slaves tremble in fear of being sold or passed on. Hearing the early rumor that Rit and her family will remain together, the Ross family may feel some relief, deciding to believe the rumors, at least until they hear differently.

But uncertainty rules their lives, and their unease does not diminish. Eliza is known to be very devilish. No one knows what she may do.

Harriet finds no comfort in the whispers. Since having called down death upon the master, her inner life has deepened and she has moved from a strictly religious faith into one that includes something like mysticism. She has begun hearing voices more often, receiving messages that seem to her the very darkest, direst kind of warning. The visions she has always had during her blackouts begin to fit into a pattern that only she can make out.

Anytime she closes her eyes and tries to go to sleep, she sees "the horsemen coming" and hears "the screams of women and children" being dragged away to a far worse slavery than what they have endured in

Maryland. In the night, she sits bolt upright and, whether asleep or awake, cries out, "They're coming, they're coming. I must go."

A born scoffer, John Tubman says she's like old Cudjo, who, when a joke goes around, doesn't laugh until the joke's long over and everybody else has gone on to something else. Now that the danger's past and Brodess is dead, now that she should relax and feel safe, *now*—he says—she starts talking about leaving? She is, he says, a fool.

But the visions continue, and the horsemen keep coming. And sometimes Harriet sees brighter scenes, imagining herself in flight, approaching a line on the other side of which are fields and flowers and "beautiful white ladies who stretch out their arms to me." She runs in their direction, but before reaching the line, she falls.

Her husband laughs at her.

But he is free and she is the enslaved oldest daughter, next in line.

No one else can act for her or on her behalf. She must find the courage to follow God's instructions. She has to do her part. She must choose to apply her will and be strong enough for the battle ahead. And if she makes the choice to fight, she becomes the agent of her own destiny. How, then, can she be owned? They can kill her or punish her, but they have no claim on her soul.

She thinks all of this out and, once she has surveyed her options, she makes a resolve. She will not be sold. Let the dogs come, the chain and the whip. Let death come on. *She will not be sold.*

She tells no one. Her mother is too impulsive and will raise a ruckus. Her husband is apt to betray her. Her father? At some point, she may go to Ben, ask him for advice, suggestions, help. But no one else, except her brothers, who must go with her to save their own lives. And if they have not come to the point of understanding that, then she will have to convince them.

Her illness passes. She grows strong. March ends without incident.

In April, Eliza Brodess receives a court order to sell all of her dead husband's personal property, "negroes excepted," to pay his debts. Eliza goes to the coadministrator of her husband's will, John Mills, a neighbor, to ask for a loan. He gives her one thousand dollars, which she applies to her debts. Soon afterward, however, with no indication in sight that Eliza will be able to pay the money back, the two of them petition the Dorchester County Orphans Court for permission to sell several slaves.

Permission to sell . . . whom?

The court apparently allows the sale, because in late June, Eliza and John Mills advertise the auction of a twenty-year-old woman named Harriet and her daughter, two-year-old Mary Jane, on July 6 at the courthouse. Taking into account the names of people still in bondage to Eliza, we can say with a good bit of certainty that the Harriet she is selling is Harriet Jolley, one of Linah Ross's two daughters and mother of a girl named Mary Ann, sometimes called Mary Jane.

Linah again! Her daughter, her granddaughter.

But on July 6, the sale does not take place, probably because of a new family squabble that begins during the summer session of the Dorchester County Orphans Court.

Gourney Pattison has finally figured a way to take on the widow of his nephew. In a lawsuit, he and his siblings and their children file against Eliza Brodess and John Mills, executors of Edward's estate, claiming ownership of Rit and any of her children who are forty-five years old and older. They back their claim by asserting that Gourney's grandfather, Atthow, did not specify what should happen to Rit and her increase *after* she and they reached the age of forty-five. The will, the Pattisons are claiming, is vague enough to warrant reexamination. Straining mightily for justification, the family contends that Atthow intended for those slaves to be kept by his granddaughter for the term specified only and that, afterward, they should have been returned to the Pattison estate, to be shared among Pattison sisters, brothers, and children.

As a final blow, the lawsuit also states that since Rit has legally belonged to the Pattison estate since she turned forty-five, all wages collected from hiring her out *since* then be remanded to the estate. Rit is sixty-four and has been hired out regularly for the past nineteen years, bringing the Brodesses a tidy sum, which the Pattisons claim belongs to them.

They also contend that because Edward sold Linah and Soph illegally beyond state lines, the Pattison heirs are entitled to compensation for loss of *their* labor since their sales, as well.

In one final brazen grab, the suit asks the court to prohibit the sale of any of Rit's children until the matter is legally resolved and ownership determined. Thus are Harriet and young Mary Ann temporarily saved from the auction block.

On August 6, the Gourney Crow Pattison suit is dismissed. But Pattison and his lawyer—the wealthy plantation and slave owner, future U.S. congressman and fiery proslavery spokesman James A. Stewart, brother to John T.—will not be dissuaded. They appeal.

Fierce Eliza doesn't wait for the court's subsequent decision: On August 29, she and John Mills advertise in the *Cambridge Democrat* that a "public sale to the highest bidder for cash" will be held on Monday, September 10, in which "a negro woman named Kizziah, aged about 25 years," will be sold "for life and a good title will be given."

This Kizziah is Rit's granddaughter, Kessiah, older daughter of Linah Ross and wife of the manumitted John Bowley, who has worked for the Stewart family for years as a skilled and respected sailmaker and shipbuilder.

Harriet's visions continue. The horses have come to get Kessiah; they will come for them all, the women especially. Like her dead husband, Eliza Brodess is selling off females, but she is now moving on to the next generation, putting the daughters of Linah on the auction block.

The night after the ad appears, the thirtieth, is a night of the new moon. The sky is black, the stars undimmed by moonlight. A good night for running away. But Harriet waits for a sign, and for her resolve to transform itself into the determination to go. Most slaves who run for their freedom are younger men, who go in a group. Before she takes off, she will have to become convinced that she has no other choice, that there is nothing else to do. She waits, prays, works, listens.

Her brothers do the same. They are all waiting

NEGRO FOR SALE.

I WILL sell at public sale to the highest bidder for cash, at the Court house door in the town of Cambridge, on MONDAY the 10th day of September next, a negro woman named KIZZIAH, aged about 25 years. She will be sold for life, and a good title will be given. Attendance given by

JOHN MILLS,
Agent for Elizabeth Brodess.
August 29th 1849.   2w

Auction announcement for the illegal sale of Harriet Tubman's niece, Kessiah Jolley Bowley.

to see what will happen next, the whole family. Waiting is all they can think about. The several stories told of how, in the end, it all transpired and who went and when wildly contradict one another, the various threads weaving together eventually, but in an unshapely lump. All we can do is pick one out and follow it, taking into account as we go the others, the varying colors, warp, woof, depending primarily, as always, on *her.*

The 1840s move beyond the midpoint. From western New York and across the state, throughout New England and down into Baltimore, abolitionists are organizing, gathering, making speeches. Frederick Douglass has published the first issue of his newspaper *North Star* and has moved to Rochester, New York, directly across Lake Ontario from Canada. Wealthy abolitionist entrepreneur Gerrit Smith of Peterboro, New York, offers Douglass forty acres and announces plans to give land to black people in New York State. A reform movement emphasizing Christian perfectionism spreads. The building of a suspension bridge to connect Niagara Falls, New York, with Niagara Falls, Canada, has been designed for use of carriage and pedestrian traffic.

Abolitionist John Brown moves to eastern New York State. The Women's Rights Convention meets in Seneca Falls, New York, Frederick Douglass attending. William and Ellen Craft escape from slavery, re-markably enough, from Georgia, she in men's clothes, light-skinned enough to pass as a white gentleman, he disguised as her slave. William Lloyd Garrison is making fervent antislavery speeches and publishing *The Liberator.*

The enslaved are listening.

A shift is occurring. The ground beneath their feet has opened, if only by a crack.

In August, two weeks before Kessiah Jolley is advertised for sale by Eliza Brodess, the *Easton Star,* published in Talbot County, reports an increase in runaway slaves. Every week, the paper reports, property owners hear of one or more slaves making an escape, and it further warns that if something is not speedily done to put a stop to it, "that kind of property will hardly be worth owning." Abolitionists are suspected of organizing a system of assistance to the fugitives. And the newspaper suggests that a telegraph line be run up and down the shoreline of Maryland as a way of spreading information from one plantation owner to the next, and that an efficient police force be put into action, since efforts to recover slaves once they have escaped has been, or appears to be, fruitless.

September 10 falls on a Monday. Once again, the sale date passes, probably blocked by the Pattison appeal.

Eliza must be particularly furious at Harriet at this juncture, since surely her prying is at least partially responsible for the Pattisons having pulled themselves together and consulted the old will in the first place. If Harriet hadn't hired the lawyer, Gourney Pattison would not necessarily have hired his own to help him come up with a scheme to bankrupt the widowed Eliza and steal property that rightfully belonged to her eight children—who, after all, are Pattison blood kin.

That following Saturday, Harriet either hears, or imagines that she hears, that her nieces Harriet and Kessiah are gone, having been sent off with the chain gang, and that she is next, along with some of her brothers.

The time has come for resolve to live out to the edge of its promise and become action. She has no other choice now except to leave. That same morning, she hurriedly consults with three of her brothers—Robert, Ben, and Henry—and tells them it is time.

Go? they might well ask. How? When? What path? To where? Who will help them? Maybe the situation will improve; maybe they should wait for winter, when nights are longer, or see how the Pattison fight works out. Maybe they will all be free in twenty years if they stick it out, and what about their mother?

Tonight, is her answer, Saturday night, when most escapes are made, since no one will notice until Monday and it will take another day or so after that for an ad to appear.

The brothers have reason to balk:

December is a better month for running.

The moon is full. The night sky will illuminate their profiles and make running shadow slaves on the ground.

John Tubman will betray them.

Their mother will cook up a fuss.

An engraving from *The Underground Railroad* by William Still, showing a man making his escape through the water, on horseback, risking life, limb, and capture, as he ventures through a dark night on his way to Philadelphia and freedom.

Their sister is a little bit crazy.

They will all be killed.

Benjamin's a father, with an infant son. If he turns his back on his family, they may be sold away, since Eliza's been keen on getting rid of women and children.

But their bullying sister will not negotiate or back down. Surely overriding all arguments to the contrary, she regales them with her visions of horsemen riding toward them, the screams and cries. And as well, there is the Quaker meeting house not five miles from the Thompson place. Helpful white people live across the line.

How to resist, especially now that God has struck down Edward Brodess as she requested? Her resolve and conviction—the conviction maintained only by the visionary and the mad—overwhelm the brothers, and that very Saturday night, surely feeling as muddled and fearful as she is certain and seemingly without qualms, they go. Ben and Harry, at any rate, perhaps without Robert, who, at age thirty-three, and the eldest of the brothers, may feel obliged to stay. He will marry Mary Manokey within the next two years and will become a devoted husband and father. He may, in fact, be married now, perhaps a newlywed, unwilling to abandon his young wife (she is twenty-one), especially this soon after her baby sister was sold away.

Harriet. Two brothers, or three. They prepare to leave.

When voices told the teenaged girl Jeanne d'Arc she had to gather an army in order to save France, she convinced an army to go with her. Harriet is not commanding an army, but it is astonishing indeed to think of her, a small, strange woman of twenty-seven, convincing grown men— Henry is about nineteen, Ben twenty-five, Robert thirty-three—to take off into the dangerous dark night of proslavery Maryland and head for freedom, with only the North Star and their own desires to help them, and even the North Star a dim guide, as the light of the moon overpowers its intensity.

They set off, their sister taking the lead, possibly along the banks of Marshy Creek toward Dr. Thompson's sawmill, where their father likely works, to the Marshy Creek Methodist Church. Or they may travel alongside the Choptank Road, keeping to the small streams that run beside it, toward Preston, where there is a Quaker meeting house, which Harriet will say she knew about. Or . . .

Terrified, they lurch into the darkness. But how can they shake off the ingrained feeling—the certainty—that someone is behind them, after them, watching, knowing, and, most important, in charge?

The brothers lose their faith in their sister's certitude and, after going only a short distance, disagree about the right way to go.

One says it's this way; the other says no, that.

Harriet remembers a particular tree marking the way.

About them they hear the squawks of sudden owls and feral cats, imagine an endless network of cold streams to cross. The tree cover obscures Polaris, the moon too bright. . . . How can they possibly find their way to a place they know so little of, only the name of a state perhaps, Pennsylvania, but not where it is or what, or if black people are really free there?

Fearful of being captured, "appalled by the dangers before and behind them," the brothers decide to go back.

Harriet protests and keeps going, heading away from them, citing voices and her own unshakable certainty. But her brothers overpower her and drag her unhappily back to Poplar Neck.

She remains—sulking, plotting—overnight and through the weekend. Sunday, the sixteenth, she assesses the situation. On Sundays, white people and black take a pause from work and commerce. No auctions, no sales, no courts. She can cool her heels through the night.

But on Monday, Eliza Brodess and John Mills return to court to petition for the right to sell Kessiah Bowley and her two children, this time not as slaves for life but until they "arrive at the age of forty-five years," which the court grants them the right to do, "at public sale to the highest bidder." This, despite the popularity of and general community respect for Kessiah's husband, John Bowley, who works with his brothers as a shipbuilder and blacksmith and is co-owner of a schooner docked in John T. Stewart's shipyard.

John Bowley may well go to Eliza himself to try to buy his family, but Eliza has no time for complications, sympathy, or distraction. She has her own family to think about.

She presents her petition.

Later that same day, a "negro from another part of the plantation" goes to Harriet privately to tell her that she and her brothers will be next.

Tonight, whispers the informant. Tonight.

In her mind, Harriet has become free already. Her decision has been made. Time to hold to it, to follow the North Star. Alone, if she has to. Her brothers will have to judge for themselves, but she will not be brought back against her will this time, however the North Star, in Frederick Douglass's words, "might flicker and fade behind some craggy hill, however doubtful and half-frozen the seductive reality of freedom might be."

Going. With no knowledge of what the North is, having only heard of Pennsylvania and New Jersey as places where nobody is a slave, not knowing what they are, exactly. Or where, exactly. Just names she has heard.

September 17, 1849. Tonight. Whatever it takes.

Scene 8.

Over the Line

One night . . . she walked off and used her strength and craft,
which were great, to make her way to Philadelphia.

—FRANKLIN B. SANBORN, "THE LATE ARAMINTA DAVIS,"

UNPUBLISHED MANUSCRIPT, 1913

She can't just go. She has to leave a message of some kind, some hint of her intentions for family and friends so that they won't worry. But she has to plan carefully, and make sure her mother won't find out too soon. Rit is impulsive and, having already lost three children, determined to hold on to the rest. She took that hotheaded stand when Brodess tried to sell Moses; she might react with equal emotion if she hears that her daughter is leaving, especially alone. She might even beg to be taken along, now that it's clear that Eliza Brodess means for her to be a slave for life, in practice if not legally.

Harriet is in no way prepared to take a sixty-four-year-old woman with her on a trip she's never before made. On the other hand, if she tells her mother about her plan, Rit might shout and groan and bring the Thompsons running. If Harriet's not already long gone and far up the road by the time her mother sets up a commotion, she'll be stopped dead in her tracks.

She has to have a strategy and be well prepared. During the weekend, after her return to Poplar Neck, she seems to have told only one person of her plans, a white woman who lives nearby, a woman widely known to be a trustworthy antislavery activist, unafraid to help enslaved people escape.

Now she has to leave a message for her family.

In mid-September, by late afternoon the day is worn out with itself. Sulky, it waits for the hot sky to turn to pink evening.

Milking time, Rit's job. When she comes across the yard, Harriet stops her. She'll do the milking tonight, she tells her mother, and take it to the house. Rit can go on back to the cabin, where it's cool.

If Rit casts a beady eye on her runaway-minded daughter, finding reason to wonder why she is making the offer on this particular day, only two nights after the escape attempt with her brothers, she doesn't let her suspicions get in the way of saying yes.

Turning her back, she makes her way toward the bend in the Choptank where she and Ben live in a cabin, leaving Harriet standing there, for all she knows watching her mother walk off for the last time in her life.

Most runaway slaves left without telling anyone. Not parents, spouses, children. For safety's sake, they simply went. And the ones left behind lamented the loss but understood, and in one way or another, went on with their lives. And when a property owner then questioned them about the whereabouts of the one who'd absconded, they could answer honestly, I don't know where, I don't know when. I don't know who with or by which route. She just *went.*

Unlike her mother, Harriet is not of an impulsive nature. She's bold, unpredictable, but not impulsive. The white woman she consulted is almost certainly one of the many Quakers who have settled in Caroline County, in or quite near to Poplar Neck. A useful accomplice.

Taking down her sunbonnet, Harriet goes to do the milking.

Now she needs to confide in a family member. For that, she's chosen a young black woman named Mary—perhaps Mary Manokey—who works in the main house and is someone Harriet feels she can trust.

She hauls the milk pail to the kitchen. Mary is there, but the room is full of people, perhaps fixing supper for the Thompsons, including the doctor, who still calls Cambridge his legal residence but who is on the premises today. There is no way for Harriet to whisper confidences in anyone's ear with so much going on and so many others around.

Undeterred, she sets the pail down, then makes her way toward the unknowing Mary. Improvising, adjusting to the needs of the situation, a natural underground fighter, she sets about creating a bit of theater to serve as a diversionary tactic.

The Quaker woman whom Harriet has visited is almost certainly Hannah Leverton, who, with her husband, Jacob, is a dedicated, activist abolitionist. Prosperous farmers and mill owners, the Levertons live slightly east of Poplar Neck, near Preston, where there is a Quaker meeting house. Their abolitionist stance is well known, as is their willingness to defy the law and the wishes of their neighbors by giving assistance to fleeing slaves. Their son Arthur will eventually be forced to flee Caroline County for taking part in a slave escape. Harriet has another reason to be acquainted with the Levertons: Barely two months from now, Dr. Thompson's son, A. C. Thompson, Jr., will marry Jacob and Hannah's daughter, Mary Elizabeth. The couple will live in Poplar Neck, near his father and his brother. Mary Elizabeth would be known to the Thompson laborers already.

Hannah Leverton has provided Harriet with whispered directions to the first safe house she should go to. She's also given her a piece of paper with two names on it. Harriet is to give the paper to the people at the safe house. They will then send her to the next one. While she will have to make much of the journey on her own, on foot, she can trust the people in each safe house to feed and care for her, then hand her on to the next family and then the next, like a bucket in a fire brigade. In return, either as a measure of her gratitude or as a form of personal payment, Harriet has given Leverton a bed quilt she pieced together herself.

There is not much reason to believe that Harriet ever sat still long enough to turn herself into much of a seamstress, and as we know, she refused to learn to weave. Nonetheless, however she managed to make one quilt and however it turned out, she prized her handiwork greatly, perhaps having forced her blunt fingers to get the job done just before she and John Tubman married, for the two of them to sleep under. In any case, an escaping slave clearly could not pack up a quilt to take with her and expect not to be noticed. She could no more easily have bestowed it on any of the slaves, who, once the quilt was found in their possession, would be questioned and punished.

Some believe Harriet may have sewn hidden messages into the quilt, secret signals for other fugitives from slavery, to let them know where to stop for help and when to keep going in the face of danger. If she did, then no wonder she gave the quilt to Hannah Leverton.

In the Thompson kitchen, she challenges Mary to some kind of rough-and-tumble frolic, something like tag-you're-it horseplay. Mary's young and she takes Harriet on. The game begins, creating way too much ruckus in a busy place at a hectic time. But Harriet stays in pursuit, playfully shoving Mary across the room, then flying out the door, swift- and surefooted, into the yard

Her tactics work. Mary flies out behind her, chasing Harriet to the corner of the house, around which they can find a place to speak privately. But there, the two young women come to a sudden halt when they see, approaching them on horseback, the master.

A. C. Thompson may well have been a fairly ridiculous-looking man, as Ben Ross suggested; nonetheless, he was said to be particularly adept at instilling fear in the hearts of his slaves. Whenever he rode his horse up to where they were, whether in the fields, the woods, or around the house, a hush rolled forward among them, sharply cutting off conversations and song as word passed. The workers continued at their tasks, but silently, staring at the ground until he passed on by.

Well aware that slaves are not supposed to converse freely with one another, especially if one has been rumored to be headed for the selling block, the terrified Mary wheels around, darts back around the corner of the house, and disappears into the kitchen.

Her eyes steady upon the doctor, Harriet stands her ground.

Thompson clicks his horse closer.

The sky deepens. Mosquitoes gather, creating a prelude to the night. She can wait no longer; it is time to take her first steps down the road. But first there is Thompson, sitting on that horse of his, between her and the gate leading east.

Once again, Harriet resorts to political theater. Suddenly, as if struck by a commandment from on high, she lifts her chin, opens her mouth, and begins to sing. Not quietly or to herself, but forcefully, without a trace of embarrassment or self-consciousness, using the rich resonant tones everybody who ever heard her sing or talk will comment on.

> "I'm sorry I'm gong to leave you,
> Farewell, oh farewell . . ."

From his saddle, Thompson eyes her . . . querulously, perhaps even bemusedly? Such a strange creature is this young slave woman, sometimes a little balmy, but such spunk, to have hired herself out the way she did. Perhaps the doctor even feels something akin to admiration for her eccentric ways, since despite her rascally behavior and regular bouts of illness—and possibly out of spiteful feelings toward the Brodess family— he continues to hire her and to keep her on the place, instead of returning her to her rightful owner in Bucktown.

> ". . . But I'll meet you in the morning.
> Farewell, oh farewell."

The doctor is used to hearing the laborers sing. They chant as they work, walk, gather up their tools, come out in the morning and go home at night. One voice rings out, then another, until an entire field of men and women joins in. The resulting harmonies resonate through the countryside and are quite beautiful and moving. The songs tell of Moses, the Promised Land, the Chariot that is going to swing down and take them all to Canaan.

Methodist songs. Bible songs, gospel hymns. Songs a minister like himself would find comforting. He might even congratulate himself, believing that his lessons have sunk in . . . not understanding that the Promised Land the black people long for is not spiritual heaven but New Jersey, or even Canada.

He walks his horse a few steps toward Harriet. She bows as they pass but does not pause as a slave might be expected to in order to pay her respects and see if he might have something to tell her, some job he needs her to perform.

Instead, she walks toward the gate, moving on to the next chorus of her song, which she sings even louder:

"I'll meet you in the morning.
I'm bound for the Promised Land
On the other side of Jordan.
Bound for the Promised Land."

With darkness coming on and her brothers done with work for the day, they cannot but know what their sister's song is telling them, especially Ben and Harry, if they are in Poplar Neck, who would be only too well aware of her intentions. Their father would also understand the message. Only Rit remains in the dark, perhaps protected from the truth by other family members, as she will be in other times, when other children take the road north.

Reaching the gate, Harriet looks back. But the doctor sits as before, twisted around in his saddle, watching her, as if slightly puzzled, perhaps even bedazzled by her effrontery.

When he makes no sign, she opens the gate, goes through, latches it behind her.

The doctor waits.

She goes on resolutely, as if with a job to do. Several steps, then several more. Then she turns around and comes back a step or two, hoping perhaps that Thompson has ridden on, leaving her safe to make one more attempt to alert Mary.

But Thompson sits as if frozen.

Undaunted, Harriet lifts the gate latch again, as if having neglected to secure it properly the first time, and firmly relocks it, as if to say, *There.* And then, after giving Thompson a cheeky wave good-bye, she turns her back and rolls on down the road, triumphantly exploding once again into song.

"I'll meet you in the morning,
Safe in the Promised Land,
On the other side of Jordan
Bound for the Promised Land."

The last notes of the song drift behind her.

And Thompson? He sits, watches. Later—after she's gone—he will say that as her voice floated back in the evening air, to his mind, "a wave of trouble never rolled across her peaceful breast."

Confidence is hers. She goes in peace.

Thompson's behavior is peculiar. Is it possible he *knows?* That he *allows* her to go?

In a nerve-wracked time, word travels fast. Everybody on this part of the Eastern Shore—whether enslaved or free, black or white—would have heard about Harriet's escape attempt of only two nights ago with her brothers. They have heard about Eliza Brodess's financial troubles and about the lawsuit and John Mills's and Eliza's attempts to sell some of her slaves, especially the females. They know that Edward Brodess tried many times to sell Harriet. And that she will likely be the next Ross daughter to be taken off by a trader. It is rumored that John Tubman may have informed on his wife for one reason or another, either to rescue her from her own instincts or to save his own skin by disassociating himself from her.

Might A. C. Thompson suspect? And if he does, wouldn't he at least stop her long enough to ask her where she is off to?

Is it possible he would sit on his horse and watch her go, in full knowledge of what her song means and why she is singing it and for whom? The financial loss, after all, is not his, but Eliza Brodess's. Family grudges little respect the grave. Resentment against an ungrateful step-brother may have only festered over time. In matters concerning slaves and slavery, slaveholders generally display a unified front, but from time to time, the wall of cohesion crumbles. From spite. The need for cash. Old wars, particularly those fought among members of a family.

Whatever his thoughts and inclinations, the bewigged, spare-built man turns his back on the escaping slave and, riding on, says nothing.

This is how Harriet tells the story to Sarah Bradford in 1868, in Auburn, New York.

And the black people who hear Harriet's song, both the free black and the enslaved, whisper among themselves and—fully understanding the coded message beneath the words—by nightfall have sent the news on, as they are obliged to do, through Caroline County and south, across the Choptank, down to Dorchester. To the Brodess place. Bucktown.

She is gone. Pray for her.

Night. The moon two nights past full. Alone, Harriet walks into the unknowable dark, barefoot in her slave dress, heading perhaps along Marsh Creek. The Quakers have given black people land for their own church and cemetery up by Preston, the Marshycreek Methodist. She may head there, or pass on by, not wanting to lose time so early on the journey. Keeping to the wetlands, allowing the streams and creeks that run beside the Choptank to guide her, she may well have her sights set on a spot near Greensboro, where the river narrows enough that it can be crossed on foot, at the Red Bridge.

Slaveholders were careful to emphasize the great distance and difficult terrain that lay between their property and the North, creating an imaginary landscape that, for illiterate slaves, loomed, if anything, larger and more dangerous than the real one. Leaving was like leaping from the edge of the earth. But slaves who worked the bays and rivers knew more and heard more about currents and distances. In truth, only about one hundred miles lay between Poplar Neck, in Maryland, and the Pennsylvania line, but the slavers made the distance seem greater by far, more fraught with dangers than the worst nightmare. Slaves went anyway, but the landscape of their imagination may have been more terrifying than any they would have to face in reality.

Harriet keeps her mind on her business, leaving fantasy to the fearful. She has memorized Hannah Leverton's instructions and may repeat them with every step to make sure she stays on the right path. She checks the Choptank, keeping it on her left, to the west. And she has her piece of paper with the names on it to give to other people, who can read. She knows the importance of a walking stick, to poke along the ground in front of her, helping her to feel out what she can't see: rabbit holes, sinkholes, logs, tree roots, animal traps set by farmers. Nobody walks into alien territory without a stick.

The first night, she makes as many miles as she can, so that by the time she is discovered missing, she will be far from Poplar Neck and even farther from Bucktown. By midnight, she is still making her way.

A Probably her favorite route: from Poplar Neck in Caroline County to Denton and then into Delaware; from there up to Wilmington, home of Harriet's friend, the Quaker abolitionist Thomas Garrett, and from there across the Pennsylvania State line to Philadelphia.

B The daring route of James and Kessiah Bowley and their children, from the courthouse steps in Cambridge and into the Choptank River on a small boat, in which they rowed their way into the Chesapeake and up to Baltimore, where Harriet awaited their arrival in order to whisk them on to Philadelphia. After which they made their way across New York State and into Canada.

C The route from Cambridge to Poplar Neck, which Harriet used when facilitating rescues from Bucktown and other Dorchester communities.

D The extraordinary rescue of Tilly: from Philadelphia, Harriet traveled through the Delaware Canal and down the Chesapeake to Baltimore, where she gathered up Tilly. The two women then went by steamboat even farther south, beyond Cambridge to the southern Dorchester County line, where, after passing through the Hooper Strait, they steamed up the Nanticoke River to Seaford, Delaware, then took a land route north to Wilmington and, finally, Philadelphia.

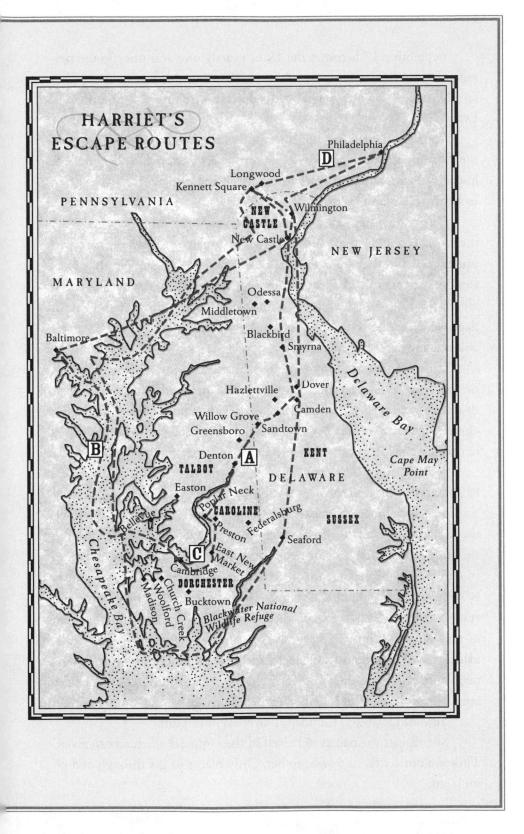

HARRIET'S
ESCAPE ROUTES

PENNSYLVANIA

MARYLAND

Baltimore

NEW CASTLE

New Castle

NEW JERSEY

Philadelphia

D

Longwood
Kennett Square
Wilmington

Odessa
Middletown

Blackbird
Smyrna

Hazlettville
Dover
Camden

Willow Grove
Greensboro
Sandtown

Denton
A

TALBOT

Easton

Poplar Neck
CAROLINE

Preston
Federalsburg

Bellevue

C

East New
Market

Cambridge
DORCHESTER

Woolford
Madison
Church Creek

Bucktown

Blackwater National
Wildlife Refuge

KENT

DELAWARE

Cape May
Point

SUSSEX

Seaford

Delaware Bay

Chesapeake Bay

B

September 17 becomes the 18th, exactly one year prior to the passage of the Fugitive Slave Act. Next year, when other members of her family make their own flight to freedom, everything will be different. Everything.

Harriet may fall sleep in the woods in the early-morning hours of the first night, waiting until late afternoon to approach the first safe house. When a woman comes to the door, she displays the paper given to her by Hannah Leverton.

The woman responds by telling Harriet to get a broom and sweep the yard. People in the South often sweep their yards when there isn't much grass and they want the dirt neatly packed and smooth, but Harriet doesn't care for the idea of stopping; nonetheless, she does as she is asked, figuring that the request is probably for the purpose of camouflage, so that a passerby will assume the woman has hired her out, and will not suspect her as a runaway.

That evening, when the woman's husband comes in from farming, he loads up his wagon and, after nightfall, helps Harriet in and then thoroughly covers her up. She crouches down, remains quiet. They bump along. Watching out for patrollers and slave catchers, the farmer drives her to the outskirts of the next town, where she gets out.

Keeping to the shadows, speaking in whispers, he advises her where to go and how to find the next station.

In this manner, she makes her way through Maryland. She follows the waterways in place of roads, through thickets and snake country, sleeping within the cradle of tree roots and in homemade caves, hiding in dense, clinging foliage, marking the navigable creeks in her memory as she goes. In Maryland, she will say—turning to metaphor—the brooks run north. Steadily, she follows their lead. There is no organized system of assistance for runaway slaves at this time, beyond the loosely established web of abolitionists, Quakers, and some Methodists, who will pass people from one meeting house or home to the next, careful to avoid the areas where slave catchers and vigilantes hide out.

Toward Delaware: Camden, Dover, Wilmington.

She repeats the names to herself in the sequence she has been given. They are not states, or towns, to her. Only places to get through and go on from.

Slaves who leave must throw themselves into the journey without knowing what is ahead. They lose one another and wander in circles, trying to find a way out. They don't look back, only ahead. They find the Big Dipper and the North Star. And go.

In his autobiography, *My Bondage and My Freedom,* Frederick Douglass wrote of his own dream of escape: "We had heard of Canada, the real Canaan of the American bondsmen, simply as a country to which the wild goose and the swan repaired at the end of winter . . . but not as the home of man. I knew something of theology but nothing of geography. I really did not, at that time, know that there was a state of New York, or a state of Massachusetts."

Behind her, the news of her escape eventually reaches Eliza Brodess, who responds oddly. She waits until October 3—almost two weeks *after* Harriet has crossed the Pennsylvania line—to post an ad offering a three-hundred-dollar reward for the return not just of Harriet but of three runaway slaves: "Harry, aged about 19 years . . . Ben, aged about 25 years . . . and Minty, aged about 27 years. . . ." All three escaped, according to the ad, on Monday, September 17. Eliza describes Harriet as fine-looking and of a chestnut color, about five feet high. She offers a hundred-dollar reward for each of the fugitives if taken out of Maryland; fifty dollars if taken within the state. Eliza runs the ad locally in the *Cambridge Chronicle* and duplicates it in the Wilmington, Delaware, *Gazette.*

Her assumption is that runaways take the Choptank route north and east to Delaware and then to New Jersey or Pennsylvania, instead of the mountainous route west, through the Appalachians.

The runaway ad is puzzling, as are various stories the Ross brothers told about Harriet's flight, accounts that occasionally crisscross and often contradict one another.

Henry will tell the 1863 interviewers in Canada that during this time, he and Ben escaped as well, and stayed away for six months before returning to Bucktown. Eliza's ad says the two brothers left together with their sister on that Monday. It's possible Eliza is confusing the earlier, September 15 escape attempt with Harriet's two days later. It's possible she didn't find out about either one until after Monday, September 17, and, even then, either misheard or misinterpreted the report, thinking the three had left Poplar Neck together.

Harriet says she went alone. After his first interview with her, Franklin Sanborn simply writes, "she walked away one night alone."

And maybe Eliza's ad has it both right and wrong. Perhaps Ben and Henry Ross did leave on that same night, the seventeenth, but not with their sister. Maybe they went looking for Harriet after she sang her song and left, thinking either to bring her back or to go with her, in either case failing to find her. Most people who fled bondage did not make it out of slavery altogether, but only stole away for a time, living for a while in nearby swamps and woodlands, then returning. The brothers might have lost their way, or their nerve, but stayed away from Poplar Neck.

A few other possibilities come to mind: Eliza holds off running the ad until two weeks and two days after the escape, first of all because she may not have known of their departure until after it occurred and, second, because she has her hands full dealing with court orders, her cousin's lawsuit, and a deteriorating financial situation. Third, she probably thinks the escapees won't succeed and will come back on their own.

There are several routes through Maryland that Harriet might have taken, perhaps moving quickly into Delaware, following the Choptank to its headwaters near Camden, where there were active African American abolitionists who would give her shelter. Or she may have traveled on farther north in Maryland, closer to Wilmington. Either way, this last leg was perhaps the most dangerous, and her friends must have taken special care to get her through it. There were bands of slave catchers who roamed the countryside there, and with fewer areas of wetlands, the bounty hunters had a better chance of spying a runaway slave making her way through the territory. Although what would later be called the Underground Railroad had not yet been systemically organized, the people willing to assist runaways were dedicated and knowledgeable. With their help, Harriet made her way through Delaware.

Pragmatic, she takes help from whoever will freely give it.

Pennsylvania is the goal—wherever Pennsylvania may be—Philadelphia. When she arrives at the state line, someone is with her who points it out to her and says, Look, you have made it. Walk over that line and you are free.

She steps across.

Everything becomes new. Even the light seems to change. She looks down at her hands to make sure she is the same person. When she looks up, she sees the sun coming over the fields and through the trees and imagines the light as "a glory over everything," as if her farewell songs have come true and she has arrived at the Promised Land.

"I felt like," she will tell Sarah Bradford in 1868, "I was in heaven."

But her feelings of euphoria quickly dissipate.

"I had crossed the line," she will tell Bradford. "I was *free,* but there was no one to welcome me to the land of freedom. I was a stranger in a strange land."

There is no one to talk to, no one to tell. No one knows where she is or what she is feeling or precisely how far she has come, all the way from the frolic with Mary in the Poplar Neck kitchen through the swamps and woodlands, to here. No one knows what life was like in Bucktown and on the A. C. Thompson place. No husband, no family.

She compares her situation to that of a man who was sent to prison for twenty-five years, who longed for home the whole time he was there, only to return and find that his house has been pulled down and a new one put up in its place, his family and friends having gone nobody knows where. No one is there to take him by the hand. No one to welcome him home.

By the laws of the slave-holding states, she is still enslaved, still the property of Eliza Brodess. But for the next year, until the passage of the Fugitive Slave Act, in the free states she can live a free life. She can make choices for herself, decide how to live her life. Still, she can't shake off her disappointment. With no one to celebrate with, no one to welcome her, "I was a stranger in a strange land; and my home, after all, was down in Maryland because my father, my mother, my brothers, and sisters, and friends were there."

As she heads toward Philadelphia, she settles her mind with a moral decision: She has no right to individual freedom while others—those who are a part of her and in whose presence her life belongs—are bound. Since she is free, so should her family be. She is the first daughter, after all, the one who has come out successfully, the one who hears the voices and has the insight. Having been chosen, she believes, she has no right to do anything but obey, no choice but to use her gifts, to take on responsibility for others.

She makes a new resolve. Once she's made a home in the North, with God's help, she will bring her family there. Before crossing the bridge into Philadelphia, she prays.

"I said to the Lord, 'I'm going to hold steady on to you, and I know you'll see me through.'"

She is the same person, but with a new resolve and a new name. From now on she is Harriet. Harriet Tubman.

She crosses the Delaware. Holding steady.

Follow her.

Scene 9.

Family

*After many adventures she reached Philadelphia, where she
found work and earned a small stock of money.*
                    —FRANKLIN SANBORN, "HARRIET TUBMAN,"
              THE *COMMONWEALTH* (BOSTON), JULY 1863

Retrospect flattens time, rendering it conveniently compressed. *For a year,* we might say, having consulted various texts and interviews describing Harriet's first months in the North, *she works.*
Doing what? *Cooking and cleaning.* Where? *In hotels and private homes
in Philadelphia and, that summer, in the resort hotels of Cape May, on the
New Jersey shore.*

And there we would have it: her year, 1849–1850.

But life happens day to day and minute to minute. Loneliness
challenges clock time, and, using bully tactics, wins.

From Harriet's perspective, time grinds on. The year becomes
lonely minutes, days, weeks without family and home. Her brothers'
children growing up without her, her parents marching steadily toward
the end of their lives, her mother yet illegally enslaved, as are all her
people except her father. Her brothers, her last sister, Rachel—now the
mother of two children—her nieces Kessiah and Harriet, all apt to be
sold off and carried away at the flick of Eliza Brodess's say-so. And Harriet is far away, on the other side of the line, unable, for now, to help.

Haunting the riverfront, she goes in search of jobs—day work,
and night—friends, and news from the Eastern Shore, salting away

what money she can manage to pinch from her earnings in some hidden place, tied up perhaps in a ticking bag she secures around her waist, or stashed in a room she's rented in a trusted rooming house.

Her resolve makes time tolerable, alleviating loneliness and the tedium of work, giving life direction and purpose beyond the day-to-day. It is not clear, at this point, how she expects to bring her people out, or if she even knows. She says she waited for God to provide instructions. During this time of uncertainty, then, she must be praying hard, staying steady, as she promised she would at the Pennsylvania line, so that the Lord will see fit to see her through, as, in exchange, she requested.

The Lord will provide instructions and armor, but she has to do her share. She has to think hard and be ready, so that when the time comes, she will have sorted through details and settled on a plan. The dark months are the best time to go, December and January, when nights are long and people who have homes stay in them, when crops are harvested and laborers are less closely observed.

Her plan may be to hoard her savings until the seasons pass. In the meantime, she considers tactics: how to alert people that she is on her way, where they should meet up when she gets there, whom to tell, how to get the message to the Eastern Shore, what to do about babies on the trip, as well as those who may grow too fearful or too ill to complete the journey. If she is to be in command—as it seems she must be—then she has to set the rules in advance, and be willing to put them into practice without compromise or mercy.

Her brothers were wrong to turn back. When she brings people out, she will tell them in advance, Either you go or you stay. She will carry a gun and be ready to use it. Anyone weak enough to turn back is weak enough to spread tales.

Once she sets a schedule to meet up, she will stick to it. Whoever's not there won't go. Even family.

They will do as she says or she will not take them.

When asked how she summoned up the courage to go back to Dorchester the first time, her answer is unflinching: "I started with this idea in my head. There's two things I've got a right to, and these are Death or Liberty. One or the other I mean to have. No one will take me back alive; I shall fight for my liberty and when the time has come for me to go, the Lord will let them kill me."

The words of a born warrior.

The black community in Philadelphia is quite large. Using her great warmth and her ability to make friends, Harriet quickly finds cohorts, especially along the Delaware River, where there are boatmen who can help keep her in touch with the Eastern Shore, through messages received from Wilmington and Baltimore. John Tubman's brothers, Tom and Evan, work on and live near the Baltimore docks, as do a number of Bowleys and Manokeys. When ships arrive from the Eastern Shore, they quietly collect information and send it on. She can then send return messages back to Baltimore and on down to Wilmington and Cambridge.

The news from home slogs on in the same direction, but with a few surprises.

On October 24, 1849, a little over a month after Harriet's departure and only three weeks after the appearance of Eliza Brodess's runaway ad, the Dorchester court rescinds permission to sell Harriet's niece Kessiah Bowley, then inexplicably grants a new order authorizing the sale of Kessiah's sister, Harriet, and her two-year-old child, Mary Jane, whom the court calls Mary Ann. Harriet will bear another daughter—Sarah, or Sarah Ann—sometime during the following year, 1850, and she may be pregnant now, as she faces the auction block.

On that same October day, at least twenty-four slaves escape from Talbot County. Some will be apprehended; others of this remarkably large group—labeled by the *Easton Star* a "stampede"—make it out. They take a route different from Harriet's. Instead of following the Choptank north, they travel southeast across Caroline County through Preston and Federalsburg. At the Delaware state line, they cross over, then proceed straight up the Nanticoke River, paralleling a trail that is now State Road 13. North of Lewes, they cross the Delaware River into New Jersey.

The *Easton Star* blames outsiders for the stampede, implying that enslaved people would not know how to leave without enticement; would not, in fact, want to.

Two weeks later, in early November, the unpredictable Dr. A. C. Thompson reduces the bondage time of twenty-seven slaves, mostly women and children—including twenty-one-year-old Mary Manokey. He schedules all slaves to be set free on the New Year's Day following their thirtieth birthday. Thompson may well be responding to the October flight by encouraging his own slaves to stay put and wait out their shortened terms. Or he is yielding to the appeals of Mary Elizabeth Leverton, his son's Quaker fiancée, whose marriage to A. C. Thompson, Jr., will take place on November 20.

Harriet spends Christmas alone, perhaps serving or cooking a meal in a hotel or private home, saving a good part of her wages to assure her of a different Christmas next year.

By the first of the year, she and all members of her race, whether enslaved or free, are paying close attention to national news.

Beginning in January and lasting through the summer, the U.S. Congress will debate the Compromise of 1850. Proposed by Henry Clay of Kentucky, the bill proposes to settle differences among pro- and antislavery forces, in order to keep the union together. It deals with a number of slavery-based territorial issues, but the most controversial section is the Fugitive Slave Act, which requires citizens of all states to help recover fugitive slaves and turn them in, so that they can be returned to their owners, failure to do resulting in a fine and imprisonment. It also denies a fugitive's right to a jury trial, increases the number of federal officials authorized to enforce the law, and makes life easier for slave owners filing claims to recover the people they consider property.

Supporters of the bill include John C. Calhoun of South Carolina, Daniel Webster of Massachusetts, and Stephen A. Douglas of Illinois. In spite of increasing threats of secession by slave states, President Zachary Taylor—himself a wealthy slave owner from Virginia—continues steadfastly to oppose the Fugitive Slave Act.

By asking questions and eavesdropping on conversations, Harriet keeps up with relevant politics. Although unsure of her exact birth date, she always remembered that the year she walked away from slavery was the last year of the James K. Polk administration. She and others like her, who are making a new life for themselves in the North, follow the progress of the compromise bill closely. They pray for Zachary Taylor's continuing support. For abolitionists and all black people, Daniel Webster's backing of the bill makes for a particularly devastating blow, since Massachusetts has previously enjoyed a reputation as a bastion of anti-slavery opinion.

In February or March, Harriet turns twenty-eight.

In June, while she is working in resorts in Cape May, on the southern tip of New Jersey—where white people go to relax, take the baths, and escape city heat—her niece Harriet is sold with her young daughter to a Dorchester County merchant, Thomas Willis, for $375. Mother and child are taken away as term slaves, to be kept in bondage until they are forty-five years old, thus indicating that, for one thing, they are not Keene slaves, but members of the Ross family, and that, for another, Eliza has at least temporarily yielded to the instructions of Atthow Pattison's will, possibly under court orders, until the appeal of Gourney Pattison and James A. Stewart is finally settled.

Harriet has been in Philadelphia less than nine months at this time, and even if she had been told of the forthcoming sale, she might not have been prepared to save her niece and her child. She can comfort herself somewhat, however, with the knowledge that mother and child will remain in the county, close to their family and, as yet, within her territory of future rescue.

The Fourth of July is a big day in Cape May, with fireworks displays and parades. Harriet works long hours. In Washington, D.C., President Taylor attends an entire afternoon of festivities and speeches, after which he takes a walk in the blistering heat and then, exhausted, goes home and gulps down a bowl of cherries, accompanied by a pitcher of cold milk. Later that same day, he develops crippling stomach cramps, eventually diagnosed as cholera morbus, caused by Washington's contaminated water. After doctors administer calomel and opium, Taylor rallies, then worsens. More calomel is followed by quinine, blistering, and bleeding, but the president's health continues to decline.

On July 9, Taylor dies; the next day, Vice President Millard Fillmore, a former U.S. Congressman from Buffalo, New York, is sworn in as president. Fillmore quickly falls in with the compromise bill's advocates, and a little more than two months after becoming president, citing his deter-

The immovably dedicated and altogether spectacular Frederick Douglass, "magnificent in his wrath."

mination to keep the union together, he signs the Compromise of 1850, including the Fugitive Slave Act, also known as the "Bloodhound Bill."

Life changes utterly . . . for Harriet, for Frederick Douglass, for all of those who have escaped slavery and those who should have been manumitted but are still living in bondage, for those who are considering taking flight, for all black people, whether free or enslaved, and for all who oppose slavery. In response, abolitionists throughout the East and Midwest join forces, forming the more systematized network of assistance for fugitive slaves that will be known as the Underground Railroad. In many cities, biracial vigilance committees are formed, which pledge to protect any fugitive who enters one of these cities. Many of those who have been working to assist runaways destroy their records and send word to colleagues to intensify their secrecy. Having traveled from Rochester to Boston to speak against the Bloodhound Bill, Frederick Douglass describes roads filled with terrified black people making their way to Canada. The abolitionist visionary, John Brown, gives voice to a contrary point of view, declaring the Fugitive Slave Act a godsend to the antislavery cause, predicting that it will create more abolitionists than years of speeches.

In November 1850, Eliza Brodess further culls her assets. She sells another slave, a man named Dawes Keene—from her family's estate—for life. And in December, fifteen months after Harriet's escape, she posts a notice of the coming sale of Kessiah Bowley, twenty-five, and her children, James Alfred, six, and Araminta, one, who will be auctioned off together on the courthouse steps in Cambridge.

Through the waterfront wires, Harriet quickly receives the news. Determined to prevent the sale—perhaps haunted by her inability to save Kessiah's sister, Harriet—and to bring Kessiah and her family north, she immediately leaves Philadelphia for Baltimore, where her brother-in-law, Tom Tubman, provides her with a place to stay. A return to Maryland is clearly fraught with dangers, especially now, but from Baltimore, she can communicate more directly with John Bowley so that together they can devise a workable strategy. There is no other way.

A skilled waterman, John Bowley knows the waters of the Eastern Shore and how to maneuver his way through its sometimes treacherous tides and currents. Because of which, he and Harriet decide on an escape up the Chesapeake to Baltimore, where she will meet the family and take them to Philadelphia. The escape will be extremely perilous. Winter is upon them, and if the Bowleys are to get to Baltimore safely, they must go in a small boat, unstable in a high wind, apt at any moment to toss its passengers into an icy, unfriendly bay, there to drown, all four. And if they run aground and are captured, John Bowley will be arrested for aiding a fugitive and will himself be returned to slavery, as well.

The risks are huge, the odds of success unspeakably low, but the admirable John Bowley has committed himself to saving his family, whatever the risks to his own life and personal liberty. He gathers up all the money he has. Harriet may send some. Other waterfront workers may contribute. He also engages the help of someone whom his as-yet-unborn son, Harkless, will one day call simply a "lady." His brother Richard, a ship's carpenter, may well help him build a small boat—perhaps a log canoe, made of scooped-out logs strapped together and fitted out with a sail—which he hides somewhere near the river until the time comes to use it.

Waiting in Baltimore, Harriet will have to spend long hours hearing nothing, knowing nothing about Kessiah and John's whereabouts or if they are alive, drowned, or caught. She will have to pray and hope for many hours. She will have to calm her heart and incline herself toward patience instead of action, trusting in the Lord, her voices, and John Bowley.

On the day of the auction, Eliza Brodess's son John takes Kessiah and the children from Bucktown to Cambridge. Shortly before noon, they are delivered to the courthouse steps.

Kessiah stands on the top step, where she can best be observed, Araminta in her arms and James by her side. James is an intelligent child, who will receive an education and become a teacher. His mind clicks away as he looks out at the gathered crowd. His father is among the group gathered beneath him. John Bowley keeps his eyes and his attention on his family, comforting them as best he can with his presence, which in some measure walls them off from humiliation and shame, turning their minds to iron.

The six-year-old James would likely have been told of their plans. Soon they will fly. He and his mother and sister will not be sold. And if the Choptank sinks their boat or the Chesapeake takes them, so be it.

The auctioneer begins the bidding. John Brodess stands close by, representing his mother's interests. A woman in her twenties like Kessiah, her fertility made obvious by the presence of two healthy children, might bring as much as five hundred dollars, maybe more.

The auctioneer keeps the bidding going until it reaches a price that John Brodess finds satisfactory, at which point mother and children are declared sold.

But before any money exchanges hands, the courthouse clock chimes the noon hour. Obviously, the auctioneer works by the hour, for without further negotiation, he orders a break for a meal, and after setting Kessiah aside, he goes off to eat his dinner.

The crowd disperses.

When John Bowley makes a move toward his family, no one pays much attention. He is, after all, a free man and Kessiah's husband, and not only that: He is the auction's high bidder. The purchase of a slave of his own is a perfectly acceptable transaction for a free black man to make—if not one many people would prefer—assuming he has the asking price, in this case a particularly significant question.

At any rate, incredible as it may seem, John Bowley has purchased his wife and children. All he has to do now is pay for them.

When the auctioneer returns and calls for payment to John Brodess, no one comes forward. And when he calls again and Bowley still fails to comply, the auctioneer and the other officials start to suspect that they have been gulled, that the purchase was only a delaying tactic foisted on them by the woman's husband.

He calls for Kessiah and her children to be brought back to the block to be sold once again. While waiting, he begins the bidding.

But the woman and her children cannot be found. Brodess and the others conduct a search through the courthouse and around its perimeter. No one has custody of Kessiah; no one has seen her. She seems to have vanished from under their very noses. After much scurrying about, the men realize they have been brazenly duped. John Bowley has stolen his wife and children from their rightful owner and has either hidden them away somewhere or run away with them, without paying Brodess a cent.

Nobody doubts but that they will be found. How far can they have gotten during an hour's recess?

The courthouse is located on High Street, only one long block from the harbor and the Choptank River. On both sides of that one block there are large homes graced with sizable front porches and shaded by giant trees. The neighborhood is one reflecting the prosperity of its owners, who were then, and are now, all white.

During his lifetime, Kessiah and John Bowley's son, Harkless, will hear the story of his parents' daring escape many times over, and in a letter to Tubman biographer Earl Conrad, he will report that his father shepherded his family from the courthouse to a "lady's house," only a five-minute walk away. Presumably, then, one of the families who lived on High Street either took in the fugitive black family or told them where to go on their own to hide out. The Josiah Bayley family on High Street were known to have educated and manumitted their slaves; they had a small shed in the backyard where the family could have stayed.

There, perhaps in a potato hole or a root cellar, they wait out the daylight hours, John holding James close, Kessiah nursing the baby to keep her quiet while John Brodess and the others continue their search.

When we cast back and consider how easily Harriet managed to walk away from A. C. Thompson, and note, as well, how Edward Brodess's uncle Gourney Pattison stubbornly continued to pursue a lawsuit that would rob his own nephew's sons and daughters of their inheritance, despite his grandfather's emphasis on the sanctity of blood relationships, it is hard not to conclude that if Edward Brodess was not particularly well liked or respected, his widow was even less wholeheartedly admired.

Perhaps this is an oversimplification. In Edward's case, part of the general disfavor may have stemmed from his brash ill treatment of his stepfather, but class awareness may also have perked up its sharp eyes and ears among the white folk. Within the circle of Dorchester's landowning tribe, Brodesses were not highly considered. Except for Edward, they all gave up on making a success in Maryland anyway and, like others of their station, headed for the bigger, quicker profits to be made in the Deep South. Eliza's family, the Keenes, had a better reputation; nonetheless, the Pattisons—who were, after all, blood relatives to her children—went after her. Nothing worked out to her advantage. She kept getting stopped in her tracks, one way or another and from all sides.

Perhaps she wasn't a brilliant manager of her affairs. Maybe she was ill-tempered in a way that rubbed men particularly wrong. But none of that wholly accounts for the relentless litigious attack by Pattison and his lawyer, James A. Stewart. There had to be something else. In his 1863 Canadian interview, Harriet's brother described Eliza as "very devilish," and perhaps she was, and not just to her slaves.

Maybe there was one simple reason why people were willing to turn their heads away from her financial distress—and looked in another direction when her slaves escaped: They didn't like her.

In the matter of the Bowleys, it's possible that some good white people in Cambridge had been scandalized by her treatment of John Bowley, a man for whom the white community had developed respect and even, despite his race, admiration.

It's not that they thought slaves should escape. Or that they actively helped John Bowley. They simply pointed out where a person might hide for a few hours.

Or maybe Harriet used her contacts with the Eastern Shore Quakers to find quick refuge for the family.

Who knows where they went or who helped them and why. Whoever knew at the time certainly never said.

At any rate, the Bowley family went somewhere and no one found them.

December darkness arrives before six o'clock, at which time John and Kessiah bundle up the children and slip away down High Street to the river. In the darkness, John slides their little boat into the cold, lapping waters of the Choptank, and they sail northwest, past Irish and Bread creeks, into the great, broad Chesapeake.

The trip will take all that night and much of the next, assuming that, of necessity, they travel only at night, finding shelter during the day, perhaps with black people living on the shores of the bay, perhaps huddling together in the scrub and bushes until nightfall, when they push off again. And if little Araminta cries out in her sleep, her shrill voice will fade into the winds of the bay and merge with the shrieks of gulls and night owls. And those who have homes are sleeping bundled up within them and have no reason to startle up out of sleep to go out into the cold night to investigate, or even to wonder if the cry was human or some-

This engraving from William Still's book might have been an illustration for the escape of John and Kessiah Bowley and their children, as they sailed from Cambridge up the Chesapeake, to Baltimore, where Harriet awaited their arrival.

thing from a dream . . . until, perhaps, the next morning, by which time, the fugitives have long before sailed on.

They sail past the islands of Talbot and Queen Anne counties, then eventually slip into nighttime or predawn Baltimore, where between large schooners and barges, John Bowley slides their boat into the sandy bank and ties it up.

There, the anxious Harriet runs up to meet them and—such relief for them all, so many congratulations and tears and groans of happiness— draws them close, meeting her namesake, little Araminta, for the first time. Then, urging them to move swiftly and without speaking until they have quit Maryland, she takes them to a place to stay until nightfall, when they head for Philadelphia.

And so Harriet's year of loneliness ends. She has family with her again. She could not save her sister Linah, but she has done her part to help John Bowley bring out Linah's daughter and her grandchildren, and now they are all safely tucked away, close to her.

Harriet is often given credit for the Bowleys' brash run for freedom. But surely John Bowley deserves most of the praise for charting and conduct- ing what may have been the most dangerous part of the flight—from the auction block in Cambridge up the bay to Baltimore. While depending on Harriet's example and advice and perhaps, in part, her funding, he, in fact, replicated her act of September 1849 by simply turning his back and—taking charge of his own life, giving himself a measure of autonomy—wrested control of his family away from the slaveholder Brodess.

Simply put, he walked off, then sailed to the north, in defiance of the Fugitive Slave Act.

Flush with success, Harriet, within months of escorting Kessiah and her family to Philadelphia, returns to Baltimore to help arrange the escape of her youngest brother, Moses, and two other men. There is not much to go on regarding these escapes, other than the stories saying that Moses left and his sister Harriet helped him, corroborated by the disappearance of Moses Ross from the records and Anthony C. Thompson's court testimony that indeed Moses ran away sometime before the spring of 1852 and was never captured.

We put the several sources together, then, and reasonably deduct that between December 1850, when Harriet traveled to Baltimore to facilitate Kessiah's escape, and the fall of 1851 when she, as Sanborn reports, went back to Dorchester for the first time, she returned to Baltimore to help her brother Moses come north with two other enslaved men.

During these two rescues, she is developing her navigational and intelligence skills, moving people through unspeakable dangers, which she does from afar—an ability she will put to use during the Civil War, when she works for the Union as a scout and a spy. Working her sources, unafraid to give orders, she sends messages to her brother. These messages contain very specific instructions, which she expects him to follow. She may provide some funding for the trips, as well, but her more important responsibility is to act as guide and commander.

Moses Ross may or may not come through Baltimore on his way north; more than likely, he does not. He may go to Philadelphia. Harriet may take him in for a while. She doesn't say. Perhaps he simply goes off on his own. After this, except for an intriguing 1854 county chattel record showing Dr. Anthony C. Thompson's purchase of a slave named Moses Ross—who may or may not, of course, be the *same* Moses Ross— the young man vanishes. None of the brothers mentions him again, nor does Harriet herself.

Kessiah and John Bowley remain in Philadelphia for the better part of a year, but because the Fugitive Slave Act is being put into practice there and in Boston, they are working and saving up money to get them out of the country—to Canada. Harriet is saving money also, to finance a plan she is putting together, this time to go back to Dorchester for the first time—not to rescue her enslaved blood kin, but to bring out her husband.

John Tubman does not seem to have been particularly good to Harriet when they were together, deriding her fears of being sold and even— according to some—doing what he could to betray her when she escaped. Nonetheless, she clearly considers her marriage inviolable, thereby considering him part of her family, included in the bounds of its sanctity.

Unquestionably, she misses him, or she wouldn't go back for him. She may also be longing for another chance to bear a child.

By the fall of 1851, she has saved up enough money to make the trip, but she has spent some of it on a new suit for John so that on their way back to Philadelphia, no one will suspect him of being a slave and take him away for the reward money. She stores her money in the ticking bag she ties around her waist, somehow packs up the suit, and sets off.

She doesn't say what route she takes, whether over the same inland trails as before or going part of the way by boat. Cape May is located so far south in New Jersey that it lies below the Mason-Dixon line. She sometimes leaves from there, and perhaps she does so this time, taking a ferry across the Delaware Bay to Lewes, from which point she could then set off south toward Maryland.

Since slave catchers focus on fugitives going north, she can depend on being fairly safe, whichever route she takes. However she goes, she escapes notice and makes her way down through eastern Maryland and over to Caroline County.

Home: the smells she knows, the feel of the ground, the color of the air. Her mother and father only a few miles away, Rit now living full-time with Ben. Her brothers in Bucktown, along with her sister Rachel and Rachel's young children, Ben and Angerine. But Harriet is nothing if not single-minded and she doesn't take the risk of being caught by indulging her heart and going to visit them. She concentrates on John.

When she arrives in the Harrisville area where she and John lived as man and wife, she establishes a place for herself some eight or so miles away—a tactic she will continue to employ throughout her rescue years—and finds somebody to send word that she has come to take him north with her. She will wait for him where she is.

But the courier quite stuns Harriet. In her absence, it seems, John Tubman has taken in a free woman whose name is said to be Caroline. The couple are living together as man and wife, even though Harriet considers herself, until death, married to him.

The news knocks her flat. Nothing she knows has prepared her for the shock of this development. Scotching her natural tendency toward confrontation, she forces herself to stay where she is instead of venturing into the new woman's presence, for fear of causing a ruckus. Still, she cannot reconcile the information she's just received with her basic beliefs. And so, certain that John, too, regards their marriage vows as sacrosanct, she sends word anyway, notifying him of her whereabouts and her intention to take him from Maryland to Philadelphia, where they can resume married life.

Her courier flies off into the night. Harriet waits. So many messages sent and received between Philadelphia and the Eastern Shore, and yet no one let her know of her husband's faithlessness, not even John's Baltimore brother, Tom? After she has bought the suit and come all this way?

The messenger returns.

John, it seems, has declined to join her.

Humiliated, Harriet blows her top, revealing a volatility she otherwise suppresses, falling into a fit of jealousy and anger so excessive that she craves nothing more than to burst into John's house and make all the trouble she can—regardless of what might happen to her if she is discovered—just to show Caroline what's what and to "see her old man once more." And as she remembers how he laughed at her and derided her for her fears of being sold, she must imagine him laughing at her now, lying in wait for him out in the cold dark. He may even encourage the new wife—whoever she may be—to join in.

But Harriet curbs her impulse and stills her anger, realizing how foolish it would be for her to allow her temper to take over and make such noisy mischief that someone might come and clap her in chains. She doesn't say how she manages to do that, but one way or another, she calms herself, and once she does, she makes a pact with herself to turn her face away from John Tubman forever.

In 1865, Harriet will tell Ednah Dow Cheney that at that moment, she decided, if her husband could do without her, she could do without him. And so, like that, John Tubman "dropped from her heart."

But the pain of sexual betrayal burns like a scorpion's sting, lasting long beyond the original hit. While we cannot, in good conscience, speculate on Harriet's erotic life, we can surely make some fair assumptions about it from her passionate response to her husband's double-cross.

It is at this point, she will later say, that she moves beyond personal aims, understanding that God wants her to focus on brave deeds and the needs of a great cause.

"I can't die but once" becomes her creed.

From then and until emancipation, she is married to a cause.

Before she sets off to go back north, however, people who have heard she is in the county come to her. They want to go to freedom. Will she take them and tell them how to go?

In Harriet's mind, she has no choice. Since she *can* guide them out, she must.

In December of this same year, it is said that she brings out a group of eleven slaves, "among them," according to Franklin Sanborn, "her brother and his wife." But no brother goes north with her, as far as we know, and Harriet often uses familial terms to denote those she is close to without being blood kin. Whoever they are, they come together to make their request.

She might have gone back to Philadelphia first, then returned for the fugitives. In the future, she will make back-to-back round-trips when necessity demands it. But given her final response to John Tubman's betrayal, it makes sense to think that once she'd dropped him from her heart, she decided to make use of her journey and to begin her new life right away.

In which case, there would have been only one trip.

In December, then, on a Saturday night, she and eleven unknown others start off together, more than likely using the route she knows, up the Choptank to Camden and Dover, then to Wilmington and into Pennsylvania. And when they reach Philadelphia, even though the eleven fugitives may think they have gone far enough, she says no, they have to go to Canada.

Since passage of the Fugitive Slave Act, she has decided, she can no longer leave her family and friends in Philadelphia or any other city in the north. From now on, as she will later say, she can no longer trust Uncle Sam with her people. Instead, she must escort them all the way out of the country. To accomplish this, she needs help, specifically from the organized system of assistance called the Underground Railroad (UGRR).

Usually, on these longer trips, she "proceeded by steam railroad to New York, and from there she took the train to Albany," where she boarded a train for Rochester. There, Frederick Douglass often saw that she "got on the train for the Suspension Bridge and St. Catharines in Canada."

So far, nothing tells us exactly how Harriet made these extensive contacts with antislavery activists throughout western New York. This absence of information should come as no surprise, however, in part because at that time, people were afraid to name names or speak above a whisper about such things. And so the information was passed on by word of mouth and through documents that were quickly destroyed. The Underground Railroad was, as its name implies, a secret organization, a web of guerrilla fighters dedicated to the cause of freedom for the enslaved people of the South.

Fugitives were hidden in root cellars and attics. They were disguised and, in unfamiliar clothing, were taken from one safe house to the next by any means available, including boats, trains, wagons, carts, and of course, on foot down secret paths and unmarked trails. Harriet identified some of her helpers as the brothers William and Nathanial Brinkley of Camden, William Still of Philadelphia, Stephen Myers of Albany, and Frederick Douglass in Rochester.

However she travels, she is setting off into new territory, beyond Philadelphia, toward New York, and eventually across the Niagara River to present-day Ontario, which at that time was called Canada West.

Slave catchers are good at their job, and they are everywhere. They watch freight and passenger trains to the north with exceeding care, as do federal agents, who also hope to collect a bounty. Any black person boarding a northbound train will be searched and questioned. Most will be kidnapped and taken away.

But Harriet has made her arrangements with people who will hide all twelve of them safely along the route, sometimes in freight cars among hay bales and boxes of goods. There will be someone to meet her and her group when they arrive at the next stop, and the next.

In Rochester, they stay in the home of Frederick Douglass, who will not speak of their visit until long after emancipation, in 1881, when he writes:

On one occasion I had eleven fugitives at the same time under my roof, and it was necessary for them to remain with me until I could collect sufficient money to get [them] on to Canada. It was the largest number I ever had at any one time, and I had some difficulty in providing so many with food and shelter, but as may well be imagined, they were not very fastidious in either direction, and were well content with very plain food, and a strip of carpet on the floor for a bed, or a place on the straw in the barn loft.

Having safely crossed the Niagara to gather under what she calls "the protection of the British lion's paw," the fugitives find their way to the nearby town of St. Catharines. There, in time, Harriet will rent a home located on North Street, in a district where black people have established a community.

By now, Kessiah and John Bowley have already taken flight from Philadelphia, and are settled in Canada. But they have gone on to Chatham, some 140 miles to the west of St. Catharines, where there is a large settlement of black people, farming and working on the waterfront. They have brought the baby, Araminta, with them, leaving James in Philadelphia, to continue his education.

The Canadian winter of 1852 is bitter. Since none of the eleven freed men and women are acquainted with the kind of snow and ice they encounter there, Harriet takes on responsibility for their care. For money, she chops wood and begs.

She stays in Canada until the spring, when she returns to Philadelphia to earn money enough to begin bringing out the rest of her family.

That summer, she goes down to Cape May to work as a cook, establishing a routine she will follow for the next five years: From spring through early fall, she cooks and cleans, earning money for trips; winters, when nights are long and those who have homes stay in them, she heads south toward what she will continue to think of as home as long as her family lives there.

The seasons, then, accumulate their rituals, bracketing time, giving structure and purpose to her year.

Scene 10.

RESCUES, PROMISES

Her imagination is warm and rich, and there is a whole region of the marvelous in her nature, which has manifested itself at times remarkably. Her dreams and visions, misgivings and forewarnings ought not be omitted in any life of her . . .
—FRANKLIN SANBORN, QUOTED IN SARAH BRADFORD,
SCENES IN THE LIFE OF HARRIET TUBMAN, 1869

A man who has been in slavery knows, and no one else can know, the yearning to be free, and the fear of making the attempt.
—INTERVIEW WITH JOHN ATKINSON, IN BENJAMIN DREW,
*A NORTH-SIDE VIEW OF SLAVERY. THE REFUGEE: OR
THE NARRATIVE OF FUGITIVE SLAVES IN CANADA,* 1856

In December 1854, Harriet begins to feel a troubling in her spirit about her three brothers, Ben, Henry, and Robert. Some great evil, she feels, shadows their lives and hangs over their heads. She is too far away to know whether or not they have received the forewarning, or, even if they have, whether or not they will be able to take their lives in their own hands and act upon the message.

By default and self-appointment, she has become the head of her family, a position she has held for some five years. Given that charge, there is only one thing to do: go down and bring them out herself. She has already been to Maryland twice this year, but her brothers need her now; she has no choice but to go again.

Life on the Eastern Shore has been fraught and rocky for every-one. During the past two years, the Ross brothers had made further attempts to escape on their own, and sometime in late 1852 or early 1853, the three of them managed to make their way beyond Bucktown, into the uninhabited wetlands. Once there, however, no matter how elated they felt to be away, they sensed trouble: patrollers and slave catchers lurking in the distance. They started back, then stopped. In the woods, they set themselves up in a secluded spot and stayed there, perhaps for six months or so.

For provisions, they sent word home of their whereabouts, un-doubtedly to their father, while they decided what to do next. Having created a hideout, they settled in, as if intending to stay. Clearly, with-out their sister's certainty and assistance, the three men were unable to convince themselves to break out and go.

At some point, an unidentified "white gentleman" showed up, offering to buy all of them from Eliza, promising that, if they agreed to the sale, the brothers would live near their parents, their wives, and their children. Perhaps also—although there was no way to be sure of it—the move would save them from sale to a trader.

Apparently, the unnamed white man was somewhat trusted by the brothers, since they agreed to his offer, considering it an acceptable compromise.

But when the man went back to Bucktown, Eliza would not give him the time of day. If she could not hold on to the Ross brothers, she snapped, she'd rather see them sold to Georgia.

And so the man returned to the brothers' hiding place and, in an astonishing break with slaveholder solidarity, advised them that, since the woman would not budge, if they could get away, they should go; otherwise, they'd soon find themselves in chains on the auction block. The brothers then sent that message on to their father, probably through the white man. Ben was still living on the Thompson place, settled in with Rit. Without telling his wife, he contacted a man he knew, who promised to take his sons to safety. Ben may even have paid his friend for his help. But when the Ross brothers arrived at the meet-ing place, the man either didn't show up or wouldn't take them out.

And so, disappointed once again, they couldn't figure out what else to do but go back to Bucktown.

A few questions come to mind. One concerns the identity of the white man. Considering the fact that their parents as well as Robert's family—Mary and their two children—live on the Thompson place, the most likely candidate seems to be Eliza Brodess's nemesis, A. C. Thompson himself. He has known the entire family since childhood and has already hired out Robert Ross during this time. He has given his slaves early manumission. His operation is bigger and better organized than Eliza's. However rough he is on his laborers, he seems a better choice by far than Eliza. Whose curt response also points to the doctor.

In less than two years, Thompson will face the possibility of a bankruptcy he's been staving off since he first purchased all that land. Maybe he makes Eliza a lowball offer. Perhaps, in turn, the edgy Eliza bristles, considering a bottom-dollar offer from a man who may be down, but not as far down as she, an even bigger insult than it otherwise might be. And so she gives him the brush-off, despite the financial mess she's in, and tells him to take his offer on back home, secretly assuming that if she waits them out, the men will return on their own.

As things turn out, Eliza is right: They do come back. But why? Their sister managed to keep going once she set out. So did their little brother, Moses, and those eleven others from the Eastern Shore. The Ross brothers, meantime, keep turning back, not just once but three or four times.

Ben, Robert, and Henry have families to take into account—children, wives. Perhaps they don't feel right leaving their aging parents. Maybe they can't *see* freedom as an actual place, the way Harriet can. All they can foresee is punishment.

There are so many understandable reasons to falter, so much to be afraid of. Perhaps because of the ordinary rivalries and doubts among siblings, they tend to cook up fear among themselves as they go, tripling their apprehension instead of finding a sense of safety in numbers. If one brother entertains one kind of reservation, another stirs a different kind

into the mix. For instance, Robert, in time, will admit to a fear of abolitionists. Having heard they are cannibals, he may be on constant lookout, convincing his brothers as they go not to trust *any* white person,
even a Quaker, who offers help.

Maybe they do not have their sister's instinct for survival, her nose
for the right path, her exquisite flair for dramatic deception. Confounded
by the unknown darkness, they sabotage their own best interests by con-
tradicting one another.

Perhaps they are too bonded to the status quo to imagine any other
life.

Possibilities. Fear seduces the heart. Momentum sputters, stalls, sinks
into inertia. They return to known horrors. To Eliza.

When they arrive in Bucktown, the "old woman" is awful glad to see
them. "Boys," she says. "You have come back again."

"Again" is triumphant, a crow.

"Awful glad" meaning what? And "old woman"? Having known only
trouble and a pinched life since her marriage, having borne eight children, four of them still under eighteen, Eliza—in her fifties, menopausal,
her hormones causing her no telling what kind of grief—might well appear old, even scraggly and a she-devil, especially to a strong young man.
But it's hard to imagine her expressing anything but vindication when
the brothers return. If she manages to appear awful glad to see them, she
probably is. Now she can sell them to Georgia.

In the meantime, the Gourney Pattison lawsuit and its sidebar
shenanigans continue to drag on, and will for another year. Since 1852,
there have been several bizarre—although, by now, hardly surprising—
twists to the case.

First off, in a presumably unrelated incident, on Sunday, May 9, the
day before the lawsuit was scheduled to come before the court, an arson-
ist set fire to the Dorchester County courthouse, totally destroying it: two
hundred years of probate, land, tax, and some criminal and civil court
documents, burned to a crisp. No clue as to who set the fire, despite a
one-thousand-dollar reward offered for information.

But on the Friday preceding the fire, in preparation for the Monday-
morning docket, the court clerk had removed two volumes of documents

to work on over the weekend. Among those documents were the minutes of Chancery Record #249—that is *Pattison et al. vs. Brodess and Mills.*

On Tuesday, May 11, then, when court came into session in the Dorchester House hotel, the Pattison appeal was called first. Attorney James A. Stewart again pressed his case, demanding the return of Rit and any of her children of forty-five years of age or older to the Pattison heirs, asking for restitution of wages accumulated during their hires. He also demanded the distribution of shares of profits made from the sale of Rit's children.

Within three months of that date and despite the fact that the court has requested that no member of the Ross family be sold until resolution of the suit, James Stewart purchased Linah Ross's daughter, Harriet Jolley, from Thomas Willis, who had brought her from Eliza Brodess in 1850. Stewart already owned more than forty slaves, over half of them women. Why would he buy Harriet? Certainly his choice was not co-incidental. He did it either to taunt Eliza or to prove that members of the Ross family could be bought and sold at will. In 1855, when the politics of slavery fire up even hotter, Stewart will ship all of his slaves to south Texas for safekeeping, perhaps including Harriet Jolley, whose recorded story ends with her forced removal from Maryland. As did her mother's.

Turning a sad story into a tragedy, Harriet's little daughter, Mary Jane, remained behind with the Willises, who at that time owned only one other slave, two-year-old Sarah Ann, who may well be Mary Jane's little sister. Since the little girls were the only slaves in that household, we have to wonder where they lived, who took care of them, and what kind of life they led. In 1860, Willis will sell Mary Jane.

Anything more is as yet unknown.

But Stewart had not appeased his obsession with the Ross family. Two months after buying Harriet Jolley, he purchased the "right, title, claim and demand" to her grandmother—Rit, that is—not from Eliza but from John R. Brown, a Pattison heir, for thirty dollars. Seven months later, he paid seventy-five dollars for the same rights, this time to Elizabeth Pattison's daughter Acsah.

Until the lawsuit is settled, neither of these men has the right to claim ownership of Rit and her children, but obviously, Stewart has advised the Pattisons to divvy up shares anyway, awarding larger cuts to older members of the family. Stewart might have been gambling that if the case went his way, he would stand to make large profits from the ownership of Rit's family. Or—an even greater likelihood—he was playing games with the defendants, demonstrating his belief in the foregone conclusion of winning the case. A fierce competitive spirit can gnarl the soul of a lawyer, twisting his own best interests and those of his clients to accomplish his one overweening goal: to win.

It is that simple desire that seems to have settled itself into James A. Stewart's mind like a rat in a pile of moldering newspapers. And it will not stop gnawing until the judge finally dismisses the case for good, in September 1854.

The case has yielded some advantage to the Ross family.

Eliza has answered Stewart's parries by agreeing to sell Rit to her own husband for twenty dollars. The sale won't be officially registered for three more years, but when it is, Eliza will acknowledge her delay in filing the bill. The Dorchester County Assessment Records of 1852 show her owning six slaves: Harry (Henry), twenty; Ben, twenty-three; Robert, thirty-five; Rachel, twenty-seven; Angerine, five; and Ben, three. Since Rit is not listed, presumably by that time Eliza had received her money and had relinquished ownership to Ben.

And so it is that Ben Ross becomes the owner of his wife, who is too old to be manumitted.

And the slaveholders rock on, viciously pursuing their own best interests. In addition, Eliza is working up a case against her partner, John Mills, who she believes has robbed her of her rightful share of profits accumulated from the sale of Negroes—the same ones being claimed by Gourney Pattison—and other property.

Given the circumstances fueling her paranoia and downright meanness, it's not hard to understand why, by the time Harriet goes to Dorchester to bring out her brothers, Eliza has become a woman who can be fairly described as very devilish by Benjamin Ross when he finally makes it to Philadelphia.

No sooner had the brothers returned to Bucktown than they began to make new plans to escape, but only when time and circumstances were

To protect his wife from the auction block (even though she is legally too old to be sold), Ben Ross purchases her. He may have done so many months before Eliza Brodess got around to filing the petition—perhaps even years. (*Transcription of bill of sale appears at bottom of page.*)

right. In the meantime, they resumed their duties, Henry and Ben in Dorchester County for Eliza and her large brood; Robert for Dr. Thompson in Caroline County.

(*Transcription*)

Benjamin Ross paid from X
Eliza Brodess

Be it remembered and it is hereby certified that the following Bill of Sale was received and recorded on the 11th day of June in the year of our Lord one Thousand Eight hundred and fifty five. To wit:

Know all men by these presents, that I Eliza Brodess of Dorchester County and state of Maryland, for and in consideration of the sum of Twenty dollars current money to me in hand paid by Benjamin Ross, (col[ore]d man) of Dorchester County and state of

Maryland have granted, bargained and sold, and by these presents do grant, bargain and sell unto the said Benjamin Ross (col[ore]d, man), his heirs and assigns, the following negro woman named Ritty aged about fifty-five years, slave for life and sound in body and mind, To have and to hold the same Negro woman Ritty aged about fifty-five years as above bargained and sold unto the said Benjamin Ross, his heirs, executors, administrators and assigns, against me the said Eliza Brodess my heirs, executors and administrators, and against all and every other person or persons whatsoever, shall and will warrant and forever defend.

In Testimony whereof, I Eliza Brodess have hereto set my hand and affixed seal, this eleventh day of June eighteen hundred and fifty five.

Eliza A. Brodess. Signed, sealed and delivered in the presence of Whitefield Woolford, Charles Corkran.

Delivered to Benjamin Ross October 20, 1855

After about a year, sometime probably late in 1853, the whole thing happened again. Having been warned of a coming sale, the brothers again prepared to leave. Then did not, or could not, go. The sale didn't take place, but that it eventually would seemed a foregone conclusion.

Having kept her ear to the ground, Harriet decided in the spring of 1854 to take matters into her own hands. But when she arrived on the Eastern Shore to bring them out, the brothers balked. She had come, they protested, in the wrong season—spring, when farms were busy and slaves more closely observed. She should have come during the dark months of winter, when agricultural life had gone quiet and nights were long. They refused to go with her.

Once she had left, their hearts mourned, and they were filled with shame and regret. But Harriet had warned them: She waited for no one. By the time Ben, Robert, and Henry had second thoughts, she was long gone, accompanied by other enslaved people who, having heard of her arrival, had chosen to follow her out.

And so when, in December 1854, Harriet perceives the shadow hanging over her brothers' heads in a vision that is as vivid as the one of horses riding toward her in 1849, she prepares to go to Maryland once again. This time, in the right season.

She has been busy since the December 1851 rescue of eleven, not only helping the enslaved find their way from Dorchester, Caroline, and Talbot counties to the Pennsylvania line but also making friends among abolitionists, and becoming a contributing and permanent member of the Underground Railroad. In about 1853, she became acquainted with Thomas Garrett, the courageous Quaker abolitionist from Wilmington, whose house served as a safe house for escaping slaves. A hardware merchant, Garrett had pledged himself to spending his last penny to helping others on their way out of bondage, even in defiance of the law. By this time, he has become Harriet's great supporter and fan, helping her accumulate money to finance her trips, even doing fund-raising for her by writing to abolitionists in England.

The General Vigilance Committee of Philadelphia has come back into being, with abolitionist William Still pretty much in charge. Harriet has become a regular there, as well.

Unlike most Underground Railroad agents, who favored secrecy, once his Anti-Slavery Society office became important as fugitives' first stop in Philadelphia, Still kept detailed records. He supplied the slave names of the individuals seeking help, as well as the names of their enslavers. Sometimes the freed men and women supplied their new names. He included a general description of the appearance of the person sitting across from him, as well as the main reasons for the escape. And while these records supply us with invaluable information, Still was acting as much in the interest of proficiency and pragmatism as for historical purposes: He wanted to make certain that the people who came to him were genuinely in need and not informers or spies.

During the past two years, when not making actual trips, Harriet has been busy arranging rescues from Philadelphia. In 1853, several Eastern Shore runaways passed through the Still office, telling of the help they had received from Tubman. One, Winnibar, or William, Johnson from Tobacco Stick, testified to Still that it was through the "kindness of Harriet Tubman" that knowledge of the Underground Railroad and Canada came to him and "suddenly illuminated his mind." She is also said to have aided Dorchester blacksmith Samuel Green, Jr.—whose father, Rev. Samuel Green was a free black man, well known on the Eastern Shore—who then traveled on to Canada.

Since becoming acquainted with Frederick Douglass and Thomas Garrett, Harriet has gained notoriety, as well, as she makes contacts along her route. People are starting to know her name and to speak of her accomplishments. The African American novelist and abolitionist William Wells Brown, for one, reported on having met her in Boston during these years.

During the fall of 1852, Harriet returned again to Maryland from lush Cape May to bring out nine slaves (who remain unidentified, indicating they did not go through Still's office). That time, she didn't have to fund the trip alone, having received supplemental financing from Thomas Garrett. Since her family is not mentioned, presumably she either received word of nine people wishing to make their way out of slavery or she went down on her own.

Perhaps once Garrett had raised the money, she simply went and waited for whoever wished to leave to show up.

To notify people of her presence, she belted out lines from songs and spirituals. "When that old chariot comes, who's going with me? I'm going with you. . . ." This tune was perhaps the one that caused Harriet to be tapped with a new name: "Ole Chariot." When people heard the song, they knew that Harriet, or the Ole Chariot, had arrived and was making ready to go, and whoever wanted to get on board better come on now.

Another was cloaked in a heavier veil:

Hail, oh hail ye happy spirits,
Death no more shall make you fear,
No grief nor sorrow, pain nor anguish
Shall no more distress you there . . .

The song goes on, but the important verse is the last one, in which is hidden a message alerting them to postponement because of nearby danger:

Moses go down in Egypt,
Tell ole Pharaoh let me go;
Hadn't been for Adam's fall,
Shouldn't have to go at all.

The codes have been worked out. "Adam's fall" means wait; don't come yet; danger.

And so when she prepares to bring out her brothers in December 1854, she is even clearer on details: how to go and when, which roads to take or avoid, different routes to take when trouble arises, dramas to create to divert suspicion, whom to go to for help, including money for the trip.

Well acquainted with her brothers' hesitations, she takes precautions before setting off. In Philadelphia, she asks a friend to write a letter addressed to a free black man in Dorchester, Jacob Jackson, who can read and write. Jackson is already under suspicion for having participated in numerous escapes from the area, and so Harriet dictates a carefully coded letter. It makes its way to Dorchester, where the self-appointed postal inspectors—who read all mail addressed to black people—peruse it with diligence. If there is a code, they aim to break it.

The letter opens with a friendly salutation to Jacob, followed by some general chatter, nothing of any import. At its conclusion, the message urges Jackson to, "Read my letter to the old folks, and give my love to them, and tell my brothers to be always watching unto prayer and when the good old ship of Zion comes along, to be ready to step aboard."

The letter is signed "William Henry Jackson," who is Jacob Jackson's adopted free son, who went north after the death of his parents.

The inspectors are flummoxed. They know that William Henry Jackson has no parents and no brothers. What can the letter mean?

To our ears, the "good old ship of Zion" seems a phrase easy enough to decode. But somehow the white men don't catch on, and, in Bradford's words, "white genius having exhausted itself, black genius was called in, and Jacob's letter was at last handed to him."

Jacob Jackson knows in an instant who sent the message and for whom it is intended. After a quick glance, he plays the black man's most effective game against white suspicion: He acts dumb.

"That letter can't be meant for me . . ." he proclaims. "I can't make head nor tail of it." And he throws the letter to the ground, then takes immediate measures to alert Ben, Robert, and Henry of Harriet's impending arrival and their need to be ready to leave at a moment's notice for the North.

Now that she can tap into a supply of money, Harriet sometimes rides the train from Philadelphia to Baltimore, then takes passage on a boat from there to the Choptank landing. Garrett and others may secure papers for her, giving her the right to board, or she may know boatmen and railroad workers who swathe her in protective gear and act as her escorts. She has purchased men's clothing; she may disguise herself as a sailor, as did Frederick Douglass in Baltimore.

She disembarks on Christmas Eve, a Sunday.

In Bucktown and Poplar Neck, holiday plans proceed as usual, with Ben and Rit's children expected to show up at their cabin on Christmas Day for the annual meal. But upon her arrival in Cambridge, Harriet spies a notice announcing the public auction of her brothers, to be held on the day after Christmas, Tuesday, the twenty-sixth.

She sends word: They must meet immediately, as soon after dark as possible, gathering somewhere in the Cambridge area, from whence they will make their way the forty miles to their father's cabin in Poplar Neck.

Once again, the brothers prepare to leave.

Ben and Henry meet up with Harriet at the appointed time and place. Ben has arranged for his fiancée, Jane Kane, to come there, as well. Jane is enslaved to the exceedingly cruel Horatio Jones, who had beaten her until the blood ran from her nose and mouth and who once whipped her brother until his back, she said, looked like raw beef. He has refused to allow Jane to marry Ben, and so they are running away together, Jane in a man's suit procured by Ben and hidden in Horatio Jones's garden. As fearful of Jones as anyone else she might meet on her escape, Jane donned the suit before leaving his plantation.

The four of them assemble somewhere in the uninhabited swamps and forests of Dorchester County, waiting for Robert.

But Robert doesn't show up. Presently, he isn't working in Bucktown, having been hired out to a family in Trappe, a few miles north of

Cambridge, across the Choptank. More important, Robert's wife, Mary Manokey, is about to give birth to their third child.

When the appointed hour arrives, Harriet—who "never waited for no one," not even a brother—strikes out towards Poplar Neck with Henry, Ben, and Jane Kane. They move quietly, crossing the Choptank, heading through the wetlands into Caroline County.

Mary Manokey, at that very moment, is in labor and in need of a midwife. But the baby starts to come too fast, and Robert refuses to leave, preferring to stay and take care of his wife himself. Mary doesn't know of Robert's plans to escape with his brothers, but if not for the coming of the child, she might have been suspicious and asked questions. After all, Robert and the other two have tried many times before. And it is Christmas, the season for auctions and escapes. Robert may seem particularly jumpy about how long the baby's arrival will take.

The hour for his meeting with Harriet passes. Darkness falls. Mary's labor proceeds. Within another hour, she gives birth. The baby is a girl, her first.

Robert is an attentive husband. He makes certain that his wife and the baby are well. And then, as time presses in on him, he becomes noticeably edgy. His choice is simple: Either go now or face lifelong slavery in the Deep South, away from his family. But when he tries to slip away, Mary calls out to him.

"Where are you going, Robert?" she asks.

He stops, comes back, waits awhile. When Mary's breathing deepens, he backs toward the door again.

But Mary is not sleeping. She calls to him again, asking where he is off to.

Robert concocts an unlikely story about going to see if he can get hired out on Christmas Day to another man. And he heads out the door.

Outside, he stops at the corner of the house nearest the head of her bed. Rain is falling. The night is cold.

Mary, who does not believe that Robert is about to be sold, begins to sob loudly.

Unable to endure her sorrow and grief, his clothes clinging to his wet skin, Robert returns to his wife's bedside.

"Oh, Robert," Mary cries. "You are going to leave me. But wherever you go, remember me and the children."

His heart heavy, Robert once again makes his way out the door, and this time he does not stop, but races off full speed toward his father's cabin, his wife's farewell plea shadowing his every footstep.

He runs into the night, through a heavy, chilling downpour. When he arrives at the Thompson place on Christmas morning, dawn is breaking. There, clustered in a bunch in the corncrib near his parents' cabin, are his brothers and sister, along with Jane Kane and two other men, John Chase and Peter Jackson, both of whom are also enslaved in the Cambridge area. Rain drips through the rude ceiling of the corncrib and seeps in through chinks in its walls. But the seven people inside lie quietly among the ears of corn, making no sound.

When they first arrived, Harriet sent Chase and Jackson—strangers to Ben and Rit—to the cabin door to let Ben know they were there, exhausted and famished. Rousing from sleep, Ben gathered up provisions. Making certain not to waken Rit, he slipped out of the house to take food and water to the corncrib. But when he got to its door, he turned his back to hand the bag inside, so as not to lay eyes on his sons and daughter.

Ben Ross has worked his entire life to establish a reputation for honesty, not just in his own people's eyes but—more important, in a practical sense—in the mind of the white man. He must not tarnish his reputation, for fear of losing the hard-earned respect that makes life tolerable for himself and his family.

If he doesn't look at his children, he has reasoned, he won't have seen them. And so, when their flight is discovered and he is asked if he has seen his sons, Ben, Robert, and Henry, he can respond honestly. No, he will say to the white people and to Rit, I have not seen them.

Robert joins his brothers and sister.

Rain falls without letup.

When day breaks, casting light through wide gaps in the corncrib, Harriet and her brothers can see their parents' cabin. All day long, they take turns watching for Rit. Like a restless cat, she comes out regularly and, shading her eyes, looks long and hard down the road to see if her children are coming yet.

Each time, she sighs and, disappointed, turns back into the cabin.

She has slaughtered and cooked a pig for the holiday feast, surrounding it with vegetables from her garden. She has made preparations for a great Christmas celebration. If she has heard rumors of the coming sale of her three sons, she may be even more anxious when her sons don't show up, wondering if Eliza Brodess has already locked them up for safekeeping, violating the sanctity of the religious holiday.

If Eliza has done that, and they are sold away, Rit may never see them again. Out of nine children, then, only one would remain, Rachel, in Bucktown with her two children, Ben and Angerine.

Rachel is not scheduled to come for Christmas dinner, nor are Ben and Angerine. As domestic servants, they may not have been given the holiday off, but are instead cooking and serving for Eliza and her family.

Rit sits by the fire, smoking her pipe, rocking back and forth. But no mother can sit still for long when she is waiting for and fretting over her children. She rises again, goes to the door, as if standing there looking will make them come. She peers from under the awning of her hand, gazing down the road.

Harriet has seen neither of her parents for five years. She watches Rit.

During the day, Ben comes to the corncrib several times to leave more food.

After nightfall, he ties his handkerchief across his eyes before reaching the crib. He wants to accompany his children a little of the way out. Two of his sons take him by his arms and turn him in the right direction.

But before leaving, they bid a silent farewell to their mother, watching her through the little window of her cabin as she sits by the fire with her head on her hand, as is her custom when trouble is in the works. As if the thoughts and memories inside are too heavy to bear. Pipe clenched between her teeth, she rocks back and forth, wondering what new evil has befallen her sons and whether or not she will ever see any of them again.

Silent, weeping, the brothers and their sister take turns watching Rit. But they must make their next station by daybreak, and so, wrenching themselves away, they leave.

Ben goes with them for a mile or so, but he can't leave Rit for long. His sons release him and they all bid him farewell and go on off, leaving their father alone in the middle of the road, standing in the darkness. When he can no longer hear their footsteps, he unties his blindfold. Nothing is there, only leftover rain dripping from the pines and poplars. Ben turns back toward the cabin and his grieving wife, who must never know where he has been or what he has been doing.

Mary Manokey names her newborn daughter Harriet.

Robert will fulfill the promise his wife asked of him as he left—never to forget her or his children. In the years to come, he will bring his sons to live with him in New York State.

On Tuesday, the twenty-sixth, the day of the sale, John Brodess and other men come to take Ben, Henry, and Robert to the auction block. But they are nowhere to be found. Ben and Henry are not in Bucktown, nor is Robert in Trappe. No one knows where they are, nobody has seen anything. Presumably, everyone assumes, they went to Poplar Neck to have their annual Christmas dinner with their parents.

The men ride to the Thompson place.

Has the doctor seen the brothers?

Thompson says no, that ordinarily they come for Christmas dinner, but this year they didn't.

Has he been down to Old Ben's?

Thompson says yes, but that Old Rit told him that not one of them came this Christmas. "She was looking for them almost all day," Thompson says, "and most broke her heart about it."

"What does Old Ben say?"

"Old Ben says that he hasn't seen one of his children this Christmas."

"Well . . ." one of the men says. "If Old Ben says that, then they haven't been around."

And the slave hunters ride off.

There are safe houses along whichever route Harriet chooses to guide her party, whether east to Federalsburg and north or along the Choptank, going more immediately north. In Wilmington, they stop at the home of Thomas Garrett, who provides them with food, shelter, and clothing. When Harriet tells him that one of the men has walked his shoes clear off his feet, Garrett gives him two dollars to buy new ones.

He then secures a carriage and sends them across the state line at last, to the home of Allen Agnew in Kennett, Pennsylvania. From there, they make their way to Philadelphia.

They arrive at William Still's Anti-Slavery Society on Friday, December 29. Three other men have joined them en route. And so nine people crowd into the office to be interviewed. Still talks first to John Chase, then to Ben Ross, whom he describes as twenty-eight years old, of chestnut color, medium size, and intelligent. After

William Still's journal entry of December 29, 1854, noting the arrival of Harriet and her brothers—Benjamin, Robert, and Henry—from the Eastern Shore. (*Transcription of journal entry appears at bottom of page.*)

declaring that Eliza Brodess was his owner, Ben describes her as "very devilish" and says they left Maryland because of the difficulty of three slaves having to take care of a family of eight whites, and the constant threat of being sold. He also tells Still of leaving behind a sister who wants to come away, as well. He identifies the sister as Mary Ann Williams, perhaps a name Rachel has chosen to take on once she makes it out.

(*Transcription*)

Harriet Tubman, Dec. 29/54
ARRIVED: John Chase (now Daniel Lloyd), Benj Ross (now James Stewart) Henry Ross (now Levin Stewart), Peter Jackson (Now Tench Tilghman), Jane Kane (now Catherine K), Robert Ross.

John is 20s of age, chestnut color, spare built, smart. He fled from John Campbell Henry, farmer, who resided at Cambridge, Dorchester Md. John spoke of his master as being a hard man, owned 140 slaves. Some he sells occasionally. The owner would not allow John to seek his own master, this was the cause of his escape. Left behiind Mother, brothers and sisters, all slaves.

Benj. is 28 yrs of age, chestnut color, medium size, intelligent, was owned by Eliza Ann Brodess, lived near Bucktown, Cambridge. . . .

Still describes Henry Ross as smart, twenty-two years old, chestnut color, married to a woman named Harriet, whom he was forced to leave behind, along with two small sons. Robert is said to be thirty-five years old, of chestnut color, and having left behind two children. Facing the necessity of changing their surnames, the brothers decide on a familiar one: Stewart. From now on, Ben will be known as James Stewart, Robert as John Stewart, and Henry as William Henry Stewart. Ben's fiancée, Jane Kane, changes her name to Catherine.

William Still provides the group enough money to get them to the next station, probably by steam railroad to New York City, where a man named Jacob Gibbs might well be the one to take care of them and send them on to Albany, into the hands of the black abolitionist Stephen Myers.

From there, they travel either to Troy, where John H. Hooper, a cousin of the Rosses, lives, or to Syracuse, where Jermaine Loguen, a minister and former Kentucky slave, would

William Still from *The Underground Railroad*, 1871.

meet them and guide them to Rochester. From Rochester, they travel to the town called Suspension Bridge (later Niagara Falls), New York, where they cross the Niagara River—only fourteen days after their departure from Poplar Neck—to the sister city of Suspension Bridge, in Canada West. From there, they go to St. Catharines, where family and old friends from the Eastern Shore await their arrival and welcome them heartily.

As for Eliza Brodess, accepting an estimated assessment of about $1,150 for the Ross brothers, this Christmas escape costs her more than one-third of the value of her entire estate, which nets out at approximately $3,450. The Pattison case against her has been dismissed for good, leaving her free to sell, hire out, or keep her slaves. But she is now down to only one adult—Rachel Ross—and her two children. Penury grinds hard; under its wheel she flails about, searching for a cause of, and solution to, her problems. Someone to blame and then go after. A lawsuit of her own.

Her belief is in the system as it now operates and stands. In the institution of slavery, and her right to *own*—buy, sell, trade, hire out—certain people, even the ones who have absconded, whom, though far away and living in a different country, she still claims as her own property.

A year from now, in December 1855, Eliza will formally file a suit she has been preparing for some time—against her former business partner and coexecutor of her husband's estate, her neighbor, John Mills, whom she accuses of fraud, theft, and breach of promise.

Like hungry possums thrown into a trash barrel, they scramble and draw blood.

PART III.

MOSES

Scene 11.

Becoming Moses

I am from the eastern shore of Maryland. I never belonged but to one master; he was very bad indeed. I was never sent to school, nor allowed to go to church. They were afraid we would have more sense than they . . .

—INTERVIEW WITH CATHERINE KANE STEWART
(AKA JANE KANE), IN BENJAMIN DREW, *A NORTH-SIDE
VIEW OF SLAVERY. THE REFUGEE: OR THE NARRATIVE
OF FUGITIVE SLAVES IN CANADA,* 1856

While in Canada in 1860, we met several whom this woman had brought from the land of bondage, and they all believed that she had supernatural power. Of one man we inquired, "Were you not afraid of being caught?"

"O, no," said he, "Moses has got the charm."

"What do you mean?" we asked

He replied, "The whites can't catch Moses, cause she's born with the charm. The Lord has given Moses the power."

. . .

. . . Yes, and the woman herself felt that she had the charm and this feeling . . . nerved her up, gave her courage and made all who followed her feel safe in her hands.

—WILLIAM WELLS BROWN, *THE RISING SON,* 1873

After Tubman's death in 1913, people dredged up memories of her, often gleaned from childhood experiences. The Reverend R. A.

Ball of the British Methodist Episcopal Church in St. Catharines remembered the arrival of Harriet with her brothers, as well as with other refugees. A boy at the time, he recalled that after guiding her party safely across the river, upon disembarking from the train, Harriet would say, "Shout, shout, you are free!" And sometimes the refugees who had come with her clapped their hands and knelt in prayer, even kissed the ground, saying, "This is British soil."

By the winter of 1855, when Harriet, her brothers, Catherine Kane, and the others arrive, droves of escaping slaves are coming across the border, especially now that Underground Railroad stations pepper the U.S. lakeshores, from Toledo, Ohio, on Lake Erie's western edge, to Lake Ontario's eastern counterpart, Oswego, New York. Up and down the lakes, fugitives are being passed from one station to the next, from root cellar to church basement to barn loft, from barn to farm wagon and finally—despite the ubiquitous presence of slave catchers and Kentucky spies—to transport of one kind or another across the water. Black abolitionists are leading the cause, with white compatriots as allies, conspirators, and full participants. The Bloodhound Bill having turned every citizen into a potential slave catcher, those who oppose it are defying the very letter of that law with passion, efficiency, and daring.

It's January when Harriet arrives with her brothers. In winter, the merciless, iron-cold wind sweeps along the shores of the Great Lakes, stabbing uncovered ears and eyes. Snow piles up over doorsteps; ice coats roadways, sending wagons careering into trees and gullies. Probably the brothers trudge into St. Catharines without kissing the snowy ground.

Antislavery advocates—Quakers, Methodists—and free blacks have been working to help the enslaved break for the North since the early 1800s. But since 1850, the system has been improved, and hundreds of agents and safe houses have been added. In Buffalo, slaves on the run are rafting from the riverbank across the Niagara. Or they sail from Buffalo to Grand Island, walk the eighteen miles across the island to the opposite bank, grab hold of a log or piece of wood—one man was seen clinging to a gate—and, fighting the current, float into Canada.

Some swim, some drown or are captured. None voluntarily return. Meanwhile, others keep coming, stowing away on ferries from Black Rock, New York, to Fort Erie, Canada, a town with a settlement so heavily populated with fugitives, it is called "Little Africa." They are also banding together and, with help from those willing to risk prison and a large fine, hiding out on freighters from Cleveland or Sandusky, Ohio, across Lake Erie to Chatham and Dresden, or from Detroit across Lake St. Clair to Windsor, Sandwich, and Amherstburg.

Sometimes when fugitives arrive at the U.S. border, the waters are either frozen or so clogged with chunks of ice that boats can't run. Even the Falls are known to freeze solid, a spectacular sight. Fugitives are forced, then, to find work in shipyards and homes, along the banks. Haunted by the steady presence of bounty-hunting predators, they live a whispered existence until the ice melts.

None of the six people escorted by Harriet into St. Catharines has spent one day beyond the boundaries of the Eastern Shore, and so they can have had no experience of, or preparation for, the kind of cold they are now experiencing. Underground Railroad agents would have helped them find shoes and warmer clothes. Now they layer up, pull hats down over their ears. Still, unaccustomed, not yet acclimated, as some never will be, they shiver.

In the South, slaveholders are issuing warnings to those among their enslaved laborers who might consider running away, telling stories of cannibalistic abolitionists and insatiable man-killing Canadian beasts, of crippling taxes levied by Queen Victoria, and of frozen rivers two hundred miles wide. The warnings spray like spit into a wind. In a way, the Fugitive Slave Act, having confirmed their greatest fear—that nothing will ever change—has freed those in bondage from illusions and hope. They go.

As Harriet told Sarah Bradford, after 1850 she could no longer trust even the free states of the United States with her people. She had to take them into the protection of the British lion, and leave them safely sheltered beneath his paw.

In 1854, once Harriet's friend Samuel Green, Jr., had arrived safely, he wrote a letter home, encouraging his father, who was still living and preaching in an Eastern Shore community, to hurry up and make his way north. In Canada, he wrote, he had found "plenty of friends plenty to eate plenty to drink," and he said that his father should tell his pals Peter Jackson and Joe Bailey to come, too. "Kom on," he wrote. "Kom more."

By January 1855, when Harriet and her brothers arrive, approximately ten thousand black families are living in what is present-day Ontario. In the town of St. Catharines, out of an estimated total population of six thousand, some eight hundred are black, most of them fugitives from slavery. Since the 1829 opening of the Welland Canal connecting Lake Ontario to Lake Erie, jobs there have been more plentiful. To supply land on which to erect a church, the Canadian legislator and abolitionist William Henry Merritt has sold a section of downtown St. Catharines to black Methodists for five pounds. After building a temporary log structure, the congregation has raised funds for a permanent one. By the time Harriet arrives with her brothers, members of the BME church are finishing work on a brick edifice. Because it has been designed and built by refugees from the United States, to Harriet and her entourage, the small church has a familiar look, rather like Scott's Chapel in Bucktown.

They make their way to North Street, and Harriet's little house.

Having become a familiar figure locally, she has scoped out the territory and knows where her brothers should go to find work. The Irish have grown prickly about the growing numbers of incoming black people, as have other white working-class residents worried about their jobs. And so black people face racial discrimination there. Despite the presence of a Fugitive Aid Society and a Refugee Slaves' Friends Society, social, religious, and academic life is still racially segregated. While blacks can work at the town's famous mineral spa, patronage is limited to white customers. Still, life in Canada provides many rights previously unknown to American black people. They can vote there, sit on juries, testify in court, own property, be counted as people.

William Henry Stewart (Henry Ross) and John Stewart (Robert Ross) quickly find work as laborers. Soon after their arrival, William Henry's wife, Harriet Ann, manages—with the navigational help of

Tubman—to make her way to St. Catharines, bringing with her their son, William Henry Junior. Harriet Ann also finds work as a laborer.

James Stewart (Ben) and his new wife, Catherine Kane, decide to move west from St. Catharines to Chatham, where there is a more established fugitive community, with better opportunities for schooling and housing. John and Kessiah Bowley also live in Chatham. There, James and Catherine will start a family of their own, while John and Kessiah will add more children to theirs, eventually six in addition to the two born in Maryland, James Alfred and Araminta.

In the coming months, Harriet's brothers will manage to move up to better jobs. John hires on as a private coachman, while William Henry makes pretty good headway as a farmer, working property he has rented with one of his brothers for two hundred dollars a year. More experienced as a timber worker than a farmer, he will see his success fade temporarily when the two men get into some trouble, presumably financial. But William Henry will tough out the hard times and remain in Ontario with Harriet Ann and his growing family for more than thirty years, most of them spent on six acres of land he will purchase on the outskirts of St. Catharines.

Once her brothers are safely set up, Harriet redirects her focus.

Five of her immediate blood kin still live on the Eastern Shore; three of them—thirty-year-old Rachel and her two children—still enslaved to Eliza Brodess. By now, her parents have been pretty much excused from manual labor at the Thompson place. Both are in their seventies, Ben is free and he has manumitted his wife, and so they are of no value to the slave trade. They have their own cabin, where they can probably live out their time peaceably enough, if not ever entirely able to take their ease. Harriet would like to bring them out, but she doesn't know if they really want to face the rigors of an escape at their age, and even if they do, how she would accomplish it. They certainly couldn't walk out or cross streams on their own. She'd have to find a way to pull them or have them driven. The logistics are staggering. Besides all of that, if she rescued her parents first, Eliza and her son John would clamp down on Rachel and her children, probably—knowing Eliza—even sell them separately before Harriet has a chance to go get them.

She can't think about her parents. Her baby sister, Rachel, must come first.

After Rachel, Mary Manokey. John Stewart (Robert) yet mourns for his wife, who is practically family herself, having had a close bond with the Rosses from her first days. And then, of course, there are John's three children, his two sons and the infant Harriet, born on the Christmas Day he escaped.

All in good time. Harriet concentrates on Rachel.

By now, she has personally gone down and taken out at least forty people from the Eastern Shore, probably more. And there is no telling how many other rescues she arranged, navigated, and helped to finance. Perhaps even more important, by becoming an exemplar to others, she has emboldened those whose hearts would otherwise fail at the thought of bucking the system, taking their lives into their own hands, risking terrible consequences to break away from the only life they have ever known. If *she* can do it, they think, maybe they can, even if they don't have the "charm."

As stories of her success are whispered between one cabin and the next, her reputation spreads. None of her passengers has been caught or injured and none tossed off her Underground Railroad car. Harriet herself doesn't remember who first called her Moses, but it happens about now. In time, she will latch onto the name herself, referring to herself in the third person as "Ole Moses."

"The slaves call her Moses" is a statement often repeated in stories about Tubman. From lecterns, she is introduced as "the woman they call Moses." Later this same year—in October—when a slave named Josiah Bailey decides to flee, he will row a boat from Talbot County to Ben Ross's cabin. "Next time Moses comes," he tells old Ben, "let me know." And then he rows back.

All slaves know the song "Go Down, Moses." When Harriet goes to the South, she often announces her presence by walking up and down hidden paths between cabins and through the back swamps close to where black people live, singing:

> *Go down, Moses, way down in Egypt's land.*
> *Tell old Pharaoh, let my people go.*

Among slaveholders, the song is so widely recognized as a call for liberation that some have forbidden their laborers to sing it. But when they are alone in the fields or, on Sundays, conducting their bush-arbor church services, black people glory in the words of the Old Testament anthem. It gives them hope.

And when, in the middle of some dark Maryland night, they hear the familiar words float through the trees as if in a dream—"You may hinder me here, but you can't up there. Let my people go!"—sung solo in those warm, rich, full-throated tones, they know in that instant who it is.

Some of them sing with her: "He sits in Heaven and answers prayer. Let my people go!"

Some gather in the woods where she is, waiting until the time comes to go back with her.

> *Go down, Moses, way down in Egypt's land;*
> *Tell old Pharaoh, let my people go.*

There is no reason for them to trust secular law. Secular law belongs to the white man and works to keep the slaves down. The Jesus Testament of the Bible belongs to white Christians, as well—at least in the way they make use of it, emphasizing its messages of obedience and submission. And so enslaved black people fix their eyes on a vision beyond government laws. They look to the Moses Testament. They stake their hope on deliverance, and the coming of an anointed savior, who has both the power *and* a working knowledge of white men and geography.

In Maryland, they have found their earthly emancipator.

Harriet spends the spring and summer of 1855 in St. Catharines, making and saving money. Sometime during those months, the antislavery journalist Benjamin Drew travels to Canada West to interview fugitives from slavery about life in the United States as compared with life in Canada. Entitling his book *A North-Side View of Slavery. The Refugee,* Drew has set out to refute the claims of a book called *The South-Side View of Slavery,* which purports that slavery is good for black people and that they are happier within its bonds.

One of the first people he interviews in St. Catharines is Harriet, who, in her first public statement, testifies daringly under her own name, Harriet Tubman. Thus she announces her whereabouts to those who would track her and return her to slavery, as well as her intention to go by that name from now on, whatever the consequences.

By name now, the hero identifies herself to her contemporaries as well as to the historical record. In her last years, she will insist that interviewers get it right. Posterity is hers, earned and identified.

Drew's interviews are formally structured in a sequence of ready questions.

Harriet's answer to his question about her upbringing is brief: "I grew up like a neglected weed," she begins, "—ignorant of liberty, having no experience of it."

Unlike almost every other person who interviewed freed slaves, Drew doesn't encode their testimony in thick dialect, instead using standardized English spelling and sentence structure. But sometimes he goes too far. "Ignorant of liberty, having no experience of it" sounds like written text, penned by a well-educated northerner. As a spoken response, it doesn't ring true. Besides which, most freed slaves testify that they had fixed on the *idea* of freedom from early on, before they had any experience of it.

Harriet then provides a nuanced view of the value of perspective and distance. "Now I've been free," she tells Drew, "I know what a dreadful condition slavery is. I have seen hundreds of escaped slaves, but I never saw one who was willing to go back and be a slave."

One request Drew made of each interviewee was to supply a general opinion or definition of slavery. Harriet's is short and to the point: "I think slavery is the next thing to hell." But she makes a distinction between the hell of slavery and the place where it is practiced. "I have no opportunity to see my friends in my native land," she reflects. "We would rather stay in our native land, if we could be as free there as we are here."

James and John Stewart (Ben and Robert Ross) and Catherine Kane Stewart also talk to Drew, all three using Seward as their surname instead of Stewart, presumably for protection.

John opens with a no-holds-barred opinion of Edward Brodess: "The man that owned me, was not fit to own a dog." And he goes on to say that by the time he left Maryland, he had been grieving and groaning over his condition for twenty years, all that time thinking about how to get away.

He also confesses to an uncontrollable fear of abolitionists, especially when they treated him with decency, "they used me so well," he explains, "I was afraid of a trick."

Like his brother, James also provides a blunt opening statement: "Where I came from, it would make your flesh creep and your hair stand on end, to know what they do to slaves." And he tells the story of being in jail when the young mother he calls his niece is brought in, to be carried off by a trader and sold away from her children.

James's wife, Catherine, relates horrific stories about her enslavement to the barbarous Horatio Jones and ends by saying she has been wanting to come away from slavery for eight years. She did not want to come away alone. Since Jim (James) promised to take her away and marry her, she'd been waiting for him to get ready to go.

Other interviewees describe slavery as a bottomless pit, the wickedest thing a man can do, the worst kind of robbery—horrible, horrible, horrible!—the worst evil that ever was.

"A man who has been in slavery knows," says John Atkinson from Norfolk, "and no one else can know, the yearning to be free, and the fear of making the attempt."

Christopher Nichols, from Virginia: "All the time I was in slavery, I lived in dead dread and fear. If I slept it was in dread, and in the morning it was dread—dread, night and day." And he finishes by guessing that if he hadn't gotten away, he'd be dead by now, since his master "was killing me as fast as he could" when he left.

When the summer ends and the nights begin to lengthen, Harriet heads back across the Niagara.

By the middle of October, she's in Philadelphia, where—along with Frederick Douglass and other colleagues, among them Stephen Myers, her Underground Railroad agent in Auburn, New York, and Rev. Samuel Green from the Eastern Shore—she probably attends the National Colored Convention. During the proceedings, like other delegates, she pays a visit to Passmore Williamson, a white abolitionist and colleague of William Still. Williamson, who had helped a slave woman escape and then had refused to give her up to authorities, is being held in Moyamensing Prison on charges of contempt. Samuel Green's wife, Kitty, accompanies Harriet to the prison and signs her name in the visitor's book.

From there, she heads back down to Dorchester to get Rachel.

She stays for an astonishing three months, waiting for an opportunity to carry out her mission. Along the Eastern Shore, as in all of the slave-owning South, the atmosphere among slaveholders has grown electric with apprehension, activity, and suspicion: slave catchers on the prowl; property owners on an increased watch, not just for potential runaways but for those who would incite them—abolitionists, free blacks—spies of every skin color on the lookout for possible bounties.

To combat what they call "an epidemic of escapes," Maryland slave owners have held meetings, during which they discussed the possibility of outlawing assembly among black people and expelling the troublemaking free blacks. They are urging one another to search the homes of black people, slave and free, and to keep their slaves at home during all holidays, including Christmas.

They keep coming up with new tricks and rougher punishments. The enslaved people ignore the threats, avoid the snares, and keep going.

Despite all of this, for three months, the wily Harriet is able to remain in the counties where she is best known, undetected. To accomplish this, she must remain several steps ahead of white people at all times.

On one occasion, she runs into A. C. Thompson somewhere in the fields, perhaps on her way to visit her parents or to find out where Rachel's children are. Whatever her mission, Thompson doesn't recognize her. Thomas Garrett says this is because she has spent so many weeks in the North that her color has changed, presumably turning lighter as she works more indoor jobs and lives in a cold climate. Garrett is a par-

ticularly reliable reporter, but his reasoning here seems weak. Other story-
tellers come up with alternate scenarios to explain why she is not recognized.

Emma Telford: Aware that the master knows she can't read, when
she sees him, she holds a newspaper in front of her face as if reading, hoping it is right side up.

Ednah Dow Cheney: She wears silken clothes, far too fine to adorn
the body of a slave, a trick she often used during rescues, relying on the
blindness and presuppositions of slaveholders, who accommodate her reliance, seemingly without second thoughts.

In 1886, Bradford describes Harriet walking down the very streets
on which she is most likely to be seen and recognized in downtown Cambridge, carrying two live chickens she has bought from the market.
When she spies "her old master," presumably Thompson, Harriet pulls a
big sunbonnet over her face and walks bent over, like a decrepit old
woman, neck curled chin to chest so that her face is hidden. As Thompson grows near, she twitches the string holding the chickens' legs together, hard, so that the birds squawk and flap and make such a fuss that
Thompson becomes distracted and hurries past Harriet and the chickens.
As he goes, he brushes her garment, not realizing that he has just touched
the clothes of a woman who has stolen herself and other property from
him.

While details vary, even when the incident being recounted is the
same one, the end results remain consistent: Harriet sees Thompson or
some other white man or woman who has served as her boss; they don't
recognize her; she goes on, managing to remain safe for three months under the very noses of those who would most like to imprison and then
sell her.

How could they not recognize her? Why weren't they looking for
her?

Harriet has a quick answer to these questions. She went only where
the Lord told her to, and since He never sent her into danger, she never
worried about getting caught. And didn't. Thomas Garrett "never met
with any person of any color who had more confidence in the voice of
God, as spoken directly to her soul." He believed that, as a result of her

unquestioning faith, Harriet never feared being arrested by her former master or anyone else. Fearlessness enabled her to think beyond crippling odds and imagined consequences.

The charm, her faith, belief, obedience, the success of her missions—these provide anecdotal confirmation of her faith but no hard proof of how she did what she did without being captured.

Students, scholars, casual readers, and historians have struggled with these questions for more than a hundred years. Wishing to apply a modern forensic approach to Harriet's story, again and again we sift through newly discovered documentation, reread the old stories, listen once again to oral histories, struggling to see beyond the tale telling, longing to uncover the practical truth behind unfathomable events. A reporter is a trained skeptic: *But what happened really?* We apply deductive reasoning; dig and dig.

So far, no investigation, proof, or speculation has provided rational evidence to satisfy the question of how Harriet Tubman was able to make so many trips into slave country—as many as nineteen—and come safely back out again.

As personal assets, she had great instincts and a natural head for logistics, unusual peripheral vision, an irresistibly engaging manner, a great sense of humor, a fearless and single-focus temperament. She knew what a story was and how to tell it, a more important attribute than might be imagined, giving her the ability to distill a wide body of knowledge into a coherent, compressed narrative—one that, in her case, jelled with reality. To an undercover agent, a knack for storytelling yields a subsidiary talent for rearranging narrative and making up tales—reasons, identities—that suit the situation.

Like a shape-shifter, Harriet becomes who she must be in order to perform her duties and do what she considers the Lord's work. We might even think of her as God's own athlete, to whom had been given the rare contact-sport ability to see beyond the wall of oncoming attackers to the goal beyond, and—using fleet-footed methods of deception—to weave and bob her way through them to the established destination.

Leaving all guesses aside, an obvious assertion seems to be that whether or not she was a true psychic or seer, she was incontrovertibly *gifted,* physically and temperamentally.

As for the road: She had her regular routes and knew people at every crossroads and Underground Railroad station along the way. Having become friendly with particular steamboat captains and actual railroad conductors, she can use these connections to gain passage on trade ships and passenger trains. Much of the help she received, she couldn't speak about, for fear of landing her collaborators in jail. Without question, someone forged passes for her, authorizing free movement through dangerous territory. Or, like Frederick Douglass, she dressed like a deckhand and boarded ships casually, as if she belonged.

But what then? If anyone in Dorchester or Caroline County looked her square in the face, they would have known that there walked Araminta Ross, owned by Eliza Brodess, who stole herself away and renamed herself Harriet Tubman. Were they stupid? That easily fooled? Too busy with their own thoughts and lives to look a small, squat black woman in the eyes and note that she had a dent in her forehead? Or was it that she just was so nervy and confident in her manner, so unlike every other slave they had ever known or been around, that people assumed that she couldn't, then, be one?

The mystery lingers, and in the end, "How could she do it? What kept her safe?" are questions impossible to answer without resorting (or yielding) to spiritual or psychic generalities: She knew because she knew; she saw what others could not. She had the charm. The charm nerved her up. The Lord told her where to go and what to do. Ednah Cheney summed her up: "as economical as Dr. Franklin, and as firm in the conviction of supernatural help as Mahomet." The head wound released her from restrictive, rational thinking and put her in touch with a deeper source, a native intuition something like the experience some have during a migraine aura, or after ingesting a hallucinogenic drug.

For her, such questions are impractical, insignificant, and beside the point. She sees, hears, knows. Imagines a new life. Sees it, goes there. Calls the voice she hears God.

She postpones her return to Philadelphia as long as she can, but Rachel will not leave without her children, who are living apart from her, presumably because she is hired out. And so Harriet gives up for the time being, and in early December, she leaves Dorchester for the North, taking only one person with her, probably Henry Hooper, a nineteen-year-old man, who arrives at William Still's office from Maryland on the sixth.

As soon as Hooper has been duly forwarded to the next station, Harriet turns around and goes back to Maryland. On the way, she stops in Wilmington, where she tells Garrett that once she has brought out her last sister, she will stop making journeys to the Eastern Shore.

But Rachel still won't leave. She and Harriet may have been banking on the possibility that she, Ben, and Angerine will receive permission to go to Ben and Rit's for Christmas. But it doesn't happen, perhaps because of last year's Christmas Eve experience, when Harriet hid her brothers at her parents' home. As for Mary Manokey, Thompson has stashed her in Talbot County with his daughter Catherine Haddaway, probably for safekeeping from Harriet. Besides which, Mary has remarried and is pregnant with another man's child. She might not wish to leave.

Haunted by the thought of another sister sold away from her children and family, Harriet returns to Philadelphia.

In the spring of 1856, as border ruffians from Missouri cross into Kansas to cast proslavery votes, violence erupts in that state. The God-fearing abolitionist warrior John Brown and his men round up five proslavery men from houses along the Pottawatomie Creek and Brown orders them to be killed in cold blood. After Massachusetts senator Charles Sumner makes a speech attacking the proslavery elements in Kansas, he is brutally caned by a congressman from South Carolina. By fall, "Bleeding Kansas" will be the chief campaign issue in the U.S. presidential election. Even the mild-mannered pacifist Thomas Garrett believes that the country is on the eve of Civil War.

Threats rumble the country. Confrontations turn nasty, then bloody. Harriet might have made five trips to the Eastern Shore in 1856. Not all of them have been or can be satisfactorily documented as trips she physically took herself; some she might have arranged and supervised from Philadelphia, or she might have gone only partway. But certainly she went all the way down to her old home three times at least. The first time was in May, when Thomas Garrett advised William Still that he would be forwarding four young men from the Eastern Shore to him and that Harriet would arrive a day later.

As Garrett later wrote Bradford, when Harriet showed up at his house, she was so hoarse, she could hardly speak. About thirty minutes south of Wilmington, she explained, she was on her regular route, when God told her to stop. After obeying, she asked what she should do next and was told to go a different way, to leave the railroad tracks and turn to the left.

In 1868, when he wrote Sarah Bradford about this particular escape, Garrett was extremely ill and had been confined to bed for four weeks. But he felt so "interested" in Harriet's accomplishments that he managed to record some of the more remarkable ones.

Following orders, she took her people in the direction she was told to go and soon came to a tidal stream, where there was no bridge and no boat going across. Again, she asked what to do and the voice said, Go on through.

It was at first light, a cold spring morning. Having no knowledge of the stream, Harriet nonetheless did as she had been instructed and waded into the icy water. The men refused to follow. In no time, she had come to a deep place, where the water reached her armpits. Alarmed, the men stood their ground on the bank, waiting to see what happened. When she finally hauled herself out of the water on the other side, the men followed. On dry land, they shook off what water they could and walked on, soon coming to a cabin of black people, who took them in, put them to bed, and dried their clothes while they slept.

Harriet rested, but she was suffering from a violent toothache, and her mind was troubled. She was out of money and had to think of another way to repay the family for their kindness. When she awoke, she offered them what she could, some of her underclothing, which they gratefully accepted.

By the time she arrived at Garrett's home two days later, she was quite incapacitated and feeble. Her head was on fire with the toothache, and she was desperately ill with a respiratory ailment she would not shake off until the end of summer, possibly the result of weakened lungs from the bronchial infection that had first come on when she was six and was ordered to wade out and check muskrat traps. Before she left for Canada, she would dispatch the offending tooth with a rock.

Soon afterward, Garrett discovered that on the day Harriet instructed the men to turn left and walk through the water, one of the fugitives' owners showed up at the very depot they had avoided and there put up advertisements offering a reward for their apprehension.

She and the four men head off to Canada and she spends the summer there, working and quietly recuperating, readying herself for further trips.

Rachel. She will not rest until she brings out her sister.

In September, she returns to Philadelphia, only to find that her landlord has died and that his house has been sold by his widow, who has left for Harrisburg, taking all of Harriet's belongings, including clothes and money. Broke, she makes an appeal to Garrett, who writes Eliza Wigham, a staunch abolitionist in England, for help. Harriet tells Garrett that after a trip to Baltimore to bring two children to Philadelphia, she will once again return to the Eastern Shore to get Rachel. She leaves, presumably to deliver the children. Soon afterward, five men from the Eastern Shore arrive in Wilmington and are forwarded by Garrett to Still's office, having been helped by Harriet to make their way out, perhaps accompanied by her part of the way.

During one of her stopovers in central New York, either to obtain shelter for refugees or—as she often must—to appeal to UGRR agents for funds, she is approached by a man who escaped from slavery some seven years before.

Now that she has become Moses, people come to her with requests and stories. Believing her to be blessed, luckier than they, having the charm and the God-given anointment to be the deliverer they have been waiting for in their particular corner of the hellish world of slavery, they solicit her help.

The man tells her that seven years ago, when he was told by a friend that his master was about to sell him south, he went to his fiancée and told her that he had to leave. And while his future wife wanted to go with him, she could not manage it, and so for seven years the two have lived apart.

The man holds out money. He has been saving up and can pay. Will Harriet find his beloved in Baltimore and bring her to him in Canada?

In years to come, Harriet will tell this story twice, once to Thomas Garrett and again to Sarah Bradford years later. Bradford names the woman "Tilly" and places this rescue at a later date, but clearly the story and the rescue are the same, and so we will follow Bradford's lead.

Harriet agrees, and after an extensive search, she locates Tilly, then manages to tap into her established network of supporters to obtain papers for herself, certifying her as a free Philadelphia resident.

When the ship's captain honors the certificate, Harriet boards.

In Baltimore, she finds Tilly working as a personal servant to a wealthy woman, but she is ill and fragile, and in need of a great deal of care. From experience, Harriet knows that she cannot take a woman from Baltimore to Philadelphia by railroad or steamboat without paying a five-hundred-dollar bond. She doesn't have anything close to that kind of money, and so she proceeds to devise a new plan, the most complex and unlikely rescue of her career.

Instead of attempting to go north, she books passage for Tilly and herself on a steamboat going south down the Chesapeake, all the way past the Choptank River to the southern border of Dorchester County, then up the Nanticoke River to Seaford, Delaware—a long and arduous trip. Using her Philadelphia-Baltimore passport to get by the captain— who, being familiar with the captain of the previous ship, honors it— Harriet and Tilly board. Since two black women going south do not tend to rouse suspicion, they are not questioned.

Tilly, however, must be wondering if she shouldn't have stayed in Baltimore instead of agreeing to go along with this strange, narcoleptic woman, beyond the marshes of lower Dorchester, deep into slave country. But there is no time for second-guessing.

The boat embarks.

In Seaford, Harriet escorts Tilly to a hotel, where she books supper and lodging, which, remarkably, are provided—perhaps because, as

Bradford has it, Tilly is a mulatto and passes as Harriet's mistress. The next morning, as they walk toward the railroad station, a suspicious slave trader attempts to haul the two women to the sheriff, but when Harriet displays the certificate, he backs off.

By now, the rescued Tilly is in near hysterics. Sometime during the journey, Harriet, too, suffers from doubts. Wondering if perhaps she has somehow misread the message about leaving the far safer city of Baltimore, she prays hard, asking the Lord not to abandon her this time, but to stick with her, the same as during the six previous trips.

From Seaford, she books passage on a railroad train to Camden, a notoriously dangerous town for runaways. Once there, she contacts a known Underground Railroad agent, probably the reliable William Brinkley, a free black man who lives there. Shelling out her last penny, she engages the services of one or two men to drive them in a carriage the fifty miles to Wilmington.

Taking a direct course, the journey from Baltimore to Wilmington is about seventy-five miles. Instead, the women have more than doubled that distance, following Harriet's instincts and advice.

They arrive exhausted in every way.

Harriet immediately asks Garrett for money. She and Tilly both need new shoes, and Tilly has to have passage to Philadelphia and on to Canada. Having only just received funds from Eliza Wigham, Garrett gives Harriet twenty-five dollars.

After, presumably, purchasing new shoes, Tilly proceeds to Canada to meet up with, and marry, her long-lost lover.

Harriet takes the remaining twenty dollars and heads back to Dorchester County, where she meets face-to-face with Rachel.

But nothing has changed, and Harriet can neither find the children nor convince her sister to leave without them. And so, at the end of ten days, she gets ready to go back herself, promising to return in six weeks or so, at Christmastime, the right season for rescues.

She does not, however, leave alone.

In Talbot County, by that fall, a slave named Josiah (called Joe) Bailey had been hired out to the farmer and lumber dealer William Hughlett for six years. An imposing figure—well built, five feet ten, bald, with a notable scar down one cheek—Joe had become one of Hughlett's most valuable hands. Intelligent and capable, he led the harvest, managed the hauling of Hughlett's ship lumber, and served as his timber foreman, saving him the cost of an overseer. Joe's older brother, Bill, also worked for Hughlett, having been hired out by a different owner, John Campbell Henry.

Hughlett already owned forty slaves, but since Joe was indispensable to his operation, he made up his mind to buy him at any cost. He wound up paying one thousand dollars up front to Joe's owner, with another thousand to come—an extraordinary amount for a slave at this time in this part of the country.

The agreement between the two white men took place in mid- to late October, a few weeks before Harriet arrived.

Known as a moderate man who nonetheless was in the habit of flogging male or female adults when he felt so disposed—including Joe's brother, Bill—Hughlett had never laid a hand on Josiah Bailey. But on the very day of the purchase, he ordered his foreman to strip and take a whipping. Stunned, Joe considered resisting, but—remembering how Hughlett treated those who refused to submit—decided instead to appeal to reason.

Hadn't he always been faithful? Worked through sun and rain, from early morning until late at night? Saved him the cost of an overseer? Had Hughlett any complaint at all to lodge against him?

Hughlett said no, Joe was a good Negro and he had always worked well, but the first lesson his slaves had to learn and acknowledge was that he was master. They were not to resist or refuse to obey any order, even to be whipped. And if they resisted, they got it all the harder, and he was willing to go on and on until he killed a slave who wouldn't give in.

Joe was no exception.

The muscular Joe Bailey stripped off his shirt, lay down, and took the flogging without a word. Satisfied, Hughlett went on back to the house. But while drawing his clothes up over his ripped and bloody back, Joe made a promise to himself: never again. His wife and three children belonged also to Hughlett, but if he had to leave them, he would.

That was the night he took a boat, rowed to Ben Ross's cabin, and told Ben the next time Moses came, to let him know. Then rowed back to the Hughlett place.

Within two weeks, Harriet has arrived.

She hears the story. Joe Bailey receives the word that she is in the area. He comes to her.

When she heads back north on a Saturday night in the middle of November, Joe Bailey is with her, along with his brother, Bill, a man named Peter Pennington—owned by another Talbot slaveholder, Turpin Wright—and a woman, Eliza Manokey, about whom little information has been uncovered.

Early the next morning, discovering that Joe and his brother, Bill, have left, Hughlett sends word to the other owners and the three men form a search party. They ride out immediately, heading north along the Choptank, passing within a few feet of Harriet and the others as they are being passed from one household to the next and then, wearing various disguises, being scattered in different directions and led separately to a place where they will all meet up.

Well known in the area, Joe Bailey has a great many friends and shipyard connections. In East New Market, Harriet and her party are taken in by the free black Methodist minister Samuel Green, who knows both Harriet and Joe.

Reward posters for the three men are widely circulated. Hughlett is offering an incredible fifteen hundred dollars and all expenses for the return of Joe Bailey to the Easton jail; Turpin Wright, eight hundred dollars for Peter Pennington; John C. Henry, three hundred dollars for Bill Bailey. Dodging and darting, with the help of agents and friends, Harriet and the runaways make their way through Caroline County into Delaware, perhaps finding shelter with Harriet's friend William Brinkley in Camden. Eventually, they come to the bridge across the Christiana River into Wilmington.

But the search party has preceded them by three days, and Hughlett, Wright, and Henry have put up posters near the bridge, at railroad stations, on downtown streets of various towns, and on tree trunks, announcing the possible near whereabouts of the fugitives and the rewards for their capture. The unusually high prices on Joe's and Peter's heads have placed the men in even greater danger, and so they and the others are separated again and placed in various safe houses. Meanwhile, Harriet sends word to Thomas Garrett through her colleagues and friends that they are there and need help crossing the bridge.

Hiding out, they pass the night. All fear being captured and tortured, but Hughlett's unwarranted humiliation of Josiah Bailey has left a deeper scar than the ones on his back, making him uncharacteristically afraid. He alone among the five speaks of surrender.

The next morning, two strangers, black bricklayers, drive a wagon up to the bridge across the Christiana. Because the wagon is fully loaded, it rumbles heavily over the wooden slats of the bridge. Rolling across the river, the drivers begin to sing and shout. On the other side, they turn up the heat of their act and sing and shout even louder, tipping their hats and sending hearty greetings to the police, slave catchers, and curious onlookers who have gathered there to witness the inevitable capture of the absconded slaves.

The crowd watches them go by.

The bricklayers proceed to a designated meeting place, where Harriet, Joe, Bill, Peter, and Eliza wait. All five are loaded like sardines into a hidden compartment beneath a pile of bricks. The bricklayers then replace the bricks on top of the compartment and drive their wagon back across the Christiana, once again singing and shouting to the police and slave catchers, who once again stand watching, perhaps making comments about the carefree nature of the African, his love of song.

In Wilmington, the five fugitives are helped out of the wagon. With no time to waste, they leave again that night, and one day later, on November 26, they arrive at William Still's office in Philadelphia. In another two days, they reach New York City and the Anti-Slavery Society office of UGRR agent Oliver Johnson, who greets Joe Bailey by telling him how glad he is to see a man whose head is worth fifteen hundred dollars.

Joe's heart sinks. If the reward flyer has been posted this far north, he is sure to be captured.

How far to Canada? he asks Johnson, and when he is told how

many miles through western New York and over the bridge to Canada, his spirits flag. Certain of capture, he is tempted to surrender and go on back to Talbot County himself.

As Harriet tells Bradford, "From that time, Joe was silent. He sang no more, he talked no more, he sat with his head on his hand, and nobody could amuse him or make him take interest in anything."

They pass through New York safely, at the Niagara River boarding the train that will take them over the suspension bridge.

With Canada in sight, the others join Harriet in celebratory song, but the inconsolable Joe sits as before, with his head in his hands.

When they pull out of the town then called Suspension Bridge, New York, Harriet calls her friends to the window to see the fabulous falls. But Joe does not move.

"Joe," Harriet calls to him. "Come look at the Falls, you fool, come see the Falls, it's your last chance!"

Joe still won't budge. At the rise in the center of the bridge, marking the border between the United States and Canada, the irrepressible Harriet, bored with his petulance, springs across the aisle to his seat and shakes his big shoulder hard.

"Joe!" she shouts. *"You have shook the lion's paw!"*

Still not catching on, Joe retreats further.

But Harriet persists.

"Joe!" she says, "Joe, you're free!"

Finally, the big man lifts his head, raises his hands, looks out up toward the heavens and, his face streaming with tears, begins to sing, "Glory to God and Jesus, too. One more soul is safe!"

And when the train stops on the other side, at Suspension Bridge, Canada, Joe is the first to spring from the car after the conductor steps off. On the soil of his adopted country, accompanied by the thundering roar of the falls, he continues his song: "Oh, go and carry the news. One more soul got safe."

Surely his friend Samuel Green, Jr.—who wrote his father and encouraged him to "Kom on" to Canada and to tell Joe Bailey and the others to "Kom more"—greets him upon his safe arrival.

Joe Bailey and his brother, Bill, will remain in St. Catharines and make their lives there. A few years from now, both men will be heavily recruited by John Brown to come join his crusade to overturn slavery in the South.

For now, they find work, make a connection with the Rev. Hiram Wilson, who is running an organization to help fugitive slaves in St. Catharines, and settle in.

November ends. The nights are coming earlier, the chill setting in fast. Harriet has promised Rachel she will return in the right season, at Christmastime. If she is to get to Dorchester by then, she must head back immediately, but she does not. Understanding the importance of this particular rescue, Thomas Garrett, when he does not hear from her in December or January, begins to worry that something has happened to her.

Eighteen fifty-six has been an exhausting year, and Harriet may be feeling somewhat bruised and beaten by its rigors and demands. By the time she does go back to Philadelphia and then to the Eastern Shore, she will be thirty-five years old.

Running against the newly founded Republican party's platform, which calls for the exclusion of slavery from all territories, the bachelor Democrat James Buchanan has been elected president. Opposed to slavery on moral grounds, Buchanan will nonetheless waffle on the issue during his inauguration speech and will win the allegiance of every slave state in the country by announcing his support for popular sovereignty in the territories, including Kansas and California.

During the ceremony, some will note the whisperings of Chief Justice Roger Taney into the ear of the newly elected president.

Conspiracy, the abolitionists believe, is afoot. The conspiracy of the slave power.

Other fugitives from Dorchester include William Cornish, his wife, Delia, and his daughter Harriet, who are also making a home in St. Catharines. The Cornish family will suffer terribly in Canada, as do other refugees. Housing, food, and jobs are inadequate, winters hard. Both William and Delia suffer from serious illnesses there, and in the next eight years, three of their six children will die. Still, William will testify to the American Freedman's Inquiry Commission, "The poorest day

I ever see out here, I would rather be there than be with the best slave-holder in the south, and I have seen slaves out there that were better treated than they can treat themselves here."

Christmas passes. Eighteen fifty-seven, an important year, shuffles in.

Harriet works, rests, recuperates, puts away money for a spring trip.

Scene 12.

Escapes, Rescues: The Stampede

Suddenly and without apparent cause the slaves of the citizens of Dorchester County began to abscond. Not singly and at long intervals as before, but in gangs collected together from various parts of the county, with a concert of action and celerity of movement that defied all attempts at recapture.

—*CAMBRIDGE EAGLE*, REPRINTED IN *EASTON GAZETTE*,
AUGUST 28, 1858

Men were better than their theology and truer to humanity than to their politics or their offices.

—FREDERICK DOUGLASS ON THE UNDERGROUND RAILROAD,
LIFE AND TIMES OF FREDERICK DOUGLASS, 1881

On March 6, 1857, two days after Buchanan's inauguration, Chief Justice Roger Taney hands down his decision in the Dred Scott case. Negroes, he declares, have "no rights which the white man [is] bound to respect," and cannot ever become citizens, since the Declaration of Independence and the Constitution were never meant to include them. In addition, Congress cannot pass laws that will deprive slaveholders of their right to take human "articles of merchandise" into any part of the union, north and south, or cause them in any way to risk loss of ownership.

The response is immediate. Abolitionists close ranks and gain members. Mass protest meetings are held in the East. The movement of white voters toward the antislavery movement causes a huge stir all over the country.

In a speech about the decision, Frederick Douglass declares to the American Anti-Slavery Association, "My hopes were never brighter. . . . Judge Taney cannot bail out the ocean, annihilate the firm old earth or pluck the silvery star of liberty from our Northern sky."

Two nights after Taney's decision (although probably having nothing to do with it), on Sunday, March 8, nine Dorchester slaves—Henry Predeaux, Thomas Elliott, Denard Hughes, James Woolfley, Lavinia Woolfley, Bill Kiah, Emily Kiah, two unnamed men—strike out together from the Bucktown area on a route—which they later report Harriet supplied—north along the Choptank.

The nine fugitives do not leave impulsively. They have a plan— towns or farms to get to, people who will help. And they have money enough to secure assistance along the way. From Cambridge, they will travel to Poplar Neck, then to Milford, then Dover, Delaware, and on to Camden to the home of William Brinkley. From there, they will go

William Still entitled this engraving "Twenty-eight fugitives escaping from the Eastern Shore of Maryland," as in the late 1850s many families made their way north in what slaveholders on the Eastern Shore referred to as a "stampede."

to Thomas Garrett in Wilmington (or perhaps to the home of Moses Pinket, a free uncle of Thomas Elliott's), then to William Still in Philadelphia, and on north and west until they reach Canada and freedom.

Harriet's route.

The runaways pass through East New Market and the home of Samuel Green without stopping. The minister is already under suspicion for helping runaways and, having only recently arrived back home from a trip to see his son Sam, Jr., in St. Catharines, is now under even closer scrutiny. The fugitives make twenty miles that first night, reaching their first stop, the Caroline County home of Ben and Rit Ross, in the early-morning hours.

Ben has given the men and women directions to his cabin. The fugitives may even spend the daylight hours in the same corncrib that Harriet and her brothers used, lying among ears of corn, listening for the sound of horses' hooves and the voices of vengeful white men, taking turns napping, waiting for darkness to fall.

By housing the men and women who—after one man flees—will become known as the "Dover Eight," Ben and Rit have broken the law as laid out in the Fugitive Slave Act, leaving themselves liable for arrest, fine, and imprisonment. Rit probably doesn't know. In all likelihood, Ben manages the overnight accommodations for the fugitives on his own.

On Monday night, the fugitives head toward Milford, Delaware, where they will meet up with Thomas Otwell, a black man recommended to them as a proven friend of runaways. Otwell rents a farm near Milford. Once there, the fugitives are to pay Otwell eight dollars to guide them the next thirty miles, to Dover, the site of an especially aggressive collection of slave catchers and vigilantes.

Henry Predeaux is a giant of a man, intelligent and, as a laborer, highly prized. Hughes and Elliott are owned by the wealthy landowner Pritchett Meredith; William Kiah is the slave of the equally prosperous Benjamin G. Tubman. Denard Hughes will describe his decision to flee as simply the desire to "go where colored men are free."

The owners offer a huge reward, three thousand dollars, for the capture of all nine fugitives. The stakes thus raised, one of the men has second thoughts and turns back soon after leaving Ben's cabin. In no time, he is apprehended and arrested. When questioned, the man yields up Ben Ross's name.

The remaining eight continue on toward their next stop. Although highly respected as a UGRR agent, Thomas Otwell has given in to the persuasions of his landlord, a white man named Hollis, who has convinced Otwell to pilot the eight fugitives straight to the Dover jail, where they will be arrested. Hollis and Otwell will then split the reward. Either dazzled by the money or simply too afraid to say no, Otwell agrees.

Hollis goes to the Dover jail to alert the sheriff. Together, they wait. Midnight passes. When 2:00 A.M. arrives and the fugitives still haven't shown up, the sheriff goes to bed, joining his family in his private apartment, located within the walls of the jailhouse, leaving Hollis on the lookout.

At 4:00 A.M., Otwell arrives. He introduces the six men and two women to Hollis, calling him a great friend to slaves. Otwell advises the fugitives to go with the white man; he knows how tired and cold they are, but they will soon, he promises, have a good warming. The plan is for Hollis to herd the eight into a dark, barred room, whereupon the sheriff will come and lock them in together. But at the moment they enter the room, a ray of moonshine makes its way through a window, casting a shadow of the bars onto the floor. One of the fugitives notices and, quickly snapping to the truth of the situation, leads the group out the door and down the hall.

Having taken in the situation, the sheriff has turned back toward his apartment for his gun. But the fugitives make their way past him, hurtling blindly downstairs and into a room that turns out to be the sheriff's apartment, where his wife and children have been sleeping. While two of the female fugitives squeeze through a window, Predeaux shovels a pile of burning embers onto the floor of the room where the sheriff's wife and children lie in their beds, weeping and screaming in fright. The sheriff backs off.

The window is too small for the men to squeeze through and so, with an andiron, Predeaux smashes the glass entirely out of its frame and the five others leap twelve feet down, landing in the soft mud below. Predeaux goes last. The only remaining obstacle for the Dover Eight is a substantial wall around the jail, which, with effort, helping one another, they surmount.

Having boosted the others over the wall, Predeaux takes it last. He looks back and sees the sheriff in his stocking feet, aiming his gun at him and then shooting. But the pistol does not fire.

The fugitives scatter. Two people take one course away from the jail, while four men and two women go another way. Lost, the group of six backtracks, and, amazingly enough, they encounter the duplicitious Otwell, who begs for his life, promising this time to steer them correctly. They have no choice but to listen. Otwell guides them on and then quickly disappears. Another of the fugitives soon joins up with them.

Eventually, five of the eight escapees manage to make their way to Wilmington and then Philadelphia to Still's office, where they tell their story. Most of them travel on to Canada, though William and Emily Kiah stay in the area. When, three months later, Lavinia Woolfley finally makes her way to Still's office as well, she is forwarded on to Canada to join her husband.

Word spreads fast among the enslaved population of the Eastern Shore: All eight made it out.

Having doubtless heard of her parents' participation in the escape, Harriet, feeling now that she has no other choice, prepares to head south to get them. But she will have to devise some kind of carriage, and she needs money for that, more money than for any other trip. On her way to Philadephia, she stops in Syracuse, where she makes an appeal to her friend, UGRR agent Jermaine Loguen. But Loguen turns her down, and Harriet is forced to take odd jobs around the city before traveling on. On another occasion, she makes her way to the offices of the New York Anti-Slavery Society, to ask Oliver Johnson for funds, vowing that if he, too, doesn't come through, she will stage a protest demonstration.

Her parents are in trouble, she has told friends, and no matter what Johnson says, she will not eat, drink, or leave until she gets enough money to take her down to Maryland after the old people.

At the office, Johnson greets Harriet, then immediately asks her what she wants.

Harriet says, "Money, sir. Twenty dollars."

"Twenty dollars!" Johnson exclaims. "Who told you to come here for that much money?"

"The Lord," she says.

"Then the Lord was mistaken," Johnson replies.

Harriet guesses the Lord wasn't wrong. Anyhow, never mind discussions, she is going to sit there until she gets what she came for.

She sits all morning and afternoon, nodding off into one of her zero zones of consciousness, then rallying, falling again into catatonia, coming to again. People come and go. Spying Harriet napping, they try to rouse her, to tell her to wake up and go somewhere where she can sleep properly. When Harriet finally awakens on her own, she tells them what she wants and how long she intends to stay. Late in the day, she loses track again, overcome by a heavier sleep than usual. When she awakens, she finds that somebody has been fund-raising for her, telling her story around the office, and that she is the happy recipient of not just twenty but sixty dollars.

Praising God for having come through for her yet one more time, she goes on her way. By the end of March, she is in Philadelphia.

In early April, the sheriff of Dorchester County, Robert Bell, serves Rev. Samuel Green with a search warrant.

Maryland has passed a law against the possession by black people of "inflammatory material" that might "create discontent amongst or to stir up to insurrection the people of color of this State." In Green's East New Market home, the sheriff turns up a map of Canada, letters from Dorchester runaways, railroad schedules of routes through New Jersey, and a letter from Samuel Green, Jr., telling his father about the good life he is leading in Canada, suggesting that some of his friends—including the recent runaway Josiah Bailey—should come, too.

A copy of Harriet Beecher Stowe's 1852 novel, *Uncle Tom's Cabin,* is also collected and taken as evidence. The sheriff charges Green with illegal possession.

When the evidence is presented in court, the judge drops charges relating to the maps, schedules, and letters, ruling that those documents were not designed to create discontent, even though some of Samuel Green, Jr.'s friends have, in fact, absconded to Canada. But the fifty-five-year-old Samuel Green is given a ten-year sentence in prison for "having in his possession a certain abolition pamphlet called *Uncle Tom's Cabin,*" even though what locals know and a newspaper will soon report is that the real cause of his arrest and imprisonment is the generally accepted suspicion that he is helping runaways to escape. Nonetheless, conventional wisdom of the region has it that *Uncle Tom's Cabin* has done its work, having transformed a quiet and contented black man into a criminal and a saboteur.

His abolitionist work notwithstanding, the Reverend Samuel Green has a fair number of loyal white friends, even among those opposed to his views. They collect two thousand dollars to redeem him from his sentence and bail him out of prison. But the state refuses to release him, and Samuel Green remains locked up.

The sheriff then starts preparing a case against the next coconspirator in the Dover Eight case, Ben Ross, for harboring fugitives.

As soon as he hears this news, the unpredictable Dr. A. C. Thompson rides or walks across his property to the cabin where Ben and Rit have been living all these years.

You will soon be arrested, he warns Ben. White men are in a rage over losing their property. You must leave the state right away.

Thompson's suggestion—that a man in his seventies would defy the Fugitive Slave Act and risk facing bounty hunters and slave catchers along every route to the North—reveals a great deal about the state of mind of Dorchester slaveholders at this time. Because Thompson is one of them, he knows their thinking and, having likely attended some of their meetings, understands how far they are willing to go to hold on to the old labor system, and its rights and privileges.

It is doubtful, however, that Dr. Thompson would have issued this advice if he hadn't had an inkling that the two old people would not make the journey alone. Presumably, he believed Harriet would either come down to get her parents or arrange for their rescue.

———

This year, spring has been particularly cold, and the chill is holding, even into April. Intermittent storms darken the sky, blocking the sun, bringing daily blasts of cold air. Late frosts attack crops, turning their developing buds to jelly. Farmers sit inside looking out. Travel is even more difficult than usual.

Everybody has too much time to think, and stew.

The sheriff issues Ben a warrant.

By late April or early May, Harriet is making her way toward Poplar Neck. But the weather complicates the trip, slamming against her repeatedly, shoving her back, delaying her departure from Philadelphia. She doesn't get to the Thompson place until late May, less than a week before Ben is to be put on trial.

On her way, perhaps in Wilmington, she's made some purchases: a broken-down workhorse fitted out with a straw collar and a jury-rigged two-man sled that rolls unsteadily on two old carriage wheels, perhaps a primitive version of the trotter-race sulky, lower in back than toward the horse's rear. She's affixed a board for Ben and Rit to sit on and has looped a length of rope into something like a sulky's stirrups so that they can rest their feet.

She arrives at the cabin. Ben apparently wants to take some tools with him, and Rit says she won't leave without a favorite feather bed.

Harriet puts her foot down. They may be old and they may be her parents, to whom she owes lifelong respect, but this time she gets to be the one to say. They can't take anything; she and the horse will be laden down enough just pulling the two of them.

Her parents climb on.

Harriet will receive some criticism for taking such a chance with the old people's lives, and they may be scared—and why wouldn't they be?—and distrustful of their daughter's ability to take them to safety, despite her reputation and other people's utter faith. To them, she is still a daughter, after all, no Moses.

But Harriet brooks no parental disapproval. She assumes control.

The slaveholders of the Eastern Shore are already up in arms about absconding slaves, who are now leaving regularly and in droves, "with a concert of action and celerity of movements that defied all attempts at recapture." Property owners are wild with fury at their impotence to stop or slow the stampede. Imprisoning an aged, respected man like Ben Ross would make a statement of the lengths to which they are willing to go.

Harriet directs the horse. Her parents ride.

In 1901, Bradford will describe Rit in her last years as "querulous and exacting and most unreasonable in her temper, often reproaching this faithful daughter as the Israelites did of Moses of old, for 'bringing them up into the wilderness to die there of hunger.' "

She must complain nonstop along this trip away from the only home she's ever known, ranting into the biting wind.

When father, mother, daughter, and horse arrive at a train station—perhaps in Camden, with William Brinkley's assistance—Harriet at last manages to move Rit and Ben from the sulky into a more comfortable and secure situation . . . and out of her hair for a while. She puts them on the train and then drives the rig the rest of the way along.

In Wilmington, Thomas Garrett greets the elder Rosses and gives them shelter and, the next day, thirty dollars to get them to Philadelphia. Harriet arrives. Once she leaves, he sells the horse and either scraps or sells the last piece of evidence, the rig.

Ben tells William Still about A. C. Thompson's rough treatment of his slaves and describes him as a bald, bewigged wolf in sheep's clothing. He and Rit also share with him their delight at the prospect of rejoining their children in Canada.

After joining them in Still's office, Harriet escorts her parents to New York City and then Rochester, where they rest for a time. They may well meet up with Frederick Douglass there, since Harriet will soon pay a visit to him at his home. They then go on to St. Catharines, to be reunited with their sons, William Henry and John, and their grandchildren and great-grandchildren.

Harriet leaves her parents in her brothers' care and returns to Dorchester immediately. But Rachel is now living apart from her children by twelve miles, and once again she refuses to leave. Angerine is ten years old, Ben eight. Both are of an age to be working in the Brodess fields, chopping, picking, weeding, breaking flax.

Harriet remains until the fall, hoping to figure out a way, or that something will change. During that time, fugitives continue to take to their heels, more of them leaving slavery every day. Harriet helps make arrangements for some thirty-nine people to go north, all from Dorchester County.

Whoever goes comes to her first. Without her example and assistance, the number of escapes from the Eastern Shore would unquestionably have been far, far fewer.

In early October, a group of about fifteen abscond, arriving in Philadelphia by about the middle of the month, and on the twenty-fourth of that month, an astonishing twenty-eight men, women, and children leave together. The night is rent with furious thunderstorms that lash the fugitives as they go. When landowner Samuel Pattison goes out the next morning to check on the state of his property, he finds that almost all of his slaves have escaped. Among the entire group are twenty children, some of them infants, who are given a sleeping potion—probably laudanum—to hush their cries. Incredibly enough, they all arrive safely, eventually, at William Still's office.

Desperate Dorchester County slaveholders hold more meetings, make more plans to better protect their interests. Gourney Pattison's attorney James A. Stewart, now a U.S. congressman, makes fiery pro-slavery speeches to Congress, demanding stronger laws to protect the property of slaveholders. The number of slave catchers on the prowl throughout the county increases. Old Maryland laws are revived, including one from 1715 that prevents servants from going ten miles from their master without documentation, and one from 1806 that promises six dollars to anyone apprehending a runaway slave.

The following year, 1858, when seven runaways from Cambridge are caught in Caroline County, a mob will threaten to take the Quaker abolitionist Arthur Leverton—son of Hannah, to whom Harriet gave her handmade bed quilt—and the settled free black landowner Daniel Hubbard to Cambridge, presumably for a lynching. Having been forewarned, the two men leave before they can be captured. Soon thereafter, they will move their families out of Maryland altogether.

Life for the enslaved left behind, as a result, grows even more tedious, more restrictive, more oppressive and punishing than before.

A. C. Thompson sells Mary Manokey Ross and her three children—Harriet's nephews and niece—to his daughter, who lives in Talbot County, from which there are fewer escapes.

The Brodesses certainly know of Harriet's regular trips to Dorchester. To hold on to Rachel Ross, now thirty-two, they continue to hire her out to various farmers, keeping Angerine and Ben with them in Bucktown, knowing that, unlike others, Rachel will under no circumstances leave her children.

Harriet spends the Christmas of 1857 with her parents in St. Catharines. Unused to the nonstop snow, ice, and freezing temperatures, Ben and Rit suffer mightily. Arthritis has settled in Ben's hand, cramping his finger joints.

Never one to keep her feelings under wraps, Rit protests without ceasing throughout the winter.

Harriet works hard to remain calm. For distraction and to set herself at a distance from her mother's complaints, she begins making plans for 1858, including a January visit to Frederick Douglass in Rochester.

Her patience, she will tell Bradford, regarding her mother's grumbling, is a lesson of trust in Providence better than many sermons.

With John Brown: Dreams, Metaphor

Harriet Tubman . . . is the most of a man, naturally, that I ever met with.

—JOHN BROWN TO JOHN BROWN, JR., APRIL 8, 1858

In 1858, life changes for Harriet in many ways.

In this year, she becomes a public figure, in demand throughout the Northeast as a performer-storyteller who, by deconstructing her own life and creating it as if new to herself as well as to her audience, does one-of-a-kind stand-up for an altogether rapt and congenial audience of abolitionists and Transcendentalists. She goes from one parlor to the next and sometimes into churches. Touting her abilities, not just as a speaker but as a performer of great dramatic and comedic power, her sponsors promise audiences tales of adventure beyond anything they might have come across in fiction. Presenting her, they speak in terms of heroism, ingenuity, style, eloquence. Often, meaning well, they nonetheless reveal a patronizing attitude by describing her manner of speech as "quaint," it being conventionally ungrammatical, coming as it does from an unlettered mind, her language not just heavily accented but of a purely narrative derivation, with no inclination toward analysis beyond the story itself—which in the end becomes analysis enough.

Eventually, the presenter runs out of superlatives and the headliner makes her appearance, often launching without preliminaries into a surprise opener, a gospel or slave song, low-pitched and resonant.

In this year, Harriet is on her way to becoming, you might even say, in one tiny corner of the country's heavens, a star.

This despite the burdensome, if altogether welcome, presence in her home of her parents, for whose constant upkeep and financial support she alone is considered, by herself and her brothers, responsible. Thus is she now required to be more attentive to home and the need for even more money than before, less able, as a result, to indulge her sometimes impulsive, if always quietly self-contained, nature.

John Brown

In 1858, that is to say, she will find herself torn between the duties of a good daughter and her obligation to what she considers her overriding mission: to uphold her vow to her God and herself by rescuing Rachel, Ben, and Angerine, if no others.

In 1858, as well, she meets a man she profoundly admires, even—as Sanborn has it—venerates: the abolitionist warrior and visionary John Brown, Calvinist antislavery zealot and veteran of the bloody Kansas slavery wars. In disapproval of his notoriously violent tactics, others now call him "Osawatomie Brown," after the disastrous battle pitched in the Kansas town of that name, in which his son Frederick was shot through the heart and killed. Others call him "Old John Brown," "Old Brown," or simply, "the Old Man." Harriet can't quite settle it in her mind how and why a white man would be willing to sacrifice his own son and take on the burdens of a race other than his own. But her perplexity is matched only by her admiration for him on the same grounds.

She calls John Brown "the Captain" or "Captain Brown."

A year from now, in late 1859, when John Brown is executed, he will have grown a long white shovel-shaped beard that fans out and reaches beyond his clavicle. A fugitive from the law, he began growing the beard in mid- to late 1857 as a disguise, but in 1858, when Harriet meets him, his hair is not yet altogether white, nor perhaps is his beard quite as long as it will be. Nonetheless, in a prophetic dream, Harriet has seen him as he will look a year from now (assuming, that is, she had the dream when she told Sanborn she did, just before her first encounter with the Captain).

In his 1863 biographical piece, Sanborn records the dream: "She thought," he writes, "she was in a 'wilderness sort of place, all full of rocks and bushes' " . . . when a serpent rises up from behind the rocks. Harriet stands there. As the serpent moves upward, its head becomes the head of an old man with a long white beard, someone she does not know.

The eyes of the old man hold steady on her. And he gazes at her "wishful like," in Harriet's words, as if he has something to say to or ask of her but can't quite get the words out.

And then two other heads emerge from the serpent's body, these with the faces of young men. And as Harriet stands wondering what the old man is trying to say and what the three-headed serpent intends to do or can possibly want from her, from out of nowhere a crowd of men comes into the wilderness (she doesn't say white or black or give any further description). The men rush to the serpent, strike down the two young men's heads and then the old man's. The crowd disappears. As the bearded old man goes down, he continues to hold Harriet's gaze, still looking at her with that same wishful expression.

The dream ends there, but it keeps coming back, nudging Harriet to pay attention, a pesky presence that won't let up. Harriet has studied the dream carefully but cannot make it out.

Then she meets the Captain in person.

He has been in New York and Massachusetts, raising money for his big campaign. In late January, he spent three weeks in Rochester, where he stayed in Frederick Douglass's home. While there, he told Douglass about his plan to recruit upward of 100,000 black men to join him in an invasion meant to free slaves and, consequently, break up what he calls the conspiracy of the slave power. Three weeks turned out to be a long visit for Douglass, since the old man never talked of anything else from early rising until nightfall. And when he mentioned Harpers Ferry, Douglass—by then worn-out and bored with Brown's rant—dismissed the possibility.

In Rochester, Brown also wrote his own version of the U.S. Constitution, one that would serve all the people of the country when all were free. He and Douglass spoke of Harriet during the visit, as well. Douglass suggested that Brown go to St. Catharines to meet her, saying she could help him recruit black soldiers as well as participate in the logistics of the operation by giving him information on the trails and backwater routes she knew and used.

When Brown left Douglass's home, he insisted on paying board for his stay, which amounted to three dollars a week.

Harriet had just paid her own visit to Douglass in January, staying with him for three days, no doubt bending his ear with stories the same as Brown had. A true oral historian, she neither abbreviates nor compresses any narration no matter the circumstances, but goes on unedited until she's finished.

After she left, Douglass, clearly impressed, wrote a fund-raising letter to the Irish Ladies Anti-Slavery Association, in which he mentioned her visit and told of her daring, her shrewdness, and her potential use to the cause—thus, like Thomas Garrett, expanding Harriet's reputation and potential for name recognition across the Atlantic.

Harriet's name came up again when Brown traveled to Syracuse to meet with Jermaine Loguen, who also suggested that he travel to Canada to meet up with her and to hold his constitutional convention there, perhaps in Chatham, where he would be in no danger of being attacked or arrested.

Traveling on something like his own Underground Railroad, Brown made his way from one like-minded abolitionist and supporter to the next. From Syracuse on to Gerrit Smith's mansion in Peterboro. And after that to Boston and Concord to meet up with the ministers, thinkers, and educators who had already committed themselves financially to his mission and who would later call themselves, along with Gerrit Smith, privately "the Secret Six": the young educator and future Boston *Commonwealth* editor Franklin Sanborn, physician and educator Samuel Gridley Howe, firebrand Unitarian minister Thomas Wentworth Higginson, Unitarian minister Theodore Parker, and wealthy businessman George Stearns. Brown needed money, and he was hoping his visits would stoke his next operation with more cash and supplies.

By now, Brown has set in motion his plan to gather hundreds of slaves and take them to the safety of the Blue Ridge Mountains and there establish a new state made up of free blacks and freed slaves. He also has in mind to raid the federal arsenal at Harpers Ferry and, if necessary, engage in a battle with federal soldiers. But he has not communicated the specifics of this part of his plan to his supporters, asking them instead to trust him without knowing the details. Gerrit Smith, for one, approves of Brown's clandestine approach. In a letter to Sanborn, he expresses his hope that Captain Brown will keep his plans to himself. What they do know is that slave power is intransigent and will go to any lengths to keep what it has. Bloodshed has become a certainty.

The men of the Secret Six are of a generally pacifist nature, but having lost patience with the country's uncompromising proslavery forces, they are now willing to support Brown despite his reputation for violence, without probing too much into tactics and strategy. Anyway, as Franklin Sanborn has predicted, the day is coming when treason will be seen not as treason but as patriotism.

Before leaving the country for Canada, Brown journeys from Massachusetts to Philadelphia, where he meets with William Still and the ferocious black abolitionist Henry Highland Garnet. Douglass joins the meeting. Support from these committed African American activists boosts Brown's spirits, leading him to estimate an army of 150,000 black men from the Northeast will join with him in what the Secret Six are calling his "great experiment."

From there, he returns to New York State, where he and Jermaine Loguen board the train for Canada, their fare furnished by Gerrit Smith, who has also sent twenty-five dollars in gold to give to Harriet for recruitment expenses.

When they arrive in St. Catharines, Brown quickly retreats to a hotel room while Loguen finds his way to the heart of the black district of town, the British Methodist Episcopal Church at the corner of Geneva

George Stearns

Gerrit Smith

Frank Sanborn

Thomas Wentworth
Higginson

Theodore Parker

Samuel Gridley Howe

John Brown's "Secret Six," and Harriet's friends.

and North streets. There, he will have no trouble finding the whereabouts of Harriet, perhaps after showing some kind of underground passport to establish his identity as a friend. He then makes his way to Harriet's house on North Street, only a block from the chapel.

Always on the lookout for hostile eavesdroppers, Loguen tells Harriet in quiet tones that John Brown is in town and wants to see her.

All of this information, these conversations, of course, derive from interviews held far in the future, conducted by people who report secondhand what Harriet said. In 1896, she will tell the interviewer Lillie Chace Wyman that the minute Loguen told her Captain Brown was in town, the dream of the three-headed serpent dropped into her consciousness.

She interrupts Loguen.

I knew he was coming.

Everyone knows she is strange. Loguen waits her out. She has been, she tells him, forewarned in a dream.

Even though she has not yet met Brown and cannot quite parse the entire significance of the three heads hammered against the rocks by a crowd—and won't for more than a year—Harriet does understand the reason for the dream. It is a warning, a prophecy, telling her she is about to meet up with someone who works a harsh and perilous wilderness the same as she, and that he will ask something of her. And when Loguen tells her of Brown's presence, she makes the certain connection in a heartswelling flash.

Loguen moves on to practicalities. Will she go to Brown's hotel to meet with him?

Harriet says best not to take the risk. The Captain should come to her house and stay overnight, where no one will hurt them. She will round up trusted friends to come hear of his plans. They will gather that night: April 7, 1858. Loguen goes off to tell Brown and Harriet to spread the word.

That the religious visionary John Brown should meet the religious visionary Harriet Tubman in her home in St. Catharines seems altogether fitting and right, as if, in fact, arranged by destiny or historical necessity, or as if—as Harriet might have it—preordained by a vision. For those inclined to believe in paranormal possibilities, there is a case to be made for the less rational conjecture. Lillie Chace Wyman senses a kinship between Harriet and the Captain beyond skin color. She will characterize them as "two souls who dealt in action but were alike moved by impulses from mystical and hidden sources." The demands of historical rightness aren't always met, but sometimes the stars find a way to cross. Meteors blaze simultaneous paths. The appropriate event takes place. Can we, in a more cynical time, imagine it?

Douglass. Brown. Tubman. Activists of eloquence, honers of language, warriors. The triumvirate. Their paths cross. The sky cracks open.

When John Brown enters her house, Harriet beholds the same head, the same face, as the one in the dream. He walks toward her, this rail-thin white man with the piercing gray eyes and the wiry beard and hair, his hand outstretched. He is only five nine but seems taller, and even at that height, he is at least a head taller than she. She will have to lift her chin to return his gaze. He, of necessity, bows slightly to match her height. She offers her hand in return.

John Brown is particular about his army. Quiet men of principle and modesty make the best soldiers, he will tell Ralph Waldo Emerson, not bullies and boasters.

He shakes Harriet's hand. "The first I see," he says, "is General Tubman."

Paying tribute, giving her a new title and a commander's position.

And then he shakes hands again, saying, "The second is General Tubman." And a third time: "The third is General Tubman."

The psychic bond is formed.

Josiah Bailey is there. Peter Pennington. Thomas Elliott and Denard Hughes of the Dover Eight. Perhaps Harriet's brothers. Her parents are living with her, and so presumably they sit in. Everyone in the room is black and has lived in bondage except Brown, who then proceeds to tell them of the plan he has worked out to free hundreds of enslaved people and take them into the mountains. There will be battles to fight, obviously. Bloodshed. He needs black men willing to go with him, a phalanx of black men, as symbols of strength and determination, and exemplars to those still held in slavery.

He has pikes and Sharps rifles. Their enemy, of course, includes a mighty swell of people, not just one slaveholder or even an enclave of them. There is a nationwide conspiracy working against them, the conspiracy of slave power. It will not yield easily, but yield it must. They will be the guerrilla uprising, the insurrection to make it happen, as did the rebellion of Spartacus. After the first incursion, they will have added firepower. The enslaved population will leave bondage in droves, rallying to their cause. The Old Man stirs their hearts. Like the woman her people call Moses, he speaks irresistibly, in terms both intimate and apocalyptic.

He is not asking them to bear arms against their will, or even to fight in combat unless they wish to. But he is hoping that some of the men at Harriet's house will join him in the South to help him break the spine of the forces of slavery forever. He would also like them to attend the convention he will hold in Chatham, a settlement to the west, where he will present for adoption a new constitution, one that supports the Declaration of Independence and the Bible, therefore taking for granted the immediate end to slavery.

Following Harriet's lead, her Eastern Shore friends—Thomas Elliott, Josiah Bailey—vow to attend the convention. The Captain spends the night in Harriet's home, further conferring with her there. The next morning, he gives her fifteen dollars toward her rent and general expenses and the twenty-five dollars in gold sent by Gerrit Smith.

When he leaves, Brown repeats his ritual of the night before, shaking Harriet's hand three times, each time calling her General Tubman. She will hear from him next, he promises, through Frederick Douglass. And then he strides away on this spring morning in early April of 1858.

In a little more than nineteen months, the Captain will be dead; and Harriet will be awash in grief.

But today she stands on her doorstep, keeping her eyes on his retreating back until he enters an omnibus and she can no longer see him, then standing there yet, watching the bus until it rolls away and becomes a speck in the distance, then disappears.

The dream still nags. She still has not fully made out the significance of the three-headed serpent.

John Brown's letter to his son, written the day after his meeting with Harriet in her home in St. Catharines. (*Transcription of letter appears below.*)

(*Transcription*)

St. Catharines, Canada West, 8th April, 1858

Dear Son John,

I came on here direct with J.W. Loguen the day after you left Rochester. I am succeeding to all appearance beyond my expectation. Harriet Tubman hooked on his whole team at once. He is the most of a man, naturally, that I ever met with. There is the most abundant material, and most of the right quality, in this quarter beyond all doubt. Do not forget to write Mr. Case (near Rochester) at once about hunting up every person and family of the reliable kind, about, at or near Bedford, Chambersburg, Gettysburg and Carlisle in Pennsylvania, and also Hagerstown and vicinity, Mary-

land, and Harpers Ferry, Va. The names and residence of all I want
to have sent me at Lindensville enclosed to Alex E. Forbes. Anything you want to say to me before you leave, write so that it may
be sent at once, when I direct where, or be kept by Mr. Forbes till I
call for it. I shall write you where to direct to me as soon as I can fix
on any point. Shall direct to you at North Elba after a few days,
when I write. I shall probably be about this region some days yet.
May God bless you all.

    Your Affectionate Father,

    John Brown

The next day, April 8, Brown writes his son to say that the reception in
St. Catharines has succeeded beyond imagining. Using the masculine
pronoun to refer to her, he reports that "Harriet Tubman has hooked on
his whole team at once" and describes her as "the most of a man, naturally, that I ever met with." John Brown believes that only men can or
should conduct war. By recognizing Harriet not just the equal of a man
but a *man,* he has found a way to make her into a real soldier. He has no
doubt, furthermore, that Harriet will be a better officer than most he has
seen, equally able to command an army as to lead fugitives from slavery.
A general.

Flushed with success, Brown departs from Canada to go on a recruiting mission in Chicago and to check on his troops, which are unhappily hiding out in Iowa.

Within a week's time, Harriet falls out of touch. Clearly expecting
her either to join up with him right away or at least to send word, Brown
begins to worry that something is wrong. Knowing of her fragile health,
having doubtless witnessed at least one of her blackouts, he asks others
to intercede and, if they make contact, tell her that if she is indisposed
and can't attend the convention, she should send Thomas Elliott in her
stead. In any case, she must know that he understands and esteems her
great value, to him and their mutual cause, and, above all, "would not *on
any account fail* of having her come if she is able to do so."

No one comes to him to report her whereabouts.

In May, with a number of her friends from the Eastern Shore, Harriet heads west toward Chatham—where, during the convention, she can also visit Kessiah and James Bowley and their children, and her brother James and his wife, Catherine, and theirs. But she and her cohorts seem to have stopped over in Ingersoll and, perhaps because of a miscommunication or a lack of funds, either to have remained there or traveled on to Toronto. In any case, they become sidetracked or otherwise derailed and miss the convention.

Brown must view her absence, as well as the nonappearance of Frederick Douglass, Jermaine Loguen, and the Secret Six, with some alarm, but, undaunted by the disappointing turnout, he holds the convention as scheduled, and his constitution is adopted. It begins: "Whereas, Slavery throughout its entire existence in the United States, is none other than the most barbarous, unprovoked, and unjustifiable war of one portion of its citizens upon another portion, the only conditions of which are perpetual imprisonment and hopeless servitude or absolute extermination; in utter disregard and violation of those eternal and self-evident truths set forth in our Declaration of Independence . . ."

Unlike the U.S. Constitution, John Brown's version mentions slavery and war in the opening sentence.

After the convention, John Brown retreats to Kansas for a time, having convinced only one Canadian black recruit, Osborne P. Anderson, to join up with him. From Ingersoll, Harriet goes back home to St. Catharines.

Harriet's behavior toward Brown is oddly ambivalent. Despite her obvious bone-deep connection to him and her great regard for his dedication and courage, she doesn't show up for planned meetings and, in the end, will not join his campaign or travel with him. Why not? Possible reasons for her indecision or hesitancy abound.

For one thing, Harriet is a loner, and she has been operating solo and by personally aimed directives and promises for most of her life—at least since her childhood injury and her subsequent request to God to kill Edward Brodess. She negotiated her own contract with A. C. Thompson; when her brothers backed off, she left bondage on her own. Nobody has ever been able to keep track of her, even those who work underground with and for her—for instance, Thomas Garrett, who is constantly wondering where she is and why she hasn't come when she said she would.

They think she's one place, then, in a flash, she's up and gone, listening only to her voices, figuring out how to follow their orders on her own. Her illiteracy contributes to her silence—releasing her from the obligation of writing letters—as do her blackouts. Others depend on reasoned strategy; Harriet goes off and consults her voices, God, her instincts, or whatever we might choose to call them.

Perhaps she can't help shying away from joining someone else's experiment—even Brown's—knowing it will be run according to standards and plans with which she may or may not agree. Or she may be skeptical about the practicality of his plan. Maybe it seems somewhat too dreamy and, like Nat Turner's insurrection, without enough hard-nosed advance preparation, therefore doomed.

If Rit and Ben have anything to say about the Captain's campaign, as surely they do, they may well rail against any members of their family signing on with the right-minded but possibly foolhardy old man, and with some reason: He is white, does not know slavery and the perniciously crippling effects of fear and torture the way they do, has not lived in the South, does not truly know the slaveholder's intractable will, his capacity for evil.

Rage exists in the margins, which a white man can afford and they cannot. A white man cannot imagine what it is like to go back South voluntarily after escaping slavery. He cannot know how the heart knots in dread, imagining that return. Ben and Rit may even suspect Brown of playing a trick on black people. Why would a white man ask his sons to die—as one already has—for the good of a race not their own?

Harriet stands by the Captain, but she falls out of touch.

Anyway, that's us doing the wondering why, not her. Harriet faces more immediate, practical concerns: the constant pressure for money for her parents' care and for the care of the indigent St. Catharines refugees, as well as funds to finance her trip to Maryland to fetch her last kinfolk. When Captain Brown needs her again, she may figure, she'll be there. In the meantime, she can't afford to clutter her mind with potential possibilities and next year's plans—however noble and right—when more vexing, if mundane, tasks are staring her in the face.

The most pragmatic of visionaries, she returns to St. Catharines.

Early that fall, she travels to Boston and Concord. A letter of introduction in hand, probably from Gerrit Smith, in Concord she meets up with her first biographer, Franklin Sanborn, who acts as a kind of publicity agent for the abolitionist cause. Sanborn helps her find a room in a boardinghouse, probably one owned and operated by free blacks, and, announcing the presence in their midst of the heroine of the day, sets her up to meet with abolitionist and religious groups.

Those who come to the parlor socials and church meetings where she speaks are already believers in her cause, and so naturally they contribute. They have read *Uncle Tom's Cabin*; some have read and heard Frederick Douglass. They are partisans, devoted to the antislavery cause.

But Harriet is more than the sum of her narratives. Her audiences show up expecting to hear horrifying stories of slavery and uplifting tales of courage, but they are in no way prepared to be won over by her in the blink of an evening's performance. If asked in advance, they would be flabbergasted by such a suggestion. To be seduced by a beguiling manner, an affectionate nature, a warm imagination, to come away feeling as if they already *know* her? They are New Englanders, book readers and thinkers, distrusting of quick intimacies, used to walling themselves off from spontaneity. Yet when she rises from her seat and begins her presentation, she draws them to her, beyond even their own desires, and wows them with the immediacy of her presence, the honesty of her gaze, her natural ease with metaphor, analogy, and myth. Dumbfounded at their own inability to resist, they leave amused, charmed, and committed.

Not that she expected notoriety or set out to get it. But now that she has it, she is, above all, *casual* about its presence. To return to Sarah Bradford's description, recorded that day in 1900 on her brother's porch overlooking Lake Owasco, Harriet embodies a quiet dignity that makes her "superior or indifferent to all surrounding circumstances." Never humiliated, never elated. No time for false modesty. Taking things as they come, without comment or complaint. Using whatever assets she possesses or can come by to fulfill her mission.

Audiences spread the word, swearing to others that she is the real thing, that they must hear her for themselves, that there has never been anyone like her. When she tells her stories, using "a wealth of eloquent gesture," she creates scenes of a life her audience can barely imagine. Her voice is resonant and warm and when she sings "Go Down, Moses" or one of the other secret songs of her rescue missions, she fills the room and makes their hearts buzz.

They struggle for language equal to her skills. "She has great dramatic power . . . the scene rises before you as she saw it and her voice and language change with her different actors." She speaks "in a style of quaint simplicity, which [excites] the most profound interest in her hearers." She is "jet black and cannot read or write, only talk, besides acting."

The one-woman show continues until late fall, when she returns to St. Catharines to distribute whatever money she has earned to the refugees and to help her parents face another frigid Christmas and New Year's.

Cold settles in. The dark month arrives, December, the best month for rescues. Eliza Brodess has died of unknown causes, buried in an as-yet-unknown place, perhaps next to Edward. Rachel is thirty-three years old; Harriet, probably feeling her years, is thirty-six; Ben and Angerine, nine and eleven.

But times are trickier than ever on the Eastern Shore. Hysteria runs higher still, as more runaways are making their way to the North. One hundred and fourteen ministers of the Black River Conference of the Methodist Church send a petition to the governor of Maryland, former Dorchester sheriff Thomas H. Hicks, asking for the release from prison of the Reverend Samuel Green. But the property owners and newspapers of the Eastern Shore advise preachers to mind their own business, even white ones, and Hicks declines to free Sam Green.

Harriet might have gone to Dorchester anyway. But with Ben and Rit to care for, only their second winter in Canada, she may feel somewhat stuck.

Christmas: The Ross family can't help thinking of Rachel and her children, Mary Manokey and hers—the ones whose place of residence is, so far, still known to them. The others? They pray to meet up with them again, without much hope of it in this life.

The year turns.

In late winter or early spring of 1859, Harriet receives an offer that will change her life: U.S. senator and Republican presidential hopeful William H. Seward of Auburn, New York, offers to sell her a home.

Although Harriet may not have actually met Seward at this time, she has without doubt visited Auburn. Located in the central part of the state between Rochester and Syracuse, just north of the Finger Lakes, the town is not only situated along her regular route from St. Catharines to Philadelphia; it also has a significant abolitionist community, actively engaged in the Underground Railroad. Harriet might well have brought passengers there to hide out for a night or two on their way to Canada. She might have stayed there alone, on her way back to Philadelphia. While in town, she would have made numerous contacts and met many people, including the passionate feminist and antislavery activist Martha Coffin Wright—the sister of Harriet's Philadelphia colleague, Lucretia Mott—and her lawyer husband, David. In the years ahead, the Wrights and their daughters will become among Harriet's staunchest allies.

To hatch plans and discuss mostly unpopular (and sometime illegal) ideas, women in the abolitionist movement met often, usually in each other's living rooms, where they could pretend to be simply gabbing. Martha Coffin Wright played a big part in this kind of organizing, as did her close friend Frances Miller Seward—the senator's wife—and Frances's sister, Lazette Miller. Perhaps Harriet performed for the women, or made speeches. She might have described how her family was suffering in Canada, and told the women how she was hoping to find another place for them, perhaps in western New York, in a community where abolitionists and friends lived. Maybe the Auburn women took on Harriet's house hunting as a mission, and put the bug in Seward's ear. Or maybe he thought up the idea himself.

However it happened, William Seward sent Harriet a message. He wanted to provide her and her family with a home.

Located on a seven-acre piece of property in Cayuga County, near the tollgate on the Auburn-Fleming line, the property included a barn, some outbuildings, and a tillable plot of land in a friendly community. Plenty of room for her family. Land to grow things, feed some chickens, maybe get a cow to milk. Or pigs.

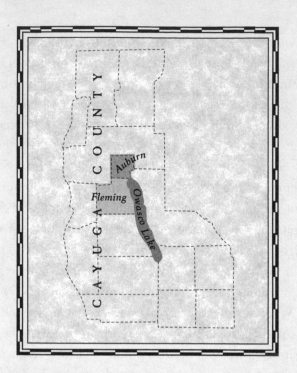

Modeled after an 1875 map of Cayuga County, showing property owners:

A The Auburn home of William Seward, which faces South Street.

B South Street, which runs between Seward's home and the acreage he sold to Harriet.

C Harriet's home and property, which on the 1875 map was mistakenly listed as belonging to "H. Tupman." Just above her home is the brickyard where her brother and second husband, Nelson Davis, probably worked. Later, her property will be listed on published maps as H. T. Davis, since by then she has legally married her second husband, Nelson Davis, who died in 1888.

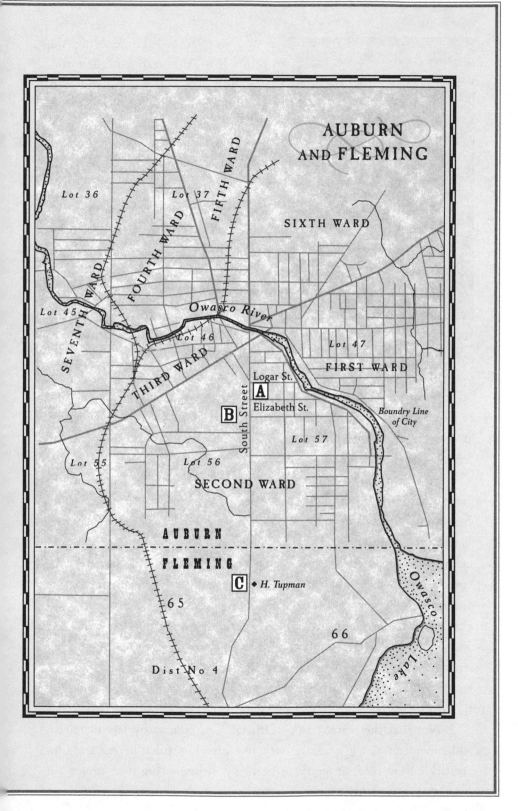

AUBURN
AND FLEMING

Lot 36

Lot 37

FIFTH WARD

FOURTH WARD

SIXTH WARD

SEVENTH WARD

Lot 45

Owasco River

Lot 46

THIRD WARD

Lot 47

FIRST WARD

Logar St.

A

Elizabeth St.

South Street

B

Boundry Line
of City

Lot 57

Lot 55

Lot 56

SECOND WARD

AUBURN

FLEMING

C ◆ H. Tupman

Owasco
Lake

65

66

Dist No 4

William Seward

Seven acres. A home. Little Araminta Ross, the strange-headed middle child of a slave woman and man, an illiterate fugitive from the law of the land, an American home owner!

Some say Seward offered to give Harriet the house but that she insisted on paying for it. Perhaps that is the case, but there is no written evidence of it. Seward had sold other homes to immigrants and families in need; later, he and his son built small frame houses to sell to black people who had come north. Since in no instance did he offer to donate land or a house to a needy family, there is no compelling reason to think he did so for Harriet.

In any case, they come to an agreement. Harriet will pay Seward twelve hundred dollars for the property, to be paid on terms he describes as "easy": twenty-five dollars down, with quarterly payments of ten dollars plus interest.

Seward has always supported abolition as well as black and immigrant rights, and he has built houses before now for people in need in his community, but none of his philanthropic offers have been as generous as the one he presents to Harriet. The recently organized (1854) Republican party is looking for a presidential candidate for 1860. Seward is favored. Perhaps he thinks a gift to Harriet will enhance his reputation among those who would vote against the extension of slavery. Or maybe either he or someone in his family has attended one of her performances and was bowled over enough to want to do something for her beyond donating money. Or perhaps cynicism is not in order. Since he is wealthy enough to afford the gesture, maybe Seward decides it is simply the right, the proper thing to do.

Not that there aren't risks. Officially, of course, by law Harriet is still considered not just a slave but a thief, having stolen herself and others from Maryland property owners. By aiding a fugitive, under the tenets of the Fugitive Slave Act, Seward risks imprisonment and a fine. By settling in the United States instead of keeping always on the dodge, Harriet risks being captured and taken back to Maryland to serve out her time in bondage.

But William Seward and Harriet Tubman take their chances and strike a deal, and Harriet transports Rit and Ben and her brother John to Auburn, where they will live in their own home, with no one looking on or making decisions for them. A long, long way from the barns and slave quarters of the many slaveholders who have owned or worked them, from Atthow Pattison to Anthony Thompson, Edward Brodess, Polish Mills, James Cook . . . and the rest.

Once the old folks are safely settled in, Harriet leaves. Even more in need of money now, for upkeep and house payments, she heads east on another fund-raising tour.

Her usual routine takes her first to Sanborn's house in Concord. The enthusiastic Sanborn starts the ball rolling. More in demand than ever, Harriet specializes in small gatherings that take place in parlors and salons, and in church vestries. The coziness works to her advantage. She is not a lecturer. She is an actor and a dramatist, and to make the most of her gifts, she needs to connect intimately with her audience. Besides, women aren't expected to speak in lecture halls.

In Boston, she makes a particularly noteworthy appearance, called by antislavery activist Lucy Osgood a "unique entertainment." In a letter, Osgood describe Harriet as coal black and says that although she was a slave only three years ago, she has taken "leg bail" and is now assisting others to do the same. Osgood quotes from stories Harriet told about her attempt to bring John Tubman north: "I had his clothes," she says. "But no husband." She also meets up at least once with John Brown, at the home of abolitionist Wendell Phillips, where Brown introduces her as General Tubman, and calls her one of the best and bravest persons on the continent. She consults with Brown, suggesting the Fourth of July as a time to "raise the mill." He requests that she return to Canada to recruit soldiers but makes no comment on the Fourth of July suggestion.

She visits Ralph Waldo Emerson, speaks to women's groups and Unitarian organizations, makes appearances with the Bronson Alcott family and Mrs. Horace Mann, is given reading lessons, which—perhaps because of her head injury, complicated by her impatience—don't take.

By early summer, she has decided not to go back to Canada to recruit for Brown, but to stay in the area and work in local hotels. She plans to return to her regular UGRR schedule, using the money she makes at summer hotel jobs to finance a rescue trip in December. Between jobs, she performs. In mid-June she speaks in Worcester, Massachusetts, at the church of Thomas Wentworth Higginson, who promotes her talk like a carnival barker, promising "tales of adventure . . . beyond anything in fiction," and, because of her ingenuity and generalship, calls her the greatest heroine of the age. Having been told by Harriet that she is going back to get her sister and her children, Higginson warns that in Maryland she will "probably be burned alive whenever she is caught, which she probably will be . . . as she is going again."

She appears again at the Fourth of July Anti-Slavery Convention in Framingham. Higginson, president of the organization, introduces her by withholding her name while he describes her adventures and rescues. When a reporter from the abolitionist journal *The Liberator* tries to describe her speaking skills, he flounders. Words, he admits, have failed him. And so the reporter refuses to further describe her particular gifts and style, urging his readers instead to take the earliest opportunity to go and hear Harriet themselves.

After her talk, Higginson again rises to ask for contributions. The money, he suggests, will enable Harriet to buy a little place for her father and mother where they can live and support themselves. This, Higginson implies, will free Harriet from that responsibility, so that she can resume her main job as an Underground Railroad conductor. He does not mention her contract with Seward.

After the Fourth, she returns to hotel work until August 1, a day when jubilees are held throughout the New England states, celebrating the twenty-first anniversary of the emancipation of West Indian slaves. On that day, she attends the New England Colored Citizens' Convention in Boston. The convention adopts a number of resolutions, including one denouncing the colonization movement, whose intent is to remove black people from the United States and send them to Africa to live in colonies.

Harriet nods off, comes back, nods. Then it is her turn.

Presumably to disguise her identity, she is introduced as "Harriet Garrison."

Coming to the speakers' platform, she moves without obligatory opening flourishes straight into a story.

There once was a man, she says, who sowed onions and garlic to feed his cows, having heard that this would increase his dairy production and bring him greater profits. But once the garlic and onions had settled in the cows' bellies, the milk took on their flavors and the butter churned up with too strong a taste. Nobody would buy it. And so the farmer returned to the old method and went back to sowing clover. But it was too late. The wind had blown onions and garlic over his fields, and they sprouted once again. And the clover came up tasting of them, as did the butter. There was no going back.

"Just so," Harriet declares, arriving at the moral of her tale, "the white people have got the 'nigger' here to do their drudgery and now they [are] trying to root them out and send them to Africa."

They can't do it, she promises the approving crowd. Like garlic and onions, "we're rooted here and they can't pull us up."

Schooled by necessity, she understands language and the elements of narration, using suspense to create narrative flow, employing metaphor, song, and symbol with the skill of a poet. Because she has been forced to disguise meaning and message from those who are in control of language, she has created her own, making skilled use of established conventions when they prove useful to her cause. As James Baldwin, speaking of the "black English" furor, will write some 120 years later, "A language comes into existence by means of brutal necessity, and the rules of the language are dictated by what the language must convey."

White supremacy and slavery make it imperative that a slave—a black man, woman, or child—learn to speak in a private tongue, crucial to communication among his or her people, while entirely unfathomable to slaveholders. A secret language, coded, the grammar and vocabulary of which include use of symbols, song, and metaphor. At which Harriet is past master.

The summer winds down. John Brown meets with Frederick Douglass, who—finally hearing of Brown's plan to raid the arsenal at Harpers

Ferry—concludes that the scheme is unworkable, if not mad. He will not participate. Harriet has dropped from sight, and when Brown asks Sanborn about her, Sanborn says she is probably in New Bedford, ill. Halfway between Providence and Buzzards Bay, New Bedford is a town with a strong community of prospering free blacks and abolitionists, one that Harriet regularly visits. But there is no documentation to support Sanborn's claim and no indication from any other source to suggest that his conjecture is based on fact. Possibly it's a guess. Or maybe he's covering for her.

The Captain heads toward Pennsylvania without summoning Josiah Bailey or any of the other Canadians who hooked up with him in St. Catharines. Harriet does not show up or respond in any way to his requests. Ten years from now, in 1869, she will tell the abolitionist Martha Coffin Wright that when Captain Brown called on her before Harpers Ferry, she *was not home*. Not that the Captain came to her house or knocked on her door. A metaphor, more than likely, revealing Harriet's growing disinclination to enlist. Like Douglass, she may have had huge doubts about Brown's plan.

Or perhaps she is waiting for a message to tell her what to do. When word doesn't come, she hides out. Is not at home for John Brown. Covers her face from her own doubts. Goes underground.

The Captain and his raiders rent a farmhouse in Maryland.

Two and a half months after her anticolonization talk, Harriet finds herself in New York City when, during the evening hours of Sunday, October 16, 1859, John Brown and twenty-one other men leave the farmhouse in Maryland to conduct a raid on the U.S. government's stockpile of weapons stored at the arsenal in Harpers Ferry, Virginia.

On that day, or perhaps the next—before the news of the raid has become public knowledge, at any rate—she tells the woman in whose house she is a guest that something is wrong, she can't tell what exactly, but she is certain that some terrible thing is happening that has to do with Captain Brown. He is in trouble and they will soon hear the bad news.

News of the shocking raid is quickly forthcoming, but John Brown is not identified as its leader until Wednesday. When Harriet hears of the failure of the raid, the wounding of the Captain, and the death of two of his sons and so many others, she finally understands the dream of the three-headed serpent. The two younger heads were those of the Captain's sons, who went down first, suffering wretchedly painful deaths. And now it is the Captain's turn.

Between October 17 and December 2, Harriet broods on Harpers Ferry and prays that some good will come of it. While she unquestionably perceives her prayers as a conversation with God as direct and practical as one with a friend, it is also possible to configure them in nonreligious terms, as a way of figuring things out, of—as she will explain to Ednah Dow Cheney about the aftermath of Harpers Ferry—*studying and studying* a situation or event until she resolves it in some way and finds some kind of epiphany. To stay on track and hold on to her faith, she requires a constructive conclusion, an explanation she can somehow categorize as hopeful enough to lift her and her people up and give them something to cling to as they ride into the next phase of their uncertain future.

During this time of uncertain and edgy apprehension, Harriet nonetheless receives a dictated letter from her brother John, who in her absence is caring for their parents in Auburn. John complains mightily about the burden of his responsibility, especially the necessity of making decisions for their father, who despite his arthritis and declining health, has it in his mind to *walk* to Canada to retrieve some of his belongings. Indicating his displeasure at her lack of communication, John wonders when Sister Harriet will be home again, to make decisions for the family and see to it that Seward receives a mortgage payment. Once again, then, the family relies on their damaged and exhausted sibling and daughter to take care of them all, all of the time.

Perhaps she goes quickly back to Auburn to settle up with her family and make a fast trip to St. Catharines to get Ben's things. Maybe she talks to someone in the Seward family about her debt.

And then she returns to Boston.

By early November, John Brown has been convicted of murder, conspiracy, and treason against Virginia and condemned to die. He spends the last weeks of his life writing eloquent letters and giving interviews, spreading the word about the necessity of military action against the slave

A dictated letter to Harriet from her brother John Stewart in which he complains about the burdens of caring for his mother and father, even though at this time, Harriet's very life is at risk as she awaits the fate of John Brown and his coconspirators, including herself. (*Transcription of letter appears at bottom of page.*)

states. Beyond politics, even his jailers and the governor of Virginia come to admire the Old Man's courage, and call him the gamest man they ever met.

On the day of his execution, December 2, 1859, he writes his final, and now famous, message to his countrymen: "I, John Brown, am now quite *certain* that the crimes of this *guilty land* will never be purged *away* but with Blood. I had *as I now think vainly* flattered myself that without *very much* bloodshed it might be done."

Harriet remains in the East, studying and praying.

At about noon on that same balmy winter day, wearing the same raggedy outfit he had on during the raid, John Brown ascends the scaffold, stepping firmly and without dread or doubt. His head hooded in white, with fifteen hundred soldiers and militiamen watching, he is hanged on a newly built gallows in a wide field in Charlestown, Virginia. His body hangs for thirty-five minutes before being cut down.

(*Transcription*)

Auburn, Nov 1st 1859

Sister Harriet Tubman

I am well and hope you are the same. Father's health is very good, for him. I received your welcome letter yesterday, which relieved my uneasiness. We thought quite hard of you for not writing before. We would like to see you much but if you can do better where you are you had perhaps better stay. Father wanted to go to Canada after his things on foot, but I would not consent as I thought it would be too much for him, and he consents to stay until he gets your advice on the subject as he has no means for going. Please write as soon as possible and not delay. We three are alone, I have a good deal of trouble with them as they are getting old and feeble. There was a man by the name of Young that promised father a stove and some things to go to keeping the house but has refused to do anything for them. Brother John has been with father ever since he left Troy and is doing the best he can. Catherine Stewart has not come yet but wants to very bad. Send what things you want father to bring if you think best for him to go. I am going to send a letter to Wm Henry if you wish me to say anything for you to him, let me know when you write. Seward has received nothing as payment since the 4th of July that I know of. Write me particularly what you want me to do as I want to hear from you very much. I would like to know what luck you have had since you have been gone, have heard that you are doing well. Hope to find it so. Direct my letter to me, Box 750, Auburn.

Truly yours,

John Stewart

[Note: Punctuation and capitalization added by author.]

Two weeks later, four other raiders will be hanged, the two white men on separate gallows from the two black. In the spring, two more will die.

As ordered in his last requests, John Brown's body is taken to Philadelphia, where it is placed in a coffin untouched by slave labor, then rolled on up to North Elba, New York. There, in the settlement established by Gerrit Smith, he is buried.

On her first visit to Concord after the Captain's execution, Harriet is taken by some of her friends into the home of George L. Stearns, a member of the Secret Six. There, they usher her into a room in which stands, on the mantel, a white marble bust of Brown, commissioned by Stearns during Brown's final days. The very sight of the statue throws Harriet into something like an ecstatic fit, and while the others stand and wait, she moans and sings her way through a kind of rhapsody of grief and veneration. Brown had cut his beard to within an inch of his jaw before he was hanged. But the bust has him fully bearded, like Moses, as he had been in Harriet's dream.

Two weeks later, on the day when the four other men are to be hanged, Harriet goes to see Ednah Dow Cheney in Boston.

At first, she says she won't take up Cheney's time, even to sit down. All she needs is an address. But she can't, she finds, leave. Her heart is too full and she needs to talk.

She's been, she tells Cheney, studying and studying the situation.

What has become clear to her is that it wasn't John Brown who died on the gallows. Because when she thinks about how he gave up his life for her people and never flinched, but remained brave to the end, she understands that those acts weren't just of mortal man, but of the God in John Brown. And that when she remembers the groans and tears and prayers she's heard on the plantation and remembers that God is a prayer-hearing God, she feels that *his* time is drawing near.

Cheney questions her about this. Does Harriet believe that God's time is near?

God's time is always near, Harriet replies.

And she goes into one of her soulful recitations, giving God credit for the gift of her own strength and voices. When God set the North Star in the heavens, she states with certainty, he meant for her to be free.

She goes on and on, speaking in a strain of what Cheney later describes as sublime eloquence, sanguine and visionary, inspired by the life and death of John Brown.

To another friend, she declares that Brown did more in dying than one hundred men would in living—a prediction that will turn out to be true.

In the aftermath of the execution, U.S. marshals discover papers in the Maryland farmhouse where Brown had quartered his troops before the raid. Mostly, these letters give the names of supporters and contacts, including Frederick Douglass, Gerrit Smith, Frank Sanborn . . . and Harriet Tubman.

Members of the Secret Six frantically burn incriminating documents. Some plan to leave the country. Douglass goes immediately from Rochester to Canada and then to England on a speech-making tour. The very emotional Gerrit Smith suffers a kind of nervous breakdown and is put in an asylum, suffering from what is called an "exaltation of the mind leading to periods of wildness."

Others of the Six leave or stay, depending upon their inclination.

As advised, Harriet goes, unhappily no doubt, to St. Catharines, perhaps after traveling to Auburn to round up her parents and take them with her, since none of them is listed in Auburn census records of 1860. December, of course, is the month she had planned to go to Maryland, but the whole of that state, and of Virginia, is in an uproar presently, so obviously she cannot go.

The year turns. A new decade arrives.

Rit and Ben remain in Canada, but within a month's time, Harriet is back in Auburn. After paying Seward $174.81 for interest and principal, reducing her debt to $876.95, she goes back on the road. First, she travels to Massachusetts, as usual. She will spend the spring as she always does, raising money to finance a rescue from Maryland, her last one.

In early 1860, the trader Thomas Willis sells away Harriet Jolley's thirteen-year-old daughter, Mary Jane/Ann, thus sundering the remaining sanctity of this family entirely, sending mother and daughters into unknown, separate futures, each alone from the other, mother from daughters, sister from sister.

Linah, her daughter, now her granddaughters, gone.

Imagine how it must tear at Harriet's heart—and at her parents'—to think of this latest violence wrought upon the life of Linah Ross and her descendants, especially when they are safe from it themselves, or will be, as long as they stay where they are.

Early that year, U.S. marshals show up in Auburn, having been advised of the presence there of runaways. Harpers Ferry raider Osborne P. Anderson, who escaped capture and found his way to Auburn, quickly leaves, headed back to Canada, where he will remain.

In the 1860 census, Richard "Broadas," twenty-eight-year-old son of Edward and Eliza, estimates that he owns three thousand dollars' worth of real estate. Still living with him in the same small house Anthony Thompson built for their father are four grown brothers, who range in age from thirty-three to twenty-one.

In the slave schedule, Brodess lists only two slaves, a female of fourteen and a male of twelve, clearly Angerine and Ben. No quarters have yet been built as housing for slaves. And there is no mention of Rachel.

Wherever her baby sister may be, by the end of the year, Harriet intends to have snatched her away, her niece and her nephew as well, and to have delivered them unto their relatives in either Canada or Auburn—where they belong.

Last Rescue

*[Harriet] loves action; I think she does not dislike fighting in
a good cause . . .*

—EDNAH DOW CHENEY, "MOSES,
FREEDMEN'S RECORD," MARCH 1865

They can only kill a dozen of us. Come on.

—"FUGITIVE SLAVE RESCUE IN TROY,"
TROY WHIG, APRIL 28, 1860

During the winter and spring of 1860, Harriet goes traveling again, first down to Auburn, where she gives Seward the house payment, then east from there, boarding a train when she can, other times
perhaps traipsing along the towpath of the Erie Canal or walking the
banks of the Mohawk. Her schedule, as always, a leapfrogging improvi-
sation, one stop to the next.

In Syracuse, she meets with pacifist-abolitionist Unitarian minister
Samuel May, who, after hearing her speak, provides her with a letter of
introduction to take with her to her next appearance. Since at this
time, no pictures of her have been published, most people don't know
exactly what she looks like, and she may need proof. Sometimes, according to Sanborn, for her own protection Harriet carries a daguerreo-
type of a well-known antislavery activist, which, upon arrival, she
presents to a potential host or hostess to identify.

From Syracuse, she continues east, then goes slightly north, probably stopping over in Peterboro to visit with Gerrit Smith.

Smith requests that she attend the large antislavery meeting to be held at the end of May in Boston. She agrees.

But Smith is a worrier and emotionally fragile. He almost certainly sends her off with a warning: She must be on the lookout and take backroads whenever possible. The countryside is rank with snoopers and spies. President Buchanan has appointed a commission to investigate the crimes for which John Brown was executed—the Mason Commission. Marshals have been sent to search for Brown's accomplices. Sanborn has been picked up and questioned, and while brief, his detention has had a chilling effect.

She leaves Smith's grand mansion.

Her timetable remains the same: raise money in the spring and fall, travel into slave country to bring out Rachel and the children when nights grow long and running away safer. While riding the train, she studies the coming months, nods off, comes to, does more studying.

A routine trip. All seems to remain the same, and perhaps she convinces herself nothing has changed. But Harriet is older, and she hasn't been to Maryland in three years. She is not stone, nor is she myth. Think back for a moment to the time when she took John Tubman a new suit of clothes, only to find him living with another woman; remember her wish to stir up a pot of trouble for the two-timer and his new woman, no matter the consequences, a completely normal human response. Beyond her public persona, her heart has needs and reasons, and hidden breaking points.

And while it is certainly fruitless to speculate on what else she might be thinking during the long hours walking and riding, it is also important to remind ourselves, she has her moments of wistfulness, regret, doubt, vanity . . . like anybody. And that she did not set out to become Moses or to be called that, but when people needed her to be the one, she knew she could do the job and took it on, even the money-scrounging dirty work.

Sometime around the middle of March, she reaches the Oneida Institute in Whitesboro, near Utica.

There she is the guest of honor at a reception given by the radical abolitionist Beriah Green. She gives her usual talk. Noting her introductory papers from Samuel May, Green sends her off with further in-troductions to friends in the town of New York Mills, where she speaks again.

She then continues east to the place where the Mohawk intersects with the Hudson. She passes through Albany, perhaps taking time to meet with her UGRR colleague Stephen Myers, then crosses the Hudson into Rensselaer County. She has family in Troy and will stop there with her cousin John H. Hooper, an Underground Railroad operator who has lived in the Albany-Troy area for thirteen years.

Last days of April. A month from now, she must be in Boston for the meeting.

Harriet does not plan to stay long in Troy. She has much to ac-complish in the coming months. By early to mid-November, she hopes to be on her way south, even though circumstances there remain chaotic. John Brown has been dead but four and a half months; the last two of his raiders were hanged within the past six weeks; the mood of the country borders on hysteria, while slaveholders remain panicked and edgy. In Douglass's opinion, since Harpers Ferry, the prevailing fierceness of mind and feeling in the South have become furious and all but uncontrollable.

Hooper hustles her into his Second Street home. Well schooled in guerrilla tactics, he knows how, when called upon, to provide safe refuge.

They exchange stories and family news. Almost certainly, Harriet has stopped at her cousin's house before, on her way from New York to Syracuse and back. Now she's going South again, her third attempt to rescue Rachel. You have to wonder: Mightn't she be entertaining some doubts this time? Her early biographers, friends, and interviewers have all said no, emphasizing her unwavering certitude, whatever the cir-cumstances. After all, she *said* she never had the least misgivings, and they took her at her word.

But it has been almost eleven years since she first escaped, and three since her last trip to Dorchester. In February or March, she turned thirty-eight. While still enormously agile and energetic, she is no longer considered young. Excluding her first trip back into slave country—which may have required the greatest store of courage and nerve—this one seems the chanciest yet, especially considering the times, her age, and the haunting possibility that she has used up her ration of luck and caginess.

Whatever her internal musings, she keeps them to herself. John Brown remained unflinching and brave to the end. She can do no less than follow the Captain's lead.

In the early-afternoon hours of April 27, she is probably readying herself for her coming journey, when a message streaks through the black community: A fugitive slave has been captured and taken into custody in downtown Troy and is about to be sent back to Virginia.

A hero brooks no pause between information and action; when Harriet hears the news, she grabs her sunbonnet and pitches headlong down the street into a situation in which, of course, the very U.S. officials looking for her will be major participants. Giving the matter no thought, she goes, aiming toward State Street, where the man, Charles Nalle, is being held prisoner.

A number of local stories and eyewitness accounts, including reports in the *Troy Whig* and the *Troy Daily Times* and a statement written by a prominent Troy attorney, Martin Townsend, provide information about Charles Nalle. His plight and subsequent rescue will make national news, and the stories will be reprinted in a number of newspapers, all of them noting the background, the history, and especially the skin color of the fugitive.

Having escaped from Virginia bondage in 1858, Nalle had lived until recently in Pennsylvania with his manumitted wife and their five children. In the past month or so, however, he'd come to Sand Lake, New York, an abolitionist community fifteen miles west of Troy, to live and work as a coachman for the wealthy Uri Gilbert, hoping soon to bring his family to live with him. Nalle is described as about thirty years old, handsome, tall, an excellent servant, possibly the son of his master, or even his half brother—in any case, a dead ringer for him and as light-skinned as a pure white man. His wife is equally pale, having been fathered and raised by her own master. Martin Townsend describes the couple as persons of refined sensibilities, and labels them "octoroons," which is to say, in the ludicrous terms of the day, seven-eighths white, one-eighth black. Some of their children, he adds, even have red hair and no trace of physical Africanness. As if Charles Nalle's white skin renders the attempt to return him to slavery that much more reprehensible.

At the moment, none of this matters. Whatever the racial cocktail of his DNA, however infused his blood with Caucasian fluids, under the terms of the Fugitive Slave Act, Charles Nalle is a slave, a runaway, a black man, and a thief.

In Troy, he has been boarding at the Division Street home of William Henry, a black antislavery activist. To remain in contact with his wife, the illiterate Nalle hired a local lawyer to read and write letters for him. But once the lawyer learned of Nalle's history, he communicated the fugitive's whereabouts to his former owner. The slaveholder then sent an agent, Henry Wall, to file with U.S. commissioner Miles Beach the necessary papers and have the man returned to him.

Early morning, April 27, 1860, a Friday. While Nalle makes his way to his job in Sand Lake, Commissioner Beach is signing off on the order. At this point, all proceedings have been conducted in private and on paper. No one knows what is about to happen except Commissioner Beach, the Virginia slaveholder Blucher Hansborough, and his agent Henry Wall, and U.S. marshal J. W. Holmes and his deputy.

All await an opportunity to seize the fugitive.

At about 11:00 A.M., the Gilberts send Nalle to a bakery to purchase bread. Since he works for the family as a coachman, presumably Nalle either goes on horseback or takes a carriage. He is followed beyond the borders of the antislavery neighborhood, then apprehended. Gilbert knows full well of Nalle's fugitive status, and when his employee fails to return home swiftly, probably in time for the midday meal, he sends his son to William Henry's home to find out what has happened.

By the time they track Nalle down, it is two o'clock. Hearing that a former slave is being held in the commissioner's custody, black citizens and all abolitionists of the city become instantly aroused, this being the first attempt in Troy to put the provisions of the Fugitive Slave Act into action. People leave their homes and jobs, some planning to stage a daring daytime rescue like the one in Syracuse in 1850, others to protest, and some for no reason other than a desire to be there. The *Troy Whig* will describe the scene as one of "unexampled excitement . . . a terrific encounter between officers and the prisoner's friends . . . a grand state of turmoil," which, that night, will dominate every other topic of conversation in the city, including the Charleston, South Carolina, nomination of Stephen A. Douglas as Democratic presidential candidate.

By the time William Henry—a former slave himself—arrives, people have already gathered in knots of ten or twelve, clogging the sidewalks and street corner. Henry works the crowd, shouting to them to keep watch of the stairs leading from Beach's office, because they will soon see a man being taken to the depot in handcuffs and placed on the first train to Virginia.

Thus exhorted and stirred, the crowd grows more restive and of one mind.

By the time Harriet gets there, wagons have congregated in the streets, and spectators have piled on top of one another in an effort to see. Women are shouting and crying. Pulling at the long brim of her sunbonnet until her face is all but covered, Harriet hunches her shoulders and hobbles toward the door of the commissioner's office as if on her last legs, thus appearing to those in charge of watching for troublemakers as an aged crone: a harmless, if not all but invisible, adjunct to the situation.

From the street, people can see Nalle at a second-story window. As Henry exhorts the crowd to keep watch, Harriet quietly arrives at the stairway. She climbs a few steps and stops, holding her position near a window. From the street, people see her sunbonnet. She is well-known among the black community in Troy, and Bradford says that once the iconic sunbonnet came into view, the people on the street knew who she was.

Word is quietly passed among them: Moses is with them, and as long as Moses is there, Nalle is safe.

Unbeknownst to those on the street, Martin Townsend has agreed to act as counsel to Nalle and has obtained a writ of habeas corpus, to be acted upon immediately in the offices of state supreme court judge Gould, some two blocks away. And so, as ordered, the U.S. marshal and his deputy place the manacled Nalle between them and proceed shoulder-to-shoulder toward the stairs. As they head down, someone cries, "Fire!"

The fire bell sounds, but the wagons can't get through. The alarm proves false, but the clanging has agitated the crowd. Still, the officers struggle down the stairs, heading into the fray. At the bottom, they meet up with the old woman in the sunbonnet, still twitching away as if utterly decrepit. At first, she refuses to move.

Then she turns to the crowd. "Here they come!" she shouts through the open door, her heavy-timbered voice carrying farther even than Henry's. "Take him!"

Pandemonium. Pulling, pushing, mauling, hauling, surging, shouting, frantic efforts by the rescuers, stern resistance from the men the *Whig* reporter calls "the conservators of the law."

Harriet darts into the crowd, heedless of consequence and as fierce as a wild thing, her low center of gravity and compact build supplying her with the leverage and athleticism needed to surprise an officer with a knee-level tackle, pulling him down while shouting, according to one observer, "Give us liberty or give us death."

Ignoring her age, a policeman clubs her in return. Harriet doesn't go down, but returns the blow, in her words, "knocking him squawking," while struggling so stubbornly and unself-consciously that most of her outer clothes are torn off.

She grabs hold of Nalle.

"Drag us out!" she cries to her compatriots. "Drag him to the river. *Drown him but don't let them have him!*"

Locked together, Harriet half-carrying Nalle, the two are shoved to the ground together, only to rise again, and then be brought down again, the helpless Nalle's wrists and head by now pouring forth blood. Twenty times, says the *Troy Daily Times*, the prisoner was snatched from the officers and twenty times returned; still, the ancient, sunbonneted colored woman held fast.

There is a Texas saying, one of those unfathomable truisms that survive despite their vague inscrutability, describing the diligence of a snapping turtle once it has locked its jaws on human flesh. "It won't let go," the saying goes, "till it thunders."

Like the Texas snapping turtle, Harriet clamps down on Nalle until, as one writer suggests, perhaps he wished to be saved from *her,* rather than from the marshals.

While the reports of the incredible rescue of Charles Nalle vary only in detail, the story still seems—as Bradford suggests—almost too good to be true. But eyewitness accounts add undeniable heft to Bradford's sometimes flowered-up narrative, corroborating it several times over. The newspaper reports do not mention Harriet by name, referring to her instead as a somewhat antiquated or venerable old colored woman who turned out to be the one most conspicuously opposed to the taking of Charles Nalle. But in his statement, Martin Townsend makes no bones about who was there that day:

> Harriet Tubman, who had been standing with the excited crowd, rushed amongst the foremost to Nalle and, running one of her arms around his manacled arm, held on to him without ever loosening her hold through the more than half-hour's struggle to Judge Gould's office and from Judge Gould's office to the dock . . . In the melee, she was repeatedly beaten over the head with policemen's clubs, but she never for a moment released her hold, but cheered Nalle and his friends with her voice, and struggled with the officers until they were literally worn out with their exertions, and Nalle was separated from them. True, she had strong and earnest helpers in her struggle, some of whom had white faces as well as human hearts . . . but she exposed herself to the fury of the sympathizers with slavery, without fear, and suffered their blows without flinching.

And didn't let go until it thundered.

Harriet and the crowd hustle Nalle down Congress Street to the waterfront, where they tumble the shackled prisoner forward into a boat and set forth across the Hudson to West Troy, in Albany County.

By then, a number of Troy policemen have broken through the crowd, as well. Arriving at the docks, they board a ferry, followed by as many as three hundred of Nalle's supporters. The jammed ferry sets off across the river.

When the boat containing the prisoner docks, Nalle attempts to run away. But West Troy policemen, having been notified by telegraph wire of the escape, are waiting, and when the handcuffed, bleeding prisoner attempts to flee, they quickly seize and arrest him.

Soon after, the ferry arrives, discharging policemen, marshals, and rescuers. Joined by supporters from West Troy, Harriet and the sympathizing crowd strike out in the direction of Judge Stewart's chambers, hoping to storm the door. Stones fly, hit their mark, then bullets.

The crowd retreats.

"They've got pistols," says one.

"Who cares," replies another. "They can only kill a dozen of us. Come on."

More stones, more pistol shots; eventually, an "immense Negro" man attacks the door to the sheriff's office. The man is quickly felled by a glancing blow of the sheriff's hatchet but not before he opens the door and then falls hard upon it, enabling the crowd to pull Charles Nalle out of the building and into the street, where Harriet and a number of other black women are waiting. Rallying, the immense man runs into the night. The women guide the exhausted and heavily bleeding Nalle into a wagon. From there, the fugitive begins his journey into western New York State and, finally, Canada.

Martin Townsend ends his story with pure lawyerly razzle-dazzle. How Harriet Tubman came to be in Troy that day, he writes, remains a mystery, as do her whereabouts after the rescue, when the crowd dispersed. After a mighty and undeniable struggle conducted within sight of a thousand—perhaps even five thousand!—spectators, she simply disappeared.

Like a mythical hero, the savior drops down at the exact moment of greatest need, fights, conquers, vanishes.

April yields to May. From Troy, Harriet makes her way to Springfield, in western Massachusetts, and then across the state to Boston and then Concord, a total of more than 170 miles. It is comforting to think she takes the train, giving her wounds time to heal as she rides.

She speaks, performs, sees old friends, gathers funds for her trip, perhaps sends money to Ben and Rit, who have returned to Auburn. When, by August, she has not collected a sufficient amount, she sends a dictated letter to abolitionist Wendell Phillips, reminding him of his promise (probably made at a July 4 suffrage meeting in Boston) to supply whatever sum she still lacked of the one hundred dollars she needed before leaving. She needs at least twenty dollars, she tells Phillips, re-questing that he send that amount to a certain Mr. Walcott, who will for-ward the money to her in Philadelphia.

She closes the letter to Phillips with a note about her health: "I am as well as usual for me and in good spirits." The comment "well as usual for me" seems to refer to her sometimes fragile health and the wounds she received in Troy, suggesting as well that she begins this arduous jour-ney with optimism, if in a somewhat compromised state of health.

By now, Abraham Lincoln has beaten out William Seward in the run for Republican presidential candidacy. Harriet hasn't sent Seward a house payment since January, but, taken up with the arduous campaign, he doesn't seem to press her. In August, the Radical Abolition party nomi-nates Gerrit Smith as its candidate for the presidency, so that he may, in Douglass's words, bear "aloft the banner of pure Abolitionism." On No-vember 6, Lincoln is elected president with only 40 percent of the vote, having adopted a moderate platform that prohibits the further extension of slavery but makes no mention of abolition.

By this time, Harriet has left Philadelphia—where she presumably picked up the twenty dollars that she had requested Wendell Phillips send to Walcott—and crossed into the South.

Winter has settled in early, snow soon to fall. Upon her arrival in Dorchester, Harriet sends word from a chilly hiding place in the woods that she is in the vicinity and is ready to take out Rachel, Angerine, and Ben.

The world she once knew has changed. The grapevine telegraph system of the enslaved does not work as efficiently as it once did. People are fearful, cautious. Since the trouble arising from the discovery of John Brown's papers, Underground Railroad agents aren't keeping the kinds of records they used to, not even William Still. People are walking with their heads down, keeping their thoughts to themselves. Many of Har-riet's associates have left the South—some with her assistance. And so news is harder to come by, less likely, even, to be sent.

All this trouble she has gone to, all those times she came and Rachel wouldn't go. So determined. Her last sister. And now she has come too late. Either she is told upon making the request or her scout goes to

Bucktown and finds out. However it arrives, the news is devastating. Harriet's last sister has died, some say only a little before her arrival, but since Rachel wasn't listed in that year's census, perhaps it happened some months earlier. In any case, Rachel has been "released from her labors some time since by that friend of the poor slave, the Angel of Death."

Too late is a stone-cold, terrible fact to face, but Harriet cannot allow herself to dwell on it. Rachel had been determined not to free herself unless she could take her children with her. Harriet now must honor her sister's commitment and find a way to take out Angerine and Ben.

But she needs thirty dollars more than she has, either for a bribe or to secure the children's transport to her one way or another. Thirty dollars is a lot of money. Harriet doesn't have that much, but in no way does she expect anyone to take on such a risky job—stealing the Brodess's last two slaves—without payment. The very air of the countryside feels agitated and threatening. Mob spirit is alive everywhere. Slave catchers prowl the backwoods and swamps. Anybody who steps out of line does so with the greatest trepidation and only for a price. Down here, Harriet has no way to come by even a dollar, much less thirty.

She may try to put one final plan into action. Bradford says that on Harriet's last trip to Maryland, a party of fugitives was supposed to meet her in a wood. When night fell, as Harriet awaited the party's arrival, a raging wind blew in, bringing with it a blinding snowstorm. Harriet hid behind a tree as best as she could, remaining exposed to the storm all night long. But the party did not show up. Might it have included thirteen-year-old Angerine and eleven-year-old Ben?

Whatever happened—whether Ben and Angerine knew Harriet was waiting for them and couldn't get away, didn't hear until after she was gone or, the worst possibility, never knew that their famous aunt, their blood kin, had come to get them—the two young people remained on the Brodess farm.

Defeated yet again, Harriet makes plans to set off north without them.

But before leaving, she is approached by six people, who ask her to help them make their way out of Maryland, at least to within reach of Wilmington. They are a family of five—Maria and Stephen Ennals and their three children, whose ages are six years, four years, and three months—and a young man named John. The children will complicate the journey, especially in such wintry conditions. But Harriet knows the family and is acquainted with the circumstances under which Stephen and Maria Ennals are forced to live—eight miles away from each other by order of Stephen's owner, from whose grasp Maria and Stephen desperately wish to deliver their children.

Harriet may want to stay in Dorchester a little longer to make another attempt at rescuing Ben and Angerine. But the Ennalses have boldly stepped away from their owners and cannot return. If they try to travel without her, they will either perish or be captured. And so, after acquiring laudanum or opium to keep the infant quiet during the day, Harriet agrees to take them.

She may plan to come back to the Eastern Shore once she has delivered them to Thomas Garrett, the way she did the last time she came down. Perhaps, she may think, when she gets to Wilmington, she can convince Garrett to loan her the thirty dollars, or he can manage to wangle it from another source.

In any case, the Ennalses cannot afford to wait, and so Harriet takes the family on, and they move into the teeth of the storm with only one light blanket for warmth, Harriet carrying the baby in a basket.

During that first night, snow gives way to a heavy, cold rain. Harriet and the others move headlong into it, the Ennalses suffering terribly for their children, even more than for themselves. At daybreak, they arrive at a safe house Harriet has frequently used, where a black member of the Underground Railroad has always lived. At the front door, she knocks out a secret rap. When no response comes, she tries it again, then again. Finally, a window flies up.

"Who are you?" a white man asks. "What do you want?"

Harriet slides past the question. She asks instead after her friend, the former tenant.

"Gone," barks the white man. "Obliged to leave for harboring niggers."

Harriet quickly backs away and, before the man can question her further, skitters into the brush where she has left her people.

But morning is upon them, a town close by, and they have nowhere to go. The white man will be sure to alert marshals and slave catchers, who will soon ride out after them. Somewhat knocked off-balance by the obvious deterioration of the Underground Railroad, Harriet can't seem to remember where to go next or how to find safe harbor until nightfall, and so, while the utterly miserable Ennalses wait for a signal, their guide stands very still for a moment, either struggling to remember or actually speaking to God the way she and her biographers describe, then waiting for the message she doesn't just hope for but *expects*.

One way or another—whether by means of a spoken message or the kind of memory flash we have all experienced, wherein a forgotten song or book title comes to us out of the seeming blue—the answer comes.

Outside of town, there is a small island in the middle of a remote swamp where the grass grows tall and rank and where no human being would voluntarily go. Harriet takes her party there and, lifting the baby's basket high, wades through the swamp. The Ennals family and the young man follow. They are cold, wet, hungry, and scared. It is Harriet's job to forage for supplies, but this time, she doesn't dare leave. There is nothing to do but wait.

Understanding this, Harriet orders everyone to lie on the wet ground. And then she prays again while the others lie on the soggy, smelly, bug-infested island, waiting all afternoon.

After dusk, when Harriet is almost ready to go on a scouting trip, they hear sounds: footsteps, a man's voice. And then they see him, a white man in Quaker garb, walking slowly along the edge of the swamp. At first, they think the man is off his head, talking to himself out there in the damp and freezing swampland. And then their trouble-sharpened ears catch his words: "My wagon stands in the barnyard of the next farm across the way; the horse is in the stable, the harness hanging on a nail. My wagon stands in the barnyard of the next farm."

He disappears.

When night has fully fallen, Harriet wades once again through the swamp, then steals to the farm. In its barn, she finds a wagon that is well stocked and ready to go. She unhooks the harness, hitches up the horse, and drives the wagon back to the swamp, where she whistles or sings a message to the Ennalses. They signal an answer and then, after pushing their way through the murky water, climb into the wagon. When they get to the next stopping place, they leave the wagon with another Quaker, a friend of Harriet's, who will return it to its owner. Harriet and her people move on, never knowing how the man walking along the swamp bank knew where they were, only rejoicing in gratitude that he came.

The trip drags on. Because of the increased vigilance, they have to hide longer and deeper in the woods than usual, and Harriet has to go out for food and supplies more often than she expected to. When she comes back, it is often pitch-dark. If the Ennals family and John have crept farther into the woods in her absence—out of fear or because of some strange sounds or vigorously approaching footsteps—she sometimes can't find them. She then has to sing to let them know she is back and needs to know where they are. They sing back their location.

On December 1, she arrives at Garrett's alone, having dropped off Stephen Ennals and young John in New Castle, on the Delaware River. She has had to leave the exhausted Maria and her three children thirty miles south of there, and needs ten dollars to pay a carriage driver to fetch them. Deeply relieved to see her, Garrett pays a man to take John and Stephen due west to Chester County, Pennsylvania, where there is an active antislavery community. He gives Harriet the money to hire the carriage for Maria and the children.

But after she leaves, Garrett worries for her safety, considering how much more risk there is on the roads now, with so many "worthless wretches" constantly on the lookout for fugitives to capture or turn in. But in a letter to Still, he says that since she seems to have a guardian angel to watch after her, he maintains hope.

Harriet retrieves Maria Ennals and her children. Either in Delaware or Pennsylvania at a train station, another fugitive shows up, a pregnant woman escaping from Baltimore. Harriet allows the woman to join them. They arrive in Philadelphia soon afterward. They are said by William Still to have been through a trip of great tribulation, but after being given clothes, food, and supplies, they are greatly cheered. Still forwards them on toward Canada.

But trouble dogs their journey, and by Christmas, when they should have been long settled in St. Catharines, Harriet and the others have gotten only as far as Auburn, where residents are relieved and happy to see her and to welcome the refugees. Well aware that Harriet made the trip specifically to rescue her sister and her children, people ask about Rachel. Word of her death passes through town; people send letters to her friends in the New York north country and Massachusetts. Ben and Rit spend yet another Christmas in grief, acknowledging the death of a daughter and the new tear in the family, probably permanent, caused by the loss of her children.

By December 1860, South Carolina has declared itself an independent commonwealth and the departing president, James Buchanan, designates himself the last president of the United States. Since Lincoln's election, southerners have been leaving Washington in droves. Let them go, says Garrison. Let them go.

"The mad winter of compromise," Sanborn calls January 1861, when state after state and politician after politician go on bended knee to beg the South not to secede. On the twelfth, Seward makes a shocking speech, in which he acknowledges a constitutional obligation to return fugitive slaves to their owners and supports an amendment to deny Congress the power to deal with slavery in those states. Some abolitionists will never trust Seward again. Harriet, however, does not lose faith, and in truth, her loyalty is well founded: Seward remains a friend and their house deal sacrosanct.

On the twenty-sixth, Louisiana secedes from the union. The dominoes keep falling.

Three days later, Harriet sits by the fire in Gerrit Smith's pillared mansion, recovering from her difficult trip and telling Smith of the expedition.

She "sits by my side," Smith writes Franklin Sanborn. Having already been in Peterboro for five days, she will remain for several more, since, Smith reports, she has badly frosted her feet, and needs time to recover. Sitting with Smith, stoking the fire, curled up and nursing her sadness over Rachel and the children, she seems also to be taking a well-deserved rest. The country is in such an upheaval, there is no way to know exactly what her next mission will be or when she will make it. Perhaps, sitting by the fire with Gerrit Smith, she is working that out.

Clearly, Harriet feels at ease in the house that reminded Frederick

Douglass of the Edward Lloyd plantation in Maryland: the "Big House," Harriet calls it. She has no duties there, no family obligations, no stories to perform. She doesn't have to listen to Rit complain about the bitterness of northern winters. She can talk to Smith when she wants to, be quiet when the mood comes upon her.

And so they sit together, the tall, majestic, if emotionally fragile, white man with the prodigiously abundant white beard, the small athletic black woman in kerchief and skirts. He admires her deeply. When she nods off, he waits.

In her last days, Harriet will recall a visit she made to Smith in Peterboro, probably this one, where she tells of being barefoot despite the cold.

"I remember," she will say, "once after I had brought some colored people from the South . . ." Her interviewer is James B. Clarke, a West Indian student from Cornell University. Sitting in the Harriet Tubman Home before a plate of chicken and rice, she tells how Gerrit Smith's son, Green, and some other boys invited her to go hunting with them. But Harriet's shoes had been ruined during her trip south, and so she said no, because she couldn't go hunting barefoot.

"It was a Saturday afternoon," she recalls in the eighty-ninth year of life. "And would you believe it? Those boys went right off to the village and got me a pair of shoes so I could go with them."

Presumably, she put on her new shoes and went hunting, since she proudly reports that the boys found her as skilled with a gun as with hoe and washboard.

Ruined shoes and frostbite belong in the same story; nonetheless, Harriet would have refuted Gerrit Smith's report. Her public position remained absolute: God kept her safe from frostbite, wrong turns, and slave catchers.

But the reliable Gerrit Smith was probably writing the truth, especially considering the cold water Harriet had to wade through on that last trip. And, to put it plainly, why would he lie?

Pain can be subjective, relative to circumstance, open to interpretation. Publicly, Harriet ignored it. At Smith's, she could heal without fuss. And unlike Smith, she had reason to insist on her imperviousness. For her to acknowledge frailty—whether physical injury, uncertainty, or despair—would be to risk curtailing her confidence.

A few days after writing Sanborn, Smith hears reports of slave catchers in Auburn and the enforced return South of a fugitive slave in Ohio, and he insists on taking his houseguest to Canada. Harriet doesn't want to go, but he somehow bundles her up and hurries her off, sorely against her will.

When abolitionist neighbors in Auburn ask how they can help, Harriet requests that they simply see that her family doesn't suffer. Through one of the refugees living in her home, she sends word asking people to please provide her family with a barrel of flour to help them make it through the winter. On her return, she vows, she will pay them back.

On March 4, Lincoln is inaugurated. On the sixth, the Confederacy calls for 100,000 volunteers, and on the eleventh, a newly formed Confederate Congress meets in Montgomery, Alabama. There, Jefferson Davis and his cabinet adopt a permanent constitution, which prohibits any law that denies or impairs the right to own Negro slaves.

Agitated, the country waits. Restless, Harriet refuses to stay in Canada, but spends the spring on the road, moving back and forth between there and Auburn. She establishes the Fugitive Aid Society of St. Catharines and staffs it with trustworthy neighbors and friends, many of them from Maryland. Once that's done, she heads back to Auburn and beyond.

A person who cannot read lives, of necessity, in memory and the moment, viewing the present within the narrow context of her own life and experiences. To compile information, she must travel where things are happening, to see and hear for herself. "Illiteracy puts you in a box" is how a woman in the twenty-first century describes it.

Harriet stays on the move.

By now, war is a foregone conclusion and both Unionists and Confederates have grown impatient to move on into it. In this season of waiting and uproar, Harriet finds reason to travel to New York, where she stays with the Presbyterian minister and abolitionist orator Henry Highland Garnet. Famous for his preaching eloquence as well as for an 1843 speech in which he advised slaves to rise up and slay their masters, Garnet, like most of the country's citizens, foresees a lengthy, difficult war; emancipation, a distant possibility.

While asleep in the Garnet home, Harriet receives a vision, perhaps in the form of a dream, or, as Bradford says, one of those glimpses into the future that were sometimes granted to her.

Upon awakening, she rises from her vision singing. In a kind of ecstatic trance, she goes downstairs to the main floor.

"My people are free!" she shouts in her rolling tones. "My people are free!"

Startled, Garnet shushes her. "Oh, Harriet!" he scolds. "Harriet! You've come to torment us before the time . . . My grandchildren may see the day of the emancipation of our people, but you and I will never see it."

But Harriet stands her ground. "I tell you, sir," she informs Garnet, "you'll see it, and you'll see it soon." When breakfast is offered, she refuses it, too filled with prophetical visions to have any interest in food.

"My people are free!" she sings again, seeing the future as it comes to her, as a real *event,* happening before her eyes, in the present tense. "My people are free!"

When emancipation does arrive, Harriet will not celebrate as ardently as others, having already staged her own private jubilee some two years before.

Energized, she keeps traveling, raising funds for the support of both her family and the refugees in St. Catharines. Knowing how easily her feelings are wrought upon, her friends parcel out their contributions, donating ten or twenty dollars at a time. The Ross family makes some adjustments. Harriet's sister-in-law Catherine Kane Stewart, wife of James, moves with her son into Harriet's home in Auburn, while her brother William Henry buys six acres on the outskirts of St. Catharines, where he settles with his wife, Harriet Ann, and their four children. There, they live in a colony of Eastern Shore refugees and perhaps spend some time reminiscing, wondering about family and friends left behind.

As for Ben and Angerine, it is easy to think of them as young people who have *disappeared,* and yet, of course, they have not. They live out lives not of their choosing, at least until the end of slavery, lives of which, so far, we have no information, no records, documents, records of sales or marriage. Who knows what happens next? They vanish into unknown lives, lost from history and from our telling of it, the same as their great-grandmother Modesty and their aunts Mariah Ritty, Soph, and Linah; their uncle Moses; their first cousin Harriet Jolley and their first cousins once removed, Mary Jane and her little sister Sarah.

On April 12, the rebel forces issue their answer to Lincoln's refusal to take down the Union flag from the federal garrison at Fort Sumter by staging a spectacular thirty-four-hour bombardment of the fort, located in the Charleston, South Carolina, harbor. Two days later, the Union surrenders the fort. Virginia secedes. The Confederates celebrate. Lincoln calls for 75,000 volunteers. Maryland remains a slave state but does not secede.

Harriet appears not to have returned to her native state again.

Except, perhaps, once.

In April, after the war begins, Harriet disappears. The country is in a frenzy, abolitionists are calling for the end of slavery, and she is surely in the thick of things—but where? Earlier in the month, on the eleventh, Gerrit Smith has written Franklin Sanborn to say that Rit has visited him in Peterboro but that he does not know where Harriet is.

She has gone, it seems, to Maryland. Because this particular trip is shrouded in clouds of mystery darkened by years of storytelling and retelling, disputed by more years of other stories, declarations, and recitations, we can only speculate. Tubman had not raised money for a trip. She had spoken of it to no one. So far, much about the journey and the reasons for it are still in dispute.

We begin with what we know.

In late April or early May, she shows up in Auburn with a nine-year-old girl. Called Margaret, the girl will be described by her daughter as "short and plump, light brown with long thick Negroid hair." "Pumpkin-skinned," a Tubman relative will describe her.

Harriet, of course, often takes children into her own home, but she chooses instead to deliver this girl to the home of Lazette Worden, the widowed sister of William Seward's wife, Frances.

"Mrs. Worden," writes abolitionist Martha Coffin Wright in late May, "has taken a contraband ten years old to live with her, a niece of Harriet Tubman."

The term *contraband* is newly being used, having been coined by Gen. Benjamin Butler in May, when three fugitive slaves crossed the Union lines and came to him at Fortress Monroe in Hampton, Virginia, asking for asylum. Although heretofore the official policy had been to return the slaves to their owners, Butler used the slave owners' terminology against them, reasoning that if the enemy has defined the men, women, and children who come to him as *property,* under the terms of war he has the right to confiscate them as contraband of war.

Martha Coffin Wright has chosen her words carefully, using *contraband* in place of the old terms: *slave, fugitive, runaway.* But in this case, the new characterization doesn't apply. The girl Harriet delivers to Lazette Worden's door has never been enslaved, or so she will claim. Neither have her mother or the twin brother she involuntarily left behind in Maryland, thanks to the purchase of family members by her great-grandfather. Margaret's father—who she says is Harriet's brother—was the only one in her immediate family born into slavery. He, too, however, is free, having found his way out of bondage.

While Lazette Worden lives on Lake Owasco, not far from the summerhouse of Sarah Bradford's brother, she also spends a good deal of time in town with her sister, especially now that William Seward is in Washington, D.C., serving as Lincoln's secretary of state.

Harriet introduces Margaret to Lazette as her niece, Margaret Stewart—the girl's surname echoing the choice of Harriet's brothers in Canada. Harriet explains her purpose: She wants to leave Margaret with Lazette Worden, to live with her and become educated while Harriet herself goes back on the road and resumes her work.

There is no written record of it, but Worden seems to have accepted responsibility for the girl, if not on the spot, then soon afterward. Harriet goes on her way, and Margaret Stewart stays in the home of the white woman. A while later, Worden takes the child to her sister's home in

Auburn, where Margaret will live, not as a servant but as a guest. There, she will learn to read, write, and sew, to do homework and speak well, to behave, in other words, like a proper lady.

But who is she, to receive this special treatment?

In 1939, Margaret Stewart's youngest child, Alice Lucas Brickler, will write a series of letters to Tubman biographer Earl Conrad concerning her mother's life. The youngest of seven, Alice Brickler tells the story as she heard it from her mother.

"My mother's life," she boldly states, as if she has been waiting to say it, "really began with Aunt Harriet kidnapping her from her home on [the] Eastern Shore [of] Maryland when she was a little girl eight or nine years old."

Kidnapping is a serious charge. We think of Harriet Tubman as a rescuer, not a child snatcher. But Brickler does not back off from the term.

Harriet, explains Mrs. Brickler, "fell in love with the girl who was my mother," perhaps, she speculates, because in Margaret she saw the child she herself might have been, if not for slavery. Or because she knew she would never be a mother herself and longed for a "little creature who would love her for her own self's sake."

Whether a thunderbolt of love or some other emotion moved Harriet, Mrs. Brickler continues, "it was stronger than her better judgment, for when her visit was ended she secretly and without so much as a by-your-leave took the little girl with her to her northern home," knowing that "she had taken the child from a sheltered good home to a place where there was nobody to care for her," leaving behind a family filled with "sorrow and anger."

Margaret told Alice the story many times: how Aunt Harriet came to her home on the Eastern Shore, where she lived with her mother and father and twin brother, and how few and what vague memories she retained of that earlier life, chiefly a shiny carriage she and her family rode in to church, pulled by a slick chestnut horse.

After Harriet gathered her up and took her away, the two of them boarded a steamer going north. And Margaret so enjoyed standing on the deck, looking out at the water, that she forgot to weep over the loss of her mother and her twin brother, the carriage and the horse.

Brickler has a curiously conflicted attitude toward the woman she calls Aunt Harriet, both critical and deeply admiring. But on one point, she is adamant: Aunt Harriet had no right to violate her brother's family by stealing his child and taking her away, knowing full well that "the warmth of this new love was not great enough to calm her restless soul and turn her into a domestic."

How and why Harriet would do such a thing remains a mystery. Undoubtedly, some of the stories Margaret Stewart Lucas told her daughter were embroidered, at the very least. For one thing, there is the matter of her being Harriet's niece. Edward Brodess owned all of Rit's children and did not set any of them free. If Margaret's father was manumitted, then he can't have been Harriet's brother. Brickler herself admits that she grew up surrounded by people she and others knew as "Aunt and Uncle," without knowing if they were actually "of the family."

Other discrepancies remain. Margaret says she was born on the Eastern Shore, but her death certificate says Baltimore. In his own letter to Earl Conrad, Harkless Bowley says that while Margaret Stewart and her husband, Henry Lucas, were dear friends of his, he never heard his aunt Harriet mention bringing Margaret to Auburn.

Facts and possibilities roll into one another. At eight or nine, a child's imagination soars. Margaret's remembrances may have been a fabulous invention. Maybe Harriet found a young girl orphaned in Baltimore or Philadelphia. Or someone brought the girl to Harriet. Perhaps in Margaret, she did—as Brickler suggested—see the girl she was at that age, before her injury, or might have been, or the child she never had.

The thing to remember is this: Whoever Margaret Stewart was, it seems that Harriet adored her.

In the Seward house, the girl will live in an environment rich with books and paintings. She will walk on fine rugs and run her hand across the warm wood of hand-carved banisters. When going out, she will ride in a fine carriage. During her childhood, whenever Harriet returns to Auburn, Margaret is dressed by Lazette Worden and Frances Seward and then sent in a carriage to Harriet's house.

There have been many theories and speculations about the birth and ancestry of Margaret Stewart Lucas, including the possibility of her being Harriet's daughter. And if we want to search for a brother who might be the father of Margaret, there's Harriet's baby brother, Moses Ross, whose life has spun out in an unknown manner. In 1870, a black man named Moses Ross lives in Maryland. He is about the age Rit's son would be at that time. Might he have secretly taken a daughter up the bay to the Baltimore docks and passed her through to Harriet?

But Margaret has light skin, indicating white ancestry. Alice Brickler also points out that besides being divided into Stewarts and Rosses, the family was also divided as to skin color, and that her mother was "proud to the point of being snobbish" of her light skin. One relative, Brickler reports, "disliked Mother very much . . . whenever Aunt Harriet was out of hearing she used to call Mother a 'pumpkin-colored hussey.' "

In the end what remains is the mystery. Margaret's ancestry matters far less than Harriet's motivations, and if we knew who Margaret really was, we could understand better why Harriet felt free to take her out of one life and insert her into another.

But we don't.

After delivering the girl to Lazette Worden, Harriet leaves for Massachusetts.

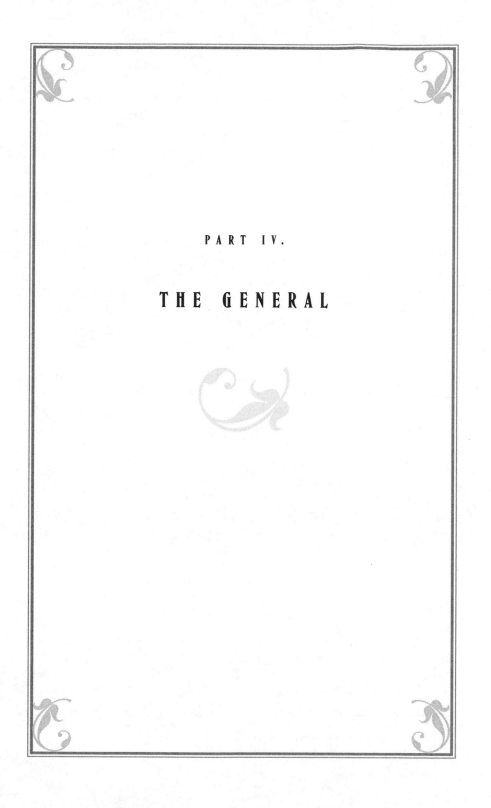

PART IV.

THE GENERAL

Scene 15.

Beaufort, South Carolina

The existing war has no direct relation to slavery.
—*NATIONAL INTELLIGENCER* (WASHINGTON, D.C.),
OCTOBER 8, 1861

Lincoln is a great man. And I am but a poor nigger. But this nigger can tell Master Lincoln how to save money and the young men: . . . by setting the niggers free.
—HARRIET TUBMAN TO LYDIA MARIA CHILD, FALL 1861

. . . the good Lord has come down to deliver my people, and I must go to help him.
—HARRIET TUBMAN, QUOTED IN SAMUEL MAY, *SOME RECOLLECTIONS OF OUR ANTISLAVERY CONFLICT*, 1869

Upon her arrival in Massachusetts in the fall of 1861, Harriet sets out on her fund-raising campaign, her twin purposes to get herself back to the South and to make sure her parents and the others living in the house in Auburn are taken care of in her absence. Ben is now about 75 years old, as is Rit. One of Ben's hands has gone all but useless, probably from chronic arthritis. Since most residents of the South Street house are either too old, too young, or otherwise unable to work, only Catherine Stewart is of an age and state of health to bring in money for food and supplies.

But she has children to see to as well, and there is no way she can do it all.

And so Harriet—as ever—struggles to keep the household afloat.

We can reasonably presume she follows her usual schedule and goes first to Concord to see Sanborn. If she requests financial assistance, he may well ask what she intends to do now that war has been declared and the Underground Railroad has all but been disbanded.

Despite the war and the great numbers of slaves leaving Virginia and Maryland, she is still aiming to make her way through the chaos and gunfire to rescue the last of her family in Maryland. But things have changed now that enslaved people are dropping their hoes and shovels, tromping barefoot through swamps and across creeks and rivers, usually at night and often on the basis of messages sent by grapevine from one African American community to the next. They are coming across Union lines and asking for asylum or to bear arms. The underground communication network has become so successful that one Confederate general believes that because of it, in only a few weeks the entire slave population of eastern Florida might become, in his term, "corrupted."

Once she brings her niece and nephew out, Harriet will have to move on. She will have to find a new way to help her people, a different job and name to go by, a new road to take to get to the South.

She takes her leave of Sanborn, certain that sooner or later she will receive instructions, a voice telling her what to do next.

By midsummer, the North is in a stew, trying to figure out what to do with the freed slaves, now gathered in contraband camps, where they wait, poorly fed, living in wretched housing. Send them back? Hire them? Put them to work? Give them arms and let them serve? *Free them* is a possibility not much discussed, not currently being a serious consideration except in the minds of abolitionists and a few rogue-minded generals.

In July, encouraged by Harriet's friend Gerrit Smith, U.S. congressman Owen Lovejoy of Illinois finally pushes through a resolution stating that U.S. soldiers are *not* required to return fugitives to their owners. That same month, the Union loses the first major battle of the war, at Bull Run. After the loss, the U.S. Congress passes the First Confiscation Act, authorizing the appropriation of rebel property, including slaves. And in late August, Maj. Gen. John Charles Fremont, commander of the Western Department, unilaterally declares that in the

HARRIET TUBMAN.

Harriet in her military attire, during her days as a Union spy and guerrilla. This engraving appeared in the 1869 edition of Sarah Bradford's biography, as a frontispiece illustration, thus giving credence to the stories of her bravery during the war, not just as a nurse but as a fully engaged—*armed*—soldier.

state of Missouri, after enemy property is confiscated, all slaves are to be declared free. But Fremont's proclamation lasts only until the president can assert his authority and water it down.

At this time, Harriet is not a particular fan of the new president. Like Frederick Douglass ("henceforth let the war cry be, down with treason and down with slavery the cause of treason"), she believes that the war must be waged for or against slavery—which Douglass calls the "source and center of this gigantic rebellion"—and that until the country stops shilly-shallying on the issue by trying to placate the border states, the hostilities will not end.

During the fall, or maybe the following winter, while raising money in Massachusetts, she takes her stand:

> They may send the flower of their young men down South to die
> of the fever in the summer and the ague in the winter. For it is
> cold down there, though it *is* down south. God won't let Master
> Lincoln beat the South till he does *the right thing*. Lincoln is a
> great man. And I'm but a poor nigger. But this nigger can tell
> Master Lincoln how to save money and the young men: He [can]
> do it by setting the niggers free."

To clarify her point, Harriet turns to metaphor.

Suppose, she says, there was a big snake curled at her feet. Then imagine that snake unwinding and shooting up to bite her. When he does that, everybody gets scared, fearing she will die. They send for the doctor. The snake rolls back into a coil. The doctor comes and begins to cut out the bite, but the snake strikes again, in a new place this time. The doctor makes another incision. The snake strikes again. Finally, somebody gets wise and realizes the doctor can't keep up with the bites and the snake is not going to stop until somebody kills him.

That, she concludes, is what Master Lincoln ought to know.

Anxious to save the last of her family in Maryland before the situation worsens, she continues stumping for financial support. Her admiring friends donate to her cause, but she can't raise anywhere near enough to cover all her needs.

Three months after Bull Run, Harriet's purposes begin to shift when a veritable armada of seventeen steam-powered frigates and gunboats, followed by some thirty-three army transports and twenty-five coaling vessels—the largest U.S. naval fleet to have landed anywhere in the world until 1944—leave Hampton Roads, Virginia. After a big send-off, loud with cheers and music, the expedition heads across the mouth of the Chesapeake and into the Atlantic. There, it turns south toward an unspecified destination. In vivid reportage, the *New York Times* and the *New York Herald* cover the expedition on a daily basis, noting weather conditions, storms, seasickness, water depths, and exact locations as the vessels make their way down the coastline of North Carolina.

People open their newspapers every morning to find out where the ships are and to speculate on their eventual destination. Rumors fly. Are they going to Charleston? To regain Sumter?

Led by the *Wabash,* under the naval command of Samuel F. Du Pont, the boats move past the Outer Banks of North Carolina—beyond Cape Hatteras and around Cape Lookout—to the point of Cape Fear, where they are smacked head-on by a vicious storm. The fleet suffers losses but moves on, past the northernmost part of South Carolina, toward Charleston Bay. But by early November, when the boats pass Sumter, intelligent rumor has it that the disembarkment point is Port Royal Sound, a large deepwater port in lower South Carolina, almost to Georgia. The sound is about two and a half miles wide, with forts on either side: Fort Walker, to the south on Hilton Head Island, and Fort Beauregard, on Bay Point.

That part of the state, from Edisto Island to the Savannah River and down to Jacksonville, make up what is called the Lowcountry. In South Carolina, this comprises the Sea Islands—Hilton Head, Saint Helena, Port Royal, Lady's, Tybee, and others—and only one town of any size, Beaufort. The Lowcountry is soggy, flat, and salty, almost equal parts water and land, much of the ground too marshy to walk through. Islands dot the raggedy coastline like scraps of paper thrown to the wind. Subject to the rhythm of ocean tides, the soil of the islands contains a

A Town of Beaufort, where Harriet lived, nursed the ill and wounded, made pies and root beer; also where she testified in the court-martial trial of Private James E. Webster, who had been accused of selling "without proper order to a colored woman named Harriet Tubman fifty pounds of brown sugar more or less, which had been delivered to him by the United States for issue to contrabands."

B Hilton Head Island, where the U.S. Commissary was located, where Harriet and her colleague William Plowden purchased flour, sugar, and other supplies.

C Harriet's route to the rice plantation where, under the command of Col. James Montgomery, she worked to liberate men and women still living in bondage, even though the Emancipation Proclamation had been passed. The military operation proceeded from the Beaufort River to St. Helena Sound, then up the Combahee (pronounced Kum-bee) River, all the way to the bridge across the Savannah River (D), which Montgomery destroyed.

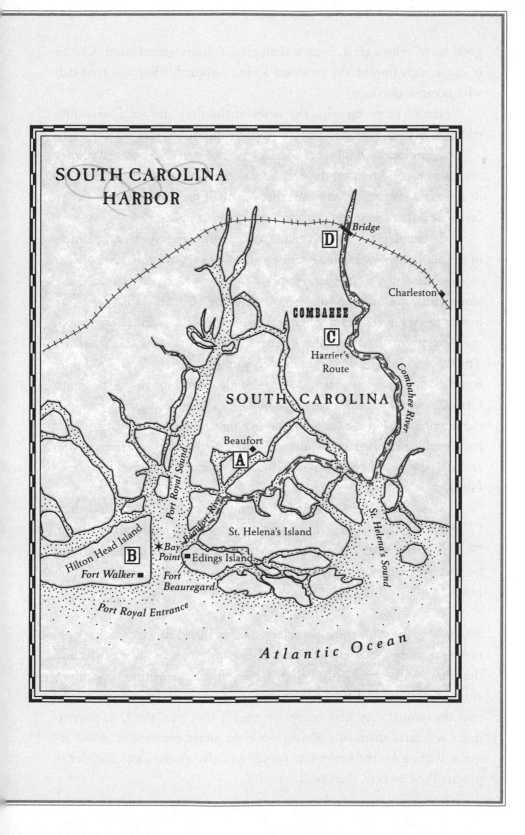

SOUTH CAROLINA
HARBOR

Bridge

D

Charleston

COMBAHEE

C

Harriet's
Route

SOUTH CAROLINA

Combahee River

Beaufort

A

Port Royal Sound

St. Helena's Island

Beaufort River

St. Helena's Sound

Hilton Head Island

B

Bay
Point

Edings Island

Fort Walker

Fort
Beauregard

Port Royal Entrance

Atlantic Ocean

good bit of yellow sand, flecked with bits of disintegrated coral. The air is staggeringly humid, the summers all but unbearably hot, the land rich with oceanic alluvium.

Harriet keeps up with the news of the fleet and its destination, which is, for her, familiar country—watery, tidal, isolated, marshy.

She will soon travel there and stay for two years. The special history and current conditions of the South Carolina Lowcountry will affect her in the most immediate way, and there she will find a new life, a way to continue doing brave, good work, serving her people.

Slaveholders of the Sea Islands have become the wealthiest planters in the South by growing long-staple cotton—expensive and silky, unique to this area. In the summer, property-owning white people escape the smothering heat of the islands by removing themselves to their fine homes in Beaufort. Slaves, of course, remain on the islands year-round, the Atlantic on one side and all around them, rivers, bays, estuaries. There are no bridges. Each island is remote and separate unto itself. Descended from grandparents and great-grandparents brought to the South Carolina islands directly from Africa—most of them from Sierra Leone—the ten thousand or more slaves who live thus isolated on the Sea Islands have established their own culture. They call themselves, their culture, and the language they speak—practically a separate tongue all its own—Gullah.

When she is there, Harriet will struggle to understand the dialect. "The language down there in the far South," she will tell Sarah Bradford, "is just as different from ours in Maryland as you can think. They laughed when they heard me talk and I could not understand them no how."

By the time the ships pass Cape Hatteras, Sea Island landowners have begun evacuating their various estates. Believing the war will be brief and that they will be gone only a short while, they leave behind their silver, china, furniture, and books. Some slaves go with their owners, fearful that the rumors they have heard are true: if they stay, the U.S. government will send them to Cuba to work the sugar plantations. Most remain, waiting for the new white people to arrive. Some leave in order to placate their owners, then swiftly return.

In the North, as arguments over the treatment of the "contraband" continues, the supporters of Negro emigration have begun drumming up business again, this time—in the face of so little government support for emancipation—calling for the colonization of Haiti.

On November 6, 1861, six months after leaving Margaret Stewart with Lazette Worden, Harriet may well be in Boston when a large group of African Americans meet to issue resolutions against colonization, suggesting that, if they are so fond of the place, those in favor of it should quit their homes and go live in Haiti themselves. Although there is no record of her presence, Harriet usually attends antiemigration meetings. Boston is her base of operations. Her friend, John S. Rock, the first black lawyer admitted to the bar of the Supreme Court, will speak at the meeting. He attended the 1859 anticolonization meeting, and so did Harriet. Two years from now, when she returns from the south, she will stay with him. The likelihood is that she's with him now.

At the meeting, John Rock decisively declares, "This being our country, we have made up our minds to remain in it and to try to make it worth living in."

If she is there, Harriet may go to the podium to tell the story of the farmer, the garlic, and the spoiled milk. Or perhaps she delivers her advice to Lincoln on how to end the war by telling the tale about the snake.

In Port Royal Sound, at 9:25 on the morning of the following day (November 7), Du Pont issues his orders and the bombardment begins. By two o'clock, Fort Walker on Hilton Head has been taken, and the ships turn their guns toward Fort Beauregard, at Bay Point. By midafternoon, both forts have fallen. Among black residents, the day will afterward be known as the day of the gun-shoot at Bay Point.

News of the capture of Port Royal travels quickly north. According to Sanborn, Harriet reacts instantaneously. In a quick flash, she comes up with "the idea of going there and working among her people on the islands and the mainlands." The good Lord, after all, has seen fit to deliver her people. The least she can do is go down there and help out.

On Friday, the eighth, army general Thomas W. Sherman, head of the newly created Department of the South, comprising South Carolina,

Georgia, and Florida, sails across Port Royal Sound and up the Beaufort River. Behind him, other vessels bear troops, horses, and supply-filled wagons, all headed to the town of Beaufort. From onboard ship, the soldiers stand ready to return fire when it comes. But they hear nothing. There are no pickets, no plantation owners, no white people. Only the Negroes remain on the plantations. When the boats pass, they come to the shore in great numbers, holding out bundles—clothing, food, belongings—as if expecting to be taken aboard.

When the troops arrive in Beaufort, they find the streets, the churches, the public library, and the fine summer homes abandoned. There has been no order to evacuate; the white people simply packed up and went, leaving their homes and furnishings, even their largest assets: their land, their field hands, and the unsold crops in the field. Soldiers march the length of the main street of town—Bay Street—without passing a soul. When they do spy a lone white man, he is staggering and incomprehensible, dead drunk.

In the Northeast, people celebrate. The *New York Herald* runs a day-by-day detailed account of the expedition. *Harper's Weekly* runs cover stories featuring maps of the area, drawings of the bombardment, sketches of the many black residents of the islands. Lincoln is said to be radiant at the news of the rout. But he, his cabinet, and especially the officers in charge are again faced with the same vexing question: If the contrabands aren't to be returned to their former owners, what then?

Frederick Douglass, among others, is happy to offer a solution. Tirelessly, he urges the immediate arming of black men so they can fight in the Union army. "We are ready and would go," he writes. "Counting ourselves happy in being permitted to serve and suffer for the cause of freedom and free institutions. But you won't let us go."

Others weigh in, supporting this position. White men—Allan Pinkerton, chief of the U.S. Secret Service and Gen. Abner Doubleday—encourage the use of fugitive slaves as spies and scouts, since they bring vital information, unobtainable from any other source.

Lincoln stands firmly against the arming of Negroes, as do most congressmen.

Once he has set up camp, General Sherman—faced with the care and dispensation of ten thousand former slaves—makes a public appeal to the disappeared whites to accept negotiation and Union protection, since the federal government has no intention of interfering with "social and local institutions." When nothing comes of his offer and nobody returns, he issues orders to his officers to hire the newly freed black people to work in the camps.

He also sends an official request for teachers to be sent from the North, as well as agents to manage the plantations and superintend the work of Negroes until they can provide for themselves. In the fields the cotton is high, a lush crop, as healthy and plentiful as anyone has seen in years. Northerners know nothing about cotton except how to buy, mill, and use it. Someone needs to come and oversee the harvesting of the crop.

Harriet can't read, and, like the Northerners, she knows nothing about cotton, so she probably isn't the kind of volunteer worker Thomas Sherman has in mind. Nonetheless, she is determined to get there, one way or another.

She begins to tap her friends, not just for money but connections— a way officially to enlist in the military program in Port Royal. Her reasoning is sound: She's been doing guerrilla work for twelve years, negotiating journeys through enemy territory, figuring the logistics of maneuvering through tidal rivers, swamps, and wetlands and up the Chesapeake. She has commanded troops and kept them safe. If the government signs her up, she can be of good use both to the country and her people. And this time she will get paid for her work, instead of having constantly to beat the bushes for handouts.

In Boston, John Albion Andrew, governor of Massachusetts and a stone abolitionist, has responded to Thomas Sherman's request by spearheading a movement to send a band of teachers to Beaufort to conduct what will be called the "Port Royal Experiment," a brave plan, not just to educate the slaves but to help move the labor system from slave- to wage-based.

Sometime during late 1861 or early 1862, Harriet is introduced by some of her influential friends—the Stearnses, the Cheneys, Garrison— to the governor. Andrew, having known previously of her accomplishments, signs on in her behalf. Because of Harriet's knowledge and experience, he declares, she will be a "valuable person to operate within the enemies lines in procuring information and scouts."

She will be a spy, a recruiter, a specialist in intelligence, a guerrilla warrior.

She will not go, however, except on one condition: that her parents be kept from want. And so before taking on the mission, she probably returns to Auburn, maybe during the Christmas season. There, applying what Ednah Dow Cheney calls "shrewd economy," she plans their household arrangements for the winter and manages to come up with the thirty dollars she figures they will need to stay comfortable during the cold months in north-central New York.

After which, she says her quick good-byes and scurries back to Boston.

The year turns. Harriet's fortieth birthday approaches.

On January 23, 1862, she may well attend the thirtieth-anniversary convention of the Massachusetts Anti-Slavery Society in Boston. Her friends are there: Ednah Cheney, the Stearnses, author and antislavery activist Lydia Maria Child.

After Governor Andrew sent word calling for "teachers of enthusiasm . . . regulated by good understanding" to go to South Carolina, abolitionists from New York and Philadelphia joined the movement, now called the Educational Commission (later to be renamed the New England Freedmen's Aid Society). They have elected John Andrew president. By the end of February, 150 people have volunteered, out of which 53 have been selected.

On a rainy March 3, 1862, following a night at the Lovejoy Hotel, where they have slept on musty sheets, the volunteers gather on the Canal Street dock in New York. Supervised and chosen by the young Boston attorney Edward Pierce—a special agent of the Treasury Department who oversaw the instruction of the contraband at Fortress Monroe—the volunteers wait to sail south on the steamer *Atlantic,* which only four months before participated in the naval expedition. Included in the group are clerks, doctors, engineers, teachers, cotton agents, and clergy—among whom, twelve are women, most of them teachers from Boston. Pierce has voiced grave doubts about taking women on so risky an adventure, but in the end, he has yielded to their insistence, calling their inclusion yet another bold experiment.

In their dark abundant dresses, buttoned to the neck, the women gather with the men in the misting rain. Dedicated Christians, the missionaries sometimes call themselves "evangels of civilization." Others have dubbed them "Gideon's Band," each one, like the Gideonites of the Old Testament, taking a pitcher of light and a trumpet into the darkness.

By this time, Sanborn says Harriet has left for South Carolina as well, and, because she has left Massachusetts, he may believe that she has. But her trip has been delayed.

Her initial orders were to go to New York and there, like the evangels, board the *Atlantic*. From there, under the direction of Col. Francis Howe, she was to sail to Beaufort, where—according to her agreement with Governor Andrew—she would work as a scout and spy. But someone has changed the program. Instead of guerrilla work, she is told, the generals want her to run a kind of clearinghouse, distributing the clothes and supplies being sent from Massachusetts and New York, to the black people of the mainland and the islands.

Scut work, in other words, certainly a demotion from Governor Andrew's initial assignment, and either an insult both to him and Harriet or a cover story devised by the military to disguise her real duties. Whatever the reasons, Harriet is dead set on going, whatever the program.

She makes her way to New York and shows up at the appointed time and place, ready to go.

At this point, there is a slight discrepancy in the accounts of her trip. In one report, it seems that Harriet leaves as scheduled, sailing from New York on the *Atlantic*. But late in her life, she will remember things differently.

"They wouldn't let no colored people go down South then," she will tell Emma Telford in 1905, "unless they went with some of the officers as a servant."

And so they find a gentleman from New York to take her with him as his servant.

The gentleman—presumably a Union officer—is staying at a big hotel on Broadway. Harriet locates the hotel and asks at the desk for the man. Dressed in her usual skirts and kerchief, carrying her belongings in a bag, she undoubtedly causes something of a stir in the hotel lobby, where she waits.

The white man comes down and makes his posturing way ("struts," she will say) to her. Upon meeting, they take each other's measure. Both seem to have reacted with instant dislike.

The officer sniffs. He guesses Harriet is young enough. She says nothing.

He instructs her to go to the quartermaster on board the ship and say he has sent her. And then he turns on his heel and leaves.

Harriet fumes. The officer has dressed the way a gentleman should. He prances about as a proper gentleman ought to. He may even *look* bold and noble enough to pass for gentlemanly. But looks don't count for everything. She is not his servant, has not been so appointed, does not wish to be treated as such, and will not go with him.

Dignity intact, she leaves the hotel.

And afterward? "I ain't seen the quartermaster yet, nor him either."

She makes her way to Baltimore on her own and there receives word that the general in Beaufort is expecting her and wants her to come on right away. When she gets to the ship, she will tell Telford, it has been docked for two days, awaiting her arrival.

Harriet does not have an official position in the military, nor has she been signed on at any particular pay scale. The general's "orders" have no official sanction or power over her or within the government structure. But in her mind, she has signed on as a soldier and, having served as a commander herself, she understands that a foot soldier must follow orders without asking questions.

She boards the ship.

Harriet arrives in South Carolina sometime during the spring, probably before the end of March. The *Atlantic* docks at Hilton Head, where naval stores have been built next to a long row of white barracks, thrown up to house former slaves. The pale yellow streets are crammed with people: black children playing games, white soldiers talking, jostling, ignoring Harriet as just one more black person among the rest.

At the port, Harriet transfers to a riverboat, probably the *Cosmopolitan,* which will navigate its way through the channels of the Beaufort River past abandoned plantations, which by the time she arrives—four months after the Union fleet—have been plundered and vandalized.

Some say the looting and destruction are the work of liberated slaves gone wild. In reports and letters, however, Union soldiers openly acknowledge that their own soldiers did most of the foraging. In June, for instance, Calvin Shedd, a first sergeant from New Hampshire, writes his wife, "Our Soldiers used most of the furniture for fire wood last winter & smashed ever[y]thing they could even to Pianos & Organs in the churches. Mirrors that cost hundreds of dollars were broken in the general ruin & all other furniture & fixtures generally found in the houses of the wealthy. The Rebels are sacrificing everything in the general ruin."

When Esther Hill Hawks, a medical doctor, arrives in October, she will observe, "The 'city' of Beaufort . . . must have been a very beautiful place previous to its occupancy by our Soldiers . . . Previous to the landing of our troops there were well kept yards and beautiful gardens, full of rare flowers—Mansions furnished with almost princely magnificence . . .

Freed slaves in Hilton Head, South Carolina, after the naval victory in the spring of 1862. Until now, these families had lived in bondage to "the Rebel Thomas Drayton."

whole libraries full of costly books—indeed, this little place contained everything which art could furnish and wealth procure." Until, she writes, "our crazy [soldiers] made sad havoc with its beauty and its wealth." The devastation is obvious: Much of the furniture stolen and sent north, more destroyed for the fun of it, private libraries trodden under foot, churches robbed of all ornament, organ keys torn off to adorn soldiers' caps, even a brick wall enclosing a cemetery torn away to build a chimney.

When the *Cosmopolitan* docks, black people push their way toward it.

Harriet steps into their midst.

"Negroes, negroes, negroes," Elizabeth Botume, a young white volunteer, will write in her diary, describing her own arrival in Beaufort. But when the diarist starts to describe how the black people are dressed, she corrects her memory. They were not *dressed,* she explains, but only partly covered with every conceivable thing they could come by: cast-off soldiers' coats, croaker sacks as skirts, strips of carpets or blankets with armholes cut through as jackets, sailcloth for kerchiefs, pants tied below and above the knees and around the waist to hold them in place. And when Botume walks through the crowd, many of the refugees raise their hands to their foreheads and salute her, as if she were an arriving soldier.

Harriet makes her own way through the crowd. Like Botume, she has never seen so many black people in one place in her life. They must wonder who she is, a black woman like them, why she has come and how to treat her. She carries with her a letter provided by Elbridge G. Dudley, an abolitionist friend of Frank Sanborn, introducing her to a number of Union officers, among them, Gen. David Hunter, who will soon replace Thomas W. Sherman as head of the Department of the South.

The chill of winter hangs on. The wet months have made for bountiful crops in the lower South, but winter rains have turned Beaufort streets into rivers of mud. Only the roads lined with crushed oyster shells are conducive to easy walking.

The shells are plentiful and, on Shell Road, for instance, make for crunchy walking. Those without shoes, however, prefer the mud.

That same month, Henry Burnell, a Union soldier from Maine, describes Beaufort as a very pretty city with neatly laid-out streets. The weather is cold, he reports; even so, orange and peach trees are in bloom, and the frosty ground has already produced some green peas. Words fail the Mainer when he tries to describe the area further; all he can think to say is that perhaps God made it for the Garden of Eden. But then he has not yet, of course, experienced a Lowcountry summer.

Where Harriet spends her first night in South Carolina is hard to pinpoint. Someone presumably sends her to stay among her people, until she can present her letter to one of the generals and make arrangements for housing.

David Hunter is almost sixty when, after recovering from a wound received at Bull Run, he accepts the assignment at Port Royal. A West Pointer and professional soldier, known as an independent thinker, an activist, and a frank, no-nonsense abolitionist, Hunter is stern-faced, with a high forehead and a bluntness of expression that is only somewhat offset by low-parted, swirled dark hair and a large, drooping mustache, the ends of which curl beneath his jaw.

Sometime during that spring, Harriet presents her letter from Elbridge Dudley to the man his soldiers sometimes call "Black Dave." Knowing of his stance regarding abolition and the arming of Negroes for battle, she must anticipate a good working relationship with the outspoken general.

As is her custom, Harriet does not waste time but goes immediately to work, setting up shop and taking charge of the Christian Commission house, which has been set up by the YMCA. There, she oversees the distribution of food, clothes, and books to Union soldiers. In no time, with two hundred dollars wangled from the government, she manages to put up what she calls a washhouse, where she teaches freed women to wash, iron, sew, and bake for the soldiers and, as a natural consequence, to support themselves with wages earned from that work and thereby establish some independence.

At first, she receives government rations like other soldiers. But to perform her job as a scout successfully, she must establish trust among the black people, and when they become standoffish because of her preferential treatment, she relinquishes the privilege. Once she gives up her government dispensation, she's on her own. In her two years of work in South Carolina, she will draw a total of only twenty days' rations.

In no time, she manages to maneuver her way through red tape and rules, the various levels of command. Once she can negotiate the streets and waterways, she finds allies, informants, and cohorts. With their help, she purchases supplies at the Beaufort wharf or across the river in Hilton Head, where a number of buildings have been constructed: a hotel, two or three eating houses, a post office, and many small naval stores. She makes friends with a man who lives across the road from the commissary. With his help, she bargains for good prices, then hauls the salt, sugar, hominy, flour, coffee—whatever she's managed to accumulate— back to Beaufort, where she either sells the provisions or uses them in the pies and root beer she makes and peddles.

Estimates of her output are pretty staggering. To keep herself and her family in Auburn going, Harriet tells Bradford, she makes about fifty pies each evening, as well as a large amount of gingerbread and two casks of root beer. She then hires "some contraband" to go through the camps, selling her wares.

She has become a teacher after all, giving practical lessons in negotiation and strategy when a labor system changes from slave to wage. Money changes hands. The former slaves learn the value of a particular bill or coin, and how the trade of goods for money works. They conduct business on their own. When they return to Harriet, they are paid for their labors. The entrepreneurial spirit that enabled Harriet to negotiate a hiring-out deal with Anthony C. Thompson blooms again.

Her eating establishment and washhouse are located around the corner from the Tabernacle Baptist Church and two blocks from the old arsenal. She lives nearby, when she is not on the move, at what she calls the Savan House, opposite the arsenal. Beaufort is a small city of compact neighborhoods. Harriet's washhouse and place of residence are in the hot middle of things, very near the general's headquarters and the military hospitals.

Spring brushes past, hardly noticed, a quick season before the onset of summer. Tireless, Harriet learns the ropes, observes, asks, listens, works pretty much all the time.

In and out the door come white soldiers and freed black people.

Lincoln still favors colonization and the separation of the races, but in April, the District of Columbia abolishes slavery. Stunned by this development, Frederick Douglass says he thinks he must be dreaming.

And on May 9, David Hunter gains permanent claim to Harriet's admiration when, ignoring possible presidential objections, he goes out on a limb and declares that since "slavery and martial law in a free country are altogether incompatible," all persons in the three states under his jurisdiction formerly held as slaves are therefore declared "forever free."

Among the black men who patronize her washhouse and eating establishment, Harriet is especially keen to meet potential scouts and spies, those who have local knowledge of the land, the water, and especially the families living in rebel territory above Saint Helena Sound and along the rivers to the north of Beaufort. There, along the Combahee (pronounced Kum-bee) River, toward the Yemassee junction of the Charleston-Savannah railroad, are sprawling rice plantations, worked by a great many slaves.

Only twenty miles long, the Combahee's a tidal river, narrow, shallow, and tortuously twisting. Rebel pickets stand guard along the riverbanks night and day. For gunboats to sail safely up the Combahee, scouts must conduct careful advance work, locating the torpedoes, the farms, the pickets.

During this time, Harriet meets Walter D. Plowden, a black man who has made his way from New York City to Beaufort by tagging along with a regiment from his home state. Clearly, Plowden is a quick study, because in no time he convinces Harriet that he knows the Combahee, the general countryside, and the mind of local planters. Together, they make plans. What Harriet needs now is a fearless and like-minded Union soldier, an all-out abolitionist warrior like John Brown, who will recognize her skills and let her either lead or colead the expedition up the river.

There is such an officer in her future, but he is still in Kansas and will not arrive in Port Royal for another seven or eight months.

Ten days after David Hunter's declaration of emancipation, Lincoln revokes it.

But by the time he does, Hunter has issued another, even more controversial order, requiring all able-bodied Negro men between eighteen and forty-five who are capable of bearing arms to go to Hilton Head at once. Days later, five hundred men are taken to the island to learn army drills and train to become armed U.S. soldiers.

The response is electric. While Governor Andrew of Massachusetts approves of Hunter's order and hopes that Lincoln will sustain it and recognize the ability and willingness of all men to be capable of loyalty, other abolitionists disapprove. They believe that by ordering the freed slaves to serve, Hunter has transcended the sphere of his duty. The freedmen themselves recoil in suspicion and terror.

In Harriet's words, because they are "as much afraid of the Yankee Buckra as of their own masters," the former slaves suspect a trap. A persistent rumor resurfaces. Once they are in Hilton Head, the black men fear, the army will round them up and send them away from their families, to Cuba, where they will be enslaved once again. No pay scale has been determined; no government order is issued approving Hunter's move; nonetheless, he orders uniforms for his new conscripts, dark blue jackets and—a critical lapse in judgment—ridiculously full scarlet Zouave pants.

Harriet does not comment on David Hunter's actions and she takes no public position about the arming of freedmen, but all black people in Port Royal are affected. The talk and rumors fly across the rivers and over the sounds. After three weeks of army drill, the black men are allowed to go home. But Hunter's heavy-handedness has unalterably alienated their trust and willingness to serve, and by the end of July, he has given up badgering the War Department for support. Secretary of War Edwin Stanton has sent a new man, Gen. Rufus Saxton, to Beaufort to take command of the plantations and their inhabitants. Ironically enough, at the end of August, Saxton himself will be authorized to raise five regiments of black troops from his jurisdiction, presumably because Lincoln and Stanton feel that he, not Hunter, is the man for the job.

About these issues and Hunter's reputation as an "ultraabolitionist," Harriet says nothing.

In June, the Garden of Eden becomes a sweat house. Accustomed to the stultifying mugginess of a wet southern climate, Harriet and the islanders make their way through it unscathed. But the soldiers—many of them from the New England states—have not experienced anything like it, and they suffer hard and fall often. In the broiling sun, their schedules seem particularly brutal. Morning bugle call for cooks is 5:30 A.M.; for soldiers, it's half an hour later. All day long, drum rolls announce roll calls, meals, and hours of drills. At 8:15 P.M., drum taps call for lights-out.

As June moves into July, the sun seems to move even closer. In their wool uniforms, the soldiers march, mount the guard, and perform drills. Battalion drills, writes Calvin Shedd, sweat the life out of the soldiers, man after man falling in a dead faint to the ground, their thick uniform coats and pants so wet that "you could wring the sweat out in streams not in drops."

On the Fourth of July, the teachers of Saint Helena Island host a big celebration at the Oaks, a plantation house where many of them live.

The day begins at 4:00 A.M., when the volunteers raise the flag and have an early breakfast with Saxton. They proceed to the Saint Helena Episcopal Church, where after a brief service, the teachers and the plantation superintendents take their seats with Saxton on a platform set up in the churchyard. There—according to the white people's journals and letters—they await the arrival of the black residents of the island, who soon approach. Filing down the road in a winding procession, the emancipated men, women, and children sway together while singing a gospel hymn, "Roll, Jordan, Roll."

Does Harriet make her way to the island to attend the celebration? Probably not. She's pretty busy. And she may not feel as if there's much to celebrate yet. On this same day, Frederick Douglass issues a savage attack at Lincoln for shielding and protecting slavery and for interfering with the antislavery policy of some of his most trustworthy generals, including, presumably, David Hunter.

Harriet may stay in her quarters in Beaufort. On the other hand, she likes gatherings and may be persuaded to ride over with others on a skiff. Once the black people have arrived at the church, the speeches begin, and more songs are sung. After the missionaries serve the freedmen lunch—crackers, dried herring, molasses, and water—they ride off to enjoy their own meal.

That night, while the Gideonites are singing old songs at the Oaks, the black people come once again to join in. Carrying lighted pitch knots to guide their way, they have come to treat the teachers to a private ritual, the "shout." In the early days of Gullah culture, dancing was banned by plantation owners, and so the workers created a kind of shuffle, keeping their toes pointed straight ahead, never crossing one foot over the other. The freed slaves still perform the traditional shuffle, mostly in the little praise houses dotted about the islands. At the Oaks, they demonstrate these steps for the teachers while singing songs in their special dialect and occasionally calling out to one another in a Sea Island version of call and response.

Entranced, the Gideonites sit watching into the late hours of the night, until finally the laborers make their way back home and their teachers retire to their own rooms.

By late July, summer clamps down.

"Fleas and vermin have been intolerable," writes one of the teachers in her diary, "but now the mosquitoes are almost unendurable." On the twenty-seventh, a company commander dies. Four of the Gideonites succumb. Others go home to recover. The hospitals—former churches and mansions in Beaufort—are filled with patients suffering from yellow fever, smallpox, malaria, dysentery. Soldiers are given cayenne pepper for fever and ague, summer pills for diarrhea, and blue pills for jaundice. Suffering from chronic dysentery, Calvin Shedd tells his family that if wounded, he would thank God if, rather than the hospital in Beaufort, he could have a place "as good as our Cow Stall" to die in.

Under the supervision of Henry K. Durant, the acting assistant surgeon in charge of contraband hospitals in Beaufort, Harriet goes to work as a nurse.

As the hospitals fill, she tends to ill soldiers and freed men and women, most of them sick rather than wounded. At this time, she is assigned primarily to the care of the people of her own race, but when necessity requires, she is often asked to give service to white people, as well.

When Harriet makes a request for some bourbon to administer to a patient, Durant provides her with signed instructions to the dispensing captain to give it to her.

Later in her life, when the war has ended and Harriet has begun her long effort to receive back pay and a government pension for this work, Dr. Durant will confirm her claims utterly. He knew her, he will write in a letter of support, for two years, and in that time he had ample opportunity to observe her general deportment, kindness, and attention to the sick and suffering of her race.

Her daily schedule is rigorous and unchanging. At night, she makes pies, gingerbread, and root beer. For patients suffering from dysentery, Harriet, while doing her cooking, boils up a concoction of roots and herbs into a tea. Every morning, she rises early and goes to one of the hospitals. There she bathes wounds, waves away the flies, helps people care for themselves, feeds those who need it her root concoction, the only cure, she says, that works.

For all of this work and during all of this time, she receives no pay.

Proceeding more judiciously than his predecessor, Rufus Saxton raises the first full-strength black regiment in the Union army—among its members some remaining Hunter conscriptees. He trains the First South Carolina Volunteers well and treats them with respect; they respond with alacrity and, to show their gratitude, give him an affectionate nickname: "General Saxby." His orders from the War Department authorize him to give the Negroes the same pay and rations allowed to all volunteers, an important stipulation, which in future will be ignored and altered many times over.

In November 1862, he invites the abolitionist minister, editor, and John Brown Secret Six supporter, Thomas Wentworth Higginson, to lead the Negro troops. Already a captain of the Fifty-first Massachusetts Volunteer Infantry, Higginson is fairly bowled over by the request. He could not have been more surprised, he will write, if invited to "take command of a regiment of Kalmuck Tartars." By this time, Lincoln has confounded his abolitionist doubters by issuing the Preliminary Emancipation Proclamation, declaring all slaves in the states in rebellion to be "forever free," effective January 1, 1863.

Harriet may be the only black person in the country who is unsurprised by Lincoln's announcement. The vision of freedom that came to her two years earlier made it clear that emancipation would come not in the far distant future but in her time. She alone takes the declaration in stride, only disappointed in its limitations, which exclude her niece and nephew and all others enslaved in Maryland, a border state still officially loyal to the Union. To hold on to their servants, some Eastern Shore farmers are even arranging to indenture them, fearing their imminent release. Lincoln's proclamation includes an equally dramatic shift in policy when he authorizes the enlistment of any able-bodied African American wishing to be of service to the Union forces in the South.

Thomas Wentworth Higginson resigns his Massachusetts captaincy and accepts Saxton's appointment. By the time he arrives in South Carolina in late November, a few days before Thanksgiving, preparations are already under way for an elaborate celebration of the dawning of emancipation in the United States, on New Year's Day.

After landing at Hilton Head, Colonel Higginson transfers to a riverboat, which takes him to the White Hall Ferry landing, a few miles south of Beaufort. There, they dock at Camp Saxton, formerly the Smith Plantation and before that Charlesfort, built by French Huguenots in 1562. Beyond the landing, the new commander of the First South Carolina Volunteers walks through an avenue of large, deep-skirted magnolia trees, their lemony blooms now having become mulch at their roots. The two-centuries-old walls of the fort have crumbled and gone to ruin, but they still stand, overgrown with tall bushes and aromatic cedars. On the other side of the wall, groves of magnificent live oaks are draped with long swags of moss so thick that they block the sun, creating a kind of permanent dusk in the campground. Within the groves are the white tents of the First South Carolina Volunteers, who are quartered there. Set on a rise, the two-storied columned house overlooks the Beaufort River, which there, at the base of the island, is deep and wide.

He reports to Saxton, who welcomes the young colonel.

A believer in the importance of discipline and regimentation, Higginson moves quickly into command, taking the regiment through a systematic course of daily drills. The volunteers respond energetically. When the emancipation celebration is held on January 1, they will be ready to display their skills.

At long last, the American black man has been allowed to participate in the war against the enslavement of himself, his family, and his descendants. Higginson's position is historic and, for a dedicated abolitionist—the sole member of the Secret Six who refused to flee after John Brown's capture—an appointment of consummate satisfaction.

Shortly after he arrives, Harriet goes unannounced to Camp Saxton to visit. Higginson seems surprised and pleased to see his old friend, whom he once described as the greatest heroine of the age. Harriet, he writes his wife, is working in Beaufort as a sort of nurse and general caretaker.

Thanksgiving falls on Thursday, the twenty-seventh. Saxton declares a holiday. According to Higginson, the daylong air is full of chronic drumming and the pop-pop of "prize-shooting" guns. William Johnson, a Union soldier from Connecticut, describes the holiday menu as stuffed chicken, roast pig, oysters, apples, pies, good coffee and tea—all in all, quite a feast, he says—and after dinner, games of all kinds, sack races being the most prominent.

Perhaps Harriet gets a taste of the chicken. Or maybe she sells the pies to the quartermaster herself and stays home. She's busy. And while she can work with and admire people like Higginson, her deeper attachments lean toward the more directly passionate kind of combatant, the all-out holy warrior, like John Brown and David Hunter. Certainly Hunter acted precipitously. After declaring martial law undemocratic, he then acted in contradiction of his statement by ignoring the freedmen's rights and fears, commanding them, against their will, to become soldiers. He might have done well to consult Harriet ahead of time. But consultation and collaboration come hard to such a man, and whatever mistakes he might have made, Harriet admires him. "Black Dave" has defined the enemy in the simplest of terms and he is as ferocious a fighter as John Brown was and—as it turns out—Harriet will be.

In late November, the sickly season passes. Christmas approaches. Holidays can be treacherous, reminding us of the past—people lost and gone.

In Harriet's case, this means people sold, enslaved, missing. She spends another Christmas lonesome for her family.

Two days before the Emancipation Proclamation goes into effect, on December 30, the stars align once again when the Union officer she has been waiting for, the ambitious and fiery Jayhawker, Col. James Montgomery, who rode with John Brown and is friends with the influential and wealthy George L. Stearns, heads for Washington, D.C. Disgruntled in Kansas, the restless Montgomery craves a commanding position in the South. Having lobbied Stearns for help, he meets in Washington with

Col. James Montgomery

the president, who, he says, receives him kindly. There's no record of Lincoln having approved of the appointment, but while in the nation's capital, the Jayhawker makes friends with a man who—disgruntled for his own reasons—will make it happen.

David Hunter, Montgomery writes Stearns, "is doing what he can for me. He wants me to go South with him. . . ."

Two weeks later—despite his indictment for having destroyed ballot boxes in Kansas and his reputation for hotheadedness, impulsiveness, and the retaliatory burning of private homes—on January 13, 1863, the former Campbellite preacher receives authorization to raise a regiment of South Carolina volunteer infantry from among the freedmen.

With General Hunter, James Montgomery heads immediately south to the Lowcountry.

Harriet awaits his arrival.

Scene 16.

The Proclamation, the Raid

Once the time was, I cried all night. . . . The next morning my child was to be sold and she was sold and I never expected to see her no more till the day of judgment. Now, no more that! No more that! . . . They can't sell my wife and child anymore, bless the Lord. No more that! . . . No more that, now! President Lincoln has shot the gate!

—EX-SLAVE, AT A MEETING OF FREEDMEN TO
CELEBRATE THE EMANCIPATION PROCLAMATION,
DECEMBER 31, 1862, WASHINGTON, D.C.;
PUBLISHED IN *THE LIBERATOR*, JANUARY 16, 1863

I had my jubilee three years ago. I rejoiced all I could den. I can't rejoice no more.

—HARRIET TUBMAN ON EMANCIPATION DAY,
AS QUOTED BY SARAH BRADFORD, *HARRIET TUBMAN,
THE MOSES OF HER PEOPLE*, 1886

Winter in the South can drive you crazy—warm as spring one day, bone-deep freezing the next. Sometimes the temperature isn't that low, especially to Northerners. But oh, the damp, merciless air, the piercing breezes!

New Year's Day of 1863—Emancipation Day—dawns blue-skied but the coldest day the volunteers have yet experienced. Harriet might have warned the Gideonites not to expect to be warm all the time, even in the lower South, where one week bluebirds and butterflies still flit about and the next the air's turned to ice. Northerners don't understand. It gets cold enough down there, Harriet has said, to bring on the ague.

But on this day, few notice.

And when the rowboats show up to bring the missionaries, the plantation superintendents, and the emancipated men and women from Saint Helena to Beaufort, everybody boards without complaint. Some freed people have stayed at home, especially many of the men, who are still suspicious of any occasion sponsored by white men. But those attending have donned their gayest holiday attire, as have the white teachers and plantation superintendents.

The boatmen sing the celebrants across to the Beaufort wharf, where they transfer to a small steamer, the *Flora,* sent by Rufus Saxton to take them downriver to Camp Saxton, where the festivities will take place. The marching band of the Eighth Maine has volunteered to contribute, and they are on board the *Flora* during the back and forthing, to keep the music going and play their passengers' way to the landing, blasting out hymns and patriotic songs all the way down the three miles of cold, calm water.

Eclipsed by preparations for the bigger event, except for prayer meetings and private shouts, Christmas Day—the greatest day of a slave's year—has been largely ignored. Harriet might be a little sulky about this. She may want to stay home; on the other hand, Higginson's troops will make their first public appearance this afternoon; she may want to cheer on the black soldiers. If she goes, she can either take the *Flora* or get there on foot, going straight west, then south down the river—altogether about three miles. Probably she walks, perhaps with her new sidekick, Walter D. Plowden, or maybe alone.

The party starts at ten o'clock, by which time all is in order. Expecting as many as five thousand people, Saxton has laid in great stores of hard bread, lemonade, and—for dessert—tobacco. Since the morning of December 31, ten whole beeves threaded on spits made of young trees have been slowly roasting. By firelight, cooks have been turning the meat and applying frequent bastings, leaning over the deeply dug pit filled with burning oak. For drink, there is molasses water—one barrel per company, ten in all. Designed to produce cheer but not

inebriation, the molasses water is made up of three gallons of molasses
to one of water, plus a half-pound of ginger and a quart of vinegar:
a burning, spicy drink, which only the men will imbibe.

The scheduled events begin. There are speeches and poems, occasional songs. On the platform, mostly white people sit, lined up and
ready to give talks and be honored. The audience—among civilians,
mostly women—sits on the ground or on blankets. Some have found a
place to sit along the low ruined wall of the courtyard. Some soldiers
watch from horseback.

Perhaps Harriet is in the audience, and since the speeches are long
and the narcoleptic episodes of her youth still come back to take her
away from time to time, she might well periodically nod off. She surely
awakens, however, when William Brisbane, a native Sea Island planter
who freed his slaves years before, reads the historic document, declaring
that on the first day of January in the year 1863, "all persons held as
slaves within any State or designated part of a State, the people whereof
shall then be in rebellion against the United States, shall be then,
thenceforward, and forever free. . . ."

Thenceforward and forever.

The proclamation is short. It ends with Lincoln's stated belief that
since this act is one of justice, warranted by the U.S. Constitution, he
asks for the considerate judgment of man and the gracious favor of
God.

The proclamation is signed by the president and his secretary of
state, Harriet's friend, William Seward.

Once those names are read out, the Camp Saxton audience rises
and cheers, and the African Americans among them sing "My Country
'Tis of Thee" for the first time in their lives.

After other ceremonial tributes and presentations, the first black
troops of the U.S. Army perform a dress parade, smartly and in perfect
order, bayonets glinting in the sun as, in their dark blue coats and red
Zouave trousers, they march and drill to the music of the Eighth
Maine. Everyone is extremely impressed with their military precision,
including white officers, who have come primarily to scoff.

A great day, declares the newly arrived African American teacher
Charlotte Forten. A day when "freedom was surely born in our land."

Harriet has many reasons to celebrate the inclusion of black men in the army, but wherever she is on this day, it's obvious she isn't into the spirit of things.

People keep coming up to ask her why she isn't rejoicing like everybody else.

"I had *my* jubilee three years ago," she replies. "I rejoiced all I could then. I can't rejoice no more."

There's a sulky sadness in that declaration, a kind of stubborn unwillingness to yield to the occasion. She's a depressing influence, insisting, as she does, on a point of honor during an otherwise upbeat, historical day. It seems unlike her to pull, in a sense, cynical rank in this fashion by reminding the celebrants of what's still left undone. But she has her reasons. For one thing, Maryland does not fall within the president's list of the states in rebellion against the United States, and so the people in bondage there—her family—remain unprotected. And if we take a careful look at some of her pictures—say the formal portrait taken in the 1860s, when she's standing in a dark dress with her hands carefully posed on the arm of a settee—we can detect a kind of sullen fury in the hard stare of those hooded eyes and the clenched set of her jaw. Lincoln's Emancipation Proclamation is a good start, but it doesn't fulfill the promise of her vision.

"My people are free!" she said. And on this day, some are—but not all.

After the meal, when dusk is falling and the festivities are ending, partygoers gather on the crumbling wall of the old fort, waiting to go home. From there, they hear the approach of the *Flora* as from on board, the Eighth Maine's band plays "Sweet Home." Moonlight streams across the river, ahead of the boat, "the perfect stillness around, the wildness and solitude of the ruins," giving the old song special poignancy. No one wants to leave. They would like to stay for the soldiers' jubilee and shouts, which will last far into the night.

On their way to Beaufort, the passengers sing with the band, and on the boat to Saint Helena, the boatmen pull their oars to the beat of Gullah hymns. All join in for what Charlotte Forten calls "the John Brown song."

The night ends in a hopeful, if wary, sigh.

At home in her little cabin, Harriet stirs and bakes for the next day's vending. Work takes her mind off homesickness. She doesn't know how her parents are, or anyone else in her family. Her sister-in-law Catherine gave birth to a son, Adam, back in August 1861, and she hasn't seen the baby since just after his birth. And she's sad for those of her family still enslaved. She's been planning a trip north for some time, but she can't leave yet. Beaufort is where she belongs, and more work lies ahead.

Alone, absorbed in her own thoughts, she rolls the pie dough, beats the gingerbread batter, sleeps little.

Within the week, as if with the snap of a finger, things change.

For some time now, Harriet has been building her own army, a band of men to serve undercover in the coming campaigns. By now, she has given Saxton the names of nine men who know the channels of the rivers around Beaufort well enough to pilot boats through those tricky waterways during high and low tide. Saxton signs off on her list, and Harriet is given one hundred dollars of Secret Service money to use as she sees fit.

Now that black soldiers are an official part of the U.S. Army, it seems, she can begin her work as a spy and a scout.

Later in January, David Hunter arrives in Beaufort after a four-month leave. He doesn't get there in time to see Higginson's men parade up and down the main streets of Beaufort on the nineteenth, conveniently, it seems, missing out on the men's second triumph. Instead, he stages a surprise visit two days later, when the soldiers are in their old clothes, conducting an ordinary battalion drill. The embittered Hunter nonetheless congratulates the men, who cheer him lustily despite their previous distrust. They become especially sanguine after he promises them muskets, pay (when it arrives from Washington), and—conceding his previous wardrobe error—blue pants.

Soon afterward, he shows up with the newly appointed commander of South Carolina's second African American regiment and Hunter's heir apparent in impulsiveness and radical abolitionism, Col. James Montgomery.

Having been born and educated in Ohio, showing no trace of the refined manners and class snobbism of the New Englanders, Montgomery, at forty-nine, brings the West to the campgrounds. Hunter, Saxton, and Higginson are West Pointers and believe in a disciplined attitude toward warfare. Montgomery, on the other hand, joined the regular service as a member of the Kansas Volunteer Infantry and has no faith in or need to abide by rules of fair play. He is, instead, an Old Testament kind of warrior, one who believes in the redemptive power of violence uninhibited by "effete notions of the rules of civilized warfare."

When Montgomery was accused of leading a band of Jayhawkers no better than murderers and robbers, he took exception. "Montgomery's *men are the people,*" he replied, "and Montgomery himself is one of them."

A man of and for the people, who calls himself by his own last name, he will not sup easily with the gentlemen officers in Beaufort.

Harvard-educated Higginson is hard-pressed not to support Montgomery, however, if for no other reason than their mutual love for John Brown. But after a couple of military experiences with the Jayhawker, he calls him an incorrigible brigand: "splendid but impulsive and changeable; never plans far ahead, and goes off at a tangent . . . embraces the conceptions of foraging." ". . . Not a harsh or cruel man but a singular mixture of fanaticism, vanity and genius" . . . and "a terrible hater."

The young Robert Gould Shaw, also of a genteel Massachusetts upbringing, will describe him as a man who "never drinks, smokes or swears, and considers that praying, shooting, burning and hanging are the true means to put down a rebellion."

A former minister of the Disciples of Christ, Montgomery believes in a social gospel and in mystical visions, something called "The Gleam," which comes to those who have faith enough to see it. Tall, weatherbronzed from exposure to Kansas wind and sun, with his full beard and burning eyes, he might pass for old John Brown's cousin.

Foreshadowing the attitude of William T. Sherman by more than a year, Montgomery brushes away criticism of his vengeful aggression. "Southerners," he will say, "must be made to feel that this is a real war and that they [are] to be swept away by the hand of God like the Jews of old."

James Montgomery knows of Harriet's reputation, perhaps from

John Brown himself. When, in time, he writes a letter in support of her pension claim, he will say that he was previously acquainted with her character and actions.

Harriet takes immediately to the Jayhawker. He arrives late in January, and in February, when General Hunter asks if she will go with several gunboats up the Combahee River on an expedition to take up torpedoes, destroy railroads and bridges, and cut off supplies from the rebel troops, she says she will, on one condition: that Colonel Montgomery is the commander.

Accordingly, infers Sarah Bradford, giving Harriet that much say-so, the colonel is appointed to lead the expedition.

Not long after his conversation with her, Hunter issues Harriet an extraordinarily inclusive military pass, giving her free passage on government transports from Hilton Head to Beaufort and wherever else she wants to go.

"Harriet," Hunter writes, "was sent to me from Boston by Governor Andrew, of Massachusetts, and is a valuable woman. She has permission, as a servant of the Government, to purchase such provisions from the Commissary as she may need." The pass is signed by Hunter. In June, when Gen. Quincy A. Gilmore succeeds Hunter as commander of the Department of the South, he will append his own signature.

She has appointed Walter Plowden her chief cohort and fellow undercover scout. Plowden, who lives across from the Hilton Head commissary, has the nerve and willingness to navigate a ship through tides and channels under duress. Plowden may or may not have been a real expert, but because of Harriet, he will become one of the most valued scouts and pilots in the government's employ.

While Montgomery searches for recruits, Harriet and Walter Plowden use the one hundred dollars of Secret Service money to buy supplies. They are simultaneously making forays outside the area of Union occupation, into rebel territory, while continuing to work together in the everyday operations of Harriet's eating establishment, taking large amounts of brown sugar, coffee, hardbread, and other supplies from the commissary to her cabin.

While they work the home front, Montgomery makes recruiting

journeys into Florida, first to Fernandina, just south of the Georgia line. When he finds that territory already mined, he sails all the way to the tip of the country, to Key West, where he signs up 130 men.

That same month, Harriet's sister-in-law Catherine Stewart buries her baby, eighteen-month-old Adam, in Auburn. There is no way to know whether or not Harriet receives this sad news. Sarah Bradford has met Rit during a Sunday School class and she may be writing letters for her. But sending word to the South is more difficult than ever now, and Harriet has lost track of many of her old contacts. And so she may not find out for some time.

In March, Montgomery takes his small regiment on a raid with Higginson and the First South Carolina Volunteers, to Jacksonville, Florida, hoping to find able-bodied Negro men willing to serve. But the slaveholders have taken most of the male slaves away, and while Montgomery does manage to confiscate several thousand dollars' worth of cotton and supplies, he returns with only thirty recruits. Whether Harriet went on this trip is not known. She will sometimes accompany expeditions as a nurse and may have done that at this time. Or she might have stayed in Beaufort to continue gathering intelligence. Since Higginson doesn't mention her presence in his very detailed diary, the latter seems more likely.

When the regiments return to Beaufort, Montgomery will receive praise from Higginson for his brilliant, if incautious, foraging of food, bricks, lumber, and sheep, as well as for the arrest of thirteen rebel soldiers, surprised while sleeping on picket duty. The successful expedition is marred only by the unnecessary torching of one section of Jacksonville during the Union withdrawal, an act of vandalism assigned to white soldiers, who set the fires in secret, led by one whose identity remains officially unspecified.

By the end of May, plans are set for a raid up the Combahee, the object of which is to destroy rebel lines of communication and to gather recruits from among the laborers. Harriet and Walter Plowden have mapped out the river channels and the effects of high and low tides. They have sent word to the bonded laborers to listen for a signal; when they hear it, they are to drop everything and run. Montgomery has raised five companies. A portion of the Third Regiment Rhode Island Heavy Artillery will also participate. For Harriet, the raid will offer her the first opportunity she has had to go head-to-head with a lifelong enemy and, using skill, deliberation, and force, to take away from them what never was theirs to begin with. The good Lord has come to deliver her people and she is taking her place in the lead gunboat of the expedition to help out.

Navigating a river like the Combahee requires patience, if not a tolerance for pure tedium. And because smoke is visible for miles, steam-driven expeditions begin under cover of darkness—usually at high tide and under a full moon—and end at the enemy's doorstep at daybreak, before he has fully awakened.

Harriet's mission, however, embarks on the night of a new moon, the sky dark but for stars. Clearly, Montgomery is depending on Plowden's expertise to navigate the boats safely upriver, even in pure darkness. The Combahee is narrow, shallow, winding and muddy, with ridges of sand that shift with the tides. Every nuance of its particular personality must be taken into account, secretly, silently and with all confidence. Under such circumstances, the military commander waits and watches, yielding to the expertise of his scouts.

On the night of June 1, 1863, a Monday, Harriet and Walter step onto the lead gunboat, the *John Adams*.

A converted old East Boston double-ender ferryboat, the *John Adams,* while unfit for sea service, is small, dependable, agile, and strong, perfect for river work—especially on a river that twists and turns. She has seen such duty before. To negotiate some of the hairpin turns, a ship's captain will sometimes run the *Adams* aground, then, after allowing the current to swing her around, reverse her engines and proceed. With front and rear paddles sturdy enough to cut through ice, she has led a number of expeditions into Florida and is known in the Sea Islands as "chief reliance." After the war, she will be sent back to Boston, where she will resume her work as an everyday ferryboat.

James Montgomery joins Harriet and Walter on the lead ship. Two other vessels will follow her, the *Harriet A. Weed* and the *Sentinel.* The troops load on.

At 9:00 P.M., the boats, carrying three hundred soldiers, slide into the river. Under Plowden's guidance, they head north along the banks of Lady's Island, then angle west into St. Helena's Sound, where, helped by the incoming tide, they move toward the mouth of the river.

Narrow and only forty miles long, the Combahee was once, ironically enough, called the River Jordan, when in 1520 Spaniards on a slave-hunting expedition discovered and claimed it. Two hundred years later, when it was regained by the Cusabo Indians, the river took on the name of the subtribe living along its banks in a village called Combe.

Undoubtedly, Harriet is the only woman on the expedition and it is a tribute to the fierce independence of spirit exhibited by both Hunter and Montgomery that they have insisted, not just on making use of her expertise, but having her on board as well. No other woman will plan and lead an armed expedition during the entire Civil War. Few women have done so in U.S. military history. A woman, a black woman, a former slave: she is essentially in charge.

General Tubman.

While trying to find her way through the sound, the *Sentinel* runs aground. The men make an effort to dislodge her from the muck, the roots, and the sea grass, but she is too caught up and remains stuck. It is past midnight now, and so Montgomery orders the *Sentinel* forces transferred into the other two boats. And quietly they proceed, the *Adams* taking a quarter-mile lead over the *Harriet.*

On the morning of June 2 at about 2:30 A.M., the boats reach the mouth of the Combahee, and there successfully cross the bar and move into the river.

In the South, June brings hot nights and an abundance of mosquitoes, the muggy darkness alleviated somewhat by the amber flicker of fireflies. Frogs gulp and yelp. Crickets sing, a sharp noise, like a ringing in the ears. Fish jump and flop, an occasional dog bays. For the sake of secrecy, Montgomery orders the steam engines cut as low as possible, riding the tide to hush their movements. When they get closer to the rice fields they can hear the burble of the bobolinks, called ricebirds, who lurk and wait for early fall, when they will fatten themselves before the harvest.

Rice farmers in South Carolina have grown even fatter than the bobolinks. In 1850, 257 plantations along ten of the state's rivers produced nearly eighty thousand tons of rice and in 1860, nine of the fourteen slaveholders in the entire country who owned more than five hundred slaves were rice planters. They have learned from their West African slaves how to put tidal culture to use, a great percentage of the enslaved workers having come from along the Gambia River and the "Rice Coast."

By dawn, the *Adams* and the *Harriet* have reached their first destination, about twenty miles up the river. They drop anchor. On the Colleton County side of the Combahee, the sun is rising over the flat fields, red and slow. Fog rolls across the land. Having just finished their breakfast, the laborers have taken up their hoes and are moving into the fields.

At first light, Montgomery orders a steady pipe of the steam whistle and simultaneously sends troops in rowboats to the bank and into the fields.

"The people was all a-hoeing," an old man named Minus Hamilton will remember. "They was a-hoeing in the field when the gunboats came."

And when the fog rolls off and the sun comes through, the workers can see the boats and the black men in blue uniforms rising from the river, armed and standing upright with their heads up (so *presumptious!* the old man will exclaim), and they drop their tools and run.

General Tubman is standing fast, watching.

From the rebels, no response. After sending several false reports of approaching troops, pickets have been warned against making precipitous alerts. And so instead of firing off warning signals, they send messengers to notify planters and drivers. "Negro troops," they report, are approaching. By the time residents and soldiers realize what is happening, the slaves are running away.

In 1905, remembering the raid, Harriet will break into convulsive laughter.

"I never seen such a sight . . . Some was getting their breakfasts, just taking their pots of rice off the fire, and they'd put a cloth on top their heads and set that on, rice a smoking, young one hanging on behind one hand round the mother's forehead to hold on, the other hand digging into the rice pot, eating with all its might."

And she laughs again, remembering women holding tied-up white blankets on their heads, with their "things" done up in them. Any woman

who didn't have a pot of rice had a child or two in her arms, or holding
on to her dress. Some were carrying two children—often twins—one on
each hip, or one hanging on her neck and the other at her forehead.
Some had pigs in bags thrown over their shoulders; some carried flapping
chickens tied by the legs. The pigs squealing, the chickens squawking, all
running, running, running to the boat.

By now, overseers, slave drivers, and plantation owners have streamed out
into the fields to threaten the escaping workers, brandishing whips and
guns, decreeing death to any man or woman who disobeys orders and
doesn't follow them back toward the woods. Some call to the fleeing
workers to run and hide, saying the Yankees have come to sell them to
Cuba!

    No one pays them any mind. Every man and woman in the field
heads the other way, straight to the boat. Weeks afterward, Minus Hamilton described the morning to Wentworth Higginson: While his master
was shouting, "Run to the wood for hide! Yankee come, see you to
Cuba . . . !" he went to the boat with his wife, he wearing only his shirt
and pantaloons, she with only the frock and kerchief she had on. They
left their two blankets tied up on the bank and ran toward the black soldiers who were so "presumptious, they came right ashore and [held] up
their heads."

    When Higginson asks Hamilton his age, he says he is eighty-eight.
"My old master keeps all the ages in a big book and when we come to
the age of sense, we mark them down every year, so I know."

    When asked if he is too old to have come away from the rice plan-
tation, Hamilton thinks Higginson must be joking. "Too old for come? . . .
Never too old for leave the land of bondage. I old . . . but give a thousand thanks every day."

    Several fleeing slaves are wounded, some killed, but most make it
safely to the riverbank. The Union expedition does not incur a single
loss.

    Montgomery orders the *Harriet* to remain where she is so that the
troops can exchange fire with the rebel pickets while boarding more
refugees. He then commands the *Adams* to sail another five miles north,
to the ferryboat landing, where there is a fine pontoon bridge.

After taking the ferry, Montgomery orders the bridge burned. North of the landing, there are obstructions in the river—either fallen trees or wooden piles placed there as a barrier by the rebels—which prevent further incursion, and so, with Harriet and Walter Plowden still aboard, the *Adams* turns back as the bridge burns and the ferry sinks, giving the rebels no way to cross the Combahee.

Montgomery's practice of redemptive torching has begun.

On the way back down the river, Montgomery orders fields and homes, mills, storehouses, and warehouses burned. The soldiers torch palatial mansions, destroying expensive furniture, paintings, china, imported rugs. The houses fall to the ground in smoldering ruins. Oak trees and palmettos are burned to a skeletal crisp, and when the soldiers break apart the sluice gates used to control tidal surges, the rice fields are flooded, leaving behind broad ponds where, only the day before, luxuriant rice crops grew. The loss is estimated at two million dollars, not counting the slaves.

When asked to describe the fires, Minus Hamilton says, "First thing I know there was a barn with ten thousand bushels of rough rice all in a blaze, then Master's great house all crackling up the roof."

Did he care?

He did not. "Didn't care, Lord . . . didn't care nothing at all. *I was going to the boat.*"

Rowboats wait to take the refugees to the steamers. People clamber on. But the boats are small, and when one fills up, people on the banks become afraid of being left behind. Panicky, they grab hold and pull the boat back. The oarsmen beat their hands, but the desperate refugees won't let go.

Standing on the deck of the *Adams,* Montgomery calls on Harriet, who in South Carolina, she says, is called "Moses Garrison."

"Moses," says the colonel, "come here and speak a word of consolation to your people."

Well, Harriet tells Emma Telford, they weren't *her* people any more than they were his, excepting they were all Negroes. For in truth, she could barely understand their Gullah dialect and didn't know any more about them than he did. But she went out on the deck close to the rowboats and, not knowing what to say that would be of consolation, stood there for about two minutes.

She stands above them on the *Adams,* waiting for something to come to her, a sign, telling her what to do.

Finally, her head clears. She lifts her voice and, instead of making a speech or trying to provide reason and calm, sings:

> *Come from the East*
> *Come from the West*
> *'Mong all the glorious nations*
> *This glorious one's the best.*
> *Come alone, come along, don't be alarmed*
> *For Uncle Sam is rich enough*
> *To give you all a farm.*

Illustration from *Harper's Weekly,* depicting Colonel James Montgomery's 1863 raid on the rice plantations on the Combahee River in South Carolina, in which at least 750 slaves were freed and brought into Union territory. Harriet served as chief spy and navigator for this campaign, and was much lauded for her part in it, by officers, freed slaves, and newspaper reporters.

The people holding on to the boat throw up their hands and shout. Once they let go, the rowboats push off, deliver that group of refugees, then go back for the next. Harriet doesn't stop singing until everyone is on board.

"We got 800 people that day," she will later boast. "And we tore up the railroad and fired the bridge!"

Others tally the count as 752, or 756. The wife of a Confederate soldier says six or seven hundred.

About Harriet's Maryland rescues, there are conflicting stories concerning the number of people she brought away. About this one, however, the count remains relatively steady.

The crowded steamers head downriver. They arrive in Beaufort the next day and there the refugees are housed temporarily in a church. Among those witnessing their return is a reporter from the *Wisconsin State Journal*, who a day or so later also attends an address given by Montgomery to the refugees.

When Montgomery is finished, he asks Harriet to speak.

And in July, the Wisconsin newspaper will publish the reporter's article, entitled "A Black She 'Moses'—Her Wonderful Daring and Tenacity," which focuses on Harriet's role in the expedition and calls her a "black heroine." He does not, however, call her by name. Nor is the writer's name recorded. He goes on to describe the raid as one in which Colonel Montgomery and his "gallant band of 300 soldiers under the guidance of a black woman dashed into the enemies' country, struck a bold and effective blow, destroying millions of dollars worth of commissary stores, cotton and lordly dwellings, and striking terror to the heart of rebellion. . . ."

Harriet's address to the refugees creates a great sensation. For sound sense and real native eloquence, the admiring Wisconsin reporter thinks her address would do honor to any man. Once again, he refers to her as "the black woman who led the raid and under whose inspiration it was originated and conducted."

In Boston, the *Commonwealth* will run excerpts of the *Wisconsin Journal* story, with comments by Harriet's friend Franklin Sanborn, who will inform his readers that the heroine of the story is none other than Harriet Tubman.

———

The day after the Combahee raid, twenty-six-year-old Robert Gould Shaw, leader of the Fifty-fourth Regiment Massachusetts Volunteer Infantry (Colored), reports to Hilton Head with his ten companies. Soon afterward, he and his regiment are sent on a raid of the Georgia coast with James Montgomery and his companies. After the pretty town of Darien, Georgia, has been conquered and pillaged, Montgomery turns to Shaw and, smiling, says, "I shall burn this town."

Afterward, he will boast that Darien "is now no more." From their campgrounds, Shaw, Montgomery, and the soldiers watch the flames rise from what once was a town, continuing to do so from three o'clock that afternoon until daylight the following morning.

Appointed by Massachusetts governor John Andrew as commander of a Northern regiment of black soldiers, the idealistic Shaw inquires as to the correctness of such action. Montgomery declares that since black troops are "outlawed," they are not bound by the rules of regular warfare.

Harriet doesn't go to Darien. She is busy taking care of the laborers from the rice plantations. She and Walter also have business in Beaufort, where they are called to testify at the court-martial of a camp superintendent, John Webster, accused of embezzling from the military by selling goods meant to be distributed among the residents of the camps. Harriet and Walter Plowden both testify that Webster did indeed sell them large amounts of brown sugar that spring. A shopkeeper verifies their story and also testifies that Harriet has personally reported the illegal sale to the general in charge, Rufus Saxton, in his home.

On June 5, 1863, ten witnesses, six of whom are black, testify in the court-martial of Pvt. John E. Webster. In Harriet's testimony, she says she twice bought about fifty pounds of brown sugar at the Hilton Head commissary, after Webster told her he had some to sell and that if she would take it, she could have the lot. Afterward, when she had agreed to the deal, she heard someone at her door call inside and say, "Here's your sugar." When she went to the door, a man was there to deliver it.

In the trial transcript, Harriet is identified as "Harriet Tubman (colored) a witness for the prosecution." Her testimony is crisp and detailed. Her friend Walter Plowden testifies, as well. They are both duly sworn in and their last names are provided for the record.

Based on the testimony of black witnesses, John Webster—a white man—is found guilty of three of the four accusations against him, then is sentenced to six months' labor without pay.

On June 30, Harriet dictates a letter to Franklin Sanborn, telling him of the raid, while making a request. Last fall, she tells him, when people in Beaufort became alarmed at the threat of a rebel invasion, she packed all her clothes and sent them to Hilton Head, where they were lost. Nobody knew what happened to them, and since she was sick at the time, she couldn't go look for them herself. And so she needs new ones.

"I want, among the rest, a bloomer dress, made of some coarse strong material to wear on expeditions."

Harriet may know about bloomer dresses from Gerrit Smith, whose daughter Elizabeth first came up with the idea and then wore one in public. Designed to promote health and ease in walking, the bloomer dress—full Turkish pantaloons under a skirt reaching a little below the knees—was named for an early, if lukewarm, supporter of the style, Amelia Bloomer. Much ridiculed, it was worn mostly by feminists and suffragists, and only for a short period of time.

Harriet had reason to order a bloomer dress. During the Combahee raid, she carried two pigs for a sick woman who had a child to carry. Montgomery's order was to move at doubletime, and so Harriet started to run. And since her dress was long, she stepped on it and, still holding the pig, fell. Her skirt tore. By the time she got on the boat, little was left of it but shreds.

"I made up my mind then," she declares to her friend, "I would never wear a long dress on another expedition . . . but would have a bloomer as soon as I could get it. So please make this known to the ladies if you will, for I expect to have use for it very soon, probably before they can get it to me."

There is no indication that she ever succeeded in obtaining a bloomer dress from Sanborn, even though Gerrit Smith was a fierce advocate of the liberating costume.

Harriet assumes that Sanborn has seen a full account of the expedition, and she wonders if he doesn't feel that "we colored people are entitled to some credit for that exploit, under the lead of the brave Colonel Montgomery?"

In her report to Sanborn, she estimates the number of "valuable live stock, known up in your region as 'contrabands' " at 756 and boasts that while they didn't lose a single life, "we had good reason to believe that a number of rebels bit the dust." Of those refugees, most of the able-bodied men have joined a colored regiment.

And then she speaks of her family: "I have now been absent two years almost, and have just got letters from my friends in Auburn, urging me to come home." But although her mother and father are old and in feeble health and need her care and attention, she does not see how she can leave at the present time with so much important work still to be done.

Among her duties is that of looking after the new refugees in the hospital, most of them destitute and almost naked. "I am trying to find places for those able to work, and provide for them as best I can, so as to lighten the burden on the Government. . . . while . . . they learn to respect themselves by earning their own living."

This may be her most difficult job yet. When the American Freedman's Inquiry Commission visits Hilton Head just after the raid, they will report that because of their extreme isolation, the slaves in the South Carolina Lowcountry have become, through the generations, markedly more degraded than those from other states.

There, the commission will report, slavery "has been darkening in its shades of inhumanity and moral degradation from year to year, exhibiting, more and more, increased cruelty, a more marked crushing out in life. . . ." Because earlier generations were treated with somewhat greater mercy and humanity, the slaves above age sixty testify more intelligently, while younger ones have descended into fear, despondency, and instilled intractability. Family names have been banned, mothers have been prohibited from eating with children, and nights spent in one-room huts have resulted in incest and defective offspring. When given a meal, younger refugees generally follow a lifelong habit and, clutching their dishes to their chests, steal off into a corner to eat in solitude.

Harriet struggles to instill in this recently liberated population some self-respect, a sense of community, family, even patriotism.

On July 10, Sanborn publishes excerpts from the *Wisconsin Journal* report and promises more stories about Harriet in the next issue. On the seventeenth, he includes excerpts of her letter in a loving biographical sketch—the first to be published—called simply "Harriet Tubman." He also issues a plea for donations to help her continue her work in South Carolina and in support of her family in Auburn. Someone seems to have responded, since that very week, one hundred dollars is deposited in her mortgage account with William Seward.

The fulsome lead paragraph ends by introducing a "poor black woman [who] has power to shake the nation that so long was deaf to her cries."

Does somebody read these words to her? Does she know what the newspapers are saying?

"We write," Sanborn continues, "of one of these heroines, of whom our slave annals are full—a woman whose career is as extraordinary as the most famous of her sex can show."

Finally, he names her: "Araminta Ross, now known by her married name of Tubman, with her sounding Christian name changed to Harriet . . ."

Named, known, acknowledged.

A pragmatist, her family's financial provider, she considers what benefits notoriety might bring, plans and thinks ahead.

Scene 17.

Raining Blood

It is of little consequence to a dying man whether any one else is to die by retaliation, but it is of momentous consequence whether his wife and family are to be cheated of half his scanty earnings by the nation for which he dies. The Rebels may be induced to concede the negro the rights of war when we grant him the ordinary rights of peace, namely to be paid the price agreed upon.

—THOMAS WENTWORTH HIGGINSON,
NEW YORK TIMES, FEBRUARY 1864

Moses Garrison alias Harriet alias General Tubman has just arrived up from Port Royal. What times.

—WENDELL GARRISON TO
WILLIAM LLOYD GARRISON II, JUNE 1864

When on June 11, Secretary of War Stanton sends Quincy A. Gilmore to replace David Hunter as commander of the Department of the South, Harriet knows what she has to do. Only days after his return from Georgia, James Montgomery writes a letter to Gilmore. "General: I wish to commend to your attention Mrs. Harriet Tubman, a most remarkable woman and valuable as a scout." He also puts in a good word for Walter D. Plowden, a "man of tried courage" who "can be made highly useful." On the back of the letter of commendation, Rufus Saxton endorses Montgomery's estimate of Harriet's skills without mentioning Plowden.

Montgomery doubtless writes at Harriet's request. By now it's clear, she is going to have to fight for every penny she might someday receive. She's not under contract to the government, has not been promised particular wages or placement on a pay scale. She works, as always, on the move and over the line of ordinary categorization. The ultimate freelancer, she has to stay ahead of the game and operate as her own agent, peddling her services the same as her root beer, however she can.

Hunter has already spoken for her. She needs the new chief to know who she is, what she did, and how she's valued.

Unfortunately, in his letter of reference, Montgomery hasn't spelled out the details of her scouting service or upon what evidence he bases his opinion of her. This is probably an oversight, since—along with Higginson and Shaw—Montgomery is a stalwart ally in the black soldiers' campaign to receive equal pay and would certainly go the distance for Harriet. Presumably, he thinks he's said enough, and that her reputation, fueled by his letter of endorsement, will do the job. After all, by now everyone in Port Royal knows about her participation in the Combahee raid. And once the article is published in the *Wisconsin State Journal,* calling her "A Black She 'Moses' " and a "black heroine," who has "penetrated the enemy's lines and discovered their situation and condition . . ." so will much of the rest of the country.

She's a hero. How much more proof does Gilmore—Stanton, Lincoln, a congressional committee—need?

Over the next thirty years, Harriet and a number of her advocates, including Secretary of State William Seward, will expend a great deal of energy lobbying the U.S. government, first for retroactive payment for services rendered to the military as nurse, scout, and spy, and then—after her husband's death—a widow's pension. In the request for back pay, letters from Montgomery, Hunter, Saxton, and Gilmore will be submitted as support. Rufus Saxton's letter will forthrightly state her case.

"I have just rec'd your letter in regard to Harriet Tubman," he writes. "I can bear witness to the value of her services rendered in the Union Army during the late war in South Carolina and Florida. She was employed in the Hospitals and as a spy. She made many a raid inside the enemy's lines displaying remarkable courage, zeal and fidelity." He goes on to say that she is as deserving of a pension from the government as any other of its faithful servants.

Her struggle will continue far into her future as, year after year, congressional committees reject her petitions, apparently refusing to believe a woman (even one who is as "extraordinary as the most famous of her sex"), a *black* woman, capable of such heroism.

Walter Plowden will fare better. In 1869, Congress approves a bill of relief for Harriet's colleague. And even though his payment is held up for six years, it does finally arrive. In 1875, Congress authorizes one thousand dollars for his services as "a colored scout and spy, for Military services rendered the army of the United States, under Major-General Hunter, in the Military District of South Carolina . . . for the repression of the rebellion." Without Harriet's endorsement, Plowden would never have participated in the Combahee raid. In addition, Montgomery is far more forthcoming on Harriet's behalf than he is on Plowden's, and so are other generals; nonetheless, he is eventually paid, while she never receives a nickel for organizing, planning, and leading the expedition.

Her campaign for back pay will begin in June 1868, when an Auburn banker, Charles P. Wood, comes to her aid and submits a claim to the congressional pension committee—including southern congressmen—for back pay amounting to several thousand dollars. He accompanies his petition with all the documentation Harriet can come up with: passes, as well as letters from Hunter, Saxton, Seward, Montgomery, Durant, and Gilmore. Harriet herself has put in for thirty dollars a month back pay for "services as a scout" for thirty-two-and-a-half months—May 25, 1862–January 31, 1865—a total of $966. She even deducts the two hundred dollars she was paid in Beaufort at the beginning of her tenure there.

No payment is forthcoming.

In 1888, after the death of her second husband, Nelson Davis, who served as a private in the Eighth Regiment U.S. Colored Troops, Harriet will apply for a widow's pension, which will be rejected on a number of counts. Before she can be declared Davis's official widow, it seems, she will first have to provide evidence of the death of her first husband, John

Tubman—to whom she was never legally married. She will also have to prove that Nelson Davis is the same man known to the army as Nelson Charles.

In November 1892, she will submit an affidavit swearing to the death of John Tubman as a result of a gunshot wound following an argument with a white man in Dorchester County in 1867. A certificate of death and newspaper clipping will accompany the affidavit.

And in November 1894, Harriet will go once again to the Cayuga County, New York, courthouse and swear that a second affidavit filed in her behalf is all true. This affidavit states that on March 18, 1869, she married Nelson Davis in Auburn, New York, in a ceremony conducted by the Reverend Henry Fowler. It then goes on give a summary of her own life as a slave, including her marriage to John Tubman, and his death, and the details of her marriage to and life with Nelson Davis. This includes the history of his military service, as well as details of his name change: "The name of his [Nelson Davis's] owner (when he was a slave) was Fred Charles. His father's name was Milford Davis."

After emancipation, Nelson Davis dropped his slave name and took on his father's surname. And so like many emancipated men and women, he had two names, Nelson Charles *and* Nelson Davis.

One year later, in 1895, seven years after Davis's death, and after many petitions and appeals submitted by Charles Wood and then congressman Sereno E. Payne, Harriet will finally be granted a widow's pension of eight dollars a month, along with a five-hundred-dollar retroactive lump-sum payment covering the years since Davis's death. Thus, after years of stubbing its collective toe on minor obstacles, will the government finally recognize her as a deserving widow.

By that time, many of her supporters will have died—Seward, Douglass, Gerrit Smith, Wendell Phillips—nonetheless, Payne will continue to apply pressure. In 1899, when Harriet is seventy-seven years old, he will finally succeed in pushing through a bill "granting a pension to Harriet Tubman Davis, late a *nurse* in the United States Army," amounting to twenty-five dollars a month. Even then, there will be objections that her pay is too high, since other Civil War nurses were paid less.

The committee will fiddle with the details and end up cutting Harriet's monthly stipend by five dollars. And then they will penny-pinch yet again: instead of adding the nurse's pay to her widow's pension, they will combine the two, so that she'll *net* twenty dollars a month: eight dollars for widowhood, twelve dollars for nursing. Nothing for being a valuable scout and spy, or for her documented displays of courage, zeal, and fidelity, while leading "many a raid."

Harriet's friends and family will maintain that Sereno Payne should have held out longer, but by then Harriet will be old and ill and Payne will either see the writing on the wall and know it's time to quit or will simply be tired of trying. In any case, he will yield to the compromise.

But we have moved far ahead of ourselves, years and years from now, into Harriet's future. In the summer of 1863, although she cannot possibly foresee such a lengthy struggle, she has already moved into a more serious campaign of letter gathering in preparation for that possibility.

Within days of his June 1863 arrival in Beaufort, General Gilmore has set his sights on the heavily defended "hellhole of secession," the Charleston harbor and Fort Sumter, where the war began. By the end of the month, he's ordered troops to head north from Hilton Head toward the Union-held Folly Island, a walking stick–shaped tongue of land in the Atlantic. From there, they'll launch an assault on nearby James Island. Once they have taken James, they will move farther north and somewhat west to take on the Confederate stronghold of Fort Wagner on Morris Island, which watchdogs the harbor and guards the southern approach to Sumter.

As Port Royal troops receive their orders, one company after the next boards steamships docked at Hilton Head. The battle will be not a raid but an all-out siege, hand-to-hand combat backed up by musketry.

On July 6, when the Fifty-fourth Massachusetts has not received orders to go, Robert Shaw writes to Brig. Gen. George C. Strong. It is time, he writes, to give black soldiers an opportunity to fight side by side with whites in an important battle, "in order that they may have other witnesses besides their own officers to what they are capable of doing." Two days later, Shaw receives orders to prepare his regiment to move at an hour's notice, and by July 9, they are anchored at the southernmost tip of Folly Island, where they join the other regiments near Fort Delafield.

James Montgomery's Second South Carolina Volunteers are there, as well, assigned to flank and back up the first-assault companies.

Harriet either follows or accompanies the Fifty-fourth to Folly Island as nurse and cook—possibly as a scout, as well, considering Saxton's "made many a raid" assessment. Whatever her duties, she goes. Having been recruited by Governor Andrews, Frederick Douglass's sons, Lewis and Charles, have reported for duty and are among the soldiers of the Fifty-fourth. Because she spent time in Douglass's Rochester home, Harriet undoubtedly knows the Douglass brothers. She would also have become familiar with other members of the regiment and their beloved commander, Shaw, who has become even more respected by his troops—and Harriet—after staging an angry protest against the inequity of pay for black soldiers. At least one soldier in the Fifty-fourth had escaped from Maryland slavery and lived in Syracuse. Charley Reason enlisted in the regiment to fight for the freedom of those who didn't have it, and he would certainly know of Harriet from her Underground Railroad days.

She moves among the men, a lone woman, bringing coffee, passing out the firm, cold biscuit known as hardtack. To soften the crackers, the soldiers dip them into their coffee. Some refuse to eat hardtack at all, despite their hunger.

From Folly Island, the Fifty-fourth moves across the Folly River and through the marshes to James Island, where in the shallows they are furiously attacked—not as soldiers but as black outlaws and fugitives—by rebels. A few days later, on the sixteenth, as a lightning storm and heavy rain sweeps across the islands, they head toward Morris Island. Through the storm, they slog through marsh and mud. By the next morning—the seventeenth—the storm has passed, leaving the air thick, hot, and sullen.

They sit in the sand, exhausted, hungry, wet. Sand fleas infest the islands. They hop into the soldiers' boots and up their pant legs, making tedious pricks, leaving tiny red welts that thicken as they multiply, becoming a rash.

That night, or perhaps the one before, Shaw feels a foreboding: At Wagner, he confides to his second in command, he believes he will fall.

The officer advises him to try to shake off the feeling. Clearly unconvinced, Shaw rises to the occasion. He says he will try.

To his men he remains upbeat, cheerful, and determined.

When the Fifty-fourth arrives on Morris Island—known locally as Coffin Island because of its previous use as a leper colony—at 5:00 P.M., they have been marching for more than two days and nights without sufficient sleep or food, going single file through swamps and mud.

Harriet insists that she was there, close by, and that she served Robert Shaw his last meal. There are no orders or eyewitness accounts to validate her claim, but she never backed down from her resolve on this point. She was *there*. And perhaps that's true.

If she cooked Robert Shaw his last meal, however, she did it at least two nights prior to the attack on Wagner. Participants in the assault and eyewitnesses to it reported unwaveringly that the Fifty-fourth, including its colonel, had been served only hardtack and coffee during the final days of the march.

And so either Harriet cooked real food for him *before* the march to Morris Island or the meal she made for him was coffee and hardtack.

Shaw is handsome, twenty-five years old, newly married.

Given her visionary nature, no matter when she brought him a meal, you have to wonder if in the young man's presence Harriet felt the same foreboding and saw death all over him that night.

On July 18, Shaw is asked if his men are ready. They are all exhausted and hungry, but—understanding the historical importance of the occasion to his men and to their race—he unhesitatingly says yes. But before riding forth, Colonel Shaw removes the personal letters and papers he has kept with him in his haversack and hands them to Edward Pierce, the first man assigned to manage Port Royal plantations. He asks Pierce to deliver the papers to his father, then moves on to join his regiment.

At 7:45 that night, at low tide, Shaw calls his troops to attention and tells them to move at quick time until they arrive within one hundred yards of the fort, then at double time, then charge.

He volunteers to carry the flag himself if the standard-bearer should fall. The men of the Fifty-fourth move forward, marching for three-quarters of a mile at double time, 180 paces per minute, through the sand.

The rebels fire, discharging musket balls, grapeshot, canisters. They hurl broken bottles, fire howitzers. A "perfect hail of shot and shell."

Illustration from *Harper's Weekly,* demonstrating the bravery and fearlessness of the newly enlisted fighting Negro regiments during the assault on Fort Wagner.

And even though gunfire is mowing down troops like "grass before a scythe," the Fifty-fourth never falters or falls back, but continues its rush to the moat and across the water, then up the parapet. Some soldiers roll back down into the ditch. When a sergeant finds the Union flag lying on the ground, its bearer shot down, he grabs the standard and carries it through the water and up the wall.

"Not a man flinched," Lewis Douglass will write. "A shell would explode and clear a space of twenty feet, our men would close up again."

Shaw makes it to the top of the parapet, brandishing his sword and calling to his men to follow ("Come on, boys! Follow me!"), when he is shot down, as are the soldiers who come to his rescue.

During the battle, Harriet is somewhere close enough to see and hear.

Here is how she describes it: "And then we saw the lightning, and that was the guns; and then we heard the thunder, and that was the big guns; and then we heard the rain falling, and that was drops of blood falling; and when we came to get in the crops, it was dead men that we reaped."

In a matter of hours, the battle is over. Union losses are 1,515 dead, wounded, missing, or captured, compared with only 174 Confederates. The Fifty-fourth will lose 256 men, including Shaw, who—even more despised by the rebels than his black soldiers—is unceremoniously stripped of his uniform and tossed into a common grave with at least forty-five of his men. Victorious, the rebel soldiers take home medals and patches of Shaw's clothing as souvenirs.

During the night, the tide comes up, washing many of the dead and wounded into the Atlantic. Dawn reveals a hellish scene: men mangled, blown apart, piled in heaps; body parts littered about the sand and clogging the marshes. *Harper's Weekly* describes the scene on the beach: "The battle is over . . . the ocean beach is crowded with the dead, the dying, and the wounded. . . . Faint lights are glimmerings in the sand-holes and rifle-pits. . . . In these holes many a poor wounded and bleeding soldier has laid down to his last sleep. . . ."

The wounded are taken to ships for transport to Beaufort. Harriet goes with them, giving what assistance she can to the resident surgeons as, on July 19, they embark on the trip from Folly Island back down the coast to Hilton Head.

There is little she can do except moisten their lips and wash their terrible wounds.

What times. What suffering.

In days to come, the martyrdom of Robert Gould Shaw and the gallantry of his regiment will make for banner headlines throughout the North. When Union officials ask that Shaw's remains be returned for proper burial, Confederate authorities refuse. He has been buried, they reply, in a mass grave with his enlisted men—his *black* enlisted men— where he belongs.

The move to secure the colonel's remains finally comes to a halt in August, when Shaw's father writes General Gilmore a public letter asking that the matter be dropped, since "a soldier's most appropriate burial-place is on the field where he has fallen."

On the morning after the battle, July 19, nurses and doctors in Beaufort receive the news from Morris Island and are told to prepare immediately

After the battle of Fort Wagner. Soldiers, many of whom are black, find a moment of peace in and around a burned-out house formerly belonging to a rebel planter, on Morris Island, near the burial sites of many of their fallen colleagues.

to receive five hundred wounded men. Since April, one of the mansions belonging to the Barnwell family has been designated General Hospital #10 for Colored Troops, the first such hospital sanctioned by the War Department. But the mansion has not yet been fitted out for medical care. There are no beds, no clean linens, no means of building a fire.

The volunteers spread blankets on the floor and wait.

Assigned to nursing duty by James Montgomery, Harriet goes to Hospital #10.

Since no medical attention has been given to the soldiers on the transports, they arrive as they were found on the battlefield. A volunteer doctor from Massachusetts, thirty-year-old Esther Hill Hawks, describes the scene as 150 men from Shaw's regiment are brought to them that first day. A graduate of the New England Female Medical College, Hawks watches the men come in, all "mangled and ghastly . . . a terrible sight." Stretcher-bearers lay the wounded on the floor, then go back to the ship for others.

There are only two doctors and one licensed nurse.

They begin their rounds, kneeling to treat their patients.

In no time, word has flashed through the islands, how many are wounded, how much help is needed. In a matter of hours, the black people of Beaufort and Saint Helena are showing up at Hospital #10, bringing buckets of broth and gruel, pitchers of lemonade, fruit, cakes, vegetables. From the farms come cartloads of melons and fresh produce for the men "wounded for we."

Missionaries cook and sew, write letters for the dying.

By July 21, the forerunner of the American Red Cross, now called the Sanitary Commission, has arrived with beds, dressings, and clean bedclothes.

Esther Hawks recalls how, only weeks before, all of Beaufort had watched the Fifty-fourth march through the streets with Shaw, and how the colored people cheered and gloried in their fine appearance. Now the smell of gangrene poisons the air. The only thing, she says, that sustains the medical crew is the patient endurance of the stricken heroes, one of whom—Charley Reason, the young man who escaped Maryland slavery and made a life for himself in Syracuse—uses a number of his last breaths to assure Hawks that he knows what he was fighting for: not *for* his country but to gain one.

Imagine Beaufort on a hot, still July night: the cries and groans drifting from open windows, an endless wail, into the mosquito-ridden darkness.

Harriet comes early every morning, bringing food she's cooked the night before. At the hospital, she finds a basin, sets a chunk of ice in it, and fills it with water, then takes a sponge and "first man I'd come to, I'd thrash away the flies," which in the thick summer air rise together like bees from a hive. She bathes wounds, changes the bloody water, gets more ice, makes her way to the next patient. By then, the flies have congregated again on the first man, black and thick upon his flesh. At the end of the day, she returns to her cabin to prepare more food and then the next morning begins her routine again.

The battle for the Charleston harbor lasts through August and into the first week of September.

The rebels remain in control. Sumter yet flies the Confederate flag, and will for another year and a half, until February 1865, when, at the end of his march to the sea, Sherman burns Columbia, the South Carolina state capital, to the ground.

The hospitals in Beaufort remain filled. Now that mosquitoes are in full swarm, the sickly season has descended like a leveling hand upon the Sea Islands.

Bone-weary doctors fall ill, as do teachers. Some of the missionaries leave. Harriet works nonstop.

In the late fall, when the hospital has released many of its patients and Harriet's work slackens—probably toward the end of October—she takes a leave. Exhausted, she sails from Hilton Head to New York, taking the train across the state to Auburn. The commanding general issues passes to soldiers and government workers who go on leave, enabling them to ride free on government transports and passenger trains. The passes are dated and valid for a limited time. In all, the trip takes her about a week, many of the hours doubtless spent either in deepest sleep or dropping off into a narcoleptic episode.

In Auburn, she makes her way down South Street to the tollgate marking the city limits, then turns left into the yard of her home, where she will see her family for the first time in eighteen months.

In her life, it's the longest time she's spent away from kin.

Has she sent word? Are they expecting her? Or does she simply show up?

It's early November, either raining or windy—in any case, cold, gray. The house shut up, a fire built, if last winter's wood's not used up, shawls and blankets drawn around. More than likely, she's in her general's garb: long striped skirt, thick three-quarter-length coat, kerchief, soldier's pouch slung across one shoulder.

Home.

She opens the door, and there they all are—family, residents, children. And there she stands, aunt, sister-in-law, only daughter. Their traveler, famous now, is keeper of the mortgage, spokesperson for the family, their connection to local employers, and provider of whatever money she can raise and send.

They exchange greetings, family remarks, about the new baby, the changes, how everybody's health is.

She can't stay. She's on leave. Like any soldier, she must follow orders.

Able family members are working hard, many of them employed by wealthy white people they may have met in church. Others struggle at manual jobs, some of them finding only day work. Catherine Stewart, wife of James, has given birth to a new baby—Esther, sometimes known as Hester, born nine month's after her son Adam's death.

Harriet surely tells them stories of where's she's been, what she's seen and done.

People returning from a war take a long time to adjust to ordinary life, one without weaponry, violent death, sounds of attack. Imagine how Harriet's family and the boarders must seem to her now. They don't have enough of anything; they're sick, worn-out, disabled. And yet life there maintains an even pulse—no basins of blood to rinse, no mangled bodies to attend to or gather like crops. Nights are quiet.

When she tells of the people running from the rice fields to the *Adams* and what it was like when the black soldiers of the Fifty-fourth stormed Fort Wagner and how horrible the scene of the battle was the next morning, they may or may not want to hear, may or may not even be able to imagine what it was like.

Ben's arthritis has worsened. To ease the pain in his joints, he walks the floor, praying aloud, praising the Lord. During this visit, Harriet may meet Sarah Bradford, who already knows Rit. Six years from now, when *Scenes in the Life of Harriet Tubman* is published, it will be illustrated with a woodcut of Harriet in her Civil War outfit.

Bradford characterizes Rit as an unending fount of complaints, especially directed toward Harriet, who, having taken the role of rescuer, can never relinquish it. Ben and Rit are in their late seventies and have aged considerably over the past eighteen months. But like her, they are sturdy. Ben will live another eight years; Rit, seventeen.

Harriet suffers with and for her aged parents. Her respect for them is that of a dutiful daughter: boundless. It is awful, seeing old people suffer, doing everything you can to make their lives easier, still coming up short.

Rit complains about winters in the north. She's talkative; Ben is not.

There's the new baby, Esther, to look at and dandle.

They sit together. Reunions can be awkward, filled with long silences. Families don't change much. They fall into patterns, which upon repetition become traditions. It is comforting, to some extent, to know what to expect—unlike life in Beaufort.

During her time on leave, Harriet goes to Canada to visit her brother William Henry and his family. He's still farming in Grantham, on the outskirts of St. Catharines. While she's there, Samuel Gridley Howe arrives, representing the American Freedman's Inquiry Commission. Harriet knows him. He was one of John Brown's Secret Six, and he may well have been in Beaufort with the Inquiry Commission in June.

In St. Catharines, Harriet can introduce Howe to refugees, William Henry, among others, who in his testimony refers to Harriet as "my sister (the one who is here now)." To Howe, he testifies about his time in Maryland, when, as Henry Ross, he was enslaved to Edward Brodess. And he tells of the sister whom Brodess sold to Georgia—Linah—and the child she left behind. He also speaks of the death of Brodess and the time when Harriet came that Christmas to lead her brothers to the North. And how Rit took her stand and wouldn't let Brodess sell her youngest child, Moses Ross.

William Henry Stewart is allowed to speak at length. After recalling the years in slavery and the sale of Linah and the others, he speaks of his own future. In Grantham, he is farming and living on six acres of land. He has done pretty well in Canada and may or may not prefer to stay there. But if "slavery remains just as it is," he tells Howe, "I will stay in Canada. I have no idea of going back unless freedom is established."

Even the Emancipation Proclamation has not convinced him that slavery does not yet remain. It is, after all, a white man's document. And even if slavery has been outlawed, freedom for black people may not have been truly *established*. He will take his chances where he is, rather than return to the land of Edward Brodess.

After a short stay in Ontario, Harriet makes a quick trip back to Auburn, then heads back east and south to continue her work.

Her family's needs prey steadily on her mind. They need money. The government must pay her. She must make a payment on the mortgage so they don't lose their home.

Seward doesn't dun her, but Harriet keeps track. And as the months roll on and interest accumulates, the debt grows.

———

As soon as she arrives in Hilton Head, Gilmore sends her back to Folly Island, where she is to talk to and work with every black person who crosses Union lines from rebel territory. Those who have been enslaved trust her. She knows what they have been through and can talk to them better than anyone else, and obtain information only they can provide. She is in, effect, Gilmore's intelligence gatherer. She assures the refugees, who are terrified when they come to her, that she has been in their position, knows what they are feeling and how they have lived. And then she asks them where pickets are and how much weaponry they are carrying and what hours they stand guard.

The refugees talk to her. In return, she takes care of them as best she can.

In February 1864, two months after her return, George Garrison, William Lloyd Garrison's son, is assigned to military duty on Folly Island. Accompanied by Boston friends on an excursion, he pays a visit to Harriet, whom they find ironing clothes in the general's quarters.

One of his friends introduces him, saying, "Here is George Garrison."

Harriet turns from her work and, instantly recognizing the young man, throws her arms around him.

She's working, she says, for General Terry, who is in command. But she wants to go back north again. Haunted by visions of her aged, ill parents, her trip home has only made her homesick. They aren't well. They could die without her. But Gilmore won't let her leave. Her services are too valuable.

She reheats the flatiron, presses it across the fabric. Everyone who knows her will say that in her forties, she began looking old. She is forty-two.

If she can't go home and the government won't pay her, she has to find other ways to lay up extra money to send her parents, as well as to pay off her debts. So she's making use of her time by taking in washing and ironing and doing any number of other jobs.

Noting the bundles of clothes around her, Garrison, with the insouciance of the privileged, speculates that Harriet has created for herself a fine opportunity to make a good deal of money on Folly Island, taking on easily fifty times more work than she can get to.

She's been saving up, she tells Garrison and the others. But last week, someone stole fifty dollars from her. She does not complain about the considerable size of this theft, but before her guests leave, she gives what's left of her savings to one of Garrison's friends to send north to Ben and Rit.

And returns to her work.

Later that same month, when James Montgomery's regiment is sent back to Florida, Harriet is ordered to return to Hilton Head and to sail to Florida with him as a nurse. She leaves Folly Island.

From now until the end of the war—a little more than a year away—she will spend most of her life in motion, going wherever she's ordered, fulfilling whatever duties she's assigned, taking leaves, then returning. Whether by steamboat, rowboat, gunboat, train, or on foot, she is once again on the move.

Other regiments, black and white, join Montgomery in Fernandina. Among the African American regiments participating in this campaign is the Eighth Regiment U.S. Colored Troops, within whose ranks serves a young soldier named Pvt. Nelson Charles. In four years, Charles will become Harriet's second husband, but by then he will have changed his surname to Davis. Given the circumstances and the fact that Harriet never mentioned this detail in her stories or affidavits, it's unlikely the two of them meet at this time, but who knows?

Whatever the case, it is worth noting that Harriet and her future husband were both in Florida at this time, taking part in the Olustee campaign.

Miscommunications between generals sabotage the Florida expedition almost immediately. As Union troops move south and west from Jacksonville toward Lake City, in the town of Olustee losses are so great and rebel fire so heavy that General Seymour orders the retreat of all Union forces.

The loss is humiliating and costly in human terms, especially for the black regiments.

Harriet may not have witnessed the battle at Olustee, but she is in Union-occupied Fernandina when the troops return, going out to the woods every day to dig up herbs for root tea for dysentery, washing wounds, providing water, fanning the flies away. When she returns to Beaufort, Acting Assistant Surgeon Henry K. Durant writes her another letter of commendation, testifying to the "esteem in which she is generally held." He backs up his comment by mentioning that he has had ample opportunity to observe "particularly her kindness and attention to the sick and suffering of her own race."

Durant writes the letter in May. In late June 1864, unpaid, tired, becoming ill, only eight months after her previous leave, Harriet takes another furlough.

In New York, she stops over and visits a few people, among them Wendell Garrison. She tells him of her visit with his brother George, who she says is well. Not being one to make casual social calls, she probably asks for a small donation or, even more likely, a letter of support. She then makes her way to Auburn, and after seeing to her parents, goes to Massachusetts. In Boston, she stays with her lawyer friend John Rock, who now lives on Beacon Hill. She also visits Frank Sanborn in Concord. Sanborn does his part. In the August 12 issue of the Boston *Commonwealth,* he announces her presence and then complains on her behalf that "her services to her people and to the arms seem to have been very inadequately recompensed by the military authorities." Any money that she has received, he notes, she has expended for others—as is her custom. Sanborn then asks for contributions, in the form of money or clothes for distribution, to be used with "fidelity and discretion for the good of the colored race."

Coincidentally, Sojourner Truth is in Boston at this same time, on her way from Michigan to Washington, where she will meet Abraham Lincoln, whom she calls the "first antislavery president."

Truth has become something of a celebrity herself, due to her fiery antislavery and Christian temperance speeches.

A meeting is arranged, probably in the home of an antislavery supporter. And there the two women sit, the bespectacled northern-born and -reared Truth sitting board-straight in her chair, lean and dignified, almost a foot taller than the earthier Harriet.

Unfortunately, neither will ever say much about this historic meeting, even though they are—even today—the two most famous freedwomen in American history. Harriet will later acknowledge that Truth invited her to accompany her to Washington. But—believing that the man in charge, the president, ought to be the one to see that she is fairly compensated—Harriet declines, saying she does not much care to meet Mr. Lincoln.

Later, after a letter from Truth is published, saying that Lincoln received her warmly, Harriet will regret not going. "I'm sorry now," she'll tell an interviewer in 1886. "But I didn't like Lincoln in them

Sojurner Truth

days. . . . You see we colored people didn't understand then he was our friend. All we knew was that the first colored troops sent south from Massachusetts only got seven dollars a month while the white regiment got fifteen. We didn't like that."

It took a while, she will eventually say, for her to understand that Lincoln was a servant of the people and had to abide by their wishes.

The two women go their separate ways and do not meet again.

Harriet continues making solicitations for testimonials and money. From Boston, she goes to Rochester, where she receives a ten-dollar donation from the Rochester Ladies' Anti-Slavery Society, and then in late November, to Peterboro to see her old friend Gerrit Smith. He writes another letter of commendation, in which he declares that, "The cause of freedom owes her much. The country owes her much." The wife of a Union general—visiting the Smiths at the time—writes a testimonial, as well.

Harriet manages to hold on to most of the letters. Many, however, are lost along the way—dropped, mistakenly thrown away, burned up in a fire, stolen with her clothes.

The past never stops asserting its claims. When on November 1, 1864, Maryland frees its slaves—the first border state to do so—some slave-holders move quickly to indenture the children of their freed slaves and thereby legally hold on to them. That same month, John Henry and Moses Ross, the sons of Harriet's brother John Stewart (Robert Ross), are indentured by Anthony C. Thompson's son-in-law, Thomas Haddaway, who purchased the boys' mother, Mary Manokey, in 1857.

When John Stewart escaped from slavery in 1854—perhaps re-membering, even haunted by, his wife's final plea that he not forget them—he did not leave his family easily or without regret. Though re-married and with a new family, he has never stopped wanting his sons to join him, either in Canada or New York State. Now that they are inden-tured, he will have to steal them away from descendants of Anthony Thompson, the man who owned his father, and his son, Anthony C., who sold his wife's sister, Susan.

After her visit to Gerrit Smith, Harriet's health fails again, this time so se-riously that she returns to Auburn. Despite knowing that her pass will run out, she remains there through Christmas and New Year's and into mid-winter, when she finally feels up to traveling again. By the time she tries to board government transports, her passes have expired. She goes to Washington, obtains a fifty-dollar loan from Seward, who applies it to her debt. He also helps her obtain another pass.

In March, Ednah Dow Cheney—secretary of the New England Freedmen's Aid Society and a lifelong reformer and devoted Harriet supporter—publishes a biographical sketch of Harriet in the *Freedmen's Record,* perhaps as a way of soliciting help for her. The article, called sim-ply "Moses," calls Harriet "probably the most remarkable woman of this age." It ends with another appeal for compensation, recognition, and jus-tice: "This society considers her labors too valuable to the freedmen to be turned elsewhere, and therefore have taken her into their service. . . ."

In April, Harriet finally receives her government pass. But before leaving for duty, she speaks to newly organized regiments at Camp

William Penn in Philadelphia, telling them of her trials and experiences among the "contrabands and the soldiers." After calling her "the great Underground Railroad woman," *The Christian Recorder* describes her account as "thrilling" and says that it elicited great applause and a liberal collection.

She sends the money to Auburn.

After her talk, she's waylaid by nurses from the U.S. Sanitary Commission, who, impressed by her lecture and her record, convince her to go with them to Hampton, Virginia, to care for hospitalized black soldiers at Fort Monroe, instead of traveling to South Carolina.

Her itinerary changes again. But she doesn't like it at Fort Monroe and will later report that she was witness to a number of abuses there. She doesn't specify exactly what kind of ill treatment or toward whom, but it's hard to imagine anything other than wounded black soldiers being neglected, insulted, or harmed. At any rate, whatever happens, she refuses to stay.

During her work in Virginia, the war ends; Lincoln is killed, and— as part of the assassination plot—William Seward is brutally attacked. In late June or early July, Harriet returns to Washington, where she speaks with the severely injured Seward. He writes David Hunter about Harriet's lack of pay and introduces her to the surgeon general, Dr. Joseph K. Barnes, who, after hearing of the abuses at Fort Monroe, appoints her "Nurse or Matron at the colored hospital" there.

Her pass is dated July 22, 1865. But when she reports once again to the hospital, her appointment is not honored. She leaves again.

By October—more than slightly flummoxed, it seems, by circumstances; exhausted; probably never completely healthy, making moves that seem either precipitous or critically delayed—she's on the move yet again.

The war is over; the slaves are free. Congress is in the process of ratifying the Thirteenth Amendment, which will abolish slavery officially. But in many ways, life now seems more complicated for her than ever before. Visions don't arrive. Voices don't tell her what to do, or even who she's to *become*. There is still much brave, good work to be done, but no certainty of getting paid for it. And no way for her family to survive if she doesn't.

Seward lends her twelve dollars toward her debt. The New England Freedmen's Aid Society pays Seward twenty dollars to apply to the mortgage.

Harriet heads toward home. On her way, she makes a few stops in Philadelphia, seeing friends from the antislavery movement. Many of the women are transferring their energies to the next great reform movement, suffrage. She tells her friends about the suffering of the freed people and how desperately she wishes to help them.

Afterward, in about mid-October, she makes her way to the Philadelphia train station.

Having missed an earlier departure, she boards a late-night passenger train, due to leave at eleven o'clock for Camden and South Amboy. When Sarah Bradford describes this moment, she makes a particular point of referring to the train Harriet boards as an "emigrant train," indicating that many of its passengers are either Irish or German natives, and almost certainly prejudiced against black people.

Harriet presents her government ticket. The conductor scans the ticket and reaches for her.

"Come, hustle out of here!" he shouts. "We don't carry niggers for half-fare!"

He orders her to the smoking car.

Harriet stands her ground. "I am," she informs the conductor, "working for the government and entitled to transportation, the same as soldiers."

The conductor takes her by the arm. "I'll make you tired of trying to stay here."

But Harriet has grabbed hold of something, a seat, hand-bar, or railing, and won't let go.

The conductor pulls her by the arm, but she is stronger, and he can't pry her loose. And so he calls on two other men, who peel her fingers one by one from their prodigious grip. When she yet resists, they twist her away, wrenching her arm and, in the process, dislocating her shoulder.

She is a small woman in her mid-forties. But no one comes to her aid. On the contrary. Several passengers—emigrants, Bradford again points out—yell insults and curses. They encourage the conductor to "pitch the nagur out!"

The three men manage to move her a few steps, but she will not go quietly. She verbally attacks the conductor for his attitude toward her race. He is, she says, a copperhead scoundrel.

As insulted as if slapped, the conductor takes her by the throat, probably with his forearm across her neck, choking her. With the help of the other men, he is finally able to remove her from the passenger car. Together, they toss her into the baggage car like a sack of meal, in the process possibly cracking one or two ribs.

Although certainly in terrible pain, she yet retains her dignity. Before the men can escape from her, Harriet issues one last bit of instruction: She doesn't, she tells the conductor, "thank anybody to call her colored person." She would instead be called black or Negro.

"I am," she informs the conductor, "as proud of being a black woman as you are of being white."

Without comment, the conductor closes her up in the baggage car and the men leave.

The train pulls out. Harriet curls up against whatever's in the baggage compartment, shielding the broken side of her body.

In New York, when she disembarks, a young man who witnessed the assault gives Harriet his card. "You ought to sue that conductor," he tells her. And he offers to serve as a witness. But, when someone reads the card for her, she will discover it is only a *carte de visite* and has no address printed on it.

She sees a doctor, who adjusts her shoulder, places her arm in a sling, and advises her to sue the railroad company, offering to act as a witness to her injuries.

Her loyal friends from the abolitionist days help nurse her. On her behalf, they explore the possibility of a lawsuit and advertise for the young witness to please come forward. But the young man is never heard from, and—knowing that on its own, a black woman's sworn testimony has no chance of standing up against a white man's word—Harriet lets the matter go.

She returns to Auburn. Now what? For the first time in her life, she is too disabled to go out to find work. Only Catherine Stewart has steady-enough employment to pay for some cold-weather provisions. And even then, the family is forced to burn fences for firewood.

One day during the winter, when Rit has been forced to go without tobacco and tea—which, Bradford says, are more essential to her than food or clothing—she spews forth a bitter diatribe, sending reproaches fast and thick in her daughter's direction.

When she can take no more, Harriet storms off and shuts herself up in a closet. In the dark, she sits. It is her habit to take time out to settle her mind down so that it will work properly and tell her what to do. Alone, she considers her options.

The house is full—even Margaret Stewart is there for a while, and perhaps John and Kessiah Bowley or others from Canada. They are all cold, hungry, and, if truth be told, probably going a bit stir-crazy, what with so many of them shut up there together for many hours at a time, especially Harriet, who is not used to staying in one place so long, surrounded by family, hectored by Rit.

In the past, Harriet has always dug them out of any hole in which they found themselves. They can't help railing at her for being unable to rescue them this time.

Eventually, her time in the closet pays off. She opens the door.

Catherine, she orders. *Put on the soup pot. Not the little one, the big one.*

Catherine protests. There is nothing to put in the pot.

But Harriet is in charge now, and she insists. *Today,* she says, *we will eat.*

Throwing a shawl across her shoulders, she hooks her shopping basket over her uninjured arm and sets off on foot, down the front steps and out into the yard, then north, to the right, toward downtown Auburn.

It's winter, and the town's a mile away. By the time she gets to the marketplace, night is coming on and the markets are about to close.

She has used the truth to trick people before. She may be too old and beat-up to go out and find work, but she can certainly still pull out the theatrical stops when she has to.

She walks among the stalls. Perhaps she's put her arm back in its sling. Or maybe she puts on the crone act that worked so well in Cambridge and Utica, stooping bent over, shuffling as if ancient. As they shut down their stalls, vendors are examining leftover hunks of meat, vegetables, and soup bones, anxious to be rid of unsold wares before heading home for the night.

As Harriet passes close to a butcher, he calls out, "Old woman, don't you want a nice piece of meat?" And he tosses the meat into her basket. She nods her thanks and moves on. She needs more.

Another butcher offers her a piece of meat for ten cents or a soup-bone for five. But Harriet explains that she has no money, then walks on. At length, a different butcher gathers from her timeworn expression what the trouble is. "Look here, old woman," he says. "You look like an honest woman. Take this soup-bone and pay me when you get some money."

Another follows suit. "Take this," he says.

She keeps going until her basket is full. Then she makes her way from the butcher stalls to the vegetable market. Now that she has bartering power, she can exchange some of the meat for potatoes, cabbage, and onions.

As the markets close, Harriet walks back home, triumphant.

Night has fallen by the time she arrives. *See!* she would remind the others, as she often does and often will. God always provides, if they will only believe.

Catherine has put the soup pot on. They fill it with Harriet's bounty. In no time, the mood of the household softens. The aromas give them much to think about, remember, and hope for. That night, as promised, they will eat.

Harriet will tell this story to Bradford in 1900, when they are sitting together on Samuel Hopkins's veranda, overlooking Owasco Lake. She will laugh at herself as she tells it, remembering how she stormed away from Rit and what kind of fuss there was.

"I guess," she says, summarizing, "I didn't go into the closet and shut the door for nothing."

That one time, she triumphed, but in truth, her body is broken and she has seen too much. Her injuries take months to heal, and she remains laid up through the winter.

Friends wonder where she is, and when they hear why she's been absent so long, they send donations. Wendell Phillips comes up with eighty dollars, enough to keep them in firewood so that they don't have to burn any more fences.

In Harriet's house, agitation and flux are constants. Boarders come and go. Ben walks the floor. Rit demands tobacco. Catherine works. A blind white woman comes to live there. John and Kessiah Bowley and their seven children move in, on their way south from Canada. Within a year or so, the Bowleys and six of their children will move back to Dorchester County, where they will live with Kessiah's father, Harkless Jolley, until they can purchase their own piece of land.

Within a few months of their arrival in Maryland, John Bowley, who rowed his family down the Chesapeake to freedom, will perform yet another act of heroism by making his way across the Choptank River to Trappe. There, under cover of night, he will steal his nephew, John Stewart's older son John Henry, away from indentureship to the Haddaways. The Bowley family will keep the boy with them in Cambridge until it is safe to send him to Auburn, where he will then move into Harriet's house.

A month or so later, Bowley will return to Trappe to take away John Henry's brother, Moses, who subsequently will be sent from the Eastern Shore to central New York. In Auburn, he, too, will live with his father in Harriet's house.

John Stewart—who now owns a fine team of horses but is crippled up with rheumatism and often confined to bed—must rejoice at the return of his sons, whom he has not seen since Christmas Eve of 1854, when he and his brothers escaped to the north. Nothing more is known, so far, of Stewart's daughter, Harriet, who was born on that same night.

In 1866, Gerrit Smith's wife, Ann Fitzhugh Smith, sends Harriet a box of clothing, including "some white things" for Rit, so that when the time comes for her to "set out for the shining shore," she will have the proper clothes to wear into the grave. In their part of the country, Smith asserts, people get ready ahead of time.

Rit is probably in ill health by now, and in her eighties. But her obstinate nature remains robust, and she may well resent Ann Smith's high-handed suggestion that it is time for her to start planning her funeral.

The next year, in September 1867, after a disagreement over the removal of ashes from a Maryland tenant house, a white farmer named Robert Vincent meets Harriet's first husband, John Tubman, on a road in Dorchester County and shoots him dead. Tried for murder, Vincent is declared not guilty by reason of self-defense by a white male jury, who have deliberated for a total of ten minutes.

In Caroline County, Dr. Anthony C. Thompson dies at seventy-five.

With help from abolitionists and suffragists, Harriet fills out a petition to the government for back pay.

The winter of 1867–68 is extremely hard, the snow many feet deep for months on end. Harriet and the others are completely snowed in. Nobody goes out except to scoop up snow for drinking water. Finally, Harriet gathers herself together and makes her way down the porch steps and into the yard. She pushes her way through snowdrifts the way she waded through cold streams in Delaware during the days of the Underground Railroad. In Auburn, she finds a way to borrow a quarter without asking for it, and when she receives it, she promises to repay the loan as soon as she can—which, in time, she does. Again, after walking through the snow to hand it over. Auburnites help out, delivering food to Harriet's door.

But Harriet keeps thinking about the freed people in the South, who are living in desperate poverty, cold and hungry, confused and hopeless. Kessiah and John Bowley's oldest son, James Alfred—called Alfred—who stood beside his mother when she was up for auction on the Dorchester County courthouse steps, is now about twenty-four years old. Educated, literate, he is working with freedmen in South Carolina. Harriet may receive messages from Alfred, whose schooling in Baltimore she helped pay for. She organizes small fairs to benefit the refugees, to be held at the Central Presbyterian Church. People drop off bundles at her door as contributions.

On Fridays, Ben, Rit, and Harriet fast until noon, the hour when Jesus came down from the cross; on Sundays, they attend the Presbyterian church, where Samuel Miles Hopkins, Jr., preaches. Sometimes the minister's sister, Sarah Hopkins Bradford, comes from Geneva to visit her brother and worship. During services, Harriet sings and shouts. Ben and Rit doze.

In the spring of 1868, at Rev. Samuel Hopkins's suggestion, Harriet begins telling her story to Sarah Bradford.

PART V.

ARAMINTA ROSS DAVIS, BETTER KNOWN AS HARRIET TUBMAN

We are all but finished going scene by scene through Harriet's extraordinary life as it *seems* (for what other choice do we have?) she might have lived it. However, she still has many years left to live.

Biographers, scholars, observers have it easy, turning time into a narrative device, rocketing past some years, then lingering long over the flicker of a moment. Years as they are lived, on the other hand, time as *we* live it, is another thing altogether, proceeding step by step, minute by minute.

Sometimes life levels out, if only for a time. Old age can make it happen, or grief, illness, depression, a bad marriage. We slog on but make few reports. Journal pages are left blank as the reflective instinct flags. We can't remember how one day differed from another or what happened at what exact point.

The General has finished her footwork and has moved into the telling of it. She goes home to Auburn, where, except for an occasional trip to Boston, Peterboro, or Rochester, she stays.

She still has work to do, of a different order, setting up for the years to come, past the end of her own life.

"Aunt Harriet," she is called by locals, white and black—an idealizing kinship term endearingly, if far too casually, applied. If Harriet herself objects to the town's presumptive familiarity, we have no word of it.

There are years, in fact, when we have no word of her at all. And then someone who knows her, or *of* her, will ask her whereabouts and about her health. And something will happen that will bring her, momentarily, back into the public notice. She will make a

Harriet at her dignified best, in a studio photo taken in Auburn just after the war, in the late 1860s. The gravity she exhibited in her daring feats of bravery is obvious here, as is the strength and nobility of her hands, even at rest.

speech or come up with a new idea, and there she is again, witnessed, noticed.

The Moses of her people. General Tubman. Our American hero.

From now on, we compress, and choose only a few more scenes to walk through with her.

Scene 18.

Auburn, Last Days

Harriet did not reason much about it but acted on the law against human slavery implanted in every heart. . . . Many who have died and will die who have used greater faculties; none who have consecrated what she had to the cause of the poor, with greater zeal or a truer heart.

—FRANKLIN SANBORN, TYPESCRIPT,
"THE LATE ARAMINTA DAVIS," MARCH 13, 1913

I am at peace with God and all mankind.

—HARRIET TUBMAN TO MARY TALBERT,
ON THE OCCASION OF THEIR LAST VISIT, 1913

In June 1868, following the winter of the waist-high snow-drifts, when Harriet goes to Sarah Bradford to tell her the story of her life, she is forty-six years old, barely past the midpoint of her life. She will live another forty-five years, during which time the country will elect eight individuals as their president, from Grant in 1868 to Wilson in 1912. Three of those men will be reelected; two will be replaced by a vice president after an assassination. One will lose his reelection campaign and return four years later to serve again. Ten men, twelve elections, fourteen inaugurations.

During her last years, there will be a thirty-year nationwide depression, the likes of which the country has never before suffered. In the South, masked white men will go night-riding during moonless hours to terrorize black people, burning their homes, leaving their mutilated bodies hanging from fat tree limbs, making certain that, although slavery is dead, white men yet reign supreme.

The freedmen suffer. Harriet organizes church fairs to benefit their relief.

Frederick Douglass will marry a white woman. He will die in 1895, the same year Booker T. Washington makes his speech in Atlanta, and becomes the most famous black man in America, invited by Teddy Roosevelt to break bread in the White House.

Black men will be given the vote. Women will not.

The African American boxer Jack Johnson will kayo the heavyweight champion of the world, Canadian Tommy Burns, in Australia, becoming not only the new boxing champ but the next holder of the title of the most famous black man in America.

During her last forty-five years, Harriet will marry, adopt a daughter, bury her father, her mother, brothers, a husband, sisters, nephews. She will participate in the women's suffrage movement and be taken for a ride by a scam artist shilling buried Confederate gold; after a long effort, she will succeed in founding an old folks home on her property. Her pigs will die. Her garden will flood. Her health will gradually decline, until she becomes first wheelchair-bound and then bedridden.

On March 10, 1913, she will die of pneumonia in the Harriet Tubman Home for Aged and Infirm Negroes.

In November 1865, after receiving an honorable discharge from the army in Brownsville, Texas, twenty-one-year-old Pvt. Nelson Davis boards a train with fellow soldier and friend Albert Thompson. They are headed for Auburn, New York, where Thompson lives, to establish life as civilians. Davis is familiar with central New York, having lived in nearby Oneida County after escaping slavery. How long would it take them to get there? Brownsville's as far south as Texas goes, down at the tip, on the Gulf of Mexico, over two thousand miles from Cayuga County. Maybe a week. Say by the first of the year, January 1866.

Exactly when Nelson Davis arrives, meets Harriet, and moves into her home is not clear. In her 1894 affidavit, Harriet will swear that when she married Davis in 1869, she had known him for "about three years," omitting any reference to where he lived when they first met. "About three years" leaves room for doubt, but is of no great importance. What matters is that, some time after early January 1866, Nelson Davis becomes a boarder, probably before the murder of John Tubman and before Harriet begins telling her life story for book-length publication.

There is but the one picture of him, the one taken in Auburn with Harriet, Gertie (Harriet's adopted daughter), and the others, in the late 1880s. A handsome, dark-skinned, muscular man, Davis smokes a stogie, wears suspenders and a porkpie hat, carries his head in a come-on tilt. Ill with tuberculosis, he nonetheless—and understandably—catches her eye and moves in. Despite his illness, he finds work, perhaps in the brickyard next door.

In the late spring of 1868, having heard about Sarah Bradford's interviews, local banker Charles P. Wood calls Harriet for an interview regarding her petitions for back pay from the government. In June, he submits a new petition, which includes a record of her service and testimonials from a number of Union officers. And late that summer or early fall, just before Sarah Bradford sails for Europe, the Auburn businessman William G. Wise organizes a subscription drive to raise money to publish *Scenes in the Life of Harriet Tubman*.

The drive brings in $430, enough to print twelve hundred copies. Bradford takes no royalties or fees; all profits are to go toward Harriet's debts. Wise hurries up publication in order to sell the book at Harriet's annual December fair for the relief of freedmen in the South. The fair raises a whopping five hundred dollars. *Scenes* is priced at one dollar and sells sixty or seventy copies. Harriet makes a wildly successful speech in which—back to doing what she *knows* how to—she dramatizes her life. Her audience is mesmerized; as good as a play, observes one witness. After the book's general release the following winter, Frank Sanborn reviews it favorably.

In March, she and Nelson Davis marry, her first legal church wedding, held at the Central Presbyterian Church and attended by family—including, presumably, Ben and Rit—and many prominent white locals. Nelson is twenty-five; Harriet, forty-seven. Soon afterward, she and Nelson open their own brickyard in the rear of her property, where Nelson can ply the masonry trade, hiring some of Harriet's kin to help out. She also works for various white women in town, doing spring cleaning and other domestic chores. Boarders come and go. Harriet sells, barters, makes deals. She and Nelson plant a vegetable garden, but unusual summer rains keep pelting down, soaking the ground, a situation that is later made only worse by the masons who pour water over the yard to make bricks. The seeds are drowned, the garden ruined.

Opinions of Nelson Davis vary considerably. One woman says he was magnificent-looking, while another calls him colorless and, because of his tuberculosis, hardly romantic. Some say Harriet married him not despite his illness but because of it, so that she could take care of him. Harriet's friend Florence Carter considered the marriage all but unworkable in any case, considering Harriet's busy schedule and her devotion to social issues. Perhaps, she suggested, a domestic life was never foremost in Harriet's mind—as presumably in a wife's mind it should be.

As a couple, admittedly they make an odd match. She is aging fast and is bent from injuries. He is fatally ill but young and still vigorous. In a photograph, he seems to be holding his own despite the debilitations of tuberculosis. Slightly defiant in attitude, he appears confident of manner, even slightly cocky.

Are they in love? Perhaps they make a deal. She will tend to him through his escalating illness and give him room and board. In return, if he dies first—which almost certainly he will—she, as the widow of someone who served in the U.S. Army, will receive a government pension for the rest of her life, even if the congressmen never give her her rightful back pay, or acknowledge her own contributions to the country.

Probably she likes Nelson Davis, drawn to both his rakish good looks *and* his eventual need for nursing. She wants to be married. She has lived such a loner's life; maybe she longs for a companion—someone who is not family—to touch her broken body every now and then and hold her during the night. Somebody besides family to talk to.

People marry for every imaginable reason.

Whatever theirs may be, they remain a couple. She takes his name.

Two years later, in 1871, Ben Ross dies at about eighty-four or eighty-five, worn down by pain, exhausted.

In 1872, William Seward dies at his home in Auburn. The following May, his son, Frederick, signs the South Street property over to Harriet for the original mortgage price of twelve hundred dollars, forgiving the remainder of the debt. At fifty-one, she becomes a full-out owner of real estate, a home on seven acres.

Only five months later—shortly after the onset of a financial panic that will bring a national depression lasting thirty years—she participates in a scheme that quickly develops into a local scandal.

Here is the story as Harriet and her brother John tell it to the *Auburn Daily Bulletin*.

On a Friday night, October 3, Harriet's brother John Stewart—who lives very near to Harriet—is in his front yard grooming his team of horses when he is approached in his yard by two black men, strangers. They are, they tell John, friends, and they give their names as John Thomas and Stevenson. They wish to have a private talk with him. When John hesitates to open himself to the opportunity, the men drop the name of a black minister who once lived in Auburn. How is he? they want to know.

John Stewart finishes grooming his horses, shuts them up for the night, and goes into his house to eat his supper. Thomas and Stevenson wait. Finally, Stewart comes back out, ready to hear what the two men have to say.

Does he, Stevenson asks, wish to do something good for himself? Make some money?

Stewart answers in the affirmative, as who would not? He always likes to do good, he tells the strangers. And to get money honestly.

At this, John reports, Stevenson "unfolded his business." He knows, he says, a contraband who has recently arrived in the vicinity of Auburn from Charleston, South Carolina, where he came into the possession of a trunk full of gold, which—afraid to use it or let any white man know he has it—he has kept since the war. The money inside is in five-, ten-, and twenty-dollar gold pieces and amounts to five thousand dollars. But the man prefers greenbacks and will turn the gold over to John for the bargain rate of two thousand dollars in cash.

John Stewart says he can't raise that much money but that perhaps his sister can. And he tells them her name.

Stevenson knows of Harriet Tubman, of course, from newspaper stories. More than likely, it is Harriet he has been looking for from the beginning. He further worms his way into John's confidence by saying he has been recommended to the family by James Alfred Bowley, the son of Kessiah and John, who is presently working in South Carolina.

The next morning, a Saturday, they meet with Harriet. The reason the Charleston man wants to relinquish the gold, they tell her, is that it belongs to the government and in South Carolina agents can seize it. Here is safer. The unnamed man—the contraband—who brought the gold from South Carolina prefers greenbacks. He will take two thousand dollars in cash. The rest will be theirs.

To further gain Harriet's trust, he drops her nephew Alfred Bowley's name once again.

She bites. The men take lodgings in her house. Stevenson stays for three nights.

If the government won't pay her outright, Harriet figures that maybe she can come by fair compensation on her own. She calls on a number of possible investors, including an ex-sheriff, who advises her to beware of the strangers, saying they are probably robbers and may even kill her. But she has by now moved beyond both rationality and skepticism. Her trust is too deeply fixed to be shaken.

She calls on bankers, who actually drive to her house with a five-hundred-dollar down payment, offering to provide the rest when the gold is produced. But Harriet tells the bankers they are too late. She needs the full amount.

In the end, it is John Stewart who comes up with the two thousand. He visits a local businessman, Anthony Shimer, for whom he has worked and who knows John to be a man of integrity. Shimer agrees to furnish the entire sum in greenbacks, in exchange for a dollar-for-dollar return in gold.

On Wednesday afternoon, October 8, Harriet meets up with Stevenson at a tavern. Her brother may or may not be with her at this point—the story is hers from here on out and she doesn't mention John's presence—but when the time comes to take the next step, to meet with the South Carolina man who will lead them to the gold, she goes alone.

It's not far, Stevenson promises. Only to Fleming Hill. And then he corrects himself, saying it's actually a little farther.

Harriet is fifty-one years old. Again we have to ask, *Why her? Why alone?* Why didn't John Stewart insist on going with her, or Nelson Davis. Why didn't somebody? Why didn't she leave the money at home and insist on going back for it only *after* the gold was produced?

Her trust in people of her race is unreserved, unshakable. She cannot *imagine* that black men would deceive her, take her for a ride, and then rob and abuse her, especially since they are friends of Alfred Bowley and, as such, practically family themselves.

Also, knowing Harriet, we have to presume she would have stood her ground had her brother and her husband raised objections, insisting that she could handle the situation on her own. And thought she could. And that since her role in the family was of the rescuer who never failed because God would not allow her to, the others gave in to her, as always.

Harriet and Stevenson get to the house where the South Carolina man is staying. He comes out, and after once again mentioning the name of Alfred Bowley, insists on being given the cash at once. Harriet will later describe the man as very dark, very troubled, and very scared. Sensing his distress, she speaks kindly to him—believing him to be only recently freed from slavery—but refuses to hand over the money. First, they must take her to the gold. Where is it?

Over the fields, says the unnamed man, in the woods.

The three of them start out on foot, making their way over plowed ground and three fences. The dark unnamed man will later be identified as an experienced confidence man from Seneca Falls, named Harris.

The moon is two nights past full. By midnight, it will have risen in the sky, round but for a slight dent on one side.

Harris asks for the money again.

The Gold Swindle.

Yesterday, Slocum Howland, Esq., of Sherwoods, at whose house Harriet Tubman was stopping, made a search in the woods where she was robbed by the "gold man," and found the box of gold.

It was a common box done up in a sack, and was full of bright, solid old fashioned—stones.

The box was sold to the strange nigger from South Carolina, some days ago, by Sidney Mosher.

—Gold is below par to-day.

One of several newspaper stories about the swindling of Harriet and her brothers, this one from the October 3, 1873, *Auburn Daily Bulletin*.

Harriet again refuses to yield it. They keep going across the fields until they come to the woods.

There. The South Carolina man points to a pile of rails. The trunk is buried there. The men begin to lift up the rails one by one.

Harriet waits.

In short order, something oblong, wooden, maybe a trunk or even just a box, appears. Wrapped in canvas, it has been covered with leaves and sunk into the ground only by inches, deep enough only to hide it. The men lift it out.

Once again, Harris asks for the greenbacks. Harriet shows him the money to prove she has it, but she refuses to hand it over until she sees the gold. The men become slightly agitated. After a heated and somewhat confused discussion, they go off together. They have, they say, forgotten the key to the trunk and must go retrieve it.

In the moonlight, alone, Harriet examines the buried prize.

When the two men first came to her and told her the story, she saw the buried trunk in her imagination. She is expecting it to be as she envisioned it, like the one she saw in Beaufort when a real cache of gold was dug up in a Confederate's yard. What she holds in her hands now is not a trunk, but only an ordinary wooden box, with no keyhole.

Now she knows. Even so, she sticks with her original instincts. She waits it out. There could still be gold inside. Besides, she can't bear not knowing how the situation will play out. After all, they have not managed to beat her out of the greenbacks.

But the years have taken a big chunk from her reserves. She is older in a way she can't yet acknowledge or perhaps even recognize. Instead of providing instructions and certainty, her imagination and visionary nature turn on her.

Waiting for the men, stories come into her mind of ghosts that haunt buried treasure and protect it from theft. Not yet fully convinced the box doesn't contain gold, she wonders if any are about.

Her heart in an uproar, she looks for a stone to break open the box. Not finding one, she lifts up one of the rails and brings it down. At which point, she seems to fall into one of her narcoleptic trances, and when she comes to, she sees something white—surely, she assumes, a ghost, there to protect the gold and keep it out of her hands. She drops the rail.

But it is a cow. A white cow, which, spooked by her presence, bolts, followed by others in the herd. The cattle take off through the woods, rumbling and snorting, moving in what she calls a "prance" through the woods. And then, simultaneously with the noise, she feels the presence once again of the two men. She doesn't exactly hear or see anything, just a blur.

And then nothing.

When she comes to, she finds herself bound and gagged. No green-backs. She makes her way to a friend's house, where she remains laid up for several days, recovering from head injuries. The story receives wide coverage in Auburn, including a lengthy newspaper report, with accounts by John Stewart and Harriet, only five days after the event. The *Auburn Daily Bulletin* entitles the story "The Gold Swindle and the Greenback Robbery."

A strange tale, it stirs a lot of gossip and a great many interpretations, including one that suggests Harriet and her brother staged the swindle to steal the money from Shimer, whom the otherwise-discreet Alice Brickler refers to as a junk dealer. "Old Man Schimer," she writes, "I believe he was a Jew."

The swindlers are not captured. They flee with Shimer's greenbacks. In partial repayment, John Stewart has to turn over his team of horses to Shimer, thereby losing his livery-rental business.

What happened? Did Harriet really think she saw a ghost? Or did she make up the ghost—and the cows—because she was embarrassed and needed a good cover story, a kind of humorous entertainment told at her own expense, the kind she always had at her fingertips, especially when white people were the audience—to distract her listeners? In the coming years, another black man will come to her door and convince her he is poor and in need of refuge. She will take him in and send him to a friend to ask for money, keeping her actions secret from her brother William Henry, knowing he would not approve.

She's gullible, and good. She once seemed invincible but is no longer.

Hard times are everywhere. People scramble for money. Perhaps John Stewart, arthritic, was looking for fast cash. His sister helped. They were taken in.

Perhaps.

In 1877, Gerrit Smith dies. With his passing, notes the *New York Times,* the "era of moral politics" has come to an end. That same year, Rutherford Hayes wangles his way into the White House by agreeing to remove all federal troops from southern states and promising not to use federal troops to prevent armed revolt against a state government, even if that state requests aid from the president.

When an AME church is founded in Auburn, Nelson Davis joins the board of trustees. Margaret Stewart marries Henry Lucas at the Central Presbyterian Church and moves into a home on Cornell Street in Auburn. They will have three children, the youngest a daughter, Alice, who will one day write long letters to Earl Conrad about—among other things—her mother's kidnapping by Aunt Harriet.

After Margaret's departure from the house, Harriet and Nelson adopt a baby girl named Gertie, whom they will raise as their own.

Who Gertie was, where she came from, who her biological parents were—all this remains a mystery. In the 1888 picture of the household, the fourteen-year-old Gertie Davis is standing between Harriet and Nelson. Already at least four inches taller than Harriet, Gertie is very light-skinned, with grayish-looking eyes. She holds her hands behind her back, has arranged her hair away from her plumpish face, and is quite attractive. In the 1875 New York State census, she is listed as Harriet and Nelson's daughter. Whether or not she had been, or ever was, legally adopted, no one knows, and in any case, the records are sealed, according to New York State law. In 1900, Gertie will marry. After becoming Gertie Davis Watson, she moves into her own, unrecorded life, without letting anyone know where she is going or what she knows about her ancestry.

In October 1879, Rit dies at ninety-four.

In 1880, Harriet's frame farmhouse burns. The February 10, 1880, issue of the *Evening Auburnian* describes the fire as a "conflagration," and reports that the house was entirely consumed, with only a "small portion of the household goods" saved. The fire is said to have been caused by a defective stovepipe that had been stuck through a hole in a lintern, to serve as a chimney. Presumably, Nelson and Harriet go next door to her brother John's house to live while a brick house is built on the ruins of the wooden one, the costs funded by townspeople. Harriet, Nelson, and the other brickyard workers may have contributed to its construction. In any case, someone inserted a Masonic symbol in the front wall, perhaps an Auburn member of the organization.

Harriet and Nelson begin attending the AME Zion church. Harriet always sits close to the front, shoulders bent forward, head down. During services, she stands and begins to shout and sing. Others follow her lead and soon everyone is shouting and singing. After her death, the minister of this church, James E. Mason, will recall these moments and remark that until her death, Harriet possessed endurance, vitality, and magnetism.

Nelson becomes more gravely ill, less able to work.

Visions occasionally return to Harriet. She calls them mysterious dreams and thoughts. The visions no longer arrive as instructions from God, but are predictions of forthcoming disasters—in one case, the sinking of a ship; in another, an earthquake.

Forty hogs on what the *Evening Auburnian* calls Harriet's "swine ranch" die in quick succession. Harriet suspects rat poisoning from refuse she has collected from all over town to feed them. Once the hogs die, garbage piles up in her yard.

When her nephew Moses Stewart is locked up in jail for petty larceny, Harriet visits him. Afterward, feeling the "power" come on her, she stands outside the jail, shouting and singing. She is taken inside the building and seen by a doctor, who settles her down.

When Grover Cleveland becomes the first Democrat to live in the White House since the Civil War, black people migrate from small towns and the rural countryside to cities, fearing reenslavement. In *Harper's* magazine, an article on "Manifest Destiny" calls the Anglo-Saxon race a powerful one that will move down upon Mexico, down upon Central and South America, out upon the islands, over upon Africa, and beyond.

Needing money, Harriet goes to Sarah Bradford and asks her to reissue *Scenes*. Bradford agrees and proceeds to update the text.

In 1886, Bradford issues *Harriet Tubman, the Moses of Her People*, a somewhat cleaned-up version of *Scenes*. In its preface, Bradford justifies the reprint by saying that the facts of Harriet's life are "unknown to the present generation" and that she needs help, not for herself but for "certain helpless ones of her people." The book ends with a description of Harriet in her home, with as many as eight or ten dependents living with her. Harriet is hoping, Bradford writes, as her "last work," to turn her home into a hospital for infirm and aged African Americans.

Emma Telford will describe the residents of Harriet's home as "the needy, the most utterly friendless and helpless of her race." In a letter to Earl Conrad, Auburnian Helen Tatlock will say that Harriet had in her care "a great number of young and old, black and white, all poorer than she." There were children she brought up, an incorrigible white woman who had a child and had served jail time, a blind woman. To pump up book sales, Harriet visits Frank Sanborn, and in Boston, she sits for a formal photograph, standing in a photographer's studio in a high-necked dress with her hands folded on the arm of a velvet settee, looking sternly out at the world. This replaces the woodcut of Harriet in her general's garb, which illustrated *Scenes*.

In 1888, Nelson Davis dies and is buried in Auburn's prestigious Fort Hill Cemetery. Harriet's brother John Stewart dies. Her younger brother William Henry leaves his six-acre farm in Grantham, Ontario, and moves to Auburn. He lives with his son for a while, then moves in with his sister, where he will stay until his death, one year before Harriet's, in 1912. Soon after William Henry moves in, his son John Isaac comes to Auburn with his baby daughter, Eva Katherine Helena Harriet Stewart, whose mother has died. John Isaac asks Harriet to raise his child. She is now sixty-eight years old. William Henry is sixty. John Isaac will die before Eva is six years old, leaving the girl's grandfather and great-aunt to raise her.

With the help of Charles Wood, Harriet petitions the U.S. pension board for a widow's pension.

She attends a number of woman suffrage meetings, where she speaks as an invited guest. At one meeting, she takes her rightful place in history. "Yes, ladies," she declares, "I was the conductor on the Underground Railroad for eight years and I can say what most conductors can't say—I never ran my train off the track and I never lost a passenger."

At the AME Zion Western New York Conference, she sings and

shouts her way up and down the aisles of the church and asks for financial assistance to open an old folks' home for black people on her property. She will call it John Brown Hall.

At the first convention of the National Association for Colored Women, she is the featured speaker, referred to as the "almost unknown, almost unsung 'Black Joan of Arc.' " After telling of her war experiences, Harriet sings a war melody and asks for contributions to her home for the aged.

She receives her widow's pension, her nurse's pension.

She speaks of having "brain surgery" without anesthesia, a procedure performed to relieve the headaches she has suffered from since her injury at the Bucktown crossroads in 1835.

In 1900, she asks Bradford for another reprint of the biography. When Bradford agrees, Harriet makes the trip across Lake Owasco, where she has lunch on the veranda with the Presbyterian minister and his sister. This book, published in 1901, is the same as the 1886 edition, except for the added scenes.

In 1906, when Ellen Wright Garrison—wife of William Lloyd Garrison, Jr., and daughter of Martha Coffin Wright—comes to call, she describes Harriet's yard as a leaking rummage heap of dry-goods boxes for kindling, old cooking utensils, a beat-up buggy in tatters, and various other

Harriet's house, located on the outskirts of Auburn, New York. This is not her original home but one that was built for her in about 1880 after a wintertime conflagration struck her kitchen and burned the house to the ground.

piles of junk. Garrison says she counted five homely cats, four puppies and their mother, a dirty pig, lots of chickens, and two white children sitting outside eating apples.

Harriet, however, emerges from the kitchen into the rummage heap looking quite well and brisk.

On a sunny June day in 1908, with an American flag draped around her shoulders, Harriet stands before a crowd of well-wishers in a celebration to mark the opening of the Harriet Tubman Home. After twelve years of planning and fund-raising, her dream has finally become a reality. There has been a big parade, with a band from Ithaca playing a quickstep, to which local young black people marched and kept time. Harriet, the hero of the day, rode in the first carriage with her brother William Henry.

At the podium, wrapped in the flag, she says, "I did not take up this work for my own benefit but for those of my race who need help. The work is now well started and I know God will raise up others to take care of the future."

That night, there is a reception, after which the young people dance the night away.

By late 1910, Harriet has become wheelchair-bound and has entered the Harriet Tubman Home. When a Cornell student, James B. Clarke, comes to call with Gerrit Smith's granddaughter Anne Fitzhugh Miller, he watches, astonished, as, despite her frailty and size, Harriet downs a full dinner of chicken, rice, pie, and cheese. Her mind, Clarke reports, is still fresh and active. After telling of the medal sent to her by Queen Victoria for having taken so many people to Canada, Harriet asks Clarke to send a letter of congratulations to the newly crowned king of England, George V.

In February 1913, a month before her death, visitors describe Harriet as thin and weak but still bright, talkative, and very clear in her mind. But when Mary Talbert, president of the Empire State Federation of Women's Clubs, visits, she says Harriet's last words to her are, "I've been fixing up for the journey for some time."

On March 10, 1913, at age ninety-one, Harriet dies of pneumonia. Some say that she directed her final rites herself, asking nurses and

Harriet (in the center, seated, dressed in a white lace shawl) and other residents of the Home for the Aged, on the grounds of her property, about 1912. She lived there from 1911 until her death in 1913.

friends to come to her bedside and sing her home. Two great-nephews were present, as well as Rev. E. U. A. Brooks of the AME Zion Church and Rev. Charles Smith, who served with the Fifty-fourth Massachusetts at Fort Wagner.

Harriet joined in the singing when her cough allowed it. After prayers and a final communion, she sank back in bed, one observer told the *Auburn Citizen,* ready to die.

March 13, 1913

After a prayer service at the Harriet Tubman Home that morning, funeral services for Harriet are held at three o'clock at the AME Zion Church. She lies in state, her casket open, the lower half covered with an American flag. Hundreds of mourners file by her coffin. She's wearing her good black dress and a waistcoat, on which is pinned Queen Victoria's medal. In her large, strong hands someone has placed a crucifix.

Representing the city in the absence of the mayor, John F. Jaeckel, president of the Common Council, calls Harriet a woman of unusual judgment and integrity, scrupulous, a woman of deep religious convictions.

"I may say I have known 'Aunt Harriet,' " he testifies, "during my whole lifetime. The boys of my time always regarded her as a sort of su-

Harriet at the end of her life, wrapped in a shawl said to have been sent to her by Queen Victoria. She is frail now, but her eyes still burn and her chin remains steady and lifted, and she seems to be looking out not from the landscape of an ordinary life, but from history itself.

pernatural being; our youthful imaginations were fired by the tales we had heard of her adventure and we stood in great awe of her."

Jaeckel continues, "Greatness in this life does not come to people through accident or by the caprice of fate or fortune; it is the reward of great zeal accompanied by great faith in the object sought and the persistent fighting against great obstacles."

He hopes that Tubman's life will serve as an inspiration to the young men and women of the congregation. In an everyday world, he says, what a "contrast we find between the average person's life filled with petty vanities, as compared with the unselfish life of our good sister. . . . If we take this contrast to heart, the example which she has set will not be entirely lost upon us."

The speeches and eulogies go on for several hours.

She is buried next to her brother William Henry in Fort Hill Cemetery. In the same plot lie her nephew William Henry, Jr., and her niece Emma Stewart. Only two small pine trees planted for the niece and nephew mark their graves. Some distance away, Nelson Davis lies beside William Henry's son John Isaac.

A year later, in June 1914, the people of Auburn unveil a bronze tablet in her memory. At the Auditorium Theater, Booker T. Washington speaks. When the seventeen-year-old daughter of Margaret Stewart, Alice Lucas, pulls aside the American flag draped over the tablet, the lights are briefly switched off. When they come back on, the tablet—a mock-up of the bronze tablet that will replace it—is displayed, surrounded by lights.

On it there is a likeness of Harriet, followed by this inscription:

IN MEMORY OF
HARRIET TUBMAN
Born a slave in Maryland in about 1821
Died in Auburn, N.Y. March 10th, 1913
Called the "Moses" of her people during the Civil War,
with rare courage she led over
three hundred Negroes up from slavery to freedom,
and rendered invaluable service as nurse and spy.

With implicit trust in God, she braved every danger and
overcame every obstacle, withal she possessed extraordinary
foresight and judgment so that she truthfully said—
"On my Underground Railroad I nebber run off
de track and I nebber los' a passenger."

THIS TABLET ERECTED BY THE CITIZENS OF AUBURN
· 1914 ·

Family, friends, and supporters gather for the dedication of a headstone for Harriet's
grave. 1915, Fort Hill Cemetery.

The tablet is later moved from the Auditorium Theater to the
Cayuga County Court House, where it has remained.

On the Fourth of July of the following year, members of the Empire State Federation of Women's Clubs, led by Mary Talbert, erect a simple marker on Harriet's grave. It will be replaced in 1937 by a granite monument.

In 1943, after many failed attempts to find a publisher, Earl Conrad, a former Auburn resident, labor organizer, and reporter, manages with the help of Carter G. Woodson to convince the African American–owned Associated Publishers of Washington, D.C., to issue his biography, *General Harriet Tubman*.

In 1944, the U.S. Maritime Commission launches the SS *Harriet Tubman* from the New England Shipbuilding Company in South Portland, Maine.

Eva Stewart Northrup, Harriet's great-niece and the granddaughter of her brother William Henry Stewart, christens the ship.

It glides out to sea.

Acknowledgments

I must first off happily extend deepest gratitude to my editor, Janet Hill, whose dream it was to publish a biography of her childhood hero, Harriet Tubman, and whose idea it was to ask me if I was interested in writing such a book. I wasn't certain I was up to such a fabulous— if rightfully daunting—opportunity, but since in writing my previous book I had already studied slavery and abolition in the United States, I thought maybe I'd like to make use of the discoveries I'd made. In addition to which, how many times does a writer come upon the chance to write about a true *hero*? Janet's enthusiasm and our immediate feelings of synchronicity and personal attachment convinced me further. We said yes to each other and here we are. Over the years of writing and revision delays on my part, her encouragement has never lagged. "A book takes as long as it takes," she would say. Big thanks also to my agent, Amanda Urban, always there.

Harriet Tubman's story has, of course, been told many times. To tell it again was to pick my way through a lot of material, some of it previously published, and to try to come up with a different version of the story, my version, and one that *seemed* to be, possibly, true. The Tubman scholar who was given me unquestioning help and support throughout the past five years, who has provided me with documents I could not find and encouragement when I needed it, is Kate Larson, whose own biography, *Bound for the Promised Land,* was published in 2004. Kate is a terrific researcher, and, unlike many, a generous historian and biographer, one who does not feel she owns her subject, permanently. As I write these words she is still providing me with information and cheerful support, not to mention some needed laughs along the way.

For all information concerning Cambridge, the Eastern Shore, and the history of the state of Maryland, I owe much to John Creighton, who is an expert in these areas. John was always willing to answer more questions and to take me on yet one more driving expedition through the back roads of Dorchester County. Like Kate, he showed me where to find things: which archive to go to, what name to look for. Jay and Susan Meredith gave me a special tour through the Bucktown store and allowed me to sit in their home for hours, combing through old Cambridge newspapers. For Caroline County information, I relied greatly upon the knowledge of J. O. K. Walsh and the terrifically sharp Patricia Guida. Pat and J. O. K. also took me on many driving tours through Quaker country and along the waterways. Gary Broadus provided much useful information about his family. Another helpful Marylander was Tubman scholar Kay McElvey. Harriet Tubman's descendant, Judith Bryant, of Auburn, provided encouragement and joy. Tubman historians Jim McGowan and Milton Sernett also contributed support, especially for the particular nature of my book. Mary Ross Taylor read a raggedy, early draft of the book and offered very insightful comments.

In the early days, Bret Schulte worked as my research assistant, providing a great deal of archival information and reportage. Another George Mason student, Christa Anderson, found things for me and did some tedious transcribing of documents, much appreciated. Paulina Vaca directed me to online archives. Jason Prokowiew tried to teach me how to use the Endnotes software, but I never figured it out. I am also grateful to archivists and librarians through the geographical areas covered in this book. These include the librarians at the Maryland State Archives, the William L. Clements Library, the Dorchester Country Public Library, the Cornell Special Collections Department, the Schomburg Library, the Library of Congress, the Buffalo Historical Society, the Buffalo Public Library, the St. Catharines Museum, the National Archives, the John Brown Home in Elba, New York, the Beaufort, South Carolina, Public Library. Extending thanks to Web sites doesn't seem exactly appropriate, but I have to say, I am very grateful they are out there, providing a huge amount of data, saving me untold hours of library work and untold amounts of money spent on travel.

Others at Doubleday for whose expertise and assistance I am grateful for are Christian Nwachukwu Jr., Daniel Romero, Rebecca Holland, and Maria Carella.

Finally, I want to thank the friends and associates who shored up my energies and propped up my confidence when it lagged. They include the mighty Susan Shreve, Lisa Page, Maxine Clair, Pati Griffith, Steve Yarbrough, Gary Fisketjon, Ann Patchett, Suzannah Lessard, Ronica Battacharya, Yolande Robbins, Tom Williams, Richard Bausch, Patty O'Toole, Roger Wilkins, Celia Morris, Michael Nussbaum, Lou Stovall, Deborah Kaplan, Steve Goodwin, Alan Cheuse, my family—Eddy, Anne, David, Gwen, Colin, Andrea, and Brandon. More gratitude than I can exactly find the words to say goes to Tom Johnson who lived with me throughout the research, the writing, and the many revisions of this book, and who put a lot of his own energies and love into our life together and, therefore, into this work.

Notes on Sources

The two best contemporary sources for resources and citations are Kate Larson's groundbreaking *Bound for the Promised Land* and Jean Humez's extremely useful *Harriet Tubman: The Life and the Life Stories*. Earl Conrad's biography, *General Harriet Tubman*, provides indispensable material, much of which was previously unrecorded in 1943 when the book was published; his papers, on microfilm at the Schomburg Library, contain letters written to him by people who actually knew Harriet, among them, Harkless Bowley, Alice Brickler, and Helen Tatlock. The most valuable—and to my mind, most reliable—of Sarah Bradford's three biographies is the first one, *Scenes in the Life of Harriet Tubman*. The third, *Harriet, the Moses of Her People*, contributes new scenes which Harriet related to Bradford, also necessary to any researcher trying to figure out how this great life was lived. Catherine Clinton's biography, *Harriet Tubman, The Road to Freedom*, yields background information on the years of Harriet's life. Jim McGowan's, *Station Master on the Underground Railroad: The Life and Letters of Thomas Garrett* provides altogether reliable primary information about Harriet and many of her rescues, in the form of letters from Garrett to William Still and other abolitionists.

Scene 1. Owasco Lake

Information about the Owasco luncheon comes from Sarah Bradford's 1901 biography. Details of Samuel Hopkins's summer home are from his grandson's book; See Adams, *Grandfather Stories*. ". . . her beloved darkies" is from Bradford, 1901. Harriet sitting at train station, waiting, is from Helen Tatlock letter to Earl Conrad.

Scene 2. Dorchester: Birth

The preponderance of background information about Dorchester County is from John Creighton's collection of documents, articles, and notes on index cards; see also, Kay McElvey, Gary Broadus, Jay and Susan Meredith, Elaine McGill. Main published historical sources are: Fields, *Slavery and Freedom on the Middle Ground;* Brackett, *The Negro in Maryland;* Jones, *New Revised History of Dorchester County;* Clemens, *The Atlantic Economy and Colonial Maryland's Eastern Shore;* and Middleton, *Tobacco Coast.* Also useful, are the Kulikoff and Walsh articles, in *The William and Mary Quarterly.* Anthony Thompson's guardian account, Atthow Pattison's will, and Equity Papers, Case 249, are all listed in the bibliography; these court documents provide invaluable information about the Ross/Green family, including names and ages of children, as well as the Pattisons, the Brodesses, and the Thompsons. Generally, sources are also included in the text. Brackett provides data on manumission laws. The U.S. Census provides details of property ownership, including slaves, by various families. Dorchester cemetery records and the Maryland census provide dates of some births and marriages. Dorchester County records yield much. Brodess genealogy, is from Gary Broadus. List of Thompson Negroes, comes from the Maryland Historical Society. ". . . always uneasy" is from Drew, *The Refugee.* Maryland law on term slaves, is from Brackett. Turning slaves into real estate, is from Polish Mills's testimony, Equity Papers, Case 249. Runaway ad is from Jay and Susan Meredith.

Scene 3. Childhood

Harriet's first memory and story of games with her baby brother are as told by Emma Telford and also Bradford, 1869. Sale of "James" and "Rhody" is in Dorchester land records. James Cook story is from Bradford, 1869, and Sanborn, 1863. "Miss Susan" is from Bradford, 1869; stolen sugar is from Bradford, 1901.

Scene 4. At Polish Mills: A Shower of Fire

Most Nat Turner material is from Oates and Greenberg. Figures on Maryland population are in Fields and Brackett. Henny story comes from Dorchester library files and the Maryland Archives. Harriet on the North Star is from Tatlock. Douglass on the North Star comes from *Life and Times.* "I was not happy . . ." is from Drew. Woolfolk quote is in Johnson, *Soul by Soul.* Polish Mills on hiring Rit is from Equity Papers, Case 249. "All which way" 1913 *Auburn Daily Advertiser.* Various stories of meteor showers, can be found on Leonid Internet sites.

Scene 5. The Weight: At the Bucktown Crossroads

"Terrorize and therefore silence . . ." is from Hart, *Slavery and Abolition.* "Worst man . . ."; ". . . set me to . . ."; and "bushel basket" are in Telford. ". . . shoulder shawl and "flutter flutter" are from Sanborn, 1863. ". . . shamed to go in,"; ". . . overseer raising . . ."; "bleeding and fainting"; and ". . . blood and sweat . . ." are in Telford. ". . . wouldn't give sixpence . . .," is from Bradford, 1869.

Scene 6. Sold and Carried Away: The Slaveholder's Choice

Sheriff's notice is from John Creighton. Anthony Thompson's will can be found at Dorchester County Courthouse. Anthony C. Thompson drugstore is from Cambridge newspaper ads. Story of hiring out and purchase of steers is in Sanborn, 1863. Ben Ross's description of Thompson, is in Still. "Half a cord . . ." is from Sanborn, 1863. William Henry Stewart story is from Howe in Blassingame's *Slave Testimony.* Benjamin (aka James Stewart/Seward) on Linah and children, is from Drew.

Scene 7. Marriage

Description of John Tubman is from McGill transcription, *Certificate of Freedom.* "Everytime I saw . . ." is from Drew. Maryland manumission law of 1835 is in Brackett. Legal search, comes from Bradford, 1869. Sale of Susan Manokey is from Dorchester County Chattel Records. Death of Brodess is from Bradford, 1869. Brodess will is in Dorchester Register of Wills. John Tubman and "Cudjo," Harriet and dreams of horses are both from Bradford, 1869. Gourney Pattison lawsuit and other matters relating to the possible sale of Kessiah, Harriet, and Mary Ann (Mary Jane) are from Dorchester Orphans Court records. ". . . flicker and fade . . .," is from Douglass, *Life and Times*.

Scene 8. Over the Line

Escape story is from Bradford, 1869, Sanborn, 1863, Helen Tatlock, and Harkless Bowley letters to Conrad.

Scene 9. Family

"I started with this idea . . ." is in Bradford, 1869. Bowleys' escape is from Harkless Bowley letters to Conrad and Polish Mills's deposition, Equity Papers, Case 249. Thompson 1854 purchase is from Dorchester County Chattel Records. ". . . proceeded by steam railroad . . ." is found in Wilbur Siebert manuscript material. "On one occasion . . ." is from Douglass, *Life and Times*.

Scene 10. Rescues, Promises

Story of Ross brothers' attempted escapes, is from Howe interview with William Henry Stewart, in Blassingame's *Slave Testimony*. Information about Equity Papers, Case 249, James Stewart's purchase of Ross family members, Eliza Brodess's property assessment and lawsuit, and the sale of Rit to Ben are all from Dorchester County records. ". . . illuminated his mind . . ." is from Still. Ross brothers 1854 escape comes from Bradford, 1869. Information about Trappe and the birth of Harriet Ross are from John Creighton. Jane Kane (aka Jane Stewart) quotes are from Still, "Journal C," and Drew. Ross brothers described and Chase and Jackson named are in Still, "Journal C." Winnibar Johnson quote is also from "Journal C." Chariot song, and coded verse come from Bradford, 1869.

Thomas Garrett and two dollars for shoes is from McGowan. Questioning of "Old Ben" is from *Baltimore American.*

Scene 11. Becoming Moses

R. A. Ball memory, comes from *Toronto Globe,* 1913. For western New York and St. Catharines information, following are the main sources: Sernett, *North Star Country;* Thomas, *Niagara's Freedom Trail;* Klees, *Underground Railroad Tales;* Pettit, *Sketches in the History of the Underground Railroad;* Sadlier, *Tubman;* Winks, *Blacks in Canada;* Buffalo public library vertical files; display, St. Catharines Museum. ". . . good headway" is from 1863 interview in Howe. Samuel Green, Jr. letter, is from Blondo. Josiah Bailey escape is in Bradford, 1869; Still, "Journal C"; and Still, *Underground Railroad;* Garrett letters are in McGowan; Siebert interview is cited in Larson. Dr. Thompson's warning to Ben, is from Garrett letters. Tilly rescue, is in McGowan and in Bradford, 1901. Garrett quote "had never met . . ." is in McGowan.

Scene 12. Escapes, Rescues: The Stampede

Story of Dover Eight, comes from Still; Garrett letters in McGowan, and *Cambridge Democrat* ad. Samuel Green is from Blondo, Still, and Creighton papers. Harriet in Syracuse is from Siebert interview in Larson. New York protest comes from Bradford, 1869. Rescue of Ben and Rit is in Taylor, Still, and Garrett letters. ". . . concert of action . . ." is from *Easton Gazette.*

Scene 13. With John Brown: Dreams, Metaphor

Dream is from Sanborn, 1863, Bradford, 1869. "worn out and bored," is from Douglass, *Life and Times.* Letter to Ladies Irish Anti-Slavery is in Foner. Smith letter is from Sanborn, *Life and Letters.* Loguen and Brown in St. Catharines, is from Wyman. Money from Brown to Harriet and her presence in Ingersoll comes from Brown Notebooks, in Larson. Harriet's storytelling abilities found in Higginson, Cheney, Telford, and

Bradford, 1901. Purchase of Seward house found in Sanborn, 1863, and in Larson.

Scene 14. Last Rescue

Nalle story, including Troy *Whig* account, is from Bradford, 1869; also, Cheney. Letter to Wendell Phillips is in Humez. ". . . aloft the banner . . ." is in Sernett. "Angel of Death" is from Sanborn papers, in Larson. ". . . for want of $30 . . ." is in Cheney. Ennals's rescue is from Sanborn, 1886; Still; Martha Coffin Wright to Ellen Wright Garrison is from Garrison Family Papers, in Humez. ". . . mad winter . . ." is in Sanborn, 1863. Harriet at Gerrit Smith's is from Sanborn papers and Clark, "An Hour with Harriet Tubman." ". . . sorely against her will . . ." is in Sanborn, 1863, and in Bradford, 1869. ". . . asking people please to provide . . ." is from Martha Coffin Wright letter, 1861, in Larson. Harriet's vision of emancipation is from Bradford, 1886. "Knowing how easily . . ." is from Bradford, 1901. Story of Margaret Stewart is from Alice Brickler, letters to Earl Conrad.

Scene 15. Beaufort, South Carolina
Scene 16. The Proclamation, the Raid

All details of Harriet's various kinds of service in South Carolina, including details of the conduct of the war and the history of African-American participation in it, are from the following sources: Rose, *Rehearsal for Reconstruction;* McPherson, *The Negro's Civil War;* Cornish, *The Sable Arm;* Trudeau, *Like Men of War;* Higginson, *Army Life in a Black Regiment;* Higginson, *Letters* and *Journals of Thomas Wentworth Higginson;* Schwartz, *A Woman Doctor's Civil War;* Kozak, *Eve of Emancipation;* Duncan, *Blue-Eyed Child of Fortune;* Pollitzer, *The Gullah People and Their African Heritage;* Linder, *Historical Atlas of the Rice Plantations of the ACE River Basin;* American Freedmen's Inquiry Commission, Beaufort, SC, found in www.civilwar.com. *Harper's Weekly* (www.harpweek.com) *Commonwealth (Boston);* Meltzer and Holland, *Lydia Maria Child.* Other sources consulted include Sanborn, 1863; Cameron, *Young Reporter of Concord;* Guterman article in *Prologue;* National Archives; Cheney; Sanborn; Bradford, 1869; Telford; Tatlock letter to Conrad; on-line manuscript collection, University of South Carolina; Forten, *A Free Negro in the Slave Era;* Holland, *Letters and Diaries of Laura Towne;* Hart, *Slavery and Abolition;* Wood, "Harriet Tubman." Manuscript History Concerning the Pension claim of Harriet's visit to Canada is found in Blassingame, *Slave Testimony.* Tubman speech at Camp William Penn, is from *Christian Recorder* in Larson. "Emigrant train" incident is from Bradford, 1869; see also Martha Coffin Wright letter to Marianna Pelham Wright. Soup-bone story is from Bradford, 1901. Story of John and Kessiah Bowley moving to Auburn and Cambridge is from Harkless Bowley letters to Conrad. Ann Fitzhugh Smith to Rit, is in Martha Coffin Wright to Ellen (see note).

Scene 17. Raining Blood
Scene 18. Auburn, Last Days

Information about Nelson Davis (aka Nelson Charles) is from Harriet Tubman Davis Civil War Pension File. Opinions of Nelson Davis found in Brickler, Tatlock, and Florence Carter letters to Earl Conrad. Reports on Harriet and Nelson's daily life found in Martha Coffin Wright letters in Larson. Gold-swindle story, is from *Auburn Daily Bulletin.* Adoption of Gertie Davis found in 1875 New York census and 1880 federal census. Harriet feeling the "power" is from *Auburn Daily Advertiser.* "Yes, ladies . . ." is from Bradford, 1901. "Brain surgery" is in Bradford, 1901, and Adams, *Grandfather Stories.* "I did not take up this work . . ." is from *Auburn Daily Citizen,* June 24, 1908. Harriet's last words to Mary Talbert and other details of funeral are from *Auburn Citizen,* March 14, 1913. Unveiling of bronze tablet is from *Auburn Citizen,* June 13, 1914. Launching of SS *Harriet Tubman,* is from *Chicago Defender* and *Baltimore Afro-American,* as cited in Larson.

Selected Bibliography

Biographies and Biographical Articles in the Order of Their Publication

Sanborn, Franklin B. "Harriet Tubman," *Commonwealth* (Boston), July 17, 1863.

Cheney, Ednah Dow. "Moses." *Freedmen's Record,* March 1865.

Bradford, Sarah H. *Scenes in the Life of Harriet Tubman,* Auburn, NY: W. J. Moses, 1869.

Sanborn, Franklin B. "A Negro Heroine—Scenes in the Life of Harriet Tubman." In *Transcendental Youth and Age,* edited by Kenneth Walter Cameron. Hartford: Transcendental Books, 1869.

Bradford, Sarah H. *Harriet Tubman, the Moses of Her People.* New York: Geo. R. Lockwood & Son, 1886.

Wyman, Lillie B. Chase. "Harriet Tubman." *New England Magazine,* March 1896.

Holt, Rosa Bell. "A Heroine in Ebony." *Chautauquan,* July 1896.

Bradford, Sarah H. *Harriet, the Moses of Her People.* Rev. ed. New York: J. J. Little, 1901.

Taylor, Robert W. *Harriet Tubman: The Heroine in Ebony.* Boston: George E. Ellis, 1901.

Telford, Emma P. "Harriet: The Modern Moses of Heroism and Visions." Typescript. Cayuga County Museum, Auburn, NY, 1905.

Drake, Frank C. "The Moses of Her People." *New York Herald,* September 22, 1907.

Clarke, James B. "An Hour with Harriet Tubman." In *Christophe: A Tragedy in Prose of Imperial Haiti,* edited by Wm E. Easton. Los Angeles; Grafton, 1911.

Sanborn, Franklin B. "The Late Araminta Davis: Better Known as 'Moses' or 'Harriet Tubman.'" Typescript, March 1913. The Franklin B. Sanborn Papers, American Antiquarian Society, Worcester, Massachusetts.

Conrad, Earl. *General Harriet Tubman.* Associated Publishers: Washington, D.C., 1943.

Petry, Ann. *Harriet Tubman: Conductor of the Underground Railroad.* New York: Thomas Y. Crowell, 1950.

Sadlier, Rosemary. *Tubman: Harriet Tubman and the Underground Railroad.* Toronto: Umbrella Press, 1997.

Humez, Jean M. *Harriet Tubman: The Life and the Life Stories.* Madison: University of Wisconsin Press, 2003.

Clinton, Catherine. *Harriet Tubman: The Road to Freedom.* New York, Boston: Little, Brown, 2004.

Larson, Kate Clifford. *Bound for the Promised Land: Harriet Tubman, Portrait of an American Hero.* New York: Ballantine Books, 2004.

Books and Other Secondary Sources

Adams, Samuel Hopkins. *Grandfather Stories.* New York: Random House, 1947.

Bancroft, Frederic. *Slave-Trading in the Old South.* Baltimore: J. H. Furst, 1931.

Berlin, Ira. *Many Thousands Gone: The First Two Centuries of Slavery in North America.* Cambridge, MA: Belknap Press, 1998.

Berlin, Ira, et al., eds. *Freedom: A Documentary History of Emancipation 1861–1867.* vol. 1, *The Destruction of Slavery.* Cambridge, MA: Cambridge University Press, 1985.

Billington, Ray Allen, ed. *The Journal of Charlotte L. Forten: A Free Negro in the Slave Era.* New York: Collier Books, 1961.

Blassingame, John W., ed. *Slave Testimony: Two Centuries of Letters, Speeches, Interviews, and Autobiographies.* Baton Rouge: Louisiana State University Press, 1977.

Blockson, Charles L. *The Underground Railroad: Dramatic Firsthand Accounts of Daring Escapes to Freedom.* New York: Berkley Books, 1987.

Blondo, Richard Albert. "Samuel Green: A Black Life in Antebellum Maryland." Masters thesis, University of Maryland, 1988.

———. "In Search of Samuel Green." *The Archivists' Bulldog,* April 30, 1990.

Bordewich, Fergus M. *The Underground Railroad and the War for the Soul of America.* New York: Amistad/HarperCollins, 2005.

Botume, Elizabeth. *First Days Among the Contrabands.* Boston: Lee and Shepard, 1893.

Brackett, Jeffrey R. *The Negro in Maryland. A Study of the Institution of Slavery.* 1889. Reprint. New York: Negro Universities Press, 1969.

Bragg, George F. *Heroes of the Eastern Shore.* Baltimore: G. F. Bragg, 1939.

Brown, William Wells. *The Rising Son; or, The Antecedents and Advancement of the Colored Race.* 1873. Reprint. New York: Negro Universities Press, 1970.

Brugger, Robert J. *Maryland: A Middle Temperament, 1634–1980.* Baltimore: Johns Hopkins University Press, 1988.

Calarco, Tom. *The Underground Railroad Conductor. A Guide for Eastern New York.* Schenectady, NY: Travels Through History, 2003.

Cameron, Kenneth Walter. *Young Reporter of Concord: A Checklist of F.B. Sanborn's Letters to Benjamin Smith Lyman, 1853–1867.* Hartford: Transcendental Books, 1978.

Campbell, Edward D. C., and Kym S. Rice, eds., *Before Freedom Came: African–American Life in the Antebellum South.* Richmond and Charlottesville: Museum of the Confederacy and University Press of Virginia, 1991.

Carroll, Kenneth. *Quakerism on the Eastern Shore.* Baltimore: Maryland Historical Society, 1970.

Clarke, Rev. James Freeman. *Anti-Slavery Days.* 1883. Reprint. New York: Negro Universities Press, 1970.

Clayton, Ralph. *Cash for Blood: The Baltimore to New Orleans Domestic Slave Trade.* Bowie, MD: Heritage Books, 2002.

Clemens, Paul G. E. *The Atlantic Economy and Colonial Maryland's Eastern Shore: From Tobacco to Grain.* Ithaca, NY: Cornell University Press, 1980.

Cohen, Stan. *John Brown, "The Thundering Voice of Jehovah,": A Pictorial Heritage.* Missoula, MT: Pictorial Histories Publishing Co., 1999.

Cornish, Dudley Taylor. *The Sable Arm: Black Troops in the Union Army, 1861–1865.* Lawrence: University Press of Kansas, 1956.

Davis, David Brion. *Slavery in the Colonial Chesapeake.* Williamsburg, VA: Colonial Williamsburg Foundation, 1986.

DiPaolo, Joseph F. *My Business Was to Fight the Devil: Recollections of Rev. Adam Wallace . . . 1847–1865.* Acton, MA: Tapestry Press, 1998.

Douglass, Frederick. *Life and Times of Frederick Douglass, His Early Life as a Slave, His Escape from Bondage and His Complete History to the Present Time.* 1881. Electronic ed. University of North Carolina "Documenting the South" Web site: http://docsouth.unc.edu.

———. *My Bondage and My Freedom.* 1855. Reprint. New York: Penguin Books, 2003.

———. *Narrative of the Life of Frederick Douglass, an American Slave. Written by Himself.* 1845. Reprint. Penguin American Library, 1982.

Drew, Benjamin. *The Refugee: A North-Side View of Slavery.* 1855. Reprint. Tilden G. Edelstein, ed. Reading MA: Addison-Wesley, 1969.

Du Bois, W. E. B. *John Brown.* 1909. Reprint. New York: Modern Library, 2001.

Duncan, Russell, ed. *Blue-Eyed Child of Fortune: The Civil War Letters of Colonel Robert Gould Shaw.* Athens: University of Georgia Press, 1992.

Eltis, David. "The Volume and Structure of the Transatlantic Slave Trade: A Reassessment." *The William and Mary Quarterly* 58, no. 1(2001).

Eltis, David, et al. eds. *The Trans-Atlantic Slave Trade: A Database on CD-ROM.* Cambridge: Cambridge University Press, 1999.

Fields, Barbara Jeanne. *Slavery and Freedom on the Middle Ground.* New Haven: Yale University Press, 1985.

Foner, Philip S., ed. *The Life and Writings of Frederick Douglass.* New York: International, 1950–1955.

Franklin, John Hope, and Loren Schweninger. *Runaway Slaves: Rebels on the Plantation.* New York: Oxford University Press, 1999.

Gara, Larry. *The Liberty Line: The Legend of the Underground Railroad.* Louisville: University of Kentucky Press, 1961.

Greenberg, Kenneth S., ed. *The Confessions of Nat Turner and Related Documents.* New York: St. Martin's Press, 1996.

Guterman, Benjamin. "Good, Brave Work: Harriet Tubman's Testimony at Beaufort, South Carolina." *Prologue: Quarterly of the National Archives and Records Administration* 32. (2000).

Hart, Albert Bushnell. *Slavery and Abolition, 1831–1841.* 1906. Reprint. New York: Negro Universities Press, 1968.

Higginson, Mary Thatcher, ed. *Letters and Journals of Thomas Wentworth Higginson, 1846–1906.* Boston: Houghton Mifflin, 1921.

Higginson, Thomas Wentworth. *Army Life in a Black Regiment.* 1870. Reprint. Mineola, NY: Dover Publications, 2002.

———. *Cheerful Yesterdays.* 1898. Reprint. New York: Arno Press, 1968.

Hinton, Richard J. *John Brown and His Men,* 1894. Reprint, New York: Arno Press and the *New York Times,* 1968.

Johnson, Walter. *Soul by Soul: Life Inside the Antebellum Slave Market.* Cambridge: Harvard University Press, 1999.

Jones, Elias. *New Revised History of Dorchester County Maryland.* Cambridge, MD: Tidewater Publishers, 1966.

Kashatus, William. *Just Over the Line: Chester County and the Underground Railroad.* West Chester, PA: Chester County Historical Society with Penn State University Press, 2002.

Kelley, William T. "The Underground Railroad in the Eastern Shore of Maryland and Delaware." *Friends Intelligencer 55,* 1898. available online at www.swarthmore.edu.

Klees, Emerson. *Underground Railroad Tales, with Routes Through the Finger Lakes Region.* Rochester, NY: Friends of the Finger Lakes Publishing, 1997.

Kozak, Ginnie. *Eve of Emancipation, the Union Occupation of Beaufort and the Sea Islands.* Beaufort, SC: Portsmouth House Press, 1995.

Kulikoff, Alan. "The Origins of Afro-American Society in Tidewater Maryland and Virginia, 1700–1790." *The William and Mary Quarterly,* 35, no. 2 (1978).

Land, Aubrey C. "The Planters of Colonial Maryland." *Maryland Historical Magazine* 67, no. 1, (1972).

Lee, Jean Butenhoff. "The Problem of a Slave Community in the Eighteenth-Century Chesapeake." *The William and Mary Quarterly,* 43, no. 3 (1986).

Levine, Lawrence. *Black Culture and Black Consciousness: Afro-American Folk Thought from Slavery to Freedom.* Oxford: Oxford University Press, 1977.

Linder, Suzanne Cameron. *Historical Atlas of the Rice Plantations of the ACE River Basin.* Columbia: South Carolina Department of Archives and History, Ducks Unlimited, and the Nature Conservatory, 1995.

Litwack, Leon, and August Meier, eds., *Black Leaders of the Nineteenth Century.* Urbana and Chicago: University of Illinois Press, 1988.

Looby, Christopher. *The Complete Civil War Journal and Selected Letters of Thomas Wentworth Higginson.* Chicago: University of Chicago Press, 2000.

Mason, James E., and Edward U. A. Brooks. *Tribute to Harriet Tubman: The Modern Amazon.* Auburn, NY: Tubman Home, 1914.

May, Samuel J. *Some Recollections of Our Antislavery Conflict.* Boston: Fields, Osgood, 1869.

Mayer, Henry. *All on Fire: William Lloyd Garrison and the Abolition of Slavery.* New York: St. Martin's Press, 1998.

McElvey, Kay Najiyyah. "Early Black Dorchester, 1776–1870: A History of the Struggle of African Americans in Dorchester County, Maryland, to Be Free to Make Their Own Choices." Ph.D. diss., University of Maryland, 1991.

McFeeley, William S. *Frederick Douglass.* New York: W. W. Norton, 1991.

McGowan, James. *The Harriet Tubman Journal,* vols. 1–3 (1993–1995). Privately printed. Available online at www.harriettubmanjournal.com.

———. *Station Master on the Underground Railroad.* Moylan, PA: Whimsie Press, 1977.

McGrath, Sally V., and Patricia J. McGuire, eds. *The Money Crop: Tobacco Culture in Calvert County, Maryland.* Crownsville: Maryland Historical and Cultural Publications, 1992.

McPherson, James M. *The Negro's Civil War: How American Blacks Felt and Acted During the War for the Union.* New York: Pantheon Books, 1965, New York: Vintage Books, 2003.

Meltzer, Milton, and Patricia G. Holland. *Lydia Maria Child: Selected Letters, 1817–1880*. Amherst: University of Massachusetts Press, 1982.

Middleton, Arthur Pierce. *Tobacco Coast. A Maritime History of Chesapeake Bay in the Colonial Era*. 2d ed. 1953. Reprint. Baltimore: Johns Hopkins University Press, 1984.

Morgan, Philip D. *Slave Counterpoint: Black Culture in Eighteenth-Century Chesapeake and Lowcountry*. Chapel Hill: University of North Carolina Press, 1998.

Mowbray, Calvin W., and Mary I. Mowbray. *The Early Settlers of Dorchester County and Their Lands*. 2 vols. 1981. Reprint. Westminster, MD: Willow Bend Books, 2000.

Oates, Stephen B. *The Fires of Jubilee: Nat Turner's Fierce Rebellion*. 1975. Reprint. New York: Harper Perennial, 1990.

———. *To Purge This Land with Blood: A Biography of John Brown*. Amherst: University of Massachusetts Press, 1984.

Painter, Nell Irvin. *Sojourner Truth: A Life, a Symbol*. New York: W. W. Norton, 1996.

Peden, Henry C., Jr. *Revolutionary Patriots of Dorchester County, Maryland 1775–1783*. 1998. Reprint. Westminster, MD: Willow Bend Books, 2000.

Petit, Eber M. *Sketches in the History of the Underground Railroad*. Westfield, NY: Chautauqua Region Press, 1999.

Pollitzer, William S. *The Gullah People and Their African Heritage*. Atlanta: University of Georgia Press, 1999. As quoted in National Park Service's *Low Country in Gullah Culture, Special Resource Study;* available online at www.nps.gov.

Pratt, John P. "Spectacular Meteor Shower Might Repeat." *Meridian Magazine*, October 15, 1999.

Preston, Dickson J. *Talbot County: A History*. Centreville, MD: Tidewater Publishers, 1983.

———. "The Tale of Absalom Christopher Columbus Americus Vespucious Thompson." *The Banner* (Cambridge, MD), August 28, 1978.

———. *Young Frederick Douglass. The Maryland Years*. Baltimore: Johns Hopkins University Press, 1980.

Quarles, Benjamin. *Black Abolitionists*. New York: Oxford University Press, 1969.

Reynolds, David. *John Brown, Abolitionist: The Man Who Killed Slavery, Sparked the Civil War, and Seeded Civil Rights*. New York: Alfred A. Knopf, 2005.

Ripley, C. Peter, ed. *The Black Abolitionist Papers*. 5 vols. Chapel Hill: University of North Carolina Press, 1991.

Robinson, John Bell. *Pictures of Slavery and Anti-Slavery.* Philadelphia, 1863.

Rose, Willie Lee. *Rehearsal for Reconstruction: The Port Royal Experiment.* New York: Bobbs-Merrill, 1964.

Sanborn, Franklin. "Harriet Tubman." *Commonwealth* (Boston), August 12, 1864.

———. *The Life and Letters of John Brown.* 1885. Reprint. New York: Negro Universities Press, 1969.

———. *Recollections of Seventy Years.* Boston: Gorham Press, 1909.

———. "The Virginia Campaign of John Brown," *The Atlantic Monthly,* January–May 1875.

Schwartz, Gerald, ed. *A Woman Doctor's Civil War: Esther Hill Hawks' Diary,* Columbia: University of South Carolina Press, 1984.

Sernett, Milton. *Black Religion and American Evangelism.* Metuchen, NJ: Scarecrow Press, 1975.

———. *North Star Country: Upstate New York and the African American Freedom Struggle.* Syracuse, N.Y.: Syracuse University Press, 2002.

Siebert, Wilbur Henry. *The Underground Railroad from Slavery to Freedom.* New York: Macmillan, 1898.

Small, Clara. "Abolitionists, Free Blacks and Runaway Slaves: Surviving Slavery on Maryland's Eastern Shore." Copyright University of Delaware, 1997; available online at www.udel.edu.

Smedley, R. C. *History of the Underground Railroad in Chester and the Neighboring Counties of Pennsylvania.* Lancaster, PA: John A. Hiestand, 1883.

Snediker, Quentin, and Ann Jensen. *Chesapeake Bay Schooners.* Centreville, MD: Tidewater Publishers, 1992.

Sprague, Stuart Seely, ed. *His Promised Land: the Autobiography of John P. Parker, Former Slave and Conductor on the Underground Railroad.* New York: W. W. Norton, 1996.

Sterling, Dorothy, ed. *Speak Out in Thunder Tones: Letters and Other Writings of Black Northerners, 1787–1865.* New York: Doubleday, 1973.

Stevenson, Brenda, ed. *The Journals of Charlotte Forten Grimke.* New York: Oxford University Press, 1988.

Still, William. *The Underground Railroad.* 1871. Reprint. Philadelphia: Johnson Publishers, 1970.

Tadman, Michael. *Speculators and Slaves: Masters, Traders and Slaves in the Old South.* 2d ed. Madison: University of Wisconsin Press, 1989.

Taylor, Susie King. *Reminiscences of My Life with the 33rd U.S. Colored Troops.* 1902. Reprinted as *A Black Woman's Civil War Memoirs: Reminiscences of My Life with the 33rd U.S. Colored Troops.* Edited by Patricia Romero and Willie Lee Rose. Princeton: Markus Wiener, 1988.

Thomas, Hugh. *The Slave Trade: The Story of the Atlantic Slave Trade, 1440–1870.* New York: Touchstone, 1997.

Thomas, Owen A. *Niagara's Freedom Trail: A Guide to African-Canadian History on the Niagara Peninsula.* Niagara, Ontario: Niagara Economic and Tourism Corporation and the Ontario Heritage Foundation, 1999.

Tilghman, Oswald. *History of Talbot County Maryland, 1661–1861.* 2 vols. Baltimore: Williams & Wilkins, 1915.

Trudeau, Noah Andre. *Like Men of War: Black Troops in the Civil War, 1862–1865.* Boston: Little, Brown, 1998.

Walls, William J. "Twenty-Second Quadrennial Session, A.M.E. Zion General Conference, 1904." In *The African Methodist Episcopal Zion Church.* Charlotte, NC: A.M.E. Zion Church, 1974.

Walsh, Lorena. "The Chesapeake Slave Trade: Regional Patterns, African Origins, and Some Implications." *The William and Mary Quarterly* 58, no. 1(2001). Also available online at www.historycooperative.org.

Wayman, A.W. *My Recollections of African M.E. Ministers, or Forty Years Experience in the African Methodist Church.* Philadelphia: A.M.E. Book Rooms, 1881.

Weeks, Christopher, ed. *Between the Nanticoke and the Choptank.* Baltimore: Johns Hopkins University Press, 1984.

Wienecke, Henry. *An Imperfect God: George Washington, His Slaves and the Creation of America.* New York: Farrar, Straus and Giroux, 2003.

Wilkins, Roger, *Jefferson's Pillow: The Founding Fathers and the Dilemma of Black Patriotism.* Boston: Beacon Press, 2002.

Winks, Robin W. *Blacks in Canada: A History.* Montreal; McGill-Queens University Press, 1997.

Wright, James A. *The Free Negro in Maryland, 1634–1860.* 1921. Reprint. New York: Octagon Books, 1970.

Newspaper Articles and Ads, Letters, and Government and Court Documents

"Another Conflagration." *Evening Auburnian,* (Auburn, NY), February 10, 1880.

"Anthony C. Thompson from Josiah Bayley, Jr." Dorchester County Court Chattel Records, Maryland Department of State Archives (here after MDSA), Annapolis.

"Anthony C. Thompson to Sundry Negroes." Dorchester County Chattel Records 1851–1860, MDSA, Annapolis.

Assessment record. Dorchester County Board of County Commissioners, MDSA, Cambridge, MD.

Assessors field book. Dorchester County Board of County Commissioners, MDSA, Annapolis.

"Benjamin Ross from Anthony C. Thompson." Dorchester County Court Chattel Records, MDSA, Annapolis.

"Benjamin Ross from Eliza Brodess." Dorchester County Chattel Records 1851–1860, MDSA, Annapolis.

"Benjamin Ross Paid Eliza Brodess." Dorchester County Chattel Records, MDSA, Annapolis,.

Bill of Complaint, Original Equity Papers, Case 249: "Gourney C. Pattison, William Pattison and Others Vs. Eliza Brodess, Eliza Brodess and John Mills Administrators of Edward Brodess, and Thomas Willis." Dorchester County Circuit Court, MDSA. Annapolis.

Bowley, Harkless. Harkless Bowley Letters. Earl Conrad/Harriet Tubman Collection, Schomburg Center for Research in Black Culture, New York, NY.

Bowley, Kessiah. Last Will and Testament of Kessiah Bowley, April 30, 1888. Registrar of Wills, Dorchester County Court House, Cambridge, MD.

Brickler, Alice. Letters to Earl Conrad, 1939. Schomburg Center for Research in Black Culture, New York, NY.

Brodess, Edward. Estate Papers of Edward Brodess. Register of Wills, Court House. Cambridge, MD.

Brodess, Elizabeth. "Negro for Sale [Harriet]." *Cambridge Democrat* (Cambridge, MD), June 27, 1849.

Brodess, Eliza Ann. "Three Hundred Dollars Reward." *Cambridge Democrat* (Cambridge, MD) October 3, 1849.

Brown, John. "Diary." *John Brown Note Books, 1838–1859.* Ms.q.1996. Boston Public Library, Boston, MA.

Carter, Florence. Letter to Earl Conrad, Schomburg Center for Research in Black Culture, New York, NY.

"Cash." *Cambridge Chronicle* (Cambridge, MD), December 25, 1830.

Census, Bureau of the. United States Federal Census, 1790–1920.

Certificates of Freedom, Dorchester County Circuit Court Records, MDSA, Annapolis.

Colonial Census, 1776.

Congress, House of Representatives. "Harriet [Tubman] Davis, Widow of Nelson Charles, Alias Nelson Davis, Pension Claim." HR 55A–D1. Papers Accompanying the Claim of Harriet Tubman. Record Group 233. Washington, D.C.: National Archives.

Conrad, Earl. Earl Conrad/Harriet Tubman Collection. Microfilm, 2 reels.

Schomburg Center for Research in Black Culture, Manuscripts, Archives and Rare Books Division: New York Public Library.

Dail, William B. "Sheriff's Sale." *Cambridge Chronicle* (Cambridge, MD), December 24, 1842.

Davis, Harriet Tubman. Papers for Harriet Tubman Davis. Records of the U.S. House of Representatives, Record Group 233, National Archives, Washington, D.C.

Davis, Nelson. Original Pension Files, National Archives, College Park, MD. 1894.

Deed—Samuel Lecompte from Richard Pattison and Wife, George Keene and Wife, and Edward Brodess and Wife. Record Books of Dorchester County Land, MDSA, Annapolis.

Dorchester County Chattel Records, 1847–1851. "Major Bowley to John Bowley, Richard Bowley, John T. Stewart." MDSA, Annapolis.

Dorchester County Levy Book. Dorchester County Board of Commissioners, MDSA, Annapolis.

———. "Thomas Willis from John Mills and Eliza Brodess." MDSA. Annapolis.

"Escape and Recapture." *Easton Gazette* (Easton), October 16, 1858.

"Edward Brodess to Dempsey P. Kane," Dorchester County Land Records. MDSA, Annapolis, July 1825.

Edward Brodess vs. Anthony Thompson, Dorchester County Court, April 24, 1827.

Edward Brodess, Jr., vs. Anthony Thompson, Eastern Shore Court of Appeals, 1823–1828. "Edward Brodess in Account with Anthony Thompson His Guardian for the Years 1821 and 1822" (1828).

Ethiop. "The Early Days of the Underground Railroad." *Anglo African Magazine,* October 1859.

"Excitement at Cambridge." *New York Tribune* (New York), August 7, 1858.

"Equity Papers 249." Dorchester County Circuit Court, MDSA, Annapolis.

Estate Papers of Edward Brodess. Register of Wills, Dorchester County Court House, Cambridge.

Estate Papers of Eliza Ann Brodess. Register of Wills, Dorchester County Court House, Cambridge.

"Fears of Insurrection." *The National Era* (Washington, D.C.), April 26, 1855.

Fitzhugh, Ann. "Harriet Tubman." *American Review,* August 1912.

"Foul Outrage." *Liberator* (Boston, MA), July 8, 1858.

"Free Negroes." *Annapolis Gazette* (Annapolis, MD), March 18, 1858.

Gourney C. Pattison to William Henson. Dorchester County Chattel Records, MDSA, Annapolis.

Harrington, Samuel. "$250 Reward." *Cambridge Democrat* (Cambridge), June 17, 1854.

Harrison, Samuel. "Meteor Shower." Harrison Collection, Maryland Historical Society, Baltimore.

Howe, Samuel Gridley. *Canadian Testimony, American Freedmen's Inquiry Commission.* Washington, D.C.: National Archives, 1863.

Howland, Emily. "Diary, October 4, 1873." Florence W. Hazzard Papers. Rare and Manuscript Collections, Carl A. Kroch Library, Cornell University. Ithaca, NY.

"James A. Stewart from Acsah Pattison." Dorchester County Chattel Records 1851–1860, MDSA, Annapolis.

"James A. Stewart from Harrison D. Barrett and Eliza Rawleigh." Dorchester County Chattel Records 1851–1860, MDSA, Annapolis.

"James A. Stewart from Thomas Willis." Dorchester County Chattel Records 1851–1860, MDSA, Annapolis.

"John D. Parker from Benjamin Ross." Dorchester County Chattel Records 1851–1860, MDSA, Annapolis.

"John D. Parker from Charles Ross." Dorchester County Chattel Records 1851–1860, MDSA, Annapolis.

Keene, Samuel of Ezekiel to Samuel Keene of Henry. Chattel Records, Dorchester County Court House, Cambridge.

Lambdin, William, and Jacob Jackson. Manumission of Jacob Jackson. Talbot County Register of Wills, Certificates of Freedom, MDSA, Annapolis.

"Maria Rayley and Aaron Manoka from Benjamin Ross." Dorchester County Chattel Records, MDSA, Annapolis.

McGill, Elaine, transcriber. *Certificates of Freedom, Dorchester County Court 1806–1864.* Privately printed, 2001.

———, transcriber. *Robert Bell's Book of Slave Statistics 1864–1868.* Privately printed, 2001.

Meredith, Pritchet. "$600 Reward." *Cambridge Democrat* (Cambridge), March 18, 1857.

Mills, Polish. "Mills Deposition." Equity Papers 249, MDSA, Annapolis.

Moxey, Debra Smith. *Newspaper Abstracts from the American Eagle and Cambridge Chronicle 1846–1857.* Cambridge, Md, 1995.

———. *Dorchester County Criminal Court Docket, 1791–1805. Volume 1.* Privately printed, 1986.

———. *Great Choptank Parish Records.* Cambridge, MD: Dorchester County Historical and Genealogical Society.

———. "Thompson Land Records." *Dorchester County Genealogical Magazine* Dorchester County, MD.

"A Negro Case." *Baltimore American* (Baltimore), May 1, 1857.

"Negroes Captured." *Easton Gazette* (Easton, MD), August 7, 1858.

"Negro Stampede." *Cecil Whig* (Elkton, MD), October 31, 1857.

New York, State of, *New York State Census,* 1855–1905.

"$1000 Reward." *Cambridge Chronicle,* Cambridge, MD. May 22, 1852.

Orphans Court Records. Dorchester County Orphans Court, Dorchester County Registrar of Wills, Cambridge.

Pattison, Atthow. Will of Atthow Pattison. Dorchester County Court House, Registrar of Wills, Cambridge.

Prisoner # 5146 Samuel Green Free Negro. Maryland Penitentiary Records—Prisoner Records, MDSA, Annapolis.

Rochester Ladies Anti-Slavery Society. Rochester Ladies Anti-Slavery Society Records. William L. Clements Library, University of Michigan, Ann Arbor, MI.

"Sam Green and Uncle Tom's Cabin." *Easton Gazette* (Easton, MD), August 28, 1858.

Seward, John. "John Seward to Sundry Negroes, January 15, 1817." Dorchester County Court Papers 1743–1849, MDSA, Annapolis.

Siebert, Wilbur. "New Jersey." Underground Railroad: Manuscript materials collected by Professor Siebert. Houghton Library, Harvard University, Cambridge, MA.

Smith, Frank R. "Muskrat Investigations in Dorchester County, 1930–1934." Report No. 474. Washington, D.C.: United States Department of Agriculture, 1938.

Stewart, James A. Estate Papers of James A. Stewart. Register of Wills, Dorchester County Court House, Cambridge.

———. "Valuable Plantation for Sale." *Cambridge Chronicle* (Cambridge), July 13, 1844.

Stewart, John. "Letter to Sister Harriet Tubman, Nov. 1, 1859." Rochester Ladies Anti-Slavery Society Papers. William Clements Library, Ann Arbor, MI.

Stewart, Levin. "Levin Stewart to Sundry Negroes." Dorchester County Court Papers 1797–1851, MDSA, Annapolis.

Still, William. Journal C of Station 2 of the Underground Railroad (Philadelphia, Agent William Still). Pennsylvania Abolition Society. Reel 32. Historical Society of Pennsylvania, Philadelphia.

————. "Vigilance Committee of Philadelphia, Accounts." Pennsylvania Abolition Society. Reel 32. Historical Society of Pennsylvania, Philadelphia.

Stutler, Boyd B. John Brown/Boyd B. Stutler Collection. West Virginia Division of Culture and History/West Virginia Memory Project. Charleston, WV.

"Suspicious." *The Public Monitor* (Easton, MD), July 8, 1858.

Tatlock, Helen. Letter to Earl Conrad, 1939. Conrad Collection, Schomburg Library, New York.

Thompson, Absalom. Last Will and Testament of Absalom Thompson. Talbot County Register of Wills, MDSA, Annapolis.

Thompson, Anthony C. Last Will and Testament of Anthony Thompson. Register of Wills, Dorchester County Court House, Cambridge.

————. Anthony C. Thompson to Sundry Negroes. Dorchester County Chattel Records, MDSA, Annapolis.

————. Anthony C. Thompson to Sarah Catherine Haddaway. Dorchester County Chattel Records 1851–1860, MDSA, Annapolis.

————. List of Anthony Thompson's Negroes, 1839. Levin Richardson Collection, 1758–1865. Maryland Historical Society, Baltimore.

————. Thompson Deposition. Equity Papers 249. MDSA. Annapolis.

"Unsuccessful Attempt to Capture Fugitive Slaves." *New York Tribune* (New York), March 20, 1857.

Wood, Charles P. "Manuscript History Concerning the Pension Claim of Harriet Tubman." Papers Accompanying the Claim of Harriet Tubman. Record Group 233. Washington, D.C.: National Archives.

Some Online Sources

University and public libraries now offer web sites containing worlds of important information. Their rich listings include special collections and archived manuscripts, soome of which are available online in their entirety. Other lush Internet sources include governmental and historical Web sites and those offering full-text newspapers and magazines. Subscription Internet services such as www.ancestry.com and www.jstor.com also provide access to an abundance of information.

The list grows longer by the day, maybe even the hour. Among the many Web sites I used, the following were particularly helpful:

www.archives.state (Maryland State Archives)

http.docsouth.unc.edu (University of North Carolina's "Documents of the South")

www.sc.edu (University of South Carolina manuscript collection) www.jeffersoninstitute.org (flax information)

science.nasa.gov and eyring.hplx.net (on Leonid shower, 1833)

www.loc.gov (Library of Congress bounteous Web site)

www.archives.com (National Archives rich Web site)

www.FirstSearch.com (eighteen databases, including library search)

www.harpweek.com (access to *Harper's Weekly*)

www.accessiblearchives.com (complete issues of *The Liberator* and many nineteenth-century African-American newspapers)

www.cornell.edu (Cornell "Making of America" Web site, including Official Records of the Civil War)

www.wvculture.org (West Virginia Memory Project, which contains the Boyd B. Sutler John Brown database)

www.kshs.org (James Montgomery and Kansas history)

www.civilwarhome.com (complete final reports of the American Freedmen's Inquiry Commission)

www.rootsweb.com/~nycayuga/maps (nineteenth-century maps of Auburn, NY)

www.ancestry.com and www.familysearch.com (genealogical information and U.S. census)

www.fultonhistory.com (contains full issues of many nineteenth-century Auburn newspapers, including the *Evening Auburnian,* the *Auburn News and Bulletin,* and the *Auburn Daily Bulletin*)

University and public libraries now have Web sites offering new worlds of important information. Their listings include special collections and archived manuscripts, some of which are available online.

Index

Italicized page numbers refer to photos and illustrations.

A

Abolition movement, 66, 82
  District of Columbia's abolition of slavery, 301
  growth of, 133, 217–18
  Harpers Ferry raid, 230–32, 235–36, 249–51
  Radical Abolition party, 266
  violence between pro- and anti-slavery forces, 206
  women's involvement, 243
  See also Underground Railroad
Adams, Samuel Hopkins, 20
Agnew, Allen, 187
Alcott, Bronson, 247
Alexander, "Pop," *15*
Anderson, Osborne P., 239, 255–56
Andrew, John Albion, 293–94, 302, 324
Anthony, Susan B., 6
  tribute to Tubman, *8–9*
Anti-Slavery Convention, 248
Atkinson, John, 201
Auburn, N.Y., 243, *244–45*

B

Bailey, Bill, 211, 212, 213, 214–15
Bailey, Josiah "Joe," 196, 198, 210–15, 235, 236
Bailey, Maria, 124
Baldwin, James, 249
Ball, R. A., 193–94
Barnes, Joseph K., 347
Barnett family, 79
Bayley, Josiah, 161
Beach, Miles, 261
Beaufort, S.C., 292
Bell, Robert, 222

Black English, 249
Black people
  colonization movement and, 248–49, 291, 301
  discrimination faced by blacks in North, 196
  educational programs for, 293, 294–95
  exodus of former slaves to North after start of Civil War, 284
  Gullah culture, 290, 304
  military participation for Union in South Carolina, 292, 302, 305, 306–7, 311, 313, 316–23, 324, 325–26, 332–38, 343
  South Carolina military expedition's impact on former slaves, 290, 292–93, *297*, 298, 301, 321–23, 326
  See also Free blacks; Slavery
Bloomer dresses, 325
Botume, Elizabeth, 298
Bowley, Araminta, 159, 160, 164, 170
Bowley, Harkless, 103, 159, 161, 278
  letter to Conrad about Tubman, *24–25*
Bowley, James, 160, 161, 170, 239
Bowley, James Alfred, 159, 353, 365
Bowley, John, 137, 165, 170, 197, 350, 352
  escape with family from slave territory, 159–64
Bowley, Kessiah Jolley, 72, 103, 106, 165, 170, 197, 239, 350, 352
  escape from slavery, 159–64
  proposed sale of, 132, *132*, 137, 155, 159, 160
Bowley, Richard, 159
Bradford, Sarah Hopkins, 1, 9, *16*, 54, 61, 62–63, 128, 144, 151, 181, 195, 203, 207, 209, 210, 214, 225, 227, 262, 264, 267, 274, 290, 300, 315, 316, 340, 348, 350, 351, 354

Tubman's visit with, 15, 20–22, 372
writings about Tubman, 4–6, 362,
    370–71, 372
Brickler, Alice Lucas, 277–78, 279, 368,
    369, 376
Brinkley, Nathanial, 169
Brinkley, William, 169, 210, 212, 218,
    225
Brisbane, William, 311
Brodess, Edward, 24, 30, 36, 37, 39,
    40–41, 54, 59, 68, 69, 91, 119,
    121, 201, 278
  death of, 50, 127–29
  financial problems, 42–44, 49, 94–96
  house construction, 41
  sales of slaves, 50–51, 104–5, 107,
    108–11
  Tubman's sale, consideration of,
    125–27
Brodess, Eliza Keene, 45, 49, 50, 54, 69,
    79, 94, 128, 129, 130–31, 132,
    134, 137, 157, 158–59, 185, 189,
    242
  neighbors' dislike for, 162
  Ross brothers' escape attempt, 172,
    173, 174
  sale of Rit Ross to Ben Ross, 176,
    177–78
  Tubman's escape from slavery, 149–50
Brodess, John, 160, 161, 186
Brodess, Joseph, 35, 36
Brodess, Mary Pattison, 31, 33, 34, 35,
    36, 37
Brodess, Richard, 256
Brooks, E. U. A., 374
Brown, Frederick, 229
Brown, John, 133, 158, 215, 229, 229,
    260, 308
  anti-slavery actions in Kansas, 206
  blacks' skepticism regarding, 240
  Douglass and, 230–31, 249–50
  execution of, 251–53
  Harpers Ferry raid, 230–32, 235–36,
    249–51
  letter to son, 237–38
  Tubman's dream about, 230, 234, 251
  Tubman's relationship with, 229–30,
    234–36, 238–40, 247, 250, 253–54

U.S. constitution proposed by, 231,
    236, 239
Brown, John R., 175
Brown, William Wells, 180
Buchanan, James, 215, 258, 271
Burnell, Henry, 298–99
Burns, Tommy, 361
Butler, Gen. Benjamin, 276

C

Calhoun, John C., 156
Canada as destination for escaped slaves,
    165, 168–70, 194–96
Carter, Florence, 363
Charles, Fred, 331
Charles, Nelson. See Davis, Nelson
Chase, John, 184, 187
Cheney, Ednah Dow, 91, 167, 203, 205,
    251, 254, 294, 346
Cheney, Lee, 15
Child, Lydia Maria, 294
Civil War
  onset of hostilities, 275
  secession by southern states, 271, 273,
    275
  Tubman's late-war activities in Vir-
    ginia, 346–47
  See also South Carolina military expe-
    dition
Clarke, James B., 272, 373
Clay, Henry, 156
Cleveland, Grover, 370
Colonization movement, 248–49, 291,
    301
Combahee raid, 301, 315, 316–23, 322,
    325–26
Compromise of 1850, 156–58
Conrad, Earl, 7, 24, 103, 161, 277, 278,
    369, 371, 377
Cook, James, 54–58, 59
Cornish family, 215–16
Craft, William and Ellen, 133

D

Dail, William, 94, 95
Davis, Gertie (HT's adopted daughter),
    15, 369
Davis, Jefferson, 273

Davis, Milford, 331
Davis, Nelson (HT's second husband),
    15, 330, 369–70, 376
    death of, 371
    marriage to Tubman, 118, 331,
        361–63
    South Carolina military expedition,
        343
District of Columbia's abolition of slav-
    ery, 301
Dorchester County, Maryland, and envi-
    rons, 26–27, 29
Doubleday, Gen. Abner, 292
Douglas, Stephen A., 156, 262
Douglass, Charles, 333
Douglass, Frederick, 28, 74, 76, 133,
    137, 158, 158, 169, 182, 202, 205,
    218, 225, 232, 235, 239, 255, 259,
    266, 271–72, 286, 292, 301, 303,
    331, 361
    Brown and, 230–31, 249–50
    dream of escape, 149
    testimonial to Tubman, 6–7
    Underground Railroad and, 169–70
Douglass, Lewis, 333, 335
Dover Eight escape of 1857, 218–21
Dred Scott case, 217–18
Drew, Benjamin, 108, 117, 200–201
Dudley, Elbridge G., 298
Du Pont, Samuel F., 287, 291
Durant, Henry K., 304, 305, 344

E

Eighth Regiment U.S. Colored Troops,
    343
Elliott, Thomas, 218, 219, 235, 236, 238
Emancipation Proclamation, 305–6, 311,
    312
Emerson, Ralph Waldo, 235, 247
Ennals family, 267–71

F

Fifty-fourth Regiment Massachusetts Vol-
    unteer Infantry (Colored), 324,
    332–38
Fillmore, Millard, 157–58
First South Carolina Volunteers, 305,
    306–7, 316

Flax-processing work, 77–79, 83–85, 84,
    85
Forten, Charlotte, 311, 312
Fort Monroe hospital, 347
Fort Wagner assault, 332–38, 335, 337
Fowler, Henry, 331
Free blacks, 66, 100
    ownership of slaves, 159
Fremont, Maj. Gen. John Charles, 284,
    286
Fugitive Aid Society of St. Catharines,
    196, 273
Fugitive Slave Act, 148, 151, 156–58,
    165, 195, 261

G

Garnet, Henry Highland, 232, 273–74
Garrett, Thomas, 6, 179, 180, 182, 186,
    202–4, 206–7, 208, 209, 210, 213,
    215, 219, 225, 231, 239, 268,
    270
Garrison, Ellen Wright, 372–73
Garrison, George, 342–43, 344
Garrison, Wendell, 344
Garrison, William Lloyd, 66, 82, 133,
    271
General Harriet Tubman (Conrad), 7,
    377
General stores, 80-81, 80
General Vigilance Committee, 179
Gibbs, Jacob, 188
Gilbert, Uri, 260, 261
Gilmore, Gen. Quincy A., 315, 328,
    332, 336, 342
"Go Down, Moses" (song), 198–99
Green, Beriah, 258–59
Green, Harriet (HT's mother). See Ross,
    Harriet Green
Green, Kitty, 202
Green, Modesty (HT's grandmother), 34,
    35, 36, 37, 69
Green, Samuel, 180, 202, 212, 219,
    222–23, 242
Green, Samuel, Jr., 180, 195–96, 214,
    222
Green, Walter, 15
Gullah culture, 290, 304
Gurney, Anne, 48

H

Haddaway, Catherine, 206
Haddaway, Thomas, 346
Hamilton, Minus, 319, 320, 321
Hansborough, Blucher, 261
Harpers Ferry raid, 230–32, 235–36,
    249–51
Harriet, the Moses of Her People (Brad-
    ford), 5, *5,* 8
"Harriet Tubman" (Sanborn), 327
Harriet Tubman, the Moses of Her People
    (Bradford), 5, 370–71
Harriet Tubman Home, 373, *374*
Harris (confidence man), 366–67
Hawks, Esther Hill, 297–98, 337, 338
Hayes, Rutherford, 369
Henny (slave), 66–67, *67*
Henry, John Campbell, 211, 212
Henry, William, 261, 262
Hicks, Thomas H., 242
Higginson, Thomas Wentworth, 231–32,
    233, 248
    South Carolina military expedition,
        305, 306–7, 314, 316, 320
Holmes, J. W., 261, 262
Hooper, Henry, 206
Hooper, John H., 188, 259
Hopkins, Samuel Miles, Jr., 15, 20–22,
    61, 354
Howe, Col. Francis, 295
Howe, Samuel Gridley, 107, 231, *233,*
    341
Hubbard, Daniel, 226
Hughes, Denard, 218, 219, 235
Hughlett, William, 210–11, 212
Hunter, Gen. David, 298, 299, 301, 302,
    307, 308, 313, 314, 315, 328, 347

I

Irish Ladies Anti-Slavery Association, 231

J

Jackson, Jacob, 181–82
Jackson, Peter, 184, 196
Jackson, William Henry, 181
Jaeckel, John F., 375–76
Johnson, Jack, 361
Johnson, Oliver, 213, 221–22

Johnson, William, 307
Johnson, Winnibar, 179
Jolley, Harkless, 72, 102, 106–7, 352
Jolley, Harriet, 103, 130, 131, 155, 157,
    175
Jolley, Kessiah. *See* Bowley, Kessiah Jolley
Jolley, Linah Ross. *See* Ross, Linah
Jolley, Mary Ann (Mary Jane), 130, 131,
    155, 175, 255
Jolley, Sarah, 155, 157, 175
Jones, Horatio, 182

K

Kane, Dempsey, 51, 70
Kane, Jane. *See* Stewart, Catherine Kane
Keene, Dawes, 158
Keene, Samuel, 32, 35
Kiah, William and Emily, 218, 219, 221

L

Leverton, Arthur, 140, 226
Leverton, Hannah, 139, 140, 141, 145,
    148
Leverton, Jacob, 140
Lincoln, Abraham, 74, 75–76, 266, 273,
    275, 286, 292, 301, 302, 303, 305,
    311, 344, 347
    Tubman's attitude toward, 345
Loguen, Jermaine, 188–89, 221, 231,
    232, 234, 239
Lovejoy, Owen, 284
Lucas, Henry, 278, 369
Lucas, Margaret Stewart, 350, 369
    ancestry of, 278–79
    Tubman's "kidnapping" of, 275–78

M

Mann, Mrs. Horace, 247
Manokey, Aaron, 124
Manokey, Eliza, 212, 213
Manokey, Jerry, 97, 98, 123
Manokey, Mary, 97, 123, 124, 135, 156,
    183–84, 186, 198, 206, 227, 242
    Tubman's escape from slavery, 139–40,
        141
Manokey, Polly, 97, 123
Manokey, Susan, 97, 123, 124
Martin, Robert P., 49, 128

Mason, James E., 370
Mason Commission, 258
May, Samuel, 257
Meredith, Pritchett, 79–80, 219
Meredith, Susan, 45, 80
Merritt, William Henry, 196
Meteor showers of 1833, 73–76, *74*
Miller, Anne Fitzhugh, 373
Mills, John, 79, 130–31, 132, 137, 176, 189
Mills, Polish, 69, 70, 71, 72, 79, 102, *102*, 103
Montgomery, Col. James, *308,* 333, 337, 343
    assignment to South Carolina military expedition, 308, 313–14
    Combahee raid, 315, 317, 318, 319, 320–21, 323
    Darien raid, 324
    letter of commendation for Tubman, 328–29
    personal qualities, 313–14
    recruiting raids, 315–16
More, Elizabeth, 98
"Moses" (Cheney), 346
Mott, Lucretia, 243
My Bondage and My Freedom (Douglass), 149
Myers, Stephen, 169, 188, 202, 259

N
Nalle, Charles, 260–65
National Association for Colored Women, 372
National Colored Convention of 1855, 202
New England Colored Citizens' Convention, 248
New England Freedmen's Aid Society, 294
Nichols, Christopher, 201
North-Side View of Slavery, The (Drew), 200

O
Osgood, Lucy, 247
Otwell, Thomas, 219, 220, 221
Owasco Lake depot, *17*

P
Parker, Blind Aunty (Sara), *15*
Parker, Theodore, 232, *233*
Pattison, Acsah, 175
Pattison, Atthow, 32, 33-34, *33,* 69, 105, 120, 121, 131
Pattison, Elizabeth, 32, 33, 34, 35, 36, 37, 69
Pattison, Gourney Crow, 33, 36, 37, 41, 121–22, 131–32, 162, 174, 176
Pattison, Mary. *See* Brodess, Mary Pattison
Pattison, Mary Keene, 94
Pattison, Richard, 94
Pattison, Samuel, 226
Pattison, Thomas, 32
Pattison, William, 33
Pattison-Brodess lawsuit, 37, 121–22, 131–32, 174–76, 189
Payne, Sereno E., 331, 332
Pennington, Peter, 212, 213, 235
Phillips, Wendell, 6, 247, 265–66, 331, 352
Pierce, Edward, 294–95, 334
Pinkerton, Allan, 292
Pinket, Moses, 219
Plowden, Walter D., 301, 310, 315, 316, 317, 318, 321, 324, 328, 330
Polk, James K., 156
Predeaux, Henry, 218, 219, 220–21

R
Radical Abolition party, 266
Reason, Charley, 333, 338
Refugee Slaves' Friends Society, 196
Robb, Peter, 1
Rock, John S., 291, 344
Rogers, Samuel, 75
Roosevelt, Teddy, 361
Ross, Angerine (HT's niece), 166, 176, 185, 225, 227, 242, 256, 266–67, 274–75
Ross, Araminta "Minty." *See* Tubman, Harriet
Ross, Ben (HT's father), 24, 29, 48, 71, 87, 99, 100, 101, 104, 122, *123,* 166, 197, 198, 211–12, 227, 240, 247, 271, 283, 340, 352, 353, 362

death of, 363
Dover Eight escape of 1857, 219, 220
escape North with Tubman, 221–22, 223, 224–25
manumission of, 96–97, 98
marriage of, 30–31
purchase and manumission of slaves, 123–24
purchase of Rit Ross, 176, *177–78*
separation of family, 41–42, 49–50
sons' escape attempt, 172
sons' escape from slavery, 184, 185–86
status within slave community, 39–40
Tubman's escape from slavery, 143
Ross, Ben (HT's nephew), 166, 176, 185, 225, 227, 242, 256, 266–67, 274–75
Ross, Benjamin, Jr. (HT's brother). *See* Stewart, James
Ross, Harriet (HT's niece), 186, 352
Ross, Harriet Green "Rit" (HT's mother), 24, 29, 43, 56, 58, 91, 99, 166, 197, 227, 240, 247, 271, 275, 283, 316, 340, 350, 352–53, 362
death of, 369
as domestic servant, 52–53
Dover Eight escape of 1857, 219
early years, 34
escape North with Tubman, 221–22, 223, 224–25
"freedom via Pattison will" issue, 32–33, 69–70, 105, 119–22, 131
hiring out to Mills, 69, 70, 71, 72, 73
marriage of, 30–31
Pattison-Brodess lawsuit and, 131
"property" status, history of, 31–40, *38–39*
sale of son Moses, prevention of, 108–11
sale to Ben Ross, 176, *177–78*
sale to Willis, 175–76
separation of family, 41–42, 49–50, 68
sons' escape from slavery, 184–85, 186
status within slave community, 39–40
Tubman's birth, 42, 44–46
Tubman's escape from slavery, 138–39, 143

Ross, Henry "Harry" (HT's brother). *See* Stewart, William Henry
Ross, John Henry (HT's nephew), 346, 352
Ross, Linah (HT's sister), 31, 43, 49, 52, 70, 71, 72, 73, 91, 99, 341
birth of, 37
naming of, 103–4
sale of, 102–8, *102*
Ross, Mariah Ritty (HT's sister), 31, 43, 49, 103, 104
sale of, 50–51, 52
Ross, Mary Manokey. *See* Manokey, Mary
Ross, Moses (HT's brother), 69, 70, 71, 279
attempted sale of, 108–11
escape from slavery, 164–65
Ross, Moses (HT's nephew), 346, 352, 370
Ross, Rachel (HT's sister), 52, 104, 166, 176, 185, 187, 189, 210, 225, 227, 242
death of, 266–67
escape attempt of 1855, 197–98, 202, 205–6
Ross, Robert (HT's brother). *See* Stewart, John
Ross, Soph (HT's sister), 31, 43, 49, 52, 91, 103, 104, 106

S

St. Catharines, Canada, 196
Sanborn, Franklin B., 4–5, 55, 86, 87, 89–90, 99, 150, 165, 168, 230, 231, 232, *233*, 241, 247, 250, 255, 257, 258, 271, 275, 284, 291, 295, 323, 325, 327, 344, 362, 371
Sanitary Commission, U.S., 338, 347
Saxton, Gen. Rufus, 302, 303, 305, 306, 307, 310, 313, 314, 324, 328, 329–30
Scenes in the Life of Harriet Tubman (Bradford), 4, *4*, 362
Scott, John, 110
Sea Islands, 290
Second Great Awakening, 126
Second South Carolina Volunteers, 333

Secret Six, 231–32, *233,* 239, 255

Seward, Frances Miller, 243, 278

Seward, Frederick, 364

Seward, William H., *246,* 266, 271, 276, 311, 329, 331, 341, 346, 347, 348, 364

    house sale to Tubman, 243, 246–47

Shaw, Robert Gould, 314, 324, 332, 333, 334, 335, 336

Shedd, Calvin, 297, 303, 304

Sherman, Gen. Thomas W., 291–93, 298

Sherman, William T., 314, 338

Shimer, Anthony, 365, 368

Slavery

    anxiety of slaveholders, 82–83

    arguments for and against, 82–83

    Christmas and, 93–95

    domestic work, 52

    Dred Scott case, 217–18

    Emancipation Proclamation, 305–6, 311, 312

    escapes by slaves, 155 (*See also* Underground Railroad)

    free blacks' ownership of slaves, 159

    Fremont's emancipation order, 284, 286

    Fugitive Slave Act, 148, 151, 156–58, 165, 195, 261

    hiring out of slaves, 43

    indenturing of emancipated slaves, 346

    manumission by slaveholders, 96–97, 98

    manumission laws, 34, 120

    marriages of slaves, 30–31, 103

    negotiating between slave and owner, 99–100

    personal records on specific slaves, absence of, 25

    rebellions by slaves, 66–67

    sales of slaves, 50–52, 70, 102–11, *102, 108,* 122–24, 157, 158–59, 160, 175, 176, *177–78*

    Sea Island slaves, 290

    singing by slaves, 142

    terminology of, 29–30

    term slaves, 40

    Tubman's definition of, 200–201

    Tubman's slave life, 54–63, 67–73, 77–79, 83–92, 99–101, 115–22, 124–30, 132–33, 134–37

    violence between pro- and anti-slavery forces, 206

    whipping of slaves, 59–60, *60,* 61, 63

    See also Abolition movement

Smith, Ann Fitzhugh, 352

Smith, Charles, 374

Smith, Elizabeth, 325

Smith, Gerrit, 1, 6, 133, 232, *233,* 253, 255, 257–58, 266, 271–72, 273, 275, 284, 325, 331, 345, 369

Smith, Green, 272

Smith, Joseph, 74, 75

South Carolina military expedition

    Beaufort's capture, 292

    blacks' participation in military actions, 292, 302, 305, 306–7, 311, 313, 316–23, 324, 325–26, 332–38, 343

    blacks' treatment as former slaves, 290, 292–93, *297,* 298, 301, 321–23, 326

    Combahee raid, 301, 315, 316–23, *322,* 325–26

    Darien raid, 324

    disease problem, 304

    education for blacks, 293, 294–95

    Emancipation Day celebration, 309–13

    fleet's voyage to South Carolina, 287

    Florida campaign, 343–44

    Fort Wagner assault, 332–38, *335,* 337

    Fourth of July celebration, 303–4

    heat problem, 303

    Jacksonville raid, 316

    looting and destruction of property, 297–98

    Lowcountry conditions, 287, 290

    maps of affected areas, *288–89*

    medical care for wounded soldiers, 336–39

    Montgomery's assignment to, 308, 313–14

    Port Royal's capture, 291

    recruiting of locals, 315–16

    Tubman's care for former slaves, 326

Tubman's clearinghouse work, 295, 299

Tubman's clothing request, 325

Tubman's command role, 318

Tubman's entrepreneurial activities, 299–301, 342–43

Tubman's inclusive military pass, 315

Tubman's interviewing of black refugees, 342

Tubman's journey to South Carolina, 295–96, 298, 299

Tubman's nursing work, 304–5, 337, 338–39, 343–44

Tubman's payment for her services, 328–32, 353, 362, 372

Tubman's relinquishing of government dispensation, 299–300

Tubman's spying and scouting work, 313, 315, 316–17

Tubman's visits home while on leave, 339–41, 344

Tubman's volunteering for, 291, 293–94

Webster's court-martial, 324–25

SS *Harriet Tubman* (ship), 378

Stanton, Edwin, 302, 328

Stearns, George L., 232, *233,* 253, 308

Stevenson (confidence man), 364–66

Stewart, Adam (HT's nephew), 313, 316

Stewart, Catherine Kane (Jane Kane; HT's sister-in-law), 197, 201, 239, 274, 283, 313, 316, 340, 350, 351, 352

escape from slavery, 182, 184

"Stewart" name, adoption of, 188

Stewart, Dora (HT's great-niece), *15*

Stewart, Emma (HT's niece), 376

Stewart, Esther (HT's niece), 340

Stewart, Eva Katherine Helena Harriet (HT's great-niece), 371, 378

Stewart, Harriet Ann (HT's sister-in-law), 196–97, 274

Stewart, James (Benjamin Ross, Jr.; HT's brother), 49, 52–53, 73, 176–77, 197, 201, 239

escape attempt in 1849, 45, *45,* 134–37

escape attempt in 1852 or 1853, 171–74

escape from slavery in 1854, 178–79, 181–89, *187–88*

imprisonment for Brodess's debts, 95–96, *95,* 99, 102, 104, 107

"Stewart" name, adoption of, 188

Tubman's escape from slavery, 143, 149–50

Stewart, James A., 132, 162, 175, 226

Stewart, John (Robert Ross; HT's brother), 31, 43, 49, 52, 124, 176–77, 196, 197, 201, 247, 346, 352, 371

escape attempt in 1849, 134–37

escape attempt in 1852 or 1853, 171–74

escape from slavery in 1854, 178–79, 181–89, *187–88*

letter to Tubman, 251, *252–53*

marriage of, 135–36

scam involving Confederate gold, 364–65, 368

"Stewart" name, adoption of, 188

Stewart, John Isaac (HT's nephew), 371, 376

Stewart, John T., 99, 101, 120

Stewart, Joseph, 72, 98

Stewart, Margaret. *See* Lucas, Margaret Stewart

Stewart, William Henry (Henry "Harry" Ross; HT's brother), 13, 14, 69, 70, 71, 105–6, 107, 108–9, 111, 128, 176–77, 196, 197, 274, 371, 376

escape attempt in 1849, 45, *45,* 134–37

escape attempt in 1852 or 1853, 171–74

escape from slavery in 1854, 178–79, 181–89, *187–88*

"Stewart" name, adoption of, 188

testimony about his life, 341

Tubman's escape from slavery, 143, 149–50

Stewart, William Henry, Jr. (HT's nephew), 197, 376

Still, William, *135, 163,* 169, 179, 187–88, *187–88,* 206, 213, *218,* 219, 225, 232, 266, 270

Stowe, Harriet Beecher, 222
Strong, Brig. Gen. George C., 332
Sumner, Charles, 206
Susan, Miss, 59–63

T

Talbert, Mary, 373, 377
Taney, Roger, 215, 217, 218
Tatlock, Helen, 371
Taylor, Zachary, 156, 157
Telford, Emma, 47, 57, 127, 203, 295, 296, 321, 371
Thomas, John, 364
Thompson, Absalom, 42, 96, 97–98
Thompson, Albert, 361
Thompson, Anthony, 24, 28–29, 30, 36, 39, 40–41, 42–44, 49, 72, 96–97
    ledger entry regarding Rit Ross, 44
Thompson, Anthony C. (A. C.), 37, 42, 96, 97–98, 99, 100, 107, 109, 120, 121, 122–24, 126, 156, 186, 202, 203, 206, 223, 225, 227, 353
    Ross brothers' escape attempt, 172, 173
    testimony regarding Rit Ross, 38–39
    Tubman's escape from slavery, 141–44
Thompson, Anthony C., Jr., 140, 156
Thompson, Barsheba, 48
Thompson, Edward, 122
Thompson, Martha Kersey, 97
Thompson, Mary Elizabeth Leverton, 140, 156
Thompson, Mary Kersey, 97
Tilly (slave), 208–10
Townsend, Martin, 260–61, 262, 264, 265
Truth, Sojourner, 344–45, 345
Tubman, Benjamin G., 219
Tubman, Evan, 155
Tubman, Harriet (Araminta "Minty" Ross), 1–2, 15, 90, 285, 358, 374, 375, 378
    acting skills, 99
    baby-sitting her brother, 52–53, 54
    birth of, 23–25, 28, 42, 44–46
    bronze tablet in memory of, 376–77
    Brown's relationship with, 229–30, 234–36, 238–40, 247, 250, 253–54

celebrity status, 180
childhood years, 47–63
colonization movement and, 248–49, 291
death and funeral, 361, 373–74, 375–76
domestic work, 59–63
Drew's interview with, 200–201
elusiveness as historical figure, 3–9
emancipation, foretelling of, 274
erotic life, 167
fieldwork, 65, 68, 71–72
first memory, 47–49
flax-processing work, 77–79, 83–85
food for her family, creative acquisition of, 349–51
"freedom via Pattison will" issue, 32–33, 69–70, 105, 119–22, 131
God's disciple, self-concept as, 127–28
hair of, 86
"Harriet" name, adoption of, 119
head injury, 17, 85–92, 372
headstone for her grave, 377
health problems, 58, 124–25, 207–8, 266, 271, 272–73, 346
hiring out her own time, 99–101
house fire and subsequent rebuilding, 369–70
house purchase in Auburn, 243, 246–47, 364
hunting incident, 272
indigent and infirm people, care for, 14, 371, 372, 373
intelligence of, 101
learning activities, 116
Lincoln, attitude toward, 345
loner personality, 239–40
marriage to Davis, 118, 331, 361–63
marriage to Tubman, 116–19, 165–67
meteor showers of 1833, 73, 76
mischievous nature, 53, 54, 78
"Moses" name, 198
muskrat-trap work, 57–58
narcolepsy of, 17, 91, 92
night sky, familiarity with, 65, 67–68
in old age, 13–17, 20–22, 361, 369–73
"Ole Chariot" name, 180

pension from U.S. government, 305, 315, 329–32, 353, 362, 363, 371, 372

performer-storyteller career, 228–29, 241–42, 247–49, 286, 362

physical appearance, 68, 86, 117

postwar wandering and confusion, 347–54

psychic abilities, 87, 91–92, 115

quiet dignity of, 241

quilt made by, 140–41

religious faith, 63, 125–26, 127, 154, 203–4, 251, 254, 370

sale by Brodess family, fear of, 125–27, 134

scam involving Confederate gold, 361, 364–68, *366*

ship named for, 378

slave life, 54–63, 67–73, 77–79, 83–92, 99–101, 115–22, 124–30, 132–33, 134–37

slavery, definition of, 200–201

sugar-filching incident, 61–63

sunbonnet trademark, 262

train assault incident, 348–49

Truth's meeting with, 344–45

Virginia activities in last days of Civil War, 346–47

visions of, 48, 92, 129–30, 207–8, 274, 370

volatility of, 167

weaving work, 54, 57, 58–59

whippings suffered by, 59–60, 61, 63

woman suffrage movement and, 371

writings about, 4–7, 323, 327, 346, 362, 370–71, 372, 377

See also South Carolina military expedition; Underground Railroad

Tubman, John (HT's first husband), *118*, 124, 130, 330–31

marriage to Tubman, 116–19, 165–67

murder of, 353

refusal to flee Maryland with Tubman, 165–67

Tubman's escape from slavery, 134, 144

Tubman, Tom, 155, 159

Tubman house in Auburn, 369–70, *372*

Turner, Nat, 64, *65*, 67, 76, 240

U

Uncle Tom's Cabin (Stowe), 222, 223

Underground Railroad, *135*

Canada as destination for escaped slaves, 165, 168–70, 194–96

Chesapeake crossings, 163–64, *163*

disbanding of, 284

discrimination faced by blacks in North, 196

Dover Eight escape of 1857, 218–21

expansion of, 194

interviews given by escapees, 200–201

Nalle's rescue in Troy, N.Y., 260–65

North Star's importance to escaping slaves, 67–68

runaways' silence to family members about escape, 139

as secret organization, 169

slaveholders' efforts to stop slave escapes, 133–34, 145, 149, 150, 156, 169, 195, 202, 212–13, 222–23, 224–25, 226

"stampede" of escaping slaves in late 1850s, 218–21, *218*, 226

Still's role, 179

systemization of, 158

Tubman's ability to survive multiple trips, 87, 154–55, 202–5

Tubman's arranging of rescues from Philadelphia, 179–80

Tubman's decision to escape slavery, 129–30, 132–33

Tubman's dedication to the cause, 167–68

Tubman's escape from slavery (1849), 45, *45*, 134–37, 138–45, 148–52

Tubman's instructions from God, 207–8

Tubman's preferred routes, *146–47*

Tubman's preparations for rescue expeditions, 154, 155

Tubman's protest demonstration for funds, 221–22

Tubman's rescue expedition of 1850 (Bowley family), 159–64

Tubman's rescue expedition of 1851
    (John Tubman incident; eleven es-
    capees), 165–70
Tubman's rescue expedition of 1851
    (Moses Ross and others), 164–65
Tubman's rescue expedition of 1852
    (nine escapees), 180
Tubman's rescue expedition of 1854
    (Ross brothers), 178–79, 181–89,
    187–88
Tubman's rescue expedition of 1855
    (Rachel Ross and children [failed]),
    197–98, 202, 205–6
Tubman's rescue expedition of 1856
    (Bailey and others), 210–15
Tubman's rescue expedition of 1856
    (Tilly), 208–10
Tubman's rescue expedition of 1857
    (Ben and Rit Ross), 221–22, 223,
    224–25
Tubman's rescue expedition of 1860
    (Rachel Ross and children [failed];
    Ennals family), 258, 259–60,
    265–71
Tubman's rescue expedition of 1861
    (Margaret Stewart), 275–78
Tubman's resolve to rescue family
    members, 52, 151–52, 153–54
Tubman's role as guide and com-
    mander, 165

Tubman's role as inspirational figure,
    198, 199, 226
Tubman's use of coded communica-
    tion, 180–82, 198–99

V

Victoria, Queen, 373
Vincent, Robert, 353

W

Wall, Henry, 261
Washington, Booker T., 361, 376
Waters, Clement, 79
Webster, Daniel, 156, 157
Webster, Pvt. John E., 324–25
Wigham, Eliza, 208, 210
Williamson, Passmore, 202
Willis, Thomas, 157, 175, 255
Wilson, Hiram, 215
Wise, William G., 362
Woman suffrage movement, 371
Wood, Charles P., 330, 331, 362, 371
Woodson, Carter G., 377
Woolfley, James and Lavinia, 218, 221
Woolfolk Brothers, 70
Worden, Lazette Miller, 243, 276, 278
Wright, David, 243
Wright, Martha Coffin, 243, 250, 276
Wright, Turpin, 212
Wyman, Lillie Chace, 234, 235

Illustration Credits

Page iv: Collection of the Cayuga Museum

Page 4:   Bradford, Sarah H. *Scenes in the Life of Harriet Tubman.* Auburn, New York, W. J. Moses, printer, 1869. From the Rare Book, Manuscript, and Special Collections Library, Duke University, Durham, North Carolina

Page 5:   Used with permission of Documenting the American South, The University of North Carolina at Chapel Hill Libraries

Page 8:   Library of Congress, Rare Book and Special Collection Division

Page 15:   Sophia Smith Collection, Smith College, Northampton, Massachusetts

Page 16:   James McGowan Collection, courtesy of Kate Larson

Page 17:   Courtesy John C. Dahl

Page 24 (L and R):   Conrad-Tubman Collection, Schomburg Center for Research in Black Culture, The New York Public Library, Astor, Lenox and Tilden Foundations

Page 33:   Dorchester County Court House, Register of Wills

Page 38:   From *Edward Brodess, Jr., v. Anthony Thompson,* Eastern Shore Court of Appeals, 1823–1828, Maryland State Archives

Page 44:   Maryland State Archives

Page 45:   From Jay and Susan Meredith Collection

Page 60:   Library of Congress

Page 65:   Library of Congress

Page 74:   Oxford Science Archive/HIP The Image Works

Page 80:   Jay and Susan Meredith Collection

Page 84:   Courtesy Pocumtuck Valley Memorial Association, Memorial Hall Museum, Deerfield, Massachusetts

Page 85:   Courtesy Pocumtuck Valley Memorial Association, Memorial Hall Museum, Deerfield, Massachusetts

Page 90:   Kate Larson Collection

Page 95:   John Creighton Collection

Page 102:   From *Edward Brodess, Jr., v. Anthony Thompson,* Eastern Shore Court of Appeals, 1823–1828, Maryland State Archives

Page 108:   Library of Congress

Page 118:   Maryland State Archives

Page 123:   Maryland Historical Society

Page 132:   From *Cambridge Democrat*

Page 135:   From *The Underground Railroad,* William Still
              (Philadelphia: Porter & Coates, 1872)
Page 158:   Library of Congress
Page 163:   From *The Underground Railroad,* William Still
              (Philadelphia: Porter & Coates, 1872)
Page 177:   Dorchester County Chattel Records 1851–1860,
              Maryland State Archives
Page 187:   Pennsylvania Abolition Society, reel 32, Historical
              Society of Pennsylvania, Philadelphia, Pennsylvania
Page 188:   Chester County Historical Society
Page 218:   From *The Underground Railroad,* William Still
              (Philadelphia: Porter & Coates, 1872)
Page 229:   Library of Congress
Page 231 (top L):   Boyd B. Stutler Collection, West Virginia State
              Archives
(top R, middle L):   Pictorial Heritage Publishers, Missoula, Missouri
(middle R, bottom L and R):   Picture History
Page 237:   John Brown/Boyd B. Stutler Collection, West Virginia
              Division of Culture and History/West Virginia
              Memory Project, Charleston, West Virginia
Pages 244, 245:   Based on map created by William Hecht
Page 246:   Kate Larson Collection
Page 252:   Courtesy William L. Clements Library, University of
              Michigan, Ann Arbor, Michigan
Page 285:   Library of Congress
Page 297:   Library of Congress
Page 308:   Courtesy Kansas Historical Society
Page 332:   *Harper's Weekly,* July 4, 1863
Page 335:   Library of Congress
Page 337:   Library of Congress
Page 345:   Library of Congress
Page 358:   Collection of the Cayuga Museum
Page 372:   National Park Service
Page 374:   Kate Larson Collection
Page 375:   Courtesy Norman F. Bourke, Memorial Library,
              Cayuga Community College, Auburn, New York
Page 377:   Kate Larson Collection
Page 378:   Schomburg Center for Research in Black Culture, The
              New York Public Library, Astor, Lenox and Tilden
              Foundations

About the Author

Beverly Lowry is the author of six novels and the non-fiction works *Crossed Over: A Murder, a Memoir* and *Her Dream of Dreams: The Rise and Triumph of Madam C. J. Walker.* The recipient of the 2007 Richard Wright Literary Excellence Award, Lowry teaches at George Mason University. She lives in Austin, Texas.